PAULINE STUDIES

Frederick Fyvie Bruce

PAULINE STUDIES

Essays presented to

Professor F.F. Bruce

on his 70th Birthday

edited by

Donald A. Hagner
Associate Professor of New Testament
Fuller Theological Seminary
Pasadena, California, U.S.A.

and

Murray J. Harris
Lecturer in New Testament
Bible College of New Zealand
Auckland, New Zealand

THE PATERNOSTER PRESS

WILLIAM B. EERDMANS PUBLISHING COMPANY

Exeter

1980

Copyright © 1980 THE PATERNOSTER PRESS LTD
Paternoster House, 3 Mount Radford Crescent, Exeter, Devon

AUSTRALIA:
Emu Book Agencies Pty., Ltd.,
63 Berry St., Granville, 2142, N.S.W.

SOUTH AFRICA:
Oxford University Press,
P.O. Box 1141, Cape Town

British Library Cataloguing in Publication Data

Pauline studies.

1. Paul, *Saint* — Addresses, essays, lectures
2. Bible, New Testament. Epistles of Paul —
Criticism, interpretation, etc. — Addresses, essays,
lectures
I. Bruce, Frederick Fyvie   II. Hagner, Donald A.
III. Harris, Murray J.
225.9'24   BS2506
ISBN 0-85364-271-0

First American edition published 1980 through special arrangement
with Paternoster by Wm. B. Eerdmans Publishing Co., Grand Rapids,
Michigan 49503

Library of Congress Cataloging in Publication Data

Pauline studies.

Bibliography: p. xii.
Includes indexes.
1. Paul, Saint, apostle—Addresses, essays, lectures.
2. Bible. N.T. Epistles of Paul—Criticism, interpre-
tation, etc.—Addresses, essays, lectures. 3. Bruce,
Frederick Fyvie, 1910- —Addresses, essays, lectures.
I. Bruce, Frederick Fyvie, 1910-   II. Hagner,
Donald Alfred. III. Harris, Murray J.
BS2506.P37 1980   225.9'24   80-16146
ISBN 0-8028-3531-7 (Eerdmans)

CONTENTS

EDITORS' FOREWORD

To mark his sixtieth birthday in 1970, Professor Bruce was presented with a *Festschrift* entitled *Apostolic History and the Gospel*. Most of the essays in that volume were contributed by his professional colleagues around the world. A decade has passed. How appropriate that this second tribute to the Professor should contain essays written by some of his former research students at the Universities of Sheffield and Manchester who are now scattered worldwide!

The habit of presenting a scholar with a collection of essays on the occasion of his birthday or his retirement is becoming more widespread, but it is still only relatively few university teachers who receive this honour. Fewer still are recipients of two *Festschriften*. But then few men have exercised a more profound influence worldwide at both the scholarly and popular levels than Professor Bruce. What is more, few scholars ever have the honour of holding the renowned Rylands Professorship, or of being the President of both the Society for Old Testament Study and the Society for New Testament Study, or of being elected a Fellow of the British Academy.

The editors are grateful for the eagerness with which the essayists agreed to contribute to the volume. It is with sorrow that we make mention of the sudden death of Rev. John H. E. Hull of the Congregational College, Manchester, in November, 1977. The volume will be the poorer without his projected contribution. The editors wish to thank the Paternoster Press and the William B. Eerdmans Publishing Company for their enthusiastic and skillful assistance in publishing these essays. Thanks are also due to Dr. Beverly S. Hagner for compiling the abbreviations and indexes.

All of us join a multitude of scholars and laymen throughout the world in warmly congratulating a splendid Christian scholar and gentleman.

October, 1980

Donald A. Hagner
Murray J. Harris

TABULA GRATULATORIA

Assemblies of God Graduate School Library, Springfield, Mo., USA
Beardslee Library, Western Theological Seminary, Holland, Mi., USA
Bethany Lutheran Theological Seminary, Mankato, Minn., USA
Biblioteca del Pontificio Instituto Biblico, Rome, Italy
Brotherton Library, Leeds, England
Christ's College Library, Aberdeen, Scotland
Covenant Theological Seminary Library, St. Louis, Mo., USA
Eastern Pentecostal Bible College, Peterborough, Ont., Canada
Library of the Faculty of Theology, Louvain, Belgium
McAlister Library, Fuller Theological Seminary, Pasadena, Ca., USA
Menighedsfakultetet, Arhus, Denmark
John Rylands University Library, Manchester, England
Trinity Episcopal School for Ministry, Ambridge, Pa., USA
Western Bible College Library, Morrison, Co., USA
Winebrenner Theological Seminary Library, Findlay, Ohio, USA
Woodstock Theological Center Library, Washington, D.C., USA
Zentrale Kath.-Theol. Seminar der Ruhr-Universität Bochum, Federal Republic
   of Germany

Abba, R.	Ap-Thomas, D. R.	Baigent, J. W.
Abba, H. M.	Arai, S.	Baird, D. A.
Adams, J. W.	Armerding, C. E.	Baird, J. A.
Adamsbaum, D.	Armstrong, M. T.	Baird, W.
Adamson, J. B.	Arnesen, N. H.	Baker, D. W.
Addy, A. J.	Asbury, R. L.	Baker, W. H.
Alcorn, W. A.	Ashby, E. G.	Baker, W. R.
Allen, L. C.	Ashley, T. R.	Bakke, R. O.
Allen, R. B.	Ashton, C. R.	Balchin, J. A.
Alsup, J. E.	Askew, J. R., Jr.	Baldwin, J. G.
Anderson, A. A.	Atherton, J. R.	Bales, J. D.
Anderson, C. W.	Aune, D. E.	Balfour, G. M.
Anderson, G. W.	Aziz, F.	Bamford, A. G.
Anderson, H.		Banks, R.
Anderson-Smith, G.	Baarda, T.	Barber, S.
Andrews, J. S.	Backhouse, H. L.	Barbour, R. S.

ix

Barclay, W.
Barker, G. W.
Barnes, P. F.
Barrett, C. K.
Bartchy, S. S.
Barth, M.
Bartlett, J. R.
Bates, A. R.
Battis, R. H., Sr.
Bauckham, R. J.
Bayes, L.
Beasley, J.
Beattie, D. R. E.
Beckwith, R. T.
Bedwell, W. L.
Beeby, H. D.
Belben, H.
Benoit, P.
Benton, W. W., Jr.
Best, E.
Betteridge, M. S.
Betz, H. D.
Beverley, J. A.
Biemen, J. D. van
Binder, H. F.
Birney, L.
Bjornstad, J.
Black, M.
Blair, P. A.
Boal, P. T.
Board, S.
Boobyer, G. H.
Borchert, G. L.
Borgen, P.
Borland, J. A.
Botha, F. J.
Bouwman, G.
Boyle, P. J.
Brady, D.

Branson, M. R. L.
Bratt, H., Jr.
Braun, D. H.
Braun, M. A.
Bray, G. L.
Bray, W. D.
Bredenkamp, V. J.
Briscoe, F. A.
Brock, S. P.
Broer, I.
Brooke, G. J.
Broughton, J. B.
Brower, K. E.
Brown, C.
Brown, C. J.
Brown, K.
Brown, M. D. E.
Brown, R. E.
Brown, R. T.
Brown, S. G.
Browning, D.
Browning, W. N.
Broyles, S. E.
Buchanan, O. B., Jr.
Budge, O. C.
Buelow, A. H.
Burdess, M.
Burdett, D. J.
Burdick, D. W.
Burge, G. M.
Burns, J. A.
Burt, R. M.
Bush, L. R.
Bustanoby, A. S.
Byrne, M.
Bystrom, R. O.

Cahill, P. J.
Caird, G. B.

Callard, D. K.
Callaway, R.
Cambier, J.-M.
Cameron, W. J.
Campbell, D. H.
Campbell, K. M.
Campbell, R.
Caragounis, C. C.
Carlston, C. E.
Carpenter, E. E.
Carson, D. A.
Cassidy, R.
Carter, C. W.
Carver, F. G.
Catchpole, D.
Causey, J. W.
Cave, C. H.
Cerk, K. R.
Chamblin, J. K.
Chapple, A. L.
Charles, H. H.
Charlesworth, J. H.
Cheesmur, R. W.
Chilcott, A. J.
Chilton, B. D.
Chirichigno, G. C.
Chow, W. W.
Christensen, R. W.
Clark, A. T.
Clark, D. G.
Clark, G. R.
Clarkson, D. E.
Clines, D. J. A.
Coad, F. R.
Coad, T. H.
Coats, G. W.
Coe, W. A.
Collins, O. E.
Collins, R. F.

Collins, T. A.
Comfort, W. M.
Condon, K.
Connell, J. C.
Cook, D. L.
Cooper, E. W.
Corsani, B.
Costello, E. E.
Cothenet, E.
Court, J. M.
Cousins, A. J.
Cousins, L. S.
Cousins, P. E.
Couve De Murville, M.
   N. L.
Cranfield, C. E. B.
Crawford, J. C.
Critchlow, J.
Crouch, L.
Cummings, J. E.
Curtis, A. H. W.

Daube, D.
Davids, P. H.
Davies, D. G.
Davies, D. P.
Davies, G. H.
Davies, G. I.
Davies, V. G.
Davis, J. A.
Davis, J. L.
Dawidow, M.
Dayton, W. T.
Dean, C. E.
Deasley, A. R. C.
Delaney, R.
Delling, D. G.
Delobel, J.
Dent, A.

Derrett, J. D. M.
Dietzfelbinger, Chr.
Dillard, R. B.
Dockery, D. S.
Donfried, K. P.
Doubles, M. C.
Douglas, J. D.
Douglas, S. L.
Drane, O. M.
Dredge, E. M. & D. J.
Drewery, B.
Dudley, M. B.
Duke, S. E.
Dul, J. A.
Dumais, M.
Duncan, R. L.
Dunham, D. A.
Dunn, J. D. G.
Dunnett, W. M.
Dyck, T. L.
Dymale, H. R.

Eady, L.
Earle, R.
Earp, J. W.
Edwards, A. D.
Eerdmans, W. B.
Eggleton, J. E.
Elbert, P. R.
Elford, R. J.
Elliott, J. K.
Ellis, D. W.
Ellis, E. E.
Ellison, H. L.
Emmerson, G. I.
Enoch, S. I.
Erdel, D. A.
Erdel, T. P.
Erickson, M. J.

Ericson, N. R.
Espinoza, H. O.
Estruth, E. J.
Evans, O. E.
Evans, R. P.
Ewert, D.

Fagal, H. E.
Fairbairn, J. W.
Faircloth, S. D.
Farmer, I. M.
Farmer, W. R.
Farnworth, R.
Farr, G.
Farrell, H. K.
Fee, G. D.
Fefegha, S. A.
Feinberg, C. L.
Feinberg, J. S.
Feld, H.
Fensham, F. C.
Ferguson, L. N.
Fields, W. W.
Fischer, K. M.
Fischer, L.
Fitzer, G.
Fitzmyer, J. A.
Foley, J. S.
Fong, B. J., Jr.
Forbes, A. & E.
Ford, J.
Fortna, R. T.
Foster, L. A.
Foster, W. R.
Foulkes, F.
Fowler, D. L.
Fraikin, D.
France, R. T.
Fraser-Smith, C. F.

Houlden, J. L.
House, H. W.
Howard, J. K.
Howard, T. L.
Howkins, K.
Hoy, W. I.
Hubbard, D. A.
Hubner, H.
Hudson, F. A.
Hughes, C.
Hughes, J. J.
Hughes, P. E.
Hughes, R. B.
Hultgren, A. J.
Humann, R. J.
Hunt, M. E.
Hurtado, L. W.
Hutchinson, G. P.
Hyland, T. M.
Hvalvik, R.

Ibach, R. D.
Ingram, E. A.
Isherwood, J. S.

Jackson, D. E.
Jenkins, D. E.
Jenkins, F.
Jensen, I. L.
Jeske, R. L.
John, E. C.
Johns, D. A.
Johnson, A. F.
Johnson, K. O.
Johnson, R. E. H.
Jones, E.
Jones, G. L.
Jones, K. E.
Jones, P.

Jones, R. G.
de Jong, J. A.
de Jonge, M.
Jonsson, J.

Kachere, R. M.
Kaiser, W. C., Jr.
Kalland, E. S.
Kalland, L. A.
Kane, J. P.
Kawamura, A.
Kearley, F. F.
Keefer, J. B.
Keiser, J.
Kellogg, W. P.
Kelly, C. G.
Kemmler, D.
Kent, H. A., Jr.
Kerr, W. F.
Kertelge, K.
Kieffer, R.
Kilde, J. C.
Kilner, J. F.
Kim, S.
Kimber, G. P.
Kinnear, A. I.
Kipping, R. H.
Kirby, G. W.
Kirk, J. A.
Kistemaker, S. J.
Kitchen, K. A.
Klein, W. W.
Klemt, C.
Klijn, A. F. J.
Knight, G. W., III
Kraft, R. A.
Kremer, J.
Krentz, E. M.
Krodel, G.

Kroll, W. M.
de Kruyf, T. C.
Kuhn, H.-W.
Kuzmič, P.

La Grand, J.
Lake, D. M.
Lane, G. E.
Lane, W. L.
Lappin, H. C.
La Rondelle, H. K.
Larsson, E. G.
La Sor, W. S.
Lattke, M.
Laws, S.
Leahy, T. W.
Leaney, A. R. C.
Learoyd, W. J.
Lee, K. S.
Legasse, S.
Le Grice, E. M.
Lehman, I. O.
Leivestad, R.
Lemcio, E. E.
Lentzen-Deis, F.
Leon-Dufour, X.
Leonard, P. E.
Lewis, L. G.
Lewis, R. A. C.
Liefeld, W. L.
Liddle, N. I.
Limb, R. A.
Lincoln, A. T.
Lindars, B.
Ling, T.
Lohse, D. E.
Longenecker, R. N.
Longstaff, T. R. W.
Love, M. B.

Palmer, E. H.
Pamplin, R. L.
Parker, P.
Pasinya, M.
Paterson, D. M.
Pathrapankal, J.
Paul-Emile, P.
Pax, W. E.
Payne, A. C.
Payne, D. F.
Payne, P. B.
Pearson, B. A.
Penna, R.
Perkin, J. R. C.
Perkins, L. J.
Perrot, Ch.
Pesch, R.
Peskett, R. H.
Petersen, W. J.
Peterson, D. G.
Pettit, B. A.
Pfammatter, J. N.
Phelps, D. R.
Pidgeon, G. M.
Pierard, R. V.
Pinnock, C. H.
Pinthus, E. I.
Piper, J. S.
Pittman, S. C.
Polkinghorne, G. J.
Polley, N. D.
Popkes, W.
Porteous, N. W.
Porter, J. R.
Porter, L. E.
Prentice, A. R.
Preston, R. H.
Pretty, J.
Procopio, A. A.

Proffitt, T. D., III
Pruitt, R. M.
Puskas, C. B., Jr.

Rack, H. D.
Radford, P. J.
Rakestraw, R. V.
Ramos, F.
Ramsay, A.
Rasmusson, B. A.
Ratcliffe, F. W.
Rawlins, C. L.
Rees, W. D.
Reese, G. L.
Reid, G. H.
Rengstorf, K. H.
Reumann, J. H. P.
Rewerts, R. M.
Reymond, E. A. E.
Riddell, C. D.
Ridder, D. R.
Ridderbos, H. N.
Riegel, S. K.
Riesenfeld, H.
Ritchie, W. J.
Roberts, D. F.
Roberts, W. E.
Robertson, A. W.
Robinson, D. W. B.
Robinson, J. A. T.
Robinson, R. D.
Robson, G. W.
Rodd, C. S.
Rogers, C. L., Jr.
Rogerson, J. W.
Roloff, J.
Romaniuk, K.
Rosenthal, E. I. J.
Royle, S. M.

Ruckstuhl, E.
Rudge, J. A.
Ruffle, J.
Russell, D. S.
Russell, R.
Russell, S. H.
Russell, W. B., III
Rusten, E. M.

Sabugal, S.
Sacon, Y. H.
Sakari, K. S.
Salom, A. P.
Sandys-Wunsch, J.
Saucy, R. L.
Sawyer, J. F. A.
Scaer, D. P.
Scharlemann, M. H.
Schenk, W.
Schippers, R.
Schneider, B.
Scholer, D. M.
Schoonhoven, C. R.
Schrage, W.
Schroeder, D.
Schwank, B.
Schwindt, P. D. G.
Scott, A. C.
Scott, J. J., Jr.
Segallia, G.
Sharpe, E. J.
Shedd, R. P.
Sheen, N. A.
Shelly, D.
Shelly, H. P.
Shelton, M. W.
Short, S. S.
Shrout, T. R.
Slater, G.

FREDERICK FYVIE BRUCE

Two Appreciations

I

To think of Fred Bruce is to be assured that the Psalmist's vision can come true:

> Mercy and truth are met together:
> Righteousness and peace have kissed each other.

I know no better example of uncompromising truthfulness wedded to that most excellent gift of charity: Fred Bruce always speaks the truth in love. Certainly the truth: he is one of the rare souls who actually do verify their references: what he says can be relied on to be correct—not that he needs to do much verification, for he is blessed with an exceptionally tenacious memory. On the granite rock of a thorough classical education (Gold Medallist in Latin and Greek at Aberdeen, senior classic of his year at Cambridge) he has built a formidable edifice of extensive and accurate learning and kept it all in good shape, from the mellow Falernian wine in the cellar to the—but no, there is no hot air or smoke escaping from the chimney. Yet, instead of the scornful condescension that this easy superiority might engender, he is conspicuously courteous and considerate; and it is not a little because of his kindly wisdom (a greater gift even than learning) that the Faculty of Theology at Manchester, like the Department at Sheffield before that, has been held together so amicably. It is no secret that the late Professor S. G. F. Brandon held and published views about Christian origins with which F.F.B. was in radical disagreement. Yet such was their friendship and mutual respect that Brandon made one of the speeches at Bruce's sixtieth birthday celebration, and Bruce was asked, and readily agreed, to say words of appreciation at Brandon's Memorial Service in Manchester Cathedral. It is the same essential loyalty on the deepest personal level that has kept him a faithful member of the Brethren, without the lowering of his rigorous academic standards. It is a loyalty shared, too, by his wife in their long and happy partnership. Beneath a rather rugged exterior, Fred conceals a ready wit. A colleague tells how Professor Gordon Rupp, then at Manchester, came to a Faculty meeting straight from attending 'Vatican II' as an observer, and sat down next to F. F. B., dumping a large attaché case on the table in front of him. 'Here comes Gordon', was the instant comment, 'bearing with him a parcel of pardons from the Pope'. It is all there and always ready—this vast stock of witty comment and information, from hilarious anecdotes, through exact knowledge of University regulations, to etymological learning (such as the origins of the word 'levirate' in Latin and Homeric Greek): apt, accurate, circumstantial, complete. It was an illustrious succession in which Bruce found himself on his election to the Rylands Chair: A. S. Peake, C. H. Dodd, T. W. Manson. It is no mean achievement to have added lustre to such a tradition. I need not recite the long list of his publications or his *cursus vitae:* others are supplying these. But I gratefully seize this opportunity, as one who has himself experienced the warmth of his loyal friendship, to add this more general little tribute and to join in a gesture which (to borrow words from one of Fred's favourite authors) 'overflows in a flood of thanksgiving to God' (2 Cor. 9:12, N.E.B.).

C.F.D. MOULE

II

For former students of F. F. Bruce to write an appreciation of their mentor is both an easy and a difficult task. Easy, because all his students feel a warm affection for him, and the mention of his name awakens a multitude of pleasant memories. Difficult, because only selected comments can be made and many significant aspects of his character and work must be left unmentioned.

The contributors to this volume, coming as they do from all around the world, are representative of the worldwide influence which Professor Bruce has had through his writings and which is now extended further through his former students. Many indeed were drawn to Manchester to study under Bruce, after having first encountered him through his writings; and it must have been the cause of some wonderment on the part of university officials that he should attract so many students from distant parts of the globe.

Writing of his "Pupils, past and present" in a recent edition of a British religious periodical, Professor Bruce comments, "As I look back over forty years of teaching, there are few things that give me such undiluted joy as the contemplation of my pupils . . . I shall be well content to have the quality of my teaching assessed by the quality of my students." A lesser man might find his greatest pleasure and pride in contemplating a shelf lined with books that he himself had written—and Bruce has such a shelf, handsomely arrayed. But for him people have always mattered more than ideas; personal relationships have always been valued over academic reputation. Rarely does one find such encyclopaedic knowledge delicately blended with patience towards beginners, or such concern for precision matched by an unashamed joy in playing with children. Not that Bruce's personal sensitivity ever blunted his critical faculties or scholarly incisiveness, but he has always shown kindly tact in dealing with the sincere efforts of others.

What was it like to do research under Bruce's direction? Bruce never hounded a research student; but the student knew that whenever he requested an appointment, he would receive not only the appointment, but also a most cordial welcome (even, perhaps, tea and biscuits, if the time were right) and careful attention to his work and progress. It came as a shock to some students that Bruce led so unobtrusively. Suggestions, though given freely, were never forced upon a student. Bruce above all served his students as a constant source of inspiration and an unfailing standard of quality. The student learned quickly enough about Bruce's concern for detail, whether in such matters as spelling peculiarities of Septuagint Greek or in attention to correct diacritical marks. The unbelievable blunders that the naive research student can be counted upon to make occasionally were always corrected with gentleness. One such student recalls an occasion when he made an error in the transcription of the unpointed Hebrew of a phrase from the Dead Sea Scrolls. Citing the passage in full from memory, the Professor drew attention to the error with the gentle remark "You will remember the whole text runs like this..." Always obvious was Bruce's uncanny ability to cut through to the heart of a complex issue. Always constant was his call to attend to primary sources, historical contexts, and careful exegesis. And yet there was always his scintillating and refreshing sense of humour.

Research students could often be seen attending Bruce's lectures to undergraduates. With his mild Scots brogue, Bruce usually lectured from a carefully prepared manuscript which was more often than not destined for publication. Unfailingly precise, he would now and then pencil in a correction without breaking stride. But awaited above all were the not infrequent interruptions when he would tug at the lapels of his gown, glance out the windows at the Mancunian skyline, and extemporize on this or that detail, often leaving his listeners breathless at his sheer mastery of the pertinent material and his penetrating, common-sense wisdom.

Bruce's phenomenal knowledge and memory are legendary. On one occasion he was serving as examiner for a Ph.D. student who had been researching aspects of French Protestantism in the nineteenth century. The candidate bears testimony to the fact that during his oral examination he discovered—to his amazement and chagrin—that Bruce already possessed certain items of information that he imagined to be his alone, as the result of his study of the original sources. Or what a surprise to chance upon a review of a volume in Dutch on early church history in which Bruce points out various spelling errors, or to have him recall with ease and accuracy the names of various streets along which he passed during a visit to Auckland, New Zealand!

One highlight of every researcher's time at Manchester is the weekly Arnold T. Ehrhardt Memorial Seminar, at which lecturers and research students in the Faculty of Theology present papers for discussion. Those attending the seminar for the first time and glancing in F. F. Bruce's direction might be tempted to think that he had finally succumbed to the pressures of his work and was nodding off. But the initial impression was short-lived. With the paper read and discussion under way, Bruce would open his eyes and respond to some question with such a remark as "I recall a relevant article in the *Expository Times* of 1930 in which Professor X propounded the view that . . ." On one occasion a faculty member of the seminar, having just read a paper, searched frantically among his notes during the discussion period for some obscure reference. F.F.B. not only came up with the reference, but was able to cite the content of the passage.

By no means, of course, does all of this knowledge remain locked in Bruce's head. His productivity was and remains a constant source of amazement for his students. At the University Library he could frequently be seen armed with little pieces of paper, tracking down this or that detail, no doubt for some current scholarly project. But how was he able to do so much? Some speculated about those daily train rides between Buxton (Bruce's home, some twenty miles away) and Manchester, during which Bruce is rumoured, for example, to have proofread *TDNT* in its entirety. If he could accomplish a task such as this on the train, one can imagine what he is able to do in the peace and quiet of his study. Yet with all this, the predominant impression a student gains of Bruce is not that he is a polymath but that he is a saintly scholar, a man whose life is being moulded by what he so thoroughly studies and so capably teaches.

None of the contributors to this volume would want the quality of Professor Bruce's scholarship or his skill as a mentor to be assessed by the quality of the essays that follow. They are, however, humbly presented to him as a slender token of the esteem and gratitude felt by a multitude of former students who have had the privilege of knowing him. And they are here presented with the best of wishes to him and his wife for an enjoyable, albeit busy, retirement.

THE EDITORS

A SELECT BIBLIOGRAPHY
OF THE WRITINGS OF F. F. BRUCE
1970–1979
Compiled by W. Ward Gasque

Note

The present bibliography continues that appearing in *Apostolic History and the Gospel: Biblical and Historical Essays Presented to F. F. Bruce on his 60th Birthday*, eds. W. Ward Gasque and Ralph P. Martin (Exeter: The Paternoster Press; Grand Rapids: William B. Eerdmans Publishing Company, 1970), 21–34; and "A Supplementary Bibliography of the Writings of F. F. Bruce," in *Journal of the Christian Brethren Research Fellowship* 22 (November 1971), 21–47.

1970

The Epistles of John. London and Glasgow: Pickering & Inglis, 1970. Pp. 160. Grand Rapids: William B. Eerdmans Publishing Co., 1979.

Tradition Old and New. Exeter: The Paternoster Press; Grand Rapids: Zondervan Publishing House, 1970. Pp. 184.

Matthew. (Scripture Union Bible Study Books). London: Scripture Union, 1970. Pp. 95. *St. Matthew.* Grand Rapids: William B. Eerdmans Publishing Company, 1971. Pp. 94.

The English Bible: A History of Translations from the Earliest English Versions to the New English Bible. (New and Revised Edition). London: Lutterworth Press; New York: Oxford University Press, 1970. Pp. XIV, 263.

"Answers to Questions" = "Question and Answer with Professor Bruce," *The Harvester*, continuing monthly feature through April 1975.

"Between the Testaments" (new article), in addition to the revision of original articles and commentaries in *The New Bible Commentary: Revised*, ed. D. Guthrie et al. (London: Inter-Varsity Press; Grand Rapids: William B. Eerdmans Publishing Company, 1970), 59–63.

"The Christ of the Scriptures," in *The Bible in the World* (London: British and Foreign Bible Society), Autumn 1970.

"Dead Sea Scrolls," in *Man, Myth and Magic*, ed. R. Cavendish (London: B.P.C. Publishing Company, 1970), 609–611.

"Exiles in an Alien World" in *The Catholic Layman's Library*, 2: Understanding the Bible—The New Testament (Gastonia, N.C.: Good Will Publishers, 1970), 265–301.

"Galatian Problems: 2. North or South Galatians?", BJRL 52 (1969–70), 243–266.

"The Origins of The Witness," The Witness 100 (January 1970), 7–9.

"Qumran," in Dictionary of Comparative Religion, ed. S. G. F. Brandon (London: Weidenfeld & Nicolson, 1970), 522–525.

"Regent College, Vancouver," The Witness 100 (November 1970), 418–420.

"Texts and Translations," in Encounter with Books, ed. H. P. Merchant (Downers Grove, IL: Inter-Varsity Press, 1970), 1–5.

Book Reviews:

The New English Bible [Old Testament] (1970); Christianity Today 14: 384–387.

The New English Bible (1970); The Christian Graduate 23: 50–51.

H. Volk, Gesammelte Schriften (1967/6); Erasmus 22: 70–72.

F. Gogarten, Jesus Christus, Wende der Welt (1966); Erasmus 22: 267–269.

W. von Schoefer, Was geht uns Noah an?; Erasmus 22: 335–337.

Leben Angesichts des Todes (Festschrift for H. Thielicke) (1968); Erasmus 22: 337–340.

A. von Speyr, Aus meinem Leben (1968); Erasmus 22: 395–396.

F. R. Bornewasser, Fels im Sturm (1969); Erasmus 22: 523–524.

E. Fuchs, Marburger Hermeneutik (1968); Erasmus 22: 524–526.

E. Benz, Die Vision (1969); Erasmus 22: 583–585.

J.-L. Leuba and H. Stirnimann (eds.), Freiheit in der Begegnung (1969); Erasmus 22: 588–591.

D. Cornu, Karl Barth et al Politique (1968); Erasmus 22: 848–850.

J. B. Taylor, Ezekiel (1969); EQ 42: 50–51.

J. N. Everett, Behold the Man (1969); EQ 42: 51–52.

D. E. H. Whiteley, 1 and 2 Thessalonians (1969); EQ 42: 52.

L. Morris, The Revelation of St. John (1969); EQ 42: 53.

M. L. Peel, The Epistle to Rheginos (1969); EQ 42: 54.

J. T. Burtchaell, Catholic Theories of Inspiration since 1810 (1969); EQ 42: 54–56.

L. H. Brockington, Ezra, Nehemiah and Esther (1969), J. W. Wevers, Ezekiel (1969), D. Guthrie, Galatians (1969), and A. L. Moore, 1 and 2 Thessalonians (1969); EQ 42: 117–119.

J. Bowker, The Targums and Rabbinic Literature (1969); EQ 42: 119–120.

J. Knox, Limits of Unbelief (1970); EQ 42: 120–121.

M. A. Jeeves, *The Scientific Enterprise and Christian Faith* (1969); *EQ* 42: 185–186.

P. Richardson, *Israel in the Apostolic Church* (1969); *EQ* 42: 186.

J. R. W. Stott, *Christ the Controversialist* (1970); *EQ* 42: 186–187.

P. von der Osten-Sacken, *Gott und Belial* (1969); *JTS* n.s. 21: 457–459.

J. A. Sanders, *The Dead Sea Psalms Scroll* (1967); *PEQ* 102: 71–72.

E. Ullendorff, *Ethiopia and the Bible* (1968); *PEQ* 102: 141–142.

Eretz-Israel, vol. 9: *Jerusalem* (1969); *PEQ* 102: 142.

A. Ben-David, *Jerusalem und Tyros* (1969); *PEQ* 102: 143–144. *Orientalia* n.s. 29: 584–585.

H. J. van Dijk, *Ezekiel's Prophecy of Tyre* (1968); *PEQ* 102: 143.

1971

The Books and the Parchments. Revised edition. London and Glasgow: Pickering & Inglis; Old Tappan, NJ: Fleming H. Revell, 1971. Pp. 287.

1 and 2 Corinthians. (New Century Bible). London: Oliphants, 1971. Pp. 262.

New Testament History. [with corrections] Garden City, NJ: Doubleday, 1971. Pp. xiv + 462. Revised edition. London: Oliphants, 1971. Pp. xiv + 434.

"Copper Scroll," "Dead Sea Scrolls," "Ein Feshkha," "Kittim," "Lies, Man of," "Lies, Prophet of," "Lion of Wrath," "Murabb'at," "Pesher," "Qumran," "Seekers after Smooth Things," "Serekh," "Shapira Fragments," "Sons of Light," "Teacher of Righteousness," "War Scroll," "Wicked Priest," "Yahad," "Zadokite Work," in *Encyclopedia Judaica*, ed. C. Roth and G. Wigoder. 16 vols. Jerusalem: Encyclopedia Judaica/Macmillan, 1971. [Bruce served as Departmental Editor for the Dead Sea Scrolls.]

"Galatian Problems: 3. The 'Other' Gospel," *BJRL* 53 (1970–71), 253–271.

"Inter-testamental Literature," in *Preface to Christian Studies*, ed. F. G. Healey (London: Lutterworth Press, 1971), 83–104.

"New Light from the Dead Sea Scrolls" (revision) and "The Early Manuscripts of the Bible," in *Holman's Family Reference Bible* (Philadelphia: A. J. Holman, 1971), appendix, 18–28, 8–17.

"Paul on Immortality," *SJT* 24 (1971), 457–472.

"St. John's Passion Narrative," *The Witness* 101–102 (January 1971– December 1972).

"Some Thoughts on Paul and Paulinism," *Vox Evangelica* 7 (1971), 5–16.

Book Reviews:

A. E. Harvey, *The New English Bible Companion to the New Testament* (1970); *The Church Quarterly* 4: 72–73.

J. Reumann, *Jesus in the Church's Gospels* (1970); *The Church Quarterly* 4: 77–78.

R. Mayer, *Christuswirklichkeit* (1969); *Erasmus* 23: 81–82.

U. Mann, *Theogonische Tage* (1970); *Erasmus* 23: 210–212.

P. V. Dias, *Vielfalt der Kirche in der Vielfalt der Juenger, Zeugen und Diener* (1968); *Erasmus* 23: 261–263.

J. Ernst, *Eschatologische Gegenspieler im Neuen Testament* (1967); *Erasmus* 23: 296–297.

U. Duchrow, *Christenheit und Weltverantwortung* (1970); *Erasmus* 23: 465–467.

J.-D. Kaestli, *L'eschatologie dans l'oeuvre de Luc* (1969); *Erasmus* 23: 650–653.

P. LeFort, *Les structures de l'Eglise militante selon Saint Jean* (1970); *Erasmus* 23: 653–655.

G. Richter, *Die Fusswaschung im Johannesevangelium* (1967); *Erasmus* 23: 717–719.

N. Schneider, *Die rhetorische Eigenart der paulinischen Antithese* (1970); *Erasmus* 23: 719–721.

P.-A. Stucki, *Herméneutique et dialectique* (1970); *Erasmus* 23: 926–928.

G. Bell and A. Koechlin, *Briefwechsel 1933–54*, ed. A. Lindt (1969); *Erasmus* 23: 975–977.

J. M. Boice, *Witness and Revelation in the Gospel of John* (1970); *EQ* 43: 53–54.

R. W. Southern, *Western Society and the Church in the Middle Ages* (1970); *EQ* 43: 184.

H. R. Rookmaaker, *Modern Art and the Death of a Culture* (1970); *EQ* 43: 186.

M. Boegner, *The Long Road to Unity* (1970); *EQ* 43: 187.

C. G. Ozanne, *The First 7000 Years* (1970); *EQ* 43: 187–188.

W. Hendriksen, *A Commentary on Colossians and Philemon* (1971); *EQ* 43: 241–242.

R. M. Grant, *From Augustus to Constantine* (1971); *EQ* 43: 242–243.

J. D. M. Derrett, *Law in the New Testament* (1970); *ExpT* 82: 121.

A. Krzyzanowska, *Monnaies coloniales d'Antioche de Pisidie* (1970); *Orientalia* 40: 360.

R. de Vaux, *Bible et Orient* (1967); *PEQ* 103: 133–134.

P. R. Ackroyd and C. F. Evans, eds., *Cambridge History of the Bible: From the Beginnings to Jerome* (1970); *The Witness* 101: 70.

I. H. Marshall, *Luke: Historian and Theologian* (1970); *The Witness* 101: 70–71.

1972

Answers to Questions. Exeter: The Paternoster Press, 1972; Grand Rapids: Zondervan Publishing House, 1973. Pp. 264.

The Message of the New Testament. Exeter: The Paternoster Press, 1972; Grand Rapids: William B. Eerdmans Publishing Company, 1973. Pp. 117.

"Biblical Authority," *RefJ* 22 (April 1972), 10–12.

"Corinthians, Second Epistle to the," in *The Encyclopedia of Christianity* 3, ed. Philip E. Hughes (Marshallton, DE: National Foundation for Christian Education, 1972).

"The Earliest Old Testament Interpretation," *Oudtestamentische Studiën* 17 (1972), 37–52.

"Galatian Problems: 4. The Date of the Epistle," *BJRL* 54 (1971–72), 250–267.

"On Dating the New Testament," *Eternity* 23 (June 1972), 32–33.

"Plymouth Brethren Worship" and other articles, in *A Dictionary of Liturgy and Worship*, ed. J. G. Davies (London: SCM Press, 1972).

Book Reviews:

J. Neusner, *The Rabbinic Traditions about the Pharisees before A.D. 70* (1971); *The Churchman* 86: 134–135.

J. Bowker, *The Targums and Rabbinic Literature* (1969); *Erasmus* 24: 83–84.

L. Peyrot, *La mort est la vie* (1970); *Erasmus* 24: 200–201.

K.-W. Thyssen, *Begegnung und Verantwortung* (1970); *Erasmus* 24: 275–278.

H. Feld, *Martin Luthers und Wendelin Steinbachs Vorlesungen über den Hebräerbrief* (1971); *Erasmus* 24: 329–332.

U. Mauser, *Gottesbild und Menschwerdung* (1971); *Erasmus* 24: 462–464.

E. Schendel, *Herrschaft und Unterwerfung Christi* (1971); *Erasmus* 24: 465–466.

J. Ernst, ed., *Schriftauslegung* (1972); *Erasmus* 24: 840–843.

K. Prümm, SJ, *Gnosis an der Wurzel des Christentums?* (1972); *Erasmus* 24: 843–845.

E. Haenchen, *The Acts of the Apostles* (1971); *EQ* 44: 48–49.

Michael Andrew, *Cyprian and the Bible* (1971); *EQ* 44: 49–50.

G. E. Ladd, *A Commentary on the Revelation of John* (1972); *EQ* 47: 53–54.

H. Riesenfeld, *The Gospel Tradition* (1970); *EQ* 44: 181–182.

A. Fawcett, *The Cambuslang Revival* (1971); *EQ* 44: 182–183.

S. Greidanus, *Sola Scriptura* (1970); *EQ* 44: 183–184.

J. A. Fitzmyer, *Essays on the Semitic Background of the New Testament* (1971); *JSS* 17: 153–154.

E. W. Nicholson, *Preaching to the Exiles* (1970); *JSS* 17: 266–267.

C. van der Waal, *Openbaring van Jezus Christus* (1971); *EQ* 44: 184–185.

Y. Yadin, *Bar-Kokhba* (1971); *PEQ* 104: 67.

1973

"Are the Gospels Anti-Semitic?", *Eternity* 24 (November 1973), 15–18.

"Bible, The," in *Webster's New World Companion to English and American Literature*, ed. Arthur Pollard (London: Compton Russell; New York: World Publishing, 1973), 54–57.

"The Corner Stone," *ExpT* 84 (1972–73), 231–235.

"Dr. G. R. Beasley-Murray: Biblical Scholar," *Spurgeon's College Record* 57 (December, 1973), 7–9.

"Eschatology in the Apostolic Fathers," in *The Heritage of the Early Church* (*Festschrift* for G. V. Florovsky), eds. D. Nieman and M. Schatkin (*Orientalia Christiana Analecta* 195; Rome: Pontifical Institutum Studiorum Orientalium, 1973), 17–89.

"Evangelism in the New Testament," *Thrust* 5 (July 1973), 5–7.

"Galatian Problems: 5. Galatians and Christian Origins," *BJRULM* 55 (1972–73), 264–284.

"The Holy Spirit in the Acts of the Apostles," *Int* 27 (1973), 166–183.

"The Humanity of Jesus Christ," *Journal of the Christian Brethren Research Fellowship* 24 (1973), 5–15.

"Jesus, Ethical Teachings," in *Baker's Dictionary of Christian Ethics* (Grand Rapids: Baker Book House; Washington, DC: Canon Press, 1973), 348–351.

"Professor Bruce Asks," *The Harvester* (January 1973–) [a continuing feature].

"Salvation History in the New Testament," in *Man and His Salvation: Studies in Memory of S. G. F. Brandon*, eds. E. J. Sharpe and J. R. Hinnells (Manchester: Manchester University Press, 1973), 75–90.

"The Spirit in the Apocalypse," in *Christ and Spirit in the New Testament: Studies in Honour of Charles Francis Digby Moule*, eds. Stephen S. Smalley and Barnabas Lindars (Cambridge and New York: Cambridge University Press, 1973), 333–344.

Book Reviews:

B. Vawter, *Biblical Inspiration* (1972); *Ampleforth J* 78(2): 77–78.

S. Lyonnet, SJ, and L. Sabourin, SJ, *Sin, Redemption and Sacrifice* (1970); *Biblica* 54 (1973), 115–118.

H. Merkel, *Die Widersprüche zwischen den Evangelien* (1971); *Erasmus* 25: 15–18.

H. Rückert, *Vorträge und Aufsätze zur historischen Theologie* (1972); *Erasmus* 25: 79–81.

H. C. Knuth, *Zur Auslegungsgeschichte von Psalm 6* (1971); *Erasmus* 25: 145–147.

O. Kuss, *Paulus* (1971); *Erasmus* 25: 147–149.

J. Eckert, *Die urchristliche Verkündigung im Streit zwischen Paulus und seinen Gegnern nach den Galaterbrief* (1971); *Erasmus* 25: 211–213.

B. Spörlein, *Die Leugnung der Auferstehung* (1971); *Erasmus* 25: 213–216.

H. D. Betz, *Der Apostel Paulus und die sokratische Tradition* (1972); *Erasmus* 25: 338–339.

H. Weinacht, *Die Menschwerdung der Sohnes Gottes im Markusevangelium* (1972); *Erasmus* 25: 461–463.

M. Bucer and T. Cranmer, *Annotationes in octo priora capita evangelii secundum Matthaeum* [1594], ed. H. Vogt (1972); *Erasmus* 25: 521–523.

E. Kränkl, *Jesus, der Knecht Gottes* (1972); *Erasmus* 25: 724–727.

O. Eissfeldt, *Kleine Schriften* 4–5 (1968, 1973); *Erasmus* 25: 779–781.

J. A. Ziesler, *The Meaning of Righteousness in Paul* (1972); *EQ* 45: 59–61; *HeyJ* 14: 72–74.

O. Eissfeldt, *Kleine Schriften* 5 (1973); *EQ* 45: 192.

J. H. Charlesworth, ed., *John and Qumran* (1972); *JTS* n.s. 24: 232–234.

1974

Jesus and Christian Origins Outside the New Testament. London: Hodder & Stoughton; Grand Rapids: William B. Eerdmans Publishing Company, 1974. Pp. 216.

Paul and Jesus. Grand Rapids: Baker Book House, 1974; London: S.P.C.K., 1977. Pp. 87.

The 'Secret' Gospel of Mark. (The Ethel M..Wood Lecture, 1974). London: The Athlone Press, 1974. Pp. 20.

"Acts of the Apostles," "Bible (English Versions)," "Epistles, Pauline," "Jesus Christ," "Manson, T. W.," "Manuscripts of the Bible," "Rowley, H. H.," in *The New International Dictionary of the Christian Church*, ed. J. D. Douglas (Exeter: The Paternoster Press; Grand Rapids: Zondervan Publishing Company, 1974).

"Exegesis and Hermeneutics, Biblical," *Ency Brit* 15 (1974), 60–68.

"The Kingdom and the Church," in *Bible Characters and Doctrines* 13 (London: Scripture Union; Grand Rapids: William B. Eerdmans Publishing Company, 1974).

"New Light on the Origins of the New Testament Canon," in *New Dimensions in New Testament Study*, eds. Richard N. Longenecker and Merrill C. Tenney (Grand Rapids: Zondervan Publishing House, 1974), 3–18.

"Paul and the Historical Jesus," *BJRULM* 56 (1973–74), 317–335.

"Remembrance of Things Past" [autobiographical reflections], *The Witness* 104–106 (January 1974–December 1976).

"The Speeches in Acts—Thirty Years Later," in *Reconciliation and Hope*, Essays Presented to Leon Morris, ed. R. J. Banks (Exeter: The Paternoster Press; Grand Rapids: William B. Eerdmans Publishing Company, 1974), 53–68.

"Which Bible is Best for You," jointly with others, *Eternity* 25 (April 1974), 27–31.

Book Reviews:

F. Laub, *Eschatologische Verkündigung* (1973); *Erasmus* 26: 332–334.

T. Gallus, *Der Nachkomme der Frau in der altlutheranischen Schriftauslegung* (1973); *Erasmus* 26: 399–402.

L. Peyrot, *Le St-Esprit et le prochain retrouvé* (1974); *Erasmus* 26: 725–727.

J.-F. Collange, *L'épitre de St Paul aux Philippiens* (1973); *Erasmus* 26: 841–843.

R. P. Martin, *Mark: Evangelist and Theologian* (1972); *EQ* 46: 57–58.

R. G. Hamerton-Kelly, *Pre-existence, Wisdom and the Son of Man* (1973); *EQ* 46: 58–59.

W. Neil, *The Acts of the Apostles* (1973); *EQ* 46: 59–60.

G. Hasel, *The Remnant* (1972); *EQ* 46: 122–123.

A. T. Hanson, *Studies in Paul's Technique and Theology* (1974); *EQ* 46: 191–192.

G. P. Wiles, *Paul's Intercessory Prayers* (1974); *EQ* 46: 247–248; *HeyJ* 15: 232–233.

R. de Vaux, *Archaeology and the Dead Sea Scrolls* (1973); *JTS* n.s. 25: 152–153.

A. H. J. Gunneweg, *Geschichte Israels bis Bar Kochba* (1972); *ThLZ* 99: 662–664.

1975

"Abraham had two Sons: A Study in Pauline Hermeneutics," in *New Testament Studies: Essays in Honor of Ray Summers*, eds. H. L. Drumwright and C. Vaughan (Waco, TX: Markham Press, 1975), 71–84.

"Apollos in the New Testament," *Ekklesiastikos Pharos* 57 (1975), 354–365.

"Aquila," "Barjesus," "Barnabas," "Elymas," "John the Baptist," "Priscilla," "Stephen," in *Wycliffe Bible Encyclopedia*, 2 vols., ed. C. F. Pfeiffer (Chicago: Moody Press, 1975).

"Corinthians, First Epistle to the," "Form Criticism," "Hebrews, Epistle to the," "Parable," "Romans, Epistle to the," in *Zondervan Pictorial Encyclopedia of the Bible*, 6 vols., ed. M. C. Tenney (Grand Rapids: Zondervan Publishing House, 1975).

"Further Thoughts on Paul's Autobiography: Galatians 1:11–2:14," in *Jesus und Paulus (Festschrift* for W. G. Kümmel), eds. E. Earle Ellis and Erich Grässer (Goettingen: Vandenhoeck & Ruprecht, 1975), 21–29.

"The Grace of God and the Law of Christ: A Study in Pauline Ethics," in *God and the Good: Essays in Honor of Henry Stob*, eds. Clifton Orlebeke and Lewis Smedes (Grand Rapids: William B. Eerdmans, 1975), 22–34.

"Introduction" to *Current Issues in Biblical and Patristic Interpretation*, Studies in Honor of M. C. Tenney, ed. G. F. Hawthorne. Grand Rapids: Eerdmans, 1975, 9–11.

"Lessons I Have Learned," *The Harvester* 54 (June 1975), 154–155.

"Paul and the Law of Moses," *BJRULM* 57 (1974–75), 259–279.

"A Reappraisal of Jewish Apocalyptic Literature," *Review and Expositor* 72 (1975), 305–315.

"Samuel Prideaux Tregelles," *The Harvester* 54 (August 1975), 211–212.

"Was Paul a Mystic?", *Reformed Theological Review* 34 (1975), 66–75.

Book Reviews:

B. M. Newman and E. A. Nida, *A Translator's Handbook on Paul's Letter to the Romans* (1974); *The Bible Translator* 26: 156–157.

C. D. Zangger, *Welt und Konversation* (1973); *Erasmus* 27: 73–76.

A. Sand, *Das Gesetz und die Propheten* (1974); *Erasmus* 27: 395–397.

W.-D. Hauschild, *Gottes Geist und der Mensch* (1972); *Erasmus* 27: 462–464.

T. Willi, *Die Chronik als Auslegung* (1972); *Erasmus* 27: 529–532.

W. Harnisch, *Eschatologische Existenz* (1973); *Erasmus* 27: 532–534.

K. M. Fischer, *Tendenz und Absicht des Epheserbriefes* (1973); *Erasmus* 27: 534–536.

E. Lohse, *Die Einheit des Neuen Testaments* (1973); *Erasmus* 27: 595–597.

W. Bujard, *Stilanalysische Untersuchungen zum Kolosserbrief als Beitrag zur Methodik von Sprachvergleichen* (1973); *Erasmus* 27: 648–650.

E. Staehelin, ed., *Die Christentumsgeschellschaft in der Zeit von Erweckung bis zur Gegenwart* (1974); *Erasmus* 27: 650–652.

H. Mohr, *Predigt in der Zeit* (1973); *Erasmus* 27: 718–719.

W. Hendriksen, *The Gospel of Matthew* (1974); *EQ* 47: 191–192.

W. S. Reid, *Trumpeter of God: A Biography of John Knox* (1974); *EQ* 47: 120–122.

P. K. Jewett, *Man as Male and Female* (1975); *EQ* 47: 242–243.

A. Ben-David, *Talmudische Ökonomie* (1974); *Orientalia* 44: 141–142.

J. N. D. Anderson, *A Lawyer Among the Theologians* (1973); *JTS* n.s. 26: 178–180.

1976

"Altar, NT," "Election, NT," "Hebrews, Letter to the," *The Interpreter's Dictionary of the Bible: Supplementary Volume*, eds. K. Crim, L. R. Bailey, and V. P. Furnish (Nashville: Abingdon Press, 1976).

"The Bible and the Faith," *Free Church Chronicle* 31 (Winter 1976), 8–16.

"Image," "Myth," "Name," "Noah," in *The New International Dictionary of New Testament Theology*, ed. Colin Brown (Exeter: The Paternoster Press; Grand Rapids: Zondervan Publishing House, 1976).

"Is the Paul of Acts the Real Paul?", *BJRULM* 58 (1975–76), 282–303.

"The Lausanne Covenant—2: The Authority and Power of the Bible," *The Harvester* 55 (November 1976), 320–323.

"Myth and History," in *History, Criticism & Faith*, ed. Colin Brown (Leicester: Inter-Varsity Press; Downers Grove, IL: InterVarsity Press, 1976), 79–100.

"The New Testament and Classical Studies," *NTS* 22 (1975–76), 229–242.

"Paul and the Athenians," *ExpT* 78 (1976–77), 8–12.

Book Reviews:

Tiburtius Gallus, SJ, *Interpretatio mariologica Protoevangelii posttridentina usque ad definitionem dogmaticam Immaculate conceptionis*, 2 vols. (1953, 1954); *Erasmus* 28: 5–7.

O. Kaiser, *Der Prophet Jesaja, Kap. 13–39* (1973) and H. Balz and W. Schrage, *Die "Katholischen" Briefe* (1973); *Erasmus* 28: 140–143.

U. Köpf, *Die Anfänge der Theologischen Wissenschaftstheorie* (1974); *Erasmus* 28: 143–145.

E. Trocmé, *The Formation of the Gospel according to Mark* (1975); *EQ* 48: 117–118.

E. Schweizer, *The Good News according to Matthew* (1976); *EQ* 48: 177–178.

J. R. McKay and J. F. Miller, eds., *Biblical Studies: Essays in Honour of William Barclay* (1975); *EQ* 48: 178–179.

J. A. Fitzmyer, *The Dead Sea Scrolls: Major Publications and Tools for Study* (1975); *JSS* 21: 185–186.

J. Neusner, ed., *Christianity, Judaism and Other Greco-Roman Cults: Studies for Morton Smith at Sixty* (1975); *JSS* 21: 194–96.

R. Banks, *Jesus and the Law in the Synoptic Tradition* (1975); *JTS* n.s. 27: 453–455.

1977

First-century Faith: Christian Witness in the New Testament. (Revised edition of *The Apostolic Defence of the Gospel = The Defense of the Gospel in the New Testament*). Leicester: Inter-Varsity Press, 1977. Pp. xi + 107. Also published as *The Defense of the Gospel in the New Testament*. Grand Rapids: William B. Eerdmans Publishing Company, 1977. Pp. 107.

Paul: Apostle of the Free Spirit. Exeter: The Paternoster Press, 1977. Pp. 491. Also published as *Paul: Apostle of the Heart Set Free*. Grand Rapids: William B. Eerdmans Publishing Company, 1978. Pp. 491.

"Christ and Spirit in Paul," *BJRULM* 59 (1976–77), 259–285.

"The Early Church's Experiment in Communism," *Shaft* 18 (1977), 6–8.

Foreword to *Dreams, Visions & Oracles*, eds. C. E. Armerding and W. W. Gasque (Grand Rapids: Baker Book House, 1977), 7–9.

"The Gospel of John," *The Witness* 107– (July 1977–).

"The History of New Testament Study," in *New Testament Interpretation*, ed. I. H. Marshall (Exeter: The Paternoster Press, 1977; Grand Rapids: William B. Eerdmans Publishing Company, 1978), 21–59.

"The Oldest Greek Version of Daniel," in *Instruction and Interpretation: Studies in Hebrew Language, Palestinian Archaeology and Biblical Exegesis = Oudtestamentische Studien* 20 (Leiden: E. J. Brill, 1977), 22–40.

"Primary Sense and Plenary Sense" (Peake Memorial Lecture), *Epworth Review* 4 (1977), 94–109.

"Titles and Descriptive Titles of God in the Old Testament," "Titles and Descriptive Titles of God in the New Testament," "Our Lord's Incarnation and Virgin Birth," in *Treasury of Bible Doctrine*, eds. J. Heading and C. Hocking (Aberstwyth: "Precious Seed" Publications, 1977), 62–69, 69–72, 148–151.

"My Father: Peter Fyvie Bruce (1874–1955)," *The Believer's Magazine* 87 (1977), 20–21.

Book Reviews:

I. H. Marshall, *The Origins of New Testament Christology* (1977); *EQ* 49: 223–224.

C. F. D. Moule, *The Origin of Christology* (1977); *EQ* 49: 224–225.

S. Sandmel, *A Jewish Understanding of the New Testament* (1977); *EQ* 49: 226–227.

R. H. Gundry, *Sōma in Biblical Theology* (1976); *HeyJ* 18: 325–327.

G. Vermes, *Post-Biblical Jewish Studies* (1975); *JSS* 22: 103–104.

D. W. Gooding, *Relics of Ancient Exegesis* (1976); *JSS* 22: 225–226.

J. T. Milik, ed. *The Books of Enoch* (1976); *PEQ* 109: 134–135.

J. A. T. Robinson, *Can We Trust the New Testament?* (1977); *RefJ* 27 (June 1977), 22–23.

1978

The History of the Bible in English. (Third Revised Edition of *The English Bible: A History of Translations.*) London: Lutterworth Press; New York: Oxford University Press, 1978. Pp. xiii + 274.

The Time is Fulfilled. Exeter: The Paternoster Press, 1978; Grand Rapids: William B. Eerdmans Publishing Company, 1979. Pp. 128.

" 'All Things to All Men': Diversity in Unity and Other Pauline Tensions," in *Unity and Diversity in New Testament Theology: Essays in Honor of George E. Ladd*, ed. R. A. Guelich (Grand Rapids: William B. Eerdmans Publishing Company, 1978), 82–99.

"Are the New Testament Documents Still Reliable?", in *Evangelical Roots: A Tribute to W. M. Smith*, ed. K. S. Kantzer (New York: Thomas Nelson, 1978), 49–61.

"Bishop Westcott and the Classical Tradition," *Spectrum* 11 (September, 1978), 19–21.

"Cecil Howley: A Tribute of Friendship," *The Witness* 108 (January 1978), 3–4.

"Christ our Hope," *The Harvester* 57 (May and June 1978), 132–133, 165–168.

"The Davidic Messiah in Luke-Acts," in *Biblical and Near Eastern Studies: Essays in Honor of William Sanford LaSor*, ed. Gary A. Tuttle (Grand Rapids: William B. Eerdmans Publishing Company, 1978), 7–17.

"Evangelical Theology Today," *Life of Faith* (February, 1978), 16–17.

"The Full Name of the Procurator Felix," *JSNT* 1 (1978), 33–36.

"George Cecil Douglas Howley: An Appreciation" and "Lessons from the Early Church," in *In God's Community*, eds. D. F. Ellis and W. W. Gasque (London and Glasgow: Pickering & Inglis Ltd., 1978; Wheaton, IL: Harold Shaw Publishers, 1979), ix–xii, 153–168.

"The Romans through Jewish Eyes," in *Paganisme, Judaïsme, Chris-*

tianisme: Mélanges offerts à Marcel Simon, eds. A. Benoit, M. Philonenko, C. Vogel (Paris: Boccard, 1978), 3–12.

"St. John at Ephesus," *BJRULM* 60 (1977–78), 339–361.

Book Reviews:

M. Künzi, *Der Naherwartungslogion Markus 9,1 par.* (1977); *Erasmus* 30: 391–393.

S. Herkenrath, *Politik und Gottesreich* (1977); *Erasmus* 30: 455–456.

K. Galling, ed., *Biblisches Reallexikon*, 2nd ed. (1977); *Erasmus* 30: 590–591.

O. Hofius, *Der Christushymnus Philipper 2,6–11* (1976); *Erasmus* 30: 718–720.

Bammel, E., C. K. Barrett and W. D. Davies, eds., *Donum Gentilicium* (1978); *ExpT* 90: 27–28.

E. P. Sanders, *Paul and Palestinian Judaism* (1977); *HeyJ* 19: 183–185.

F. Altermath, *Du Corps Psychique au Corps Spirituel* (1977); *HeyJ* 19: 308–309.

D. L. Baker, *Two Testaments, One Bible* (1976); *JTS* n.s. 29: 312.

P. E. Hughes, *A Commentary on the Epistle to the Hebrews* (1977); *JTS* n.s. 29: 544–546.

B. M. Metzger, *The Early Versions of the New Testament* (1977): *RefJ* 28 (March 1978), 24.

R. Price, *A Palpable God* (1978); *RefJ* 28 (July 1978), 21–22.

E. Wilson, *Israel and the Dead Sea Scrolls* (1978); *RefJ* 28 (December 1978), 23–24.

1979

God's Kingdom and Church. London: Scripture Union, 1979. Pp. 63.

The Work of Jesus. Eastbourne, Sussex: Kingsway Publications, 1979. Pp. 144.

Incil Nasil Yazildi? (Turkish: *What are the New Testament Writings?*). Istanbul: Seher Ofset, 1979. Pp. 30.

"Accountability in University Life," *Spectrum* 12 (September 1979), 10–11.

"Acts of the Apostles," "Age," "Colossians, Epistle to the," "Criticism," in *The International Standard Bible Encyclopedia*, Revised Edition, ed. G. W. Bromiley *et al.* (Grand Rapids: William B. Eerdmans Publishing Company, 1979–).

"Arthur Samuel Peake: Biblical Scholar," *The Methodist Recorder* (August 16, 1979).

"La Bibbia, i 'Fratelli' e la confessione di fede," *Studi di Teologia* 2 (1979), 111–116.

"The Gospel Text of Marius Victorinus," in *Text and Interpretation: Studies in the New Testament Presented to Matthew Black*, eds. E. Best and R. McL. Wilson (Cambridge: Cambridge University Press, 1979), 69–78.

"Jødenes historie hos historikeren Tacitus," in *Israel-Kristus-Kirken, Festskrift til Sverre Aalen*, eds. I. Asheim, Å. Holter, E. Larsson, Magne Saebø (Oslo: Universitetsforlaget, 1979), 15–26.

"The Main Ideas of the New Testament," *Introduction to the Bible* (London: Scripture Union, 1979), 35–40.

"The Old Testament and the Christian," "Introduction to the Wisdom Literature," "Introduction to the Poetical Literature," "A Note on Old Testament Chronology," "Ezekiel," in *A Bible Commentary for Today* (Glasgow: Pickering & Inglis, 1979); published in the USA as *The New Layman's Bible Commentary in One Volume* (Grand Rapids: Zondervan Publishing House, 1979).

"Prophetic Interpretation in the Septuagint," *Bulletin of the International Organization for Septuagint and Cognate Studies*, No. 12, Fall 1979, 17–26.

"St. Paul in Macedonia," *BJRULM* 61 (1978–79), 337–354.

"The Transmission and Translation of the Bible," in *The Expositor's Bible Commentary*, Vol. 1, ed. F. E. Gaebelein (Grand Rapids: Zondervan Publishing House, 1979), 37–57.

"The Theology and Interpretation of the Old Testament," in *Tradition and Interpretation*, ed. G. W. Anderson (London: Oxford University Press, 1979), 385–416.

Men and Movements in the Primitive Church: Studies in Early Non-Pauline Christianity. Exeter: The Paternoster Press, 1979. Pp. 159. Also published as *Peter, Stephen, James & John.* Grand Rapids: William B. Eerdmans Publishing Company, 1980. Pp. 159.

Book Reviews:

The New International Version of the Bible (1978); *Eternity* 30 (January 1979), 46–47.

J. G. Baldwin, *Daniel: An Introduction and Commentary* (1978); *EQ* 52: 115–116.

A. Lacoque, *The Book of Daniel* (1979); *EQ* 51: 116.

D. L. Emery, *Daniel: Who Wrote the Book?* (1978); *EQ* 51: 116–117.

B. Orchard and T. R. W. Longstaff, eds., *J. J. Griesbach: Synoptic and Text-critical Studies, 1776–1976* (1978); *EQ* 51: 117–118.

P. Garnet, *Salvation and Atonement in the Qumran Scrolls* (1977); *EQ* 51: 118.

C. Jones, G. Wainwright and E. Yarnold, eds., *The Study of Liturgy* (1978); *EQ* 51: 187.

D. M. Lloyd-Jones, *God's Ultimate Purpose* (1978); *EQ* 51: 245–246.

L. Ginzberg, *An Unknown Jewish Sect* (1976); *JSS* 24: 117–118.

E.-M. Laperrousaz, *Qoumrân: Histoire et archéologie du Site* (1976); *JSS* 24: 118–119.

S. Levin, *The Father of Joshua/Jesus* (1976); *JSS* 24: 282.

Forthcoming

"Altars to Unknown Gods," "Lysanias of Abilene Inscriptions," "Quirinius Inscriptions," in *Documents of New Testament Times*, ed. A. R. Millard.

"Amarna," "Amarna Letters," "Bernice," "Cenchraea," "Chorazin," "Galatia," "Hierapolis," "Maccabees," "Peter, Tomb of," "Qumran," "Solomon's Porch," "Zeno Papyri," in *Dictionary of Biblical Archaeology*, ed. E. M. Blaiklock (Zondervan Publishing House).

"Appeal," "Collection," "Hellenists," "Myth," in *Illustrated Bible Dictionary* [revised edition of *The New Bible Dictionary*] (Leicester: InterVarsity Press; Wheaton, IL: Tyndale House Publishers).

"Called to Freedom: A Study in Galatians," *Festschrift for Bo Reicke*, eds. D. A. Brownell and W. C. Weinrich, *NovTestSup* (Leiden: E. J. Brill).

"The Acts of the Apostles: Historical Record or Theological Reconstruction?" and "To the Hebrews: A Document of Roman Christianity," in *Aufstieg und Niedergang der römischen Welt*, ed. W. Haase (Berlin and New York: W. De Gruyter).

Acts (Scripture Union).

Commentary on Galatians for *The New International Greek Text Commentary* (Exeter: The Paternoster Press; Grand Rapids: William B. Eerdmans Publishing Company).

Commentary on Philippians for *The Good News Bible Commentary* (New York: Harper & Row).

Commentary on 1 and 2 Thessalonians for *Word Biblical Commentary* (Waco, TX: Word Books).

Remembrance of Things Past (Glasgow: Pickering & Inglis).

"Hittites," "Paul, the Apostle," in *The International Standard Bible Encyclopedia*, Revised Edition, ed. G. W. Bromiley *et al.* (Grand Rapids: William B. Eerdmans Publishing Company).

"St. Paul in Macedonia, 2: The Thessalonian Correspondence," *BJRULM* 62.

Places Abraham Knew; Places David Knew; Places Jesus Knew; Places Paul Knew (4 illustrated volumes. Scripture Union).

FREDERICK FYVIE BRUCE

Curriculum Vitae

Born: 12 October 1910, Elgin, Morayshire, Scotland

School: West End School, Elgin, 1915–21; Elgin Academy, 1921–1928

Universities: Aberdeen (1928–1932) M.A., Cambridge (1932–1934) B.A., and Vienna (1934–35)

Gold Medallist in Greek and Latin; Fullerton Scholar in Classics, Aberdeen, 1932

Ferguson Scholar in Classics, Scottish Universities, 1933

Croom Robertson Fellow, Aberdeen, 1933–36

Scholar of Gonville and Caius College, Cambridge, 1932–34

Sandys Studentship, Cambridge, 1934–35

Assistant in Greek, Edinburgh University, 1935–1938

Lecturer in Greek, Leeds University, 1938–1947

Crombie Scholar in Biblical Criticism, Scottish Universities, 1939

Associate Editor, *The Evangelical Quarterly*, 1942

Diploma in Hebrew, Leeds University, 1943

Assistant Editor, *The Evangelical Quarterly*, 1943–49

M.A., Cambridge, 1945

Editor, *Yorkshire Celtic Studies*, 1945–1957

Head of Department (1947–59) and Professor of Biblical History and Literature, Sheffield University, 1955–59

President, Yorkshire Society for Celtic Studies, 1948–1950

Editor, *Journal of the Transactions of the Victoria Institute*, 1949–1957

Editor, *The Evangelical Quarterly*, 1949–80

President, Sheffield Branch of The Classical Association, 1955–1958

Contributing Editor, *Christianity Today*, 1956–1978

Editor, *Palestine Exploration Quarterly*, 1957–1971

Honorary D. D., Aberdeen University, 1957

John A. McElwain Lecturer, Gordon Divinity School, 1958

Calvin Foundation Lecturer, Calvin College and Calvin Theological Seminary, 1958

President, The Victoria Institute, 1958–1965

John Rylands Professor of Biblical Criticism and Exegesis, Manchester University, 1959–1978

Joint Editor, *Bible Guides*, 1961–1965

Consulting Editor, *Eternity*, 1961–

President, Manchester Egyptian and Oriental Society, 1963–1965

General Editor, *The New International Commentary on the New Testament* = *The New London Commentary on the New Testament*, 1963–

M.A., Manchester, 1963

Dean of the Faculty of Theology, Manchester University, 1963–64

President, The Society for Old Testament Study, 1965

Payton Lecturer, Fuller Theological Seminary, 1968

Norton Lecturer, Southern Baptist Theological Seminary, 1968

Editorial Co-operator, *Erasmus*, 1970–1979

Smyth Lecturer, Columbia Theological Seminary, 1970

Earle Lecturer, Nazarene Theological Seminary, 1970

Lund Lecturer, North Park Theological Seminary, 1970

Fellow of the British Academy, 1973

Thomas F. Staley Lecturer, Ontario Bible College, 1973

President, The Society for New Testament Study, 1975

Moore College Lecturer, Sydney, Australia, 1977

Emeritus Professor, Manchester University, 1978–

Burkitt Medal in Biblical Studies, The British Academy, 1979

Festschriften: *Apostolic History and the Gospel: Biblical and Historical Essays Presented to F. F. Bruce on his 60th Birthday*, ed. W. Ward Gasque and Ralph P. Martin (1970); *Studies in Honour of F. F. Bruce*, ed. C. E. Bosworth and S. Strelcyn = *Journal of Semitic Studies* 23, No. 2 (Autumn 1978); and the present volume.

ABBREVIATIONS

AB—Anchor Bible.
ANF—The Ante-Nicene Fathers.
ASV—American Standard Version.
AThe—Acts of Paul and Thecla.
AUSS—Andrews University Seminary Studies.
BAG—W. Bauer, W. F. Arndt, and F. W. Gingrich, Greek-English Lexicon of the NT (1957; 1972²).
BASOR—Bulletin of the American Schools of Oriental Research.
BDF—F. Blass, A. Debrunner, and R. W. Funk, A Greek Grammar of the NT (1961).
BEvT—Beiträge zur evangelischen Theologie.
BHT—Beiträge zur historischen Theologie.
Bib—Biblica.
BJRL—Bulletin of the John Rylands Library.
BJRULM—Bulletin of the John Rylands University Library of Manchester.
BKAT—Biblischer Kommentar: Altes Testament.
BNTC—Black's New Testament Commentaries (= Harper's).
BWANT—Beiträge zur Wissenschaft vom Alten und Neuen Testament.
BZ—Biblische Zeitschrift.
BZAW—Beihefte zur Zeitschrift für die alttestamentliche Wissenschaft.
BZNW—Beihefte zur Zeitschrift für die neutestamentliche Wissenschaft.
CBC—Cambridge Biblical Commentary.
CBQ—Catholic Biblical Quarterly.
CD—Damascus Document.
CGT—Cambridge Greek Testament.
CH—Corpus Hermeticum.
CIL—Corpus inscriptionum latinarum.
CT—Christianity Today.
EBib—Etudes bibliques.
EGT—Expositor's Greek Testament.
Ency Brit—Encyclopedia Britannica.
Enc Jud—C. Roth (ed.), Encyclopedia Judaica (1971–72).
EQ—Evangelical Quarterly.
E.T.—English Translation.
EvT—Evangelische Theologie.
ExpT—The Expository Times.
FRLANT—Forschungen zur Religion und Literatur des Alten und Neuen Testaments.
GCS—Griechische christliche Schriftsteller.
Greg—Gregorianum.
HDB—Hastings' Dictionary of the Bible (1911–12).
HeyJ—Heythrop Journal.

HNT—Handbuch zum Neuen Testament.
HNTC—Harper's NT Commentaries.
HTKNT—Herders theologischer Kommentar zum Neuen Testament.
HTR—Harvard Theological Review.
IB—Interpreter's Bible (1952–57).
ICC—International Critical Commentary.
IDB—Interpreter's Dictionary of the Bible (1962).
IDBSup—Supplementary volume to *IDB* (1976).
Int—Interpretation.
JB—Jerusalem Bible.
JBL—Journal of Biblical Literature.
JE—I. Singer (ed.), *Jewish Encyclopedia* (1901–06).
JES—Journal of Ecumenical Studies.
JJS—Journal of Jewish Studies.
JQR—Jewish Quarterly Review.
JR—Journal of Religion.
JSNT—Journal for the Study of the New Testament.
JSS—Journal of Semitic Studies.
JTS—Journal of Theological Studies.
KJV—King James Version.
LCC—Library of Christian Classics.
LSJ—Liddell-Scott-Jones, *Greek-English Lexicon* (1940).
LXX—Septuagint.
MM—J. H. Moulton and G. Milligan (eds.), *The Vocabulary of the Greek NT Illustrated from the Papyri and Other Non-Literary Sources* (1914–29).
MNTC—Moffatt NT Commentary.
MS(S)—Manuscript(s).
MT—Masoretic Text.
NAB—New American Bible.
NASB—New American Standard Bible.
NBD—New Bible Dictionary (1962).
NCB—New Century Bible.
NEB—New English Bible.
NICNT—New International Commentary on the NT.
NIDNTT—C. Brown (ed.), *New International Dictionary of New Testament Theology* (1975–78).
NIV—New International Version.
NovT—Novum Testamentum.
NovTSup—Novum Testamentum, Supplements.
n.s.—new series.
NTD—Das Neue Testament Deutsch.
NTF—Neutestamentliche Forschungen.
NTS—New Testament Studies.
PCB—M. Black and H. H. Rowley (eds.), *Peake's Commentary on the Bible* (rev. ed., 1962).
PEQ—Palestine Exploration Quarterly.
PNTC—Penguin New Testament Commentaries.

RB—Revue biblique.
RefJ—Reformed Journal.
RelS—Religious Studies.
RevExp—Review and Expositor.
RSV—Revised Standard Version.
RV—Revised Version.
SANT—Studien zum Alten und Neuen Testament.
SBLMS—Society of Biblical Literature Monograph Series.
SBM—Stuttgarter biblische Monographien.
SBT—Studies in Biblical Theology.
SE—Studia Evangelica.
SJT—Scottish Journal of Theology.
SNT—Studien zum Neuen Testament.
SNTSMS—Society for New Testament Studies Monograph Series.
ST—Studia Theologica.
StKr—Theologische Studien und Kritiken.
Str-B—H. L. Strack and P. Billerbeck (eds.), *Kommentar zum NT aus Talmud und Midrasch* (1922–28).
SUNT—Studien zur Umwelt des Neuen Testaments.
TCNT—Twentieth Century New Testament.
TD—Theology Digest.
TDNT—G. Kittel and G. Friedrich (eds.), *Theological Dictionary of the New Testament* (1964–74).
TDOT—G. J. Botterweck and H. Ringgren (eds.), *Theological Dictionary of the Old Testament* (1974–   ).
TEV—Today's English Version.
ThHwAT—E. Jenni and C. Westermann (eds.), *Theologisches Handwörterbuch zum Alten Testament* (1971–   ).
ThLZ—Theologische Literaturzeitung.
TNTC—Tyndale New Testament Commentaries.
TQ—Theologische Quartalschrift.
TRACI/ETS—Theological Research and Communication Institute.
TS—Theological Studies.
TynB—Tyndale Bulletin.
TZ—Theologische Zeitschrift.
VD—Verbum domini.
VT—Vetus Testamentum.
VTSup—Vetus Testamentum, Supplements.
WMANT—Wissenschaftliche Monographien zum Alten und Neuen Testament.
WUNT—Wissenschaftliche Untersuchungen zum Neuen Testament.
WZKM—Wiener Zeitschrift für die Kunde des Morgenlandes.
ZNW—Zeitschrift für die neutestamentliche Wissenschaft.
ZTK—Zeitschrift für Theologie und Kirche.

Part One:

THE LIFE AND
THEOLOGY OF PAUL

Chapter 1

OBSERVATIONS ON PAULINE CHRONOLOGY

COLIN J. HEMER

THERE ARE THREE REASONS which prompt the thought that some reconsideration of the chronology of Paul's life is particularly apt. (1) There are significant places where new discussion needs to be assessed and applied and where some reformulation may assist greater accuracy of statement. (2) *Actaforschung* is a current focus of attention, and the subtle correlations of chronology provide a crucial test of the framework of the Acts narrative. He who would look for a basically sound historical sequence in it must examine whether his view is feasible on this score: he who would dispute it as tendentious must also account sufficiently for the implications of this aspect of the evidence. (3) A special case of the preceding is the bearing of Acts upon the Galatian question. Here I should wish to follow Professor Bruce's lead[1] in holding to an early dating of Galatians and a straightforward interlocking of the evidence of Acts with that of the epistle. On this ground too we need to know whether the framework of Acts will bear the weight of the hypothesis. Much may be urged against this reconstruction, but I think most of the usual objections may in principle be answered:[2] this gives the most likely total explanation, and its difficulties are the crucial ones. But if there is a potentially decisive weakness in the case, it lies in the chronology. If some plausible computations of the data are accepted, there is scarcely time to accommodate our early date of Galatians. And the possible difficulty lies, curiously enough, not in the evidence of Acts, but in that of Paul's own *Hauptbriefe*. That is a perspective to which we shall return in a moment in another connection.

The present essay will comprise two parts. In the first I shall look

3

afresh at the evidence bearing on several of the real or alleged fixed points of Pauline chronology to see whether the dates derived from them may be established or refined. In the sequel I shall try to re-examine the chronological aspect of the early dating of Galatians which Professor Bruce has so ably presented.

I

In this section I must be severely selective. There are only a few places where I have something fresh and relevant to say within the scope of this paper. The focus will be on matters bearing on the basic viability of the Acts framework. Yet some of the evident correlations will not be treated here: the death of Herod Agrippa I is approximately datable, but the narrative of Acts is not here in rigid sequence (cf. Acts 12:1); and the accession of Festus is still keenly debated—I have only indirect light to offer about it. I will only say that the case does not stand or fall on these points. If on the contrary some other dates may be clarified, the probabilities about them will suit the emerging pattern well enough.

(1) *Aretas.* The problem here derives from Paul's own words in 2 Cor. 11:32. They are naturally taken to mean that Aretas IV, king of the Nabataeans, controlled Damascus at the time of Paul's experience. But we should otherwise have assumed without question that the Romans held Damascus throughout the period. If the incident corresponds to that of Acts 9:23–25, we have a potentially important correlation. But the *prima facie* difficulty is in Paul's *Hauptbrief*, not in Acts. Paul is presum-ably a reliable authority for that which lay in his own experience. We are almost driven into an explanation which, if invoked to defend Acts, would be dismissed as special pleading. It seems likely, though very surprising, that at some stage Aretas held Damascus, unless the activity of his 'ethnarch' there may admit of some other explanation. No Roman coinage is known to have been minted at Damascus between AD 34 and AD 62. This gap may or may not be significant.[3] It is often assumed that Aretas may have been given the city by Caligula (37–41), whose policy it was to encourage client kingdoms. The Nabataeans had actually held Damascus a century earlier, and its control or commercial accessibility was a natural aspiration of Nabataean policy. So the link is an interesting one, but we can say no more. It is well to be reminded of what we do not know. The chronological options remain very open. There are possible grounds here for placing Paul's experience between 34 (or 37) and the death of Aretas in 40. If the occasion is further equated with that of Gal. 1:17–18, it may be set 'three years' after Paul's conversion, but this in

turn is an uncertain date. I am inclined to an early synthesis, but the possibilities thus far are still very flexible.

(2) *The Famine.* The approximate dating of the famine of Acts 11:28 often seems a virtually closed question. It is common to refer to the old article by K. S. Gapp.[4] This is in fact a most illuminating study, which will richly repay rereading. It draws on the then newly available papyrus documents of an Egyptian record-office with notes of transactions and expense accounts throughout the period 45–47.[5] Gapp's account of the origins, social aspects and geographical spread of ancient famine is important. It was at first a matter of prices rather than of absolute scarcity: the poorer classes were progressively priced out before the richer were seriously affected. The failure of the harvest in Egypt, consequent either upon a deficient or an excessive seasonal inundation of the Nile, had widespread and complex consequences. The heart of Gapp's specific case is that very high prices of seven or eight *drachmae* per *artaba* of wheat were current in Egypt in 45–46.[6] It is difficult to sense the emergency in these bald records, or indeed in additional ones from the same archive which have been published later.[7] I should like to see the larger picture more fully documented than even Gapp was able to do: the positive evidence for the famine here is little more than a handful of numerals, though the almost day to day records occupy parts of two published volumes. There is of course a wider circumstantial corroboration. Pliny records an exceptionally high Nile under Claudius (41–54):[8] if this corresponds with our high prices in autumn 45, we may infer either a bad harvest in 45 or the expectation of a bad one in 46. Then there is Josephus' famous account of the famine in Jerusalem relieved by Queen Helena of Adiabene.[9] This is connected with the procuratorship of Tiberius Julius Alexander (46–48), but might presumably have begun earlier under Fadus. Gapp suggests a conjunction of famine in Egypt with a slightly later failure of the harvest in Syria-Palestine: Helena was then able to obtain relief from Egypt after the worst was over in Egypt.

J. Dupont has used Josephus in an able advocacy of a later dating of this famine in Jerusalem, following Jeremias in linking its climax with the sabbatical year of 47–48.[10] This view is of some consequence, as it leads Dupont to a later chronology of the famine-relief visit of Acts 11, which he equates with Gal. 2:1ff. and the occasion of Acts 15.

The actual differences of time are relatively small, the options are again flexible, and Dupont's conclusions are not necessary. In any case the specific arguments of Gapp, of which Dupont takes no account, may be preferred to what is still only dependence on a circumstance of doubtful relevance. And the New Testament references are anticipatory, and seem likely to belong to the early stages of a complex of events culminating in famine in Greece and Rome as late as 49–50. Agabus' prophecy is not precisely placed in the sequence of Acts (11:28), but may belong to the time when the signs of trouble were first apparent in Egypt: the love of God and of his church in Antioch for the poor of Jerusalem was then seen in the promptness of the succour. It is an attractive suggestion of D. R. Hall that the aorist ἐσπούδασα in Gal. 2:10 should be rendered as a pluperfect: Paul is saying that to 'remember the poor' *had been* the actual occasion of his coming to Jerusalem in the first place.[11] Here an early chronology lends itself to a plausible and pointed construing of Paul's words. But the last word has not been spoken on this whole topic of the famine: new materials and fresh study may yet clarify some points.

(3) *Gallio.* Gallio's proconsulship of Achaia is attested independently by an inscription of Delphi which may be dated within narrow limits. This document has long been recognized as of high importance, as giving the one firmly based absolute date for Pauline chronology. I shall not repeat here the rather intricate, but clear, process of inference from the imperial titulature of Claudius which places this text in the spring or summer of AD 52: there are however complicating problems of restoration and interpretation which are not so often noticed, but which may have a material bearing on the precise application of our fixed date. I shall look briefly at two aspects: (a) implications of the recent debate over restoration; (b) the relation of the chronology of Paul's residence in Corinth with that of Gallio.

The first topic leads into somewhat technical difficulties. The text we have has been reconstructed from fragments of stone, so incomplete that even the length of the lines is doubtful. The document consists of a letter or rescript from Claudius referring to Gallio in the third person as proconsul, but the identity of the recipient or recipients of the letter is lost. The traditionally cited version of the inscription is derived from the piecing together of four fragments, and has been understood as a letter addressed to the citizens of Delphi during Gallio's year of office.[12] But three more fragments have long been known, though not always included, and there are now altogether nine to be considered. A few years ago A. Plassart published a much improved version, and drew attention to the apparent occurrence of the second person *singular* pronoun σε in the part newly restored. He suggested that Claudius's letter was addressed not to the Delphians but to Gallio's successor in office. This would not affect the probable dating of Gallio's proconsulship in 51–52, but would slightly change the basis of the inference and exclude the remote possibility of 52–53.[13] But Plassart's reading in its turn is questionable. J. H. Oliver, while accepting much of his restoration, has argued that Plassart's view depends on a false word-division: in the sequence ειασεεντελλομαιιγ the letters σε must be read as a verb ending; in any case the verb ἐντέλλομαι should take the dative σοι.[14]

The implications of the text are so important, and the problems of its reconstruction so intricate and intriguing, that some closer study is desirable. There are other difficulties in the larger context: I quote the two relevant lines in full, essentially in Plassart's form; the difficulty is compounded by the fact that neither writer indicates the length of the gaps, even where approximately known, and I have tried to supply estimates from the positioned photographs of the three fragments involved as reproduced in Plassart's plate.[15]

line 16 ανα[. . . . . .ᶜ: 12. . . . . φ]ημί < [τ]οῖς μέντ[οι? - - -
17 εἰς τῶν[. . .ᶜ.9. . . .]ειασε ἐντέλλομαι. ἵγ[α - - -

(i) The accusative σε with ἐντέλλομαι is scarcely likely unless we have licence to assume a solecism in an official and otherwise well-expressed document. (ii) On Oliver's alternative two finite verbs are to be read together: their relationship is unclear and there is a clash of vowels between them with no buffer ν. (iii) [τ]οῖς in the previous line gives a suitable (and *plural*) dative with ἐντέλλομαι, but presumably then refers to persons other than the recipient(s) of the letter. (iv) If the structure is φημί with direct speech following an angled punctuation mark, we should expect the following words to begin a complete unit of sense, but they seem to begin with a linking μέντοι (or with a μέν which cannot be easily joined with a δέ), and to require quite an elaborate and compressed construction in short space to accommodate the surviving syntactical forms. (v) This point is further reinforced by the apparent difficulty in this context of the letter group ειστων, where Plassart's word division cannot be right as it stands: if however –εἰς is a participle ending, the structure comes to look even more overloaded. (vi) We should have expected an infinitive rather than a ἵνα-clause after ἐντέλλομαι, unless the sequel were felt to have a quasi-purposive force.

The last point in fact need not delay us, for the ἵνα construction is paralleled,[16] and the unknown sequel does not affect the question whether it is practicable to restore a syntactically plausible sequence in the main clause. After some experimentation I offer the following *exempli gratia*: its content would suit the probable theme of the letter as dealing with resettlement of Delphi after depopulation:

ανα[. . . . . φ]ημί < [τ]οῖς μέντ]οι ἄλλοις οὓς ὁ Γαλλίων πεισθ-]
-εἰς τῶν [κατοίκων] ειασε ἐντέλλομαι ἵγ[α - - -

I render this: 'However to the others of the settlers, whom Gallio permitted upon being convinced, I give command that...'. This does not quite meet all the minor difficulties which seem to be contained in the surviving portions, but it does, I think, give a conceivable structure within the limits available. Now if anything like this is right, it is evident that the clause gives us no help whatever in identifying a second person, singular *or* plural. It supports the essential viability of Oliver's view; but I have not succeeded in making a comparable restoration to include the pronoun σε. I have to conclude that after all this we gain no decisive light here on the application of our document to Pauline chronology. The text really needed to be discussed afresh: it is only too easy to take our assumptions about sources at second hand. Plassart's hypothesis remains possible, but is not compelling: it gives one possible explanation of the reference to Gallio in the third person. And there are circumstantial hints that Gallio may have left his province prematurely with its affairs unsettled. But such speculations cannot overthrow the established view. In any case Gallio is likely to have left office in summer 52.

The second topic, the interpretation of the overlap between Gallio and Paul at Corinth, has been reopened in a recent study by K. Haacker.[17] Haacker questions the assumption widely made since Deissmann that Paul, near the end of his eighteen months, met Gallio at his first advent: Γαλλίωνος... ὄντος in Acts 18:12 is not necessarily 'when he became proconsul', nor are the ἡμέραι ἱκαναί of 18:18 necessarily a brief interval, nor does 18:12–17 necessarily follow sequentially upon 18:11.

These points may formally be allowed, but I suggest a slightly different evaluation of the probabilities which need not be so despondent of reaching a likely sequence. Gallio was perhaps a target for Paul's opponents precisely because he was new and untried. If Paul's residence extended from the autumn at the close of a summer journey through a full year to the spring of the next, he faced only one change of governor, in the summer of the middle year. Opposition grew over several months, and came to a head when Gallio arrived. Then Gallio's decision secured Paul's position for almost a year, and perhaps he moved before the advent of another proconsul put this facility at risk. If then Gallio came in summer 51, Paul was in Corinth from autumn 50 to early summer 52. There are several circumstantial hints which serve to confirm this hypothesis. The date of Claudius' expulsion of Jews from Italy (Acts 18:2) depends on the late testimony of Orosius, who claims to be following Josephus.[18] If he is right in assigning it to 49, this will fit well enough with Paul's meeting with Aquila and Priscilla in Corinth the next year. It also suits Professor Bruce's attractive suggestion that news of the expulsion arriving by the Via Egnatia first deflected Paul southward from his original intention of going from Macedonia to Rome.[19] And at the end of the Corinthian sojourn Gallio may have left his province abruptly for the health cruise of which his brother writes.[20] If this was likely to occasion a brief interregnum, Paul may have feared the more that Jewish opponents might use it to undermine his position, and have had the stronger reason for choosing this time to leave Corinth.

This is a crucial point at which to glance at the view of Professor John Knox.[21] Knox's work is specially pertinent to our theme in that he tries to build a structure wholly on the occasional, if 'primary', notes of time in the Epistles, while taking a sceptical stance towards the 'secondary' narrative of Acts. In the attempt he is forced to overload and schematize one aspect of the evidence at the expense of the rest: in the first form of his theory he arbitrarily equated the fourteen-year period of Gal. 2:1 with that of 2 Cor. 12:2. Having then brought Paul to Corinth no later than 45, Knox dismisses the Gallio passage in Acts as an anachronism conflicting with his scheme.[22] Further, he infers a date of 41 for the expulsion of Jews, but does so without mentioning the later date actually stated by Orosius.[23]

This is not the place for detailed criticism of Knox's arguments, but he seems to me to make a Procrustean use of the evidence to accommodate his scheme, and in the process to raise more questions against the hypothesis than against Acts. When conversely we admit the whole range of ostensible evidence, we find that it tends to the enlargement of a broadly consistent picture, within which debate may reasonably be focused on refining the reconstruction of the detailed sequence. I suggest that the ἡμέραι ἱκαναί amount virtually to Gallio's year of office, but were for Luke simply the residue of time, included in the eighteen months total, and ending with Paul's departure in 52.

(4) *The Voyage to Jerusalem.* There is a further point on which the establishment of very exact absolute dates has been canvassed since a bold hypothesis of W. M. Ramsay in 1896.[24] I will defer for the moment discussion of the difficulties and uncertainties which underlie the case. We have at least something approaching a diary by which we may trace Paul's movements over seven weeks successively. Let us forget at this stage the prospect of setting any absolute chronological value to those weeks, and simply summarize their internal relations. Between Passover at Philippi (Acts 20:6) and Pentecost in Jerusalem (Acts 21:15) Paul spent a calendar week at Philippi (the days of unleavened bread), four days to Troas (the five being reckoned inclusively in the ancient manner), six at Troas (the seven being inclusive), three days noted by details of itinerary to Miletus, where he stopped for a brief but unspecified time, two specified days between Cos and Patara, six at Tyre, one at Ptolemais (whether or not the journey involved another), one to reach Caesarea, and 'more' days (πλείους) at Caesarea before going up to Jerusalem. If we adopt the implication of the Western reading here, this final stage of sixty-four miles itself involved two days' travel.

If then we assume that this detailed and entirely plausible account is accurately reported, we have accounted for a minimum of thirty *specified* days of the seven weeks. There remain the stay at Miletus and the crossing to Cos (probably brief, but entailing the passage of messengers and visitors between Miletus and Ephesus), changing ships at Patara, and the voyage thence to Tyre, which must have occupied at least three days, the unspecified but fairly extended stay at Caesarea, and presumably arrival in Jerusalem as intended before Pentecost, in time for preliminary consultations with the apostles, for the sequel refers to Paul's conduct as a Jew at the feast.

I submit that the narrative as it stands gives a pretty full account of the lapse of time in those weeks, but it falls into two markedly different parts. The first section gives the impression of travellers impatient of delay, frustrated by the unexpectedly slow passage to Troas, counting the days, and making exceptional arrangements for Paul to prolong slightly his strategic work there (20:13). It was early in the season and the timing of the voyage was uncertain. They yet had to make transshipment at Patara without further critical delay. But when they reach Tyre, the pace relaxes. The focus changes to what awaits Paul if he ventures to Jerusalem.

Now this sequence is very natural. The journey has prospered after an anxious start, and they have time comfortably in hand. The change has been overlooked by those critics who have used the later lingerings to minimize the force of the earlier part. The days at Troas were taken out of the time of pressure, and there and at Miletus Paul organized the means of spending time with the churches whose needs he saw as specially urgent or strategic, yet without sacrificing his prior commitment to Jerusalem.[25] But at Tyre he knows there is time to spare, and he allows himself 'seven' days. When Paul reaches Caesarea, Luke is no longer concerned even to note the time. They spend the 'residue' merely: thus I render the implication of πλείους. It may have been near a week, long enough for the Agabus incident and the culmination of Paul's personal crisis, but hardly longer at most, for little time remained.

We come next to the attempts to offer an absolute chronology for this seven-week period. Apart from the fact that the date of the Passover in each relevant year is theoretically knowable, we have one solid datum. Paul spoke until midnight on the eve of his departure from Troas, and that day is denoted in the phrase ἐν τῇ μιᾷ τῶν σαββάτων (20:7). The meaning of that phrase has been debated, but it must, I think, be interpreted from Luke 24:1, where the same writer uses the identical term of what can *only* be the day following the Jewish Sabbath. The occasion was a Sunday night, not a Saturday night. If then we count back, the stay in Troas ran from a Tuesday to the following Monday morning, and the voyage to Troas from the preceding Friday to that Tuesday. That Friday marks the departure from Philippi. *If* Paul's party left Philippi *immediately* on the conclusion of the days of unleavened bread, we infer that they ended on the Thursday and that the Passover was the previous Thursday.

I do not wish to press that kind of reckoning unduly. There are undoubted uncertainties in it. Ramsay was perhaps over-confident. He calculated that the Passover of 57 fell on Thursday 7 April, and that the Passovers of neighbouring years could not have fallen on that day of the week. Plooij essentially agrees with him, but Gerhardt draws a different scheme from non-inclusive reckoning, and pushes the Passover back to a Tuesday, giving possibilities in different years.[26]

C. H. Turner, in his classic, and still important, treatment of Pauline chronology, sounds salutary cautions here.[27] (1) It is not certain, though admittedly probable, that Paul sailed from Philippi immediately after the days of the feast. (2) Ramsay treats only the years 56–59 as open to discussion, and does not for instance consider 55. (3) The uncertainty over calculating the precise day kept as 14 Nisan in a given year remains considerable in view of the observational and approximate basis of the Jewish system.

A comment may now be offered on each of these difficulties. (1) My previous remarks on the time-schedule serve to confirm the initial haste of the journey and the tightness of the narrative, and so to reduce the plausibility of finding unrecorded gaps. If there were delay at sailing, it may even be included in the five days'. And by the same token any uncertainty fostered by alternatives based on non-inclusive reckoning becomes minimal, for the available time is stretched almost to the limit. (2) Turner wrote *before* the discovery of the Gallio inscription. Whatever refinements are yet needed in our use of it, it is a fundamental datum, and it effectively excludes, on a natural reading of the texts, any option so early as that which allowed consideration of the Passover of 55 in Turner's day. (3) This is a real difficulty, which reminds us afresh of the need for caution. The Jewish month was traditionally reckoned from the observed, not the astronomical, new moon. It has long been noted, of course, that a more standardized procedure must have been adopted to fix the date in advance when pilgrims had to travel from a far-flung Diaspora, even if the traditional forms were tenaciously preserved. But even so we cannot be sure that our posthumous astronomical calculations always exactly duplicate ancient ones. Sometimes no doubt there is variation of a day or so, but we have no means of knowing.[28] A check based on a correlation with the Passover proves to be only a rough and ready one, but it is worth applying nevertheless.

The date of Felix's recall and Festus's accession is a well-known

crux, which I shall not pursue here.[29] If we accept the likelihood of 59
and interpret the διετία of Acts 24:27 as the period of Paul's Caesarean
detention, corresponding with the last years of Felix, we should presumably agree with Ramsay in placing this voyage in 57. In that case our
calculations fit exactly. If we might expect that our Passover ought to fall
on or about a postulated day of the week and it falls *on* that day, that is
as good as we can expect. It would no doubt have been nicer if the
criteria were more rigid and the coincidence more spectacular, but that is
not in the nature of the case. The test may not be worth much, but it fits.
It offers some slight corroboration of a pattern emerging from the careful
handling of many hints: if it had been more than a day adrift, it could
conversely have posed a question against our reasoning.

II

The effect of the preceding section is to illustrate that we have the
means of building, if at times tentatively, a broadly consistent picture of
the pattern of Paul's later life. The bulk of the evidence has come from
Acts, and the principal corroboration of Acts has come from external
sources of various kinds. Yet in detail many of their problems remain
unresolved, and it may yet be possible to refine their application. It is
doubtful whether dramatic advances are likely to be made unless new
sources appear: epigraphical material about Festus, for instance, is an
obvious desideratum, and a real find about him might stimulate or
change our thinking. Meanwhile there is more need for a proper use of
what we have than for ingenious hypotheses which do less than justice
to it. The epistles may mostly be placed in the general framework of
Acts, whatever the problems of detail: we are faced with acute difficulty
with the Pastorals, where the guidance of Acts is withdrawn.

The Galatian question is still the crux which faces this optimistic
view of Acts. The terms of the problem are complex, and may of course
be variously resolved, irrespective of the view held of Acts. But Professor Bruce has given definitive statement to the view which dates Galatians early, before the Council of Jerusalem, and this permits a
straightforward identification of the Jerusalem visits in Acts with those
of Galatians. Many objections may be offered to this, but I think most of
them may in principle be readily answered. The basic issue hinges upon
the chronology. Is there enough time to accommodate the periods of
three and fourteen years to which Paul himself refers (Gal. 1:18; 2:1), or
will the attempt to place them force Paul's conversion back to an impos-
sibly early date? The problem is highlighted in the important recent
study of J. van Bruggen.[30] He contends that the South Galatian view is
tenable *only* in the synthesis accepted here, but that the chronology is

fatal even to that, and he is therefore driven perforce to a later occasion and a North Galatian destination for the epistle. He feels obliged, however to date the crucifixion in 33: if we follow the common dating in 30, much of the force of this argument is removed.[31]

There are in fact several uncertain factors in the case. (1) The date of the crucifixion was probably 30, but there are advocates of 33.[32] (2) The lapse of time between the crucifixion and the conversion of Paul is never specified. The complex development of events in Acts 1–8 gives the impression of requiring considerable time. But this may be no more than an impression: the dynamic vigour of the infant Christian movement was such that the whole story *may* conceivably have been contained within the first few months. It *may* have extended into years: while guarding against assumptions which might seem to close the question prematurely, I am open to conviction either way. (3) It is debatable whether the three and fourteen years are to be reckoned concurrently from Paul's conversion, or consecutively. The former is natural to Paul's wording, if also easier in keeping the period short. (4) It may be argued whether or not these periods are to be reckoned inclusively. Ancient practice seems essentially clear here, but the inclusive reckoning should not be overplayed on dubious analogies from regnal years: a time little over twelve years *might* possibly be rendered as fourteen if it spilled over at the ends to an additional calendar year, but it is unlikely in this context. To argue for a value below thirteen would be special pleading, but we may accept thirteen plus rather than fourteen plus.[33]

If then we start from 30 and combine the shortest likely options throughout, we *might* compress the whole period from the crucifixion to the second Jerusalem visit into about fourteen calendar years, allowing only months before Paul's conversion to offset the possibility of months involved in the inclusive reckoning. We should then have time and to spare: any date after about 44 would be possible for the visit. We have seen that the questions surrounding the famine are still complex and imperfectly resolved, and its progress extended in time. Even if, as I incline to think, Paul's visit of mercy may be placed substantially earlier within the sequence than Helena's relief mission, it is not likely to have been earlier than about 46, and perhaps later.

In any case that combination of the extreme options is unlikely. There might be a lead from some readings of the Aretas episode, but our present study counsels renewed caution here. If there were secure grounds for placing it after 34 or after 37 and then linking it with the time of the first visit of Galatians 1, we could find a *terminus a quo* for Paul's conversion in about 32 or 35, and the latter would be near fatal to the early chronology. But the political background of the ethnarch's presence remains unknown, and the question cannot be decided upon the unproved assumption of Nabataean control at a date we could only guess.

There are still several ways of combining the variables. If we take a start in 33 with the later and longer reckoning of other points, that would definitely exclude our view. But various intermediate positions are at least possible. Even 33 for the crucifixion with a lapse of fourteen years all told would give a very possible 47 for the famine visit. Or consecutive reckoning from an early dating of the conversion following 30 for the crucifixion could produce a similar result. Or if the period before Paul's conversion were more extended, or if the fourteen years were near to full calendar years and the reckoning virtually non-inclusive, there is still ample time if these possibilities are combined with other shorter options. In fact each of the longer or later options in (1) to (4) might be included in a conceivable reconstruction. It seems likely that the actual truth lies in one of them or in an adjustment between two or more of them. My guess would be somewhere in the range: crucifixion in 30; conversion c. 32–34; visit c. 46–47.

It remains only to check our conclusions against other evaluations of the chronology. I have refrained from the detailed criticism of alternative views within the limits of this paper. And I pass over here those who seem to approach the evidence with a ready-made scheme. The most thorough and detailed overall treatment of the particularities is that of Ogg. If I were to tabulate a whole sequence of approximate inferential dates, as they might seem to cohere with the suggestions and probabilities outlined here, they would differ in many cases from his, but usually only by a year or two. These small differences would conceal two different phenomena. In some cases they would represent slightly variant approximations based on the same data and parallel inferences, in others they would cover substantial differences of judgment, often within a complex of interrelated alternatives or overlaid by general probabilities which tend to impose similar resultant approximations. Such differences, in a matter so elusive, are hardly surprising, but one who approaches so intricate a subject in so piecemeal and episodic a way as I have done can scarcely boast his claims to differ from Ogg's painstaking survey.

There are however two very material points which engender, directly or indirectly, some of the wider divergences in conclusions. Ogg is committed, in the light of his equally thorough study of the chronology of Jesus' ministry, to the minority view which places the crucifixion in 33, and he differs over the Jerusalem visits, a matter which involves the Galatian synthesis. These are questions not lightly resolved. Yet in equating the visit of Galatians 2 with that of Acts 15 he measures his fourteen years from a conversion in 34 or 35 to the Jerusalem Conference, not to the famine-relief visit. He accepts from Acts 11 the separate historicity of this visit, but places it *within* the fourteen years, arguing that it is omitted from Galatians: "indeed it seems that no room for it can be found there" (43).

I find this solution implausible. Paul's argument in Galatians hinges upon his frankness in confessing the total extent of his visits to the Jerusalem apostles. The omission of a visit, even if it were unimportant, would arouse suspicion.

We have seen that even the later dating of the crucifixion might possibly be accommodated within variants of our present reconstruction. But I prefer to argue from a position of which I am more fully persuaded, largely through Professor Bruce's own studies. There is time enough, on more than one plausible reading of the case, for the early chronology of the Galatian situation within an approximate framework to which the evidence of Acts and the epistles alike contributes.

Additional Note:
Observations on Pauline Chronology

The present paper had already gone to press when Professor Robert Jewett's learned study *Dating Paul's Life* (London, SCM, 1979; American ed. *A Chronology of Paul's Life*, Fortress Press, 1979) appeared, and I was unable therefore to take its arguments into account. The editors and publishers have kindly permitted me to insert a brief reaction at the proof stage.

Jewett is insistent upon the importance of an unprejudiced experimental method and a properly critical treatment of Acts in particular. In the event I find his work problematic in several ways. He has not in my view effectively explored underlying issues where he has sometimes presupposed disputable positions and thereby not really communicated with alternatives which he rejects. I think he has not penetrated the arguments for other readings of the Acts evidence, or of the Jerusalem visits, and he has simply assumed the 'North Galatian' view, which I make bold to think is radically mistaken and which subtly affects the patterns of reconstruction. He is clearly right in identifying the focal crux in the tight but uncertain chronology of Paul's earlier period, but his handling of the problems leans heavily on the recurring use of some questionable propositions: (a) that the placing of the Aretas incident after 37 is a solid datum; (b) a very lengthy reckoning of Paul's progress from Jerusalem to Corinth (Acts 15:30–18:1) as perhaps occupying four years, including a conjectured year's mission in North Galatia; (c) an insistence upon the full and consecutive reckoning of the three- and fourteen-year periods of Galatians, grounded on an artificially rigid treatment of ἔπειτα in Gal. 1:18 and 2:1.

There is much throughout which merits detailed discussion and cannot be pursued here. In some places, as in (b) above, Jewett seems to compound his own chronological dilemma unnecessarily and improbably. Overall, his varying use of Acts is a recurring focus of problems. The book is interesting, but its arguments and conclusions uncompelling. I have learnt much from reading it, and yet feel unconstrained to wish to alter materially any part of the substance of what I have written.

Notes

1. In his series of five Rylands Lectures entitled "Galatian Problems", published in *BJRL*, vols. 51-55, especially the fourth, "The Date of the Epistle", *BJRL* 54 (1971-72), 250-267.

2. See C. J. Hemer, "Acts and Galatians Reconsidered", *Themelios* 2 (1976-77), 81-88.

3. T. E. Mionnet, *Description des médailles antiques* (1811), 5.284-5: Nos. 30-32 (of AD 33/4); No. 33 (of AD 62/3). Inaccurate statements have often been made here. The coins Nos. 20-22 in Mionnet have been pressed into service in a mistaken attempt to show that Aretas actually held Damascus in 37 (H. E. Dosker, "Aretas", *International Standard Bible Encyclopedia* [1939]): these items are actually undated, but are assigned to Aretas III a century earlier, when the dynasty certainly held Damascus.

4. K. S. Gapp, "The Universal Famine under Claudius", *HTR* 28 (1935), 258-265.

5. *Papyri from Tebtunis*, Part I (*Michigan Papyri*, Vol. 2), ed. A. E. R. Boak (Ann Arbor, 1933), Nos. 123, 127.

6. No. 123, verso XI, lines 26-27; No. 127, I, lines 8, 12-14, 16, 17, 38.

7. *Papyri from Tebtunis*, Part II (*Michigan Papyri*, Vol. 5), eds. E. M. Husselman, A. E. R. Boak and W. F. Edgerton (Ann Arbor, 1944), Nos. 238-240.

8. Eighteen cubits high (Pliny, *NH* 5.10.58). Famine conditions obtained after the height exceeded sixteen, according to *NH* 18.47.168. Cf. Gapp, 259.

9. Josephus, *Antiq.* 20.2.5.51 ff; 20.5.2.101. If we read ἐπὶ τούτου in the latter passage ("in his time"), the reference is to Ti. Julius Alexander; if the plural ἐπὶ τούτων, we may include Fadus, unless we then render the phrase "in these circumstances".

10. J. Jeremias, "Sabbatjahr und neutestamentliche Chronologie", *ZNW* 19 (1928), 98-103; J. Dupont, "La Famine sous Claude (Actes, XI,28)", *RB* 62 (1955), 52-55.

11. D. R. Hall, "St. Paul and Famine Relief: A Study in Galatians 2¹⁰", *ExpT* 82 (1970-1), 309-311.

12. The fragments were first published in a Paris thesis by E. Bourguet (*De Rebus Delphicis imperatoriae aetatis capita duo*, 1905), and popularised in their bearing on Pauline chronology by W. M. Ramsay in *The Expositor*, 7th ser., 7 (1909), 467-469. Although the three further fragments were published shortly afterwards by A. Brassac, "Une Inscription de Delphes et la chronologie de Saint Paul", *RB* 13 (1910), 37-53 and 207-217, the influence of A. Deissmann (*St. Paul.*

A Study in Social and Religious History, tr. L. R. M. Strachan [1912], Appendix I, 235–260 = *Paulus* [Tübingen, 1911], 159–177) and H. Pomtow (*Sylloge Inscriptionum Graecarum*[3], 801D) has led to their exclusion from consideration in much of the large subsequent literature. The interpretation thus made familiar by Deissmann has held the field for half a century to Haenchen, but must now be reconsidered.

13. A. Plassart, *Fouilles de Delphes*, Part III, 'Inscriptions', fasc. 4 (1970), 286; cf. his "L'Inscription de Delphes mentionnant le proconsul Gallion", *Revue des Études Grecques* 80 (1967), 372–378. The precise dating hinges in part on the fact that Claudius is still "*imp.* XXVI". A *terminus ad quem* in the year 52 is set by the known datum that he had received his 27th imperial salutation by the occasion of the dedication of the Aqua Claudia in Rome. According to Frontinus (*de Aquaeductis* 1.13) this was on 1st August in a year correctly given by the eponymous consuls as 52, though wrongly also as A.U.C. 803 (for 805). The year 52 is confirmed by the dedicatory inscription (*CIL* 6.1256 = H. Dessau, *Inscriptiones Latinae Selectae*, 218). If then the inscription belongs to the earlier part of that year, it is more likely to precede than to follow the change of governor. On the traditional reading therefore Gallio held office in 51/2 or less probably 52/3; on Plassart's version the inscription refers to the beginning of the less probable 52/3 but places Gallio categorically in the preceding 51/2.

14. J. H. Oliver, "The Epistle of Claudius which Mentions the Proconsul Junius Gallio", *Hesperia* 40 (1971), 239–240.

15. Frags. 833, 728 and 2311 in the Delphi catalogue. The gaps are inaccurately placed in the publications both of Plassart and of Oliver. The placings and the length of line are now partly controlled by the observation that two of the original four fragments fit at the back of the stone.

16. Cf. e.g. Mark 13:34; John 15:17; Josephus, *Antiq.* 8.14.2.375; 7.14.5.356.

17. K. Haacker, "Die Gallio-Episode und die paulinische Chronologie", *BZ* n.s. 16 (1972), 252–255; cf. B. Schwank, "Der sogenannte Brief an Gallio und die Datierung des 1 Thess.", *BZ*, n.s. 15 (1971), 265–266.

18. The source is not known from the surviving work of Josephus, but is not likely to be of Orosius' own devising. It is possible that his source was Julius Africanus. His statement has been both challenged and ignored. See further G. Ogg, *The Chronology of the Life of Paul* (1968), 99–103.

19. F. F. Bruce, *Paul: Apostle of the Free Spirit* (Exeter, 1977), 235.

20. Seneca, *Epist.* 104. Gallio's voyage to Alexandria after his consulship was evidently a different, later occasion, starting from Italy (Pliny, *NH* 31.33.62). Recent study has thrown new light on his consulship (E. M. Smallwood, "Consules Suffecti of A.D. 55", *Historia* 17 [1968], 348).

21. J. Knox, *Chapters in a Life of Paul* (New York, 1950); cf. his articles "'Fourteen Years Later': A Note on the Pauline Chronology", *JR* 16 (1936), 341–349, and "The Pauline Chronology", *JBL* 58 (1939), 15–29.

22. *Chapters in a Life of Paul*, 81–82. It may conversely be argued that Knox's failure to give a sufficient account of this item of 'hard' evidence weighs heavily against him. The viability of his scheme in any case hinges much upon the unconvincing equation of Gal. 2:1 with 2 Cor. 12:2. This is the starting point of his earlier articles, but in his book he virtually abandons it in the face of critical objections (78n.), while elaborating the chronology it prompted.

23. *Ibid.*, 82–83. But the reference in Suetonius, *Claudius* 25, is not in chronological order, and the action of Claudius dated by Dio Cassius (60.6.6) in

41, when Jews were *not* expelled, was apparently a different occasion. See further Ogg, *Paul*, 99–103.

24. W. M. Ramsay, "A Fixed Date in the Life of St. Paul", *The Expositor*, 5th ser., 3 (1896), 336–345.

25. We may note the scrupulous Jewishness of aspects of Paul's conduct and the special importance he seems to attach to this Jerusalem visit and its timing. This may not fit some over-simplified stereotypes of the preacher to the Gentiles, but is true to the matured determination of a man 'not even in bondage to his own liberty' where the paramount interests of the gospel were at stake in sensitive areas of community relations. Our approach attempts to deal seriously with the complexity and 'reality' of the plans and motives which seem to dominate the shifting perspectives of the narrative.

26. See Ogg (*Paul*, 140–145) for discussion and criticism of these views. For calculation of the dates see now E. J. Bickerman, *Chronology of the Ancient World* (London, 1968), whose tabulations show that a new moon fell about midnight on Wednesday 23 March AD 57 (corrected to the longitude of Jerusalem) and the following one in the afternoon of Friday 22 April, and the intervening full moon therefore on the evening of Thursday 7 April. Ogg refers to D. Plooij, *De Chronologie van het leven van Paulus*, and O. Gerhardt, "In welchen Jahr wurde der Apostel Paulus in Jerusalem gefangen gesetzt?" *Neue kirchliche Zeitschrift* 33, pp. 89ff., works which I have not seen.

27. "Chronology of the New Testament. II. The Apostolic Age", *HDB* I, 415–425. Cf. Ogg, *Paul*, 143–145.

28. We should in any case expect the resultant fixing of 14 Nisan to correspond closely with the astronomical full moon (cf. n. 26 above).

29. Ogg (*Paul*, 146–170) concurs in rejecting the "antedated" chronology, but argues for somewhat later absolute dates than I prefer. His reconstruction depends however on allowing the lapse of a year for the phrase πρὸ τούτων τῶν ἡμερῶν in Acts 21:38 and a lengthier estimate of preceding events than may be necessary. It has sometimes been tentatively suggested that a change of coinage in 59 reflects a change of procurator (e.g. H. J. Cadbury, *The Book of Acts in History* [London, 1955], 9–10).

30. J. van Bruggen, *Na Veertien Jaren* (1973), accessible through an English summary, pp. 233–239.

31. In any case the chronology poses an acute problem for such a view as that of D. R. de Lacey, "Paul in Jerusalem", *NTS* 20 (1973–74), 82–86, who argues for a dating of Galatians even *before* the famine-relief visit.

32. See especially J. K. Fotheringham, "The Evidence of Astronomy and Technical Chronology for the Date of the Crucifixion", *JTS* 35 (1934), 146–162, for an impressive case offering these options. Fotheringham's supposition about a confused reference to the eclipse in 33 is however unwarranted as a ground for preferring that year, which Ogg, *The Chronology of the Public Ministry of Jesus* (Cambridge, 1941), esp. 276–277, holds for other reasons derived from the Lucan evidence.

33. Thus C. J. Cadoux, "A Tentative Synthetic Chronology of the Apostolic Age", *JBL* 56 (1937), 177–191, reduces the period to twelve years in offering a dating scheme broadly consonant with the present view. Cadoux however is driven to strain the limits of probability by an unnecessary and unwarranted attempt to force the events of Acts into an artificial annalistic pattern in five-year sequences.

Chapter 2

QUMRAN LIGHT
ON PAULINE SOTERIOLOGY

PAUL GARNET

WITHIN A FEW YEARS OF THE DISCOVERY of the Dead Sea
Scrolls, similarities were noticed between various aspects of Paul's
soteriology and individual Qumran emphases such as justification by
grace[1] or man's extreme sinfulness.[2] More recently, E. P. Sanders, in his
Paul and Palestinian Judaism,[3] has attempted a more global overview of
the relationship between the Pauline and the Qumran soteriology. He
has presented Qumran in the general context of Palestinian Judaism as a
whole, which he has surveyed, starting with the rabbinic material. He
concludes by characterizing the soteriology of Palestinian Judaism with
the term "covenantal nomism". By this he means the belief that membership of the covenant community was the primary means of salvation
and that one remained within this community by keeping the Law. This
is in contrast with the Lutheran view, which he felt had too long dominated this field of inquiry, according to which Law observance was a
primary means of salvation.

The present writer's work on Qumran soteriology was not influenced by Sanders. Indeed, it was published about the same time.[4] I
approached Qumran, not in the light of rabbinic material, but against its
own background in the Old Testament and the early intertestamental
literature. The findings certainly tend to confirm Sanders' assertion that,
for Qumran, salvation was a matter of belonging to the covenant community. Initially this community was the Qumran Community itself, but
ultimately it would be identical with Israel, because in the last days the
others would either join it[5] or be slaughtered.[6] If we are to understand
how this type of soteriology might illuminate the Jewish background of

19

Paul's thought, however, we must ask *how* the covenant community was considered to constitute a means of salvation.

At least four concrete vehicles of salvation were considered to be available in the Qumran Community:

1. The teaching or knowledge, especially of the Law, which the Community's Founder had received from God (1QH 4:5f., 23f., 27f.; 5:20–39; 8:4–26; 9:29–36).

2. The holy atmosphere prevailing in the Community, called "the spirit of holiness" (1QH 4:29–32; 16:9–12; 1QS 3:6–12; 9:3; cf. 5:1–7).

3. The exclusiveness of the Community, preserving this atmosphere from the defiling influence of the unrighteous (1QH 6:27f.; 1QS 2:25–3:12; 5:13–20).

4. The discipline of the Community, including its reproof and penalties (1QH 6:4; 1QS 8:1ff.;[7] CD 20:17f.).

It is clear that each of these becomes effective for salvation by enabling or encouraging the individual to obey God and his Law. This consideration forces us to supplement the concept of "covenantal nomism" by the following statement if we are to describe Qumran soteriology adequately:

I. Membership in the Community saves by facilitating obedience in the four ways we have just outlined. There is no salvation without obedience, even for members of the covenant (CD 20:25f.).

More than this must be added, however.

II. Qumran salvation is sometimes spoken of as a special instance of general principles of salvation (1QH 4:29–32; 9:32–36; 14:23–27).

III. Even the Community itself needed to be saved:

(a) If Israel is thought of as the covenant community, she has to be saved from her exilic condition. The promise made through the prophets for her restoration after the Babylonian exile had not been fulfilled. Second-temple Judaism was convinced of this (Neh. 9:36f.; Tob. 14:5–7; *Jub.* 1:1–18). This sense of need gave rise to what I have called "the exilic soteriology", whereby the restoration was conceived to depend on the fulfillment of certain conditions: (i) a perfect doxology of judgment, accepting God's exilic punishment as righteous, as required in Lev. 26:39–42; (ii) the separating of the submissive from the rebellious in Israel, according to Ezek. 20:33–40; (iii) the passage of a pre-determined period of time as foretold in Dan. 9:24. This exilic soteriology dominated at Qumran, as I have shown elsewhere,[8] but there are signs of it in most strands of Judaism. Exilic doxologies of judgment occur in the Prayer of Azariah (Gk. Dan. 3:26–46), the Prayer of Esther (Addns. to Esth. 14:6f.)

and the Prayer of Baruch (Bar. 1:15–3:8). The inter-testamental literature has something to say about other pre-conditions for a restoration. Tob. 13:5 and *T.Jud.* 23 demand true repentance, *Jub.* 23:17–31 an entire generation that studies and obeys the Law whilst *T.Naph.* 8 ascribes this coming salvation to the activity of God himself through priestly and kingly Messianic figures. Even Philo has allusions to the exilic soteriology.[9]

At Qumran the life of the Community was thought of as a fulfilment of Leviticus 26 and Ezekiel 20, thus providing "an acceptance", so that God would remember the land and effect the restoration. In this way Israel's salvation was an important concern for Qumran, not merely the salvation of individuals.

(b) If the Qumran Community itself is thought of as the covenant community, certain considerations should be borne in mind. (i) The Israel which is to be saved amounts to the same thing as the Community. CD 3:10–14 states that, after the first members of the covenant had sinned and been delivered to the sword, God established his covenant for Israel forever with those who kept his commandments amongst those who survived. The sequel makes it clear that this remnant is the Community. According to 1QSa 1:1–5, Israelites *en masse* will be converted to the Qumran discipline. The Community will grow to become the congregation of Israel. (ii) The Qumran Community itself was threatened with loss of salvation. It needed to keep itself free from the contamination of sinners (1QS 2:25–3:6). As the Damascus Document traces the history of the Community, a point is reached in which the members sinned: "as for them they wallowed in the transgression of man and in the ways of uncleanness and they said 'this is ours', but God in his wonderful mysteries forgave their iniquity" (CD 3:17f.). The expression used for God's forgiveness here implies sheer grace in the face of an exceptionally inexcusable transgression.[10] The Community was a means of salvation, not a source of salvation, hence a constant state of repentance, discipline and vigilance was called for.

IV. Life in the Community is sometimes viewed as an end of salvation, a sort of heaven upon earth (1QH 11:11ff.; 15:14f.)—as a preliminary of course to greater glories to come (15:16f.). Viewed as a solution to a human problem, salvation points towards its means, which we have already identified as the discipline of the Community leading to obedience. Viewed as God's act, however, salvation points towards its end, which is the manifestation of the glory of God (11:10; 15:20). The Community is ideally a place where God is glorified through obedience. The opening lines of the Manual of Discipline state that the purpose of the Community's existence is obedience to the Law and the fulfilling of righteousness. The book closes with a hymnic doxology of judgment and a meditation on the glory of God.

This attitude was not confined to Qumran. In *Jub.* 1:19ff. it is stated that Israel was appointed in order to keep the sabbath. The commandments do not exist for man, according to this perspective, but man (including the covenant community) exists for the commandment. This serves to heighten the importance of the Law and to relativize the importance of the Community as a means of salvation.

What are the consequences of all this for Pauline soteriology?

1. We can say that the term "justification by works of the Law" was meaningful in second-temple Judaism. In spite of the emphasis on the covenant community, obedience was essential if either the community or the individual were to find acceptance with God.

It may be objected that the emphasis on grace which is explicit at Qumran and implicit in covenantal nomism as a whole relativizes the notion of justification by works. I reply that at Qumran grace was operative outside of the Community as well as within it, since it is recognized that it is grace that brought the individual into the Community and even that it is grace that caused the Community to come into existence. Furthermore, we have already noted that reflection on God's grace in saving gives rise to the consciousness of his purpose in saving, and that this tends to relativize the Community as a means of salvation. Salvation itself is then thought of as a means. The Qumran emphasis on works of the Law does not necessarily carry with it the idea of personally piled-up merits, since these works had also a value in relation to the Community and to the future of Israel. The closest Qumran ever came to a merit soteriology was in the Herodian period with the idea that the sufferings of the Community would goad the divine pity into a saving intervention. Yet one cannot deny the presence of the concept of merit in intertestamental Judaism. It abounds in Tobit for example (4:8f., 14; 12:9; 14:9,11).

Sanders' evaluation of the Judaism of the time of Paul was that it "kept grace and works in the right perspective, did not trivialize the commandments of God and was not especially marked by hypocrisy."[11] One may wonder why Paul left the movement if that was the case. Sanders' answer is to assert that Paul's criticism of Judaism was based ultimately on the fact that it was not Christianity. It is not that he was dissatisfied with Judaism and found no peace until he found Christ. Rather, he found Christ and was so thrilled with His glory that Judaism appeared worthless in comparison. If Christ was saviour, there could be no salvation in the Law. Thus for Paul the solution (Christ) preceded the problem (the futility of seeking righteousness by the Law).[12] I believe Paul was more logical than this. We have now seen that it is open to us to accept that the Judaism of Paul's day could truthfully be represented as seeking justification by the works of the Law. If this was a futile quest, Paul's soteriology can be seen again in the logical order: problem, solution. In the second part of this essay I propose to examine a key passage from Paul to see whether this is indeed the case.

2. We have also seen that an important feature of second-temple Judaism was the "exilic soteriology": the idea that Israel was still in exile as regards the fulfilment of God's purposes, so that she needed to pursue the kind of behaviour, including Law observance, which would bring the promised national restoration. In *The Gospel and the Land*, [13] W. D. Davies has amply demonstrated the importance of the theme of the holy land in Judaism. The exilic soteriology is part of that theme. What Davies said about the importance of the land as background to the New Testament will serve to express the importance I attach to the theme of restoration and the perspective from which I plan to view a small section of Paul's writings in the remainder of this paper. [14]

> Christianity arose in that land at a time when, in varying degrees of emotional intensity and geographic distribution, these [convictions and expectations about the land of Israel] were the constant concern, if not preoccupation, of many Jews, inside the land especially, and also outside it. The tensions of the decades before the fall of Jerusalem in A.D. 70 made this inevitable. The earliest Christians, Jews convinced that the "end of the ages" had come upon them and that the promises of God were being fulfilled, could not have escaped the convictions and expectations to which we refer. They met them, not only in highly charged actions and words of their fellow Jews, but also in their own breasts and minds, because these convictions and expectations were rooted in and evoked by the agelong yearnings of the Jewish people. Did early Christians simply ignore or suppress or reject these? Did they confront them deliberately, to sublimate or transcend them? Or did they at times succumb to them? Such questions can only be answered by looking afresh at the documents of the New Testament from an unusual point of view.

I intend, therefore, to examine the first two chapters of the Epistle to the Galatians in order to ascertain—

1. The relationship between the gospel and Judaism according to Paul,

2. How Paul's gospel relates to the prevalent exilic soteriology.

Galatians was one of the earliest of Paul's soteriological works, if not the earliest of all his extant works of any kind. [15] The first two chapters contain accounts of Paul's own separation from Judaism (1:13–17; 2:15f.) and a discussion of its implications (2:17–21).

Paul's purpose in writing Galatians was to combat the disruptive and anti-gospel influence of the Judaizers and thus to further the unity of the church. This conclusion emerges from an analysis of the book.

1:1–2:20	Paul's independent apostleship and the validity of his gospel.
2:11–21	For a Jew to become a Christian implies death to the Law and life through faith in Christ.
3:1–4:7	Blessing is by faith not by the Law—proved by the example of the blessing promised to Abraham.
4:8–20	The Galatians are regressing in following the Judaizers!
4:21–5:6	Sundry arguments against the Judaizers.
5:7–12	Personal attack on the Judaizers: they are a bad influence.
5:13–6:10	Avoid strife. Act in love and in the Spirit.
6:11–18	Personal attack on the Judaizers: their motives are unworthy and incompatible with the cross of Christ.

There would appear to be no point in his introducing the exhortations of 5:13–6:10, if they are totally unrelated to the problem of the Judaizers, which is the concern of the rest of the epistle. Probably the presence of the circumcision teaching was adding considerably to the normal roots of strife in a community. Even if he is not concerned about the Judaizers in 5:13–6:10, his exhortations about avoiding strife contribute to his over-all purpose in writing: the unity of the church. Every piece of writing contains an implicit soteriology insofar as it is written for a purpose. The author desired to achieve some end which can always be expressed in terms of saving somebody from something. The end may be quite secular of course, but in examining religious writing it is good to look at the purpose of the work as a whole as well as the individual salvation statements if we desire to recover the author's soteriology. At this point it is sufficient to note that Paul is concerned both for the gospel and for the unity of the church.

In the opening section (1:1–2:10) Paul emphasizes the independence of his apostleship and the validity of his gospel quite apart from any other human authority. He received both directly from Jesus Christ. In the Address (1:1–5) he establishes these key notes already by describing the divine origin of his apostleship and briefly expressing the content of his gospel: God has raised Jesus Christ from the dead, the "Christ, who gave himself for our sins, that he might deliver us from the present evil age, according to the will of our God and Father" (verse 4). There are two links with the exilic theme here:

1. Resurrection is seen in the prophets as an image for the restoration of Israel (Hos. 6:1f.; Ezek. 37:12–14).

2. The statement about Christ's self-giving is full of exilic overtones:

a) "The present evil age" recalls the expression "the age of wrath" (CD 1:5), or "the reign of Belial" (1QS 2:19) by which Qumran designated Israel's exilic condition. Whereas in Judaism this connoted gentile oppression, for Paul slavery to sin and to the Law is in view.

b) The phrase "for our sins", in connection with the need for deliverance from the evil age, reminds us that Israel had been sold into exile because of her iniquities (Lev. 26:14f., 31–39; Deut. 28:15, 68; Isa. 42:24; 50:1; Jer. 5:25–29). If there was to be a restoration this sin must be dealt with.

c) The reference to Christ's self-giving for our sins in order to deliver us alludes to the solution offered in Isa. 43:3f. to Israel's plight as sold into captivity: "I have given Egypt as thy ransom . . . I will give men for thee, and peoples for thy life".[16] Qumran embraced this doctrine of Israel's coming redemption and developed it. 1Q 34 1:5f. substitutes the term "wicked" for the gentiles so that the apostates in Israel are included. Salvation is to come through the destruction of the wicked who are the enemies of God's people, and this is referred to metaphorically as an atonement or ransom (Heb. *kōper*). Paul takes up again the thought of Christ's self-giving in Gal 2:20: "the Son of God who *loved me* and surrendered himself for me." There we can see an even stronger allusion to Isa. 43:3f: "I have *loved thee*; therefore will I give men for thee." In Isaiah 43 the surrender of the gentiles is God's doing, whereas in Galatians we have the self-surrender of Christ. Nevertheless this self-surrender is "according to the will of God" (verse 4). It is not incompatible with the statements elsewhere that it was God who surrendered Christ (e.g. Rom. 8:32).

It is clear from this that for Paul what Judaism looked forward to, the giving of a ransom for Israel, had already happened in the death of Christ. Instead of the destruction of the gentiles and of sinners for the sake of "the sons of God", as the Israelites are called in Isa. 43:6, there has taken place the self-surrender of the Son of God. God has not left his Son, however, in the exile of death, but has raised him up. Thus the restoration has already begun.

In the passage which follows (1:6–10), Paul pronounces an anathema upon the Judaizers. In the LXX the term *anathema* regularly translates the Hebrew *ḥerem*, the ban of total destruction which Israel was supposed to inflict upon apostate cities (Deut. 13:12ff.), probably in order to prevent Israel herself from becoming subject to the *ḥerem* (cf. Num. 25:6–13; Josh. 6:18; Isa. 43:28; Mal. 4:6). The prophets had spoken of Israel's exile in terms of a *ḥerem* and of her restoration as that which God would bring about in spite of a general *ḥerem* upon all nations, in which Israel deserves to participate (Isa. 34:2,5; cf. ch. 35; Jer. 25:9).

The kind of zeal which Israel directed against apostates to preserve her own salvation, and which Paul himself had formerly exercised against Christians, he now directs against the Judaizers to protect the church. Probably Paul expected God to judge these people in a physical way so as to prevent their continuing to function in the Christian community.[17]

In 1:11–17 he emphasizes again the independence of his gospel by asserting that he had received it by revelation, not from men. The fact that he was formerly heavily committed to its opposite, Judaism, proves this, since he would not have changed from such a leading position in the Jewish religion unless something remarkable had been the cause. Another proof lay in the fact that as soon as he was converted he left human company and went to Arabia, not to the Jerusalem apostles. He describes this revelation of Jesus Christ whereby God converted him from Judaism (verses 15ff.) in terms reminiscent of those used to describe the call of the Servant in Isaiah 49.[18] Paul's application of Servant language to himself here is not surprising in view of the fact that he understands his conversion as a matter of God's revealing his Son in him (verse 15), that is, in his person. To understand this concept there is no need to have recourse to Greek philosophical mysticism. Paul's own Jewish background was already familiar with the idea of God acting *in* a person in the sense of the person being an agent for God or an instance of the thing God wished to reveal.[19] It means Paul is to become an instance of the new reality which God wants to proclaim amongst the gentiles: his Son. In Exod. 4:22f. and Isa. 43:3–6 Israel as God's son amongst the gentiles had been the cause of judgment for them. Here Christ as God's Son is the subject of good news amongst the gentiles.

Paul's aim in the present section is to show the independence of his apostleship from the Jerusalem church authorities and the directness of the revelation he has received. This aim is furthered considerably by the metaphor of identification between himself and Christ we have just been considering. He goes on to point out that, even when he eventually went to Jerusalem, three years after his conversion, his contact with the apostles and with the Judean Christians was extremely limited (1:18–24). A second visit (2:1–10) had not come until much later, when he was concerned to establish unity with the Jerusalem leaders. Even then he neither compromised any of his principles regarding circumcision, nor did he receive any authorization from them (as though he needed such authorization). There was simply a mutual understanding. On this occasion he met with the leaders privately, "lest I was running or had run in vain" (verse 2). This enigmatic phrase gains light from the exilic soteriology. Paul's "running" was obviously his activity in preaching the gospel, but how could a conference with the Jerusalem leaders validate or invalidate this? Not at all if we think of the gospel as only a matter of the salvation of individuals! We have to understand the term "gospel" in the light of its Jewish background. In Isaiah the term means the good news of a return from exile (40:9; 41:27; 52:7; 61:1). In the ministry of Jesus it is the gospel of the *kingdom*, an idea closely connected with that of the restoration of Israel. Jesus constantly characterized his work as "gathering", connoting a return from exile. This is one of the implications of the parables and imagery involving harvesting, fishing, shepherding and feasting. Paul's gospel too had as its aim the production of a unified entity, the church, which would correspond to God's plan for a restored Israel in the last days. If the result of his work were not brought into unity with the rest of the church he would have run in vain. Though seeking unity, however, he was not prepared to compromise the principle of liberty, which was central to the "truth of the gospel" (verse 5). The exilic soteriology again explains the origin of this emphasis: the captives must be set at liberty as well as united in their homeland.

Paul has shown the independence of his apostleship and the validity of his gospel as a direct revelation from Jesus Christ (1:1–2:10). In the next section (2:11–21) he deals with what is logically implied for a Jew to become a Christian. Peter was a clear example of one who had perceived this but for unworthy reasons had ceased to act consistently with it (2:11–14). Before the emissaries arrived at Antioch "from James", Peter had practised table fellowship with the gentiles. When the emissaries came he stopped this practice though he knew circumcision was not necessary for salvation. Peter's withdrawal from table fellowship had the effect of putting pressure on the gentile Christians to become Jews. This was probably not Peter's intention but it certainly fitted in with the purposes of the Judaizers from Jerusalem, who according to Acts 15:1 were openly teaching that circumcision was necessary for salvation.

Probably 2:15–21 represents Paul's subsequent reflection on the issue he had raised with Peter: what he would have said if the occasion had permitted this elaboration of his thought. This passage deliberately sets out to explore what is implied when a Jew becomes a Christian, particularly in the light of an objection with which Paul was familiar: Christianity is a minister of sin. To see what this objection meant and how Paul handled it, as well as the way he conceived the relationship between Judaism and Christianity, we must examine the passage phrase by phrase.

In what follows, I shall give first a translation of the text, then a paraphrase, followed by any exegetical notes which may be necessary to show how I have arrived at the interpretation presented in the paraphrase.

(15) *We, Jews by nature and not sinners of the gentiles,* (16) *knowing that a man is not justified by deeds of the Law, but only through faith in Jesus*

Christ, even we believed on Christ Jesus, that we might be justified by faith in Christ and not by the works of the Law, because by the works of the Law shall no flesh be justified.

(15) Before our conversion to Christianity we identified ourselves as Jews, in contrast to the gentiles, whom we classed as sinners. (16) It looked as though there was no problem with our status before God, yet we knew both by experience and by scripture (Ps. 143:2) that no one could be justified by the works of the Law. That is why we abandoned any such idea and instead trusted in Christ in order to be justified.

> For a discussion of the enigmatic phrase "faith of Jesus Christ", see N. Turner, *Grammatical Insights into the New Testament* (Edinburgh, 1965), 110f., where the cogent parallel "faith of the truth" (2 Thess. 2:13), which must mean "belief in the truth", leads him to the interpretation here, "faith in Jesus Christ", though he does not exclude the alternative meaning, "faithfulness of Jesus Christ." Of course, "faith in Jesus Christ" implies that Jesus Christ is faithful, worthy of faith. In any case it does not mean "the faith which Jesus Christ himself exercised."

> Obviously "to be justified" here cannot mean "getting in . . . the body of the saved" (*pace* Sanders, *Paul and Palestinian Judaism*, 544), otherwise Paul would be dangerously close to uttering a tautology. He intends to say more than that to become a Christian one must believe in Christ. Being justified for Paul means gaining a status of "righteous" before God.

(17) *But if seeking to be justified in Christ even we were found sinners, is Christ then the minister of sin? Far be the thought.* (18) *For if I build up again those things which I destroyed, I constitute myself a transgressor.*

(17) It may be objected "Christ" has caused the problem, since there was no problem when we were in Judaism. Now all of a sudden we find that we are sinners! The new factor which has come into the picture to give us this sinful status is Christianity, so Christianity must be the cause of sin. Furthermore, Christianity is simply an invitation to sin, since it constantly offers free forgiveness. I totally reject this conclusion for the following reasons. (18) What has actually happened is that there has been a complete change of direction. At one point I was destroying Christianity, now I am building it up again. This implies that I now acknowledge I was wrong before! Thus it is not "Christ" that constitutes me a transgressor. I do this myself, forced to it by the realities of life under the Law.

> Verse 17 has proved difficult to commentators. J. C. O'Neill (*The Recovery of Paul's Letter to the Galatians* [London, 1972]) proposes to omit the verse as a gloss, but there is no manuscript evidence against the verse. The objection "Christ is a minister of sin" can be interpreted in the light of two other objections Paul mentions in Romans: 6:1, "Let us continue in sin that grace may abound"; 7:7, "Is the Law sin?" The first of these helps us to understand διάκονος in this verse, as if Christ were serving up sin at the

table by giving justification to the sinner. The second resembles the objection here in so far as both identifications (Christ is sin, the Law is sin) depend upon the fact that both Christ and the Law in each case appear to have brought a consciousness of sin after a previous state of blissful ignorance of the matter (the state referred to in verse 15, "not sinners of the gentiles").

Verse 18 is often interpreted to mean "if I build up Judaism after I have abandoned it for Christianity." This was the topic of verses 12–14, but since verse 16 the topic has been the change from Judaism to Christianity. The words "I constitute myself a transgressor" are the key to the whole passage. (a) Paul is talking about the "whence" of his new-found guilty status and laying the blame on himself and on the Law rather than on Christianity. (b) He is talking about the moral implications of the change to Christianity (συνιστάνω) not about mystical incorporations. The incorporational language in the passage is metaphorical for the moral and the relational.

(19) *For I through the Law died to the Law, that I might live to God. I have been crucified with Christ.*

(19) I really tried life under the Law and it was through trying that I came to see the futility of the attempt. It is not Christ who is to blame, but the Law, for my new-found sinful status. This painful experience, however, was part of God's plan for me to find justification by the only effective way: faith in Christ. I could call this painful experience "dying to the Law in order to live to God." I died not only in the sense of seeing that I could not be justified by the works of the Law, but also in the sense of acknowledging myself a transgressor and deserving the Law's sanction: death itself. Furthermore, Christ's crucifixion can be thought of as a kind of death to the Law. He died in order to satisfy the Law's sanctions against the sinner: exile, curse and death. That Christ would need to do this, proves the insufficiency of the Law as a means of justification. I see this death as God's judgment in which I acquiesce.

Paul uses the terms "die" and "live" metaphorically for "being condemned" and "being justified" respectively; cf. Gen. 17:18, where "live before thee" means to be accepted by God. At the beginning of this section Paul prosaically talks about justification. As he becomes more lyrical he calls this "life".

The interpretation adopted here results from the perception that Paul is answering the calumny that Christianity is the minister of sin, since when they were in Judaism they did not think of themselves as sinners (verse 15). He shows that instead it is the Law (διὰ νόμου) which gave him his sinful status, though he also accepts full blame himself ("I constitute myself a sinner", "I died"). Later, in Romans 7, he will correct any false conclusion from this that there is anything intrinsically wrong with the Law.

(20) *Yet I live, but it is no longer I, but Christ lives in me. What I now live in the flesh, I live in the faith which is in the Son of God who loved me and*

surrendered himself for me. (21) *I do not set aside the grace of God, for if there is a righteousness through the Law, then Christ died for nothing.*

(20) I have been condemned with Christ, yet I am justified! I have been crucified with Christ, yet I live! But this justification has nothing to do with myself and my own works, it is due to the fact that I believe in the Son of God who loved me and surrendered himself to the exile of death by crucifixion for me. This is the secret of my present material existence in this world. I am a living demonstration of the condemning and justifying significance of the death and resurrection of Christ! This is what I meant when I said that God was pleased to reveal his Son in me. (21) I do not spurn the free gift of God's grace in Christ's self-giving for me. This is what I would be doing if I were to seek salvation through the Law, but it would be like saying Christ did not need to have died.

Paul explains the highly compressed, metaphorical and incorporational sentence, "Christ lives in me", by means of the literal and relational statement "I live by the faith of the Son of God who loved me and gave himself for me." I have already commented on the similarity of this statement to the one made in 1:4 and noted there the parallel and contrast with Isa. 43:3f. We should note too that Paul here returns to the designation "Son of God" for Jesus, an interesting contrast with Isa. 43:6 where the sons of God are the exiled Israelites on whose behalf the gentiles are to be given up as a ransom. The language is highly individual. Proverbs had individualized the idea of the ransom (11:9; 21:18); this verse individualizes the love too. W. Popkes (*Christus Traditus* [Zürich, 1967], 254) has argued that self-surrender statements developed later in the tradition than statements in which God is the one who surrenders Jesus. He thought it was highly likely that the earliest form of the tradition which has survived is to be found in Mark 9:31 (*ibid.*, 266): "The Son of Man is surrendered into the hands of men." If this is the case, there is perhaps even there an allusion to Isa. 43:4: "I will give men for thee and peoples for thy life", where the "men" are gentiles, the very ones into whose hands this "man" (son of man) was to be surrendered. Again we find the form of Isaiah 43, but the content is reversed, it is Jesus not the gentiles who are handed over.

The influence of Isaiah 43 in intertestamental Judaism is attested in an interesting way by the LXX translation of Isa. 53:9: "and I shall give the wicked instead of his doom, and the rich instead of his death", thus making the Servant the beneficiary of the wicked as a *kōper*. This version frequently uses the term παραδιδόναι in this chapter, but it emphasizes Yahweh's surrender of the Servant rather than the Servant's self-surrender as is found in the MT. If the early church's thinking on Christ's surrender was influenced by Isaiah 53, this must have taken place in circles which were not dependent upon the LXX alone.

Verse 21 explicitly presents the argument from hindsight: Christ is the solution so there must have been a need. He has already said this implicitly by means of the statement "I have been crucified with Christ". It is significant, however, that he does not use this kind of argument until he has clearly stated that he came to Christ originally because he already knew there could be no salvation through the Law (verse 15). Thus the solution does not really precede the problem for Paul. Rather reflection on the solution reinforces the analysis of the problem which originally drove him to this particular solution (Christ).

To conclude, in the light of an understanding of second-temple Jewish soteriology as exemplified at Qumran, we have examined a passage from Paul's early writings (Galatians 1 and 2), in which he gives an account of his change from Judaism to Christianity and reflects upon its significance. From Qumran we saw that the expression "covenantal nomism" only gives a partial picture of Jewish soteriology and in any case does not succeed in excluding salvation by Law observance. This enabled us to perceive that Paul is indeed expressing in Gal. 2:15–21 the futility of Judaism's seeking salvation by Law observance. It is not correct to say that for Paul this solution (Christ) precedes the problem (the impossibility of salvation through the Law). Rather, the solution vindicates the analysis of the problem which originally drove him to this particular solution.

We saw too that there was concern for the salvation of the Community as well as for the individual at Qumran: Israel herself needed to be saved from the exile of Gentile oppression and there was a desire to fulfil the conditions laid down in scripture for her restoration. We saw that this "exilic soteriology" was understood by Paul in a way radically different from that of contemporary Judaism:

1. The *herem* which Israel was to inflict upon the apostates on pain of being herself subject to the *herem*, Paul now solemnly pronounces upon the Judaizers who trouble the peace of the church.

2. Both Paul and Judaism agree that a pre-condition of salvation is that sin must be dealt with through an atonement. For Judaism this ransom was the gentiles and the wicked in Israel. For Paul it is Christ who had to be surrendered, and who had surrendered himself voluntarily.

3. This atonement of the last days would be on behalf of Israel according to Judaism, but for Paul it was both for Israel and for the gentiles, considered as individuals, not just as corporate entities: "He gave himself for me".

4. The liberation implicit in the restoration was for Judaism a liberation from gentile oppression and pollution. For Paul it is a liberation from sin and from the Law.

5. The exilic soteriology looked forward to the reunion of the Israelite tribes in the promised land. Contemporary Judaism understood this in terms of a return of the diaspora, but Paul thought of a new entity, whose unity was paramount in God's plans: the church. We

noticed that Paul uses incorporational language metaphorically to express a relational reality. Probably his purpose in doing this so often is to express the importance of the "post-exilic" unity of Christians in Christ according to God's plan.

Notes

1. S. Schulz, "Zur Rechtfertigung aus Gnaden in Qumran und bei Paulus", *ZTK* 56 (1959), 155–185.
2. H. Braun, "Römer 7, 7–25 und das Selbstverständnis des Qumran-Frommen", *ZTK* 56 (1959), 1–18.
3. London, 1977.
4. Late 1977. *Salvation and Atonement in the Qumran Scrolls*, WUNT II.3 (Tübingen).
5. IQSa 1:1–5.
6. IQM 1:1f.
7. For my interpretation of the *cruces* in this passage see *Salvation and Atonement*, 64–67.
8. *Salvation and Atonement, passim.*
9. *Praem. Poen.* xiv.79ff.; xvi.95; xix.186f.; xxviii.
10. See my "Atonement Constructions in the Old Testament and the Qumran Scrolls", *EQ* 46 (1974), 156; also *Salvation and Atonement*, 78f., 98f.
11. *Paul and Palestinian Judaism*, 427.
12. *Ibid.*, 442–444.
13. California, 1974.
14. *Gospel and Land*, 161.
15. I hold the South-Galatian theory and that the epistle was written before the events described in Acts 15:2ff. The prosopography of Galatians is that of the situation before Silas and Timothy came into Paul's *entourage* for the second missionary journey. If a later date and a northern address is accepted, however, the soteriological conclusions will not be affected.
16. Biblical quotations are from the Revised Version, except where the writer has made his own translations.
17. Cf. 1 Cor. 5:3–5; Acts 5:9; Gal. 5:12 (ἀποκόπτεσθαι, cf. Deut. 23:2, LXX [23:1, Heb.]).
18. Cf. also Acts 9:15 with Isa. 49:6f.; and Acts 26:16–18 with Isa. 42:6f.
19. Ezek. 39:27. God is sanctified *in* the returning Israelites at the restoration. 1QH 7:12 God separates *in* the Community's Founder between the righteous and the wicked according to the attitude they take towards the Founder; cf. 2 Cor. 2:16.

Chapter 3

INTERPRETATIONS OF PAUL IN THE ACTS OF PAUL AND THECLA

E. MARGARET HOWE

I. Introduction

THE APOCRYPHAL *ACTS OF PAUL*[1] was composed in Asia Minor sometime during the latter half of the second century AD. It is complete in a number of Greek manuscripts and in many versions (Latin, Syriac, Slavic, and Arabic). Parts of it also exist in Coptic and Ethiopic. Tertullian informs us that the author was a presbyter living in Asia who wrote, "as if he were augmenting Paul's fame from his own store." The presbyter, "after being convicted, and confessing that he had done it from love of Paul, was removed from his office."[2] Tertullian maintains that these writings "wrongly go under Paul's name," which suggests that some claim was being made concerning apostolic authorship. The superscription of the Coptic version reads, "The Acts of Paul [according to] the Apostle,"[3] which would support such a theory. The letter of Paul to the Corinthians, which forms a part of this literary unit, is introduced in a style similar to that of the canonical letters.[4] Tertullian rejects the possibility of Pauline authorship, and dismisses the document as being of questionable validity. Other early writers, however, seem to assume that even if not written by the Apostle, the writings do contain a core of trustworthy material. Origen makes reference on two occasions to the *Acts of Paul*, and indicates that the document is to be taken seriously.[5] Hippolytus suggests that the story in the *Acts of Paul* concerning the lion which refused to attack Paul, lends support to the truth of similarly amazing stories in the book of Daniel. In so arguing, Hippolytus seems to be classifying the *Acts of Paul* along with books more readily accepted as being canonical.[6] Eusebius, although relegating the *Acts of Paul* to his

33

list headed "spurious," nevertheless distinguishes it from inferior heretical works.[7] Further evidence of the esteem in which the *Acts of Paul* was
held in the early centuries is found in the textual tradition of the New
Testament. In at least two instances, details of information have found
their way from the *Acts of Paul* into early manuscripts of canonical
books.[8]

Indications such as these sharpen interest in Tertullian's statement
that the author of the *Acts of Paul* was removed from his ecclesiastical
office on account of this document.[9] Was the presbyter deposed because
he falsely claimed apostolic authorship for the work, or was he desposed
because the viewpoints expressed in the document were considered
heretical? Tertullian implies the former, and if this is so, we are encoun-
tering the Christian community at a time when there was a strongly
developed sensitivity to the issue of canon. The presbyter's motives may
have been sincere, but his attempt to propagate his own opinions by
claiming for them apostolic authority, met with suspicion. The church
could not approve the production of documents falsely claiming apostolic authorship. Such a situation could too easily be used by opponents
to cast doubt on the integrity of the Christian tradition.[10]

The alternative possibility, that the viewpoints expressed in the
Acts of Paul might have been considered heretical, is not without significance. However, it is clear that the presbyter himself was evidently an
admirer of Paul and would probably not have intentionally distorted the
Pauline tradition with which he was familiar. Furthermore, if his work
did represent viewpoints considered heretical, it is hard to understand
why the *Acts of Paul* maintained its popularity and standing among the
early Fathers. It seems more probable that the viewpoints expressed in
this document reflected popular religious traditions widely held in the
second century AD. The issue which must then be addressed is, to what
extent do these popular religious traditions embody an accurate interpretation of Pauline thought?

In order to explore this issue, attention will be focused on one
section of the work, the *Acts of Paul and Thecla*. This section is of particular significance because of the central role assumed by a woman in the
narrative. Tertullian suggests that the document was written in order to
establish some kind of precedent to justify participation by women in
the church's ministry of teaching and baptizing. Tertullian sees no place
for a woman in any such rôle. He states that the document is quite out of
harmony with Paul's attitude towards women expressed in the canonical material:

> How credible would it seem, that he who has not permitted a woman even
> to learn with over-boldness, should give a female the power of teaching
> and baptising! 'Let them be silent,' he says, 'and at home consult their own
> husbands.'[11]

In this statement Tertullian has isolated two issues arising from the *Acts of Paul and Thecla*. Both concern the leadership rôle of women in the church. One issue relates to the right of a woman to teach; the other concerns the right of a woman to baptize. The document also raises issues concerning human sexuality and its expression in the context of the Christian faith. Has the writer of the *Acts of Paul and Thecla* accurately represented the Pauline position in relation to these issues? Could it be that in this apocryphal document we recapture the Pauline spirit more surely than we do in the writings of Tertullian? Does the *Acts of Paul and Thecla* provide us with a "liberation document," carrying to its logical conclusion the Pauline teaching concerning the equality of men and women expressed in Galatians 3:28? The story of Thecla forms a basis for answering questions such as these.

II. Paul's Teaching on "Self-control" and "Resurrection"

The narrative begins with the arrival of Paul in Iconium,[12] where he is welcomed into the house of Onesiphorus.[13] There he presents his teaching.

> And when Paul had entered the house of Onesiphorus, there was great joy, and bending of knees, and breaking of bread, and the word of God concerning self-control and resurrection (*AThe* 5).

As in the first gospel Matthew introduces the teaching of Jesus by crystallizing the characteristics of the true disciple in a series of beatitudes, so the presbyter introduces the teaching of Paul by depicting the true Christian in a series of sayings. In most of these sayings, the protasis has reference to "self-control," while the apodosis has reference to the special rewards reserved for those whom this virtue characterizes. This can be seen in the following examples.

Happy are the pure in heart — because they will see God.

Happy are the ones who have kept the flesh pure — because they will become a temple of God.

Happy are those who exercise self-control — because to them God will speak.

Happy are the ones who have parted company with this world — because they will be very pleasing to God.

Happy are those who have wives as though not having them[14] — because they will inherit God.

Happy are the ones who have preserved the baptism — because they will rest before the father and the son.

Happy are the bodies of the virgins	because they will be very pleasing to God and they will not forfeit the reward of their purity (AThe 5–6).

It is immediately apparent that the presbyter interprets the Pauline teaching about "self-control" (ἐγκράτεια) in relation to the concept of "purity" (ἁγνεία). The understanding of purity expressed here, and in the story which follows, differs from that found in the biblical documents. Here the word is used to denote celibacy or virginity rather than abstention from unlawful sexual activity.[15] Such an interpretation indicates that the presbyter was influenced by the same encratite modes of thought which were current in the Ebionite, Gnostic and Montanist movements of his time. A dualistic concept of the universe led to the assumption that physical matter was evil. Sensual enjoyment in all its forms was therefore depreciated. The idea of ἐγκράτεια as endurance or steadfastness resulting from inner strength, has given way to the concept of ἐγκράτεια as an ascetic way of life, pursued as a means of achieving the favor of God.[16]

The presbyter interprets the Pauline teaching about "resurrection" (ἀνάστασις) in terms of a goal to which the celibate aspires. It is a reward reserved for those who live the life of "purity," and it will be attained in the future.[17] This is contrasted with the teaching which Demas and Hermogenes are propagating. They maintain that "the resurrection of which this man speaks has already taken place; it has come about in the children we have, and knowing the true God we are risen" (AThe 14). For these teachers, the resurrection is something already experienced. It involves knowledge of God and the continuance of life through childbirth. Spiritual and physical union combine to bring about this resurrection; the one does not preclude the other. But the presbyter designates Demas and Hermogenes as "hypocrites" and implies that they are false teachers (AThe 1). These two related themes, "self-control" and "resurrection," dominate the narrative which follows in the Acts of Paul and Thecla.

III. Thecla and Paul

As the story unfolds, we are introduced to Thecla. She sits at an open window, in a house adjacent to that in which Paul is teaching, "hearing by night and by day the word spoken by Paul concerning purity" (AThe 7). Her mother, Theocleia, anxiously sends for Thamyris, the man to whom Thecla is betrothed. Theocleia complains to Thamyris concerning Paul; he is teaching the women and the young men of the city that they must "fear only God and live in purity" (*AThe* 9). Thamyris, unable to distract Thecla from Paul's teaching, grieves over the situation. He concludes that Paul is "deceiving the souls of young men and misleading virgins (by suggesting) that they should not marry but remain as they are" (*AThe* 11). Demas and Hermogenes, fellow-travellers with Paul, though not his friends,[18] sympathize with Thamyris. They have listened at length to Paul's teaching and they too contend that "he deprives young men of wives and virgins of husbands, saying, unless you remain pure ones, and do not defile the flesh but keep it pure, there is resurrection for you in no other way" (*AThe* 12). This is described as "a new teaching of the Christians" (*AThe* 12). Thamyris accuses Paul of defrauding him of his marriage partner (*AThe* 10), and married men complain that Paul has corrupted their wives (*AThe* 15). When called before the proconsul to account for this, Paul maintains that he teaches only what has been revealed to him by God. His aim is to "draw (men) away from corruption, uncleanness, pleasure, and death, so that they will no longer be sinning" (*AThe* 17).

In the light of this, the relationship which comes into being between Thecla and Paul is of interest. In what has become the classic description of Paul, the writer presents him as,

> . . . a man small of stature, with a bald head and crooked legs, in good state of body, with eyebrows meeting and nose somewhat hooked, full of friendliness; for now he appeared like a man, and now he had the face of an angel (*AThe* 3).[19]

It is clearly not Paul's physical appearance which lures Thecla away from her betrothed. But there is nevertheless a powerful attraction which draws Thecla into a strange state of ecstasy. After listening at a distance to his teaching, Thecla "eagerly desired that she might be considered worthy to stand before Paul and to hear the word of Christ. For she had not yet seen Paul in person; she had only heard his word" (*AThe* 7). Theocleia, her mother, observes that:

> For three days and three nights Thecla has not risen from the window either to eat or to drink, but looking intently, as though towards an object of rapture, she so reverences the strange man who is teaching seductive and subtle words, that it amazes me how a virgin of such modesty can be so violently troubled. . . . My daughter, like a spider, is bound by his words to the window, seized by a new craving and a terrible passion (*AThe* 8–9).

Thamyris tries to fathom the nature of Thecla's attraction to Paul. To Demas and Hermogenes he confesses:

> I have no small inner conflict concerning Thecla, because she loves the stranger so much, and I am defrauded of my marriage (*AThe* 13).

The observations of Theocleia and Thamyris indicate that the natural affection Thecla once had for Thamyris has been replaced by an awesome and overwhelming passion directed towards Paul. Thecla is engulfed by this passion even before she sees Paul in person.

The first meeting between Paul and Thecla takes place in a prison in which Paul is being held for questioning. Thamyris has persuaded the proconsul to investigate the situation, and Paul is awaiting a hearing. Thecla bribes the doorkeeper with bracelets and a silver mirror and enters Paul's cell.[20] Within the prison, Thecla, "sitting at his feet, heard the great works of God ... and her faith began to grow as she kissed his chains" (AThe 18). Thamyris and his friends find her "seemingly chained to (Paul) in affection" (AThe 19). After Paul's removal from the prison cell, "Thecla rolled herself about over the place where Paul was seated as he taught in the prison" (AThe 20). Later, Thecla is called to the judgment-seat and is questioned concerning her refusal to marry Thamyris. She makes no reply, but stands "intently gazing at Paul" (AThe 20). Paul is banned from the city; Thecla is condemned to be burned. The writer comments:

> As a lamb in a desert place searches for the shepherd, so Thecla sought for Paul. And gazing into the crowd she saw the Lord, seated, in the likeness of Paul, and she said, 'As though I were not able to endure, Paul has come to watch over me.' And she stood there, gazing at him intently, but he went away into heaven (AThe 21).

As Paul had not yet died, this would seem to have been a vision of Jesus which Thecla interpreted in terms of a visitation from Paul. For her, indeed, Paul's presence would be more sustaining than that of Jesus.

The attempt to burn Thecla is thwarted—rain and hail miraculously quench the fire. Thecla is reunited with Paul, and she praises God for delivering her from the fire so that this reunion can take place. She asks Paul's permission to become his disciple and to accompany him on his travels. Reluctantly, he permits her to travel with him to Antioch. Here Thecla is accosted in a public place by a nobleman named Alexander. She looks about for Paul, hoping he will help her, but it seems she is left to defend herself. Thecla rebuffs Alexander's advances, and as a result finds herself for the second time condemned to death. Again she is miraculously preserved.

After this, Thecla is unable to settle in Antioch. "Thecla yearned for Paul, and she searched for him, sending around in every direction" (AThe 40). Evidently Paul has left no word concerning his whereabouts, but Thecla finally locates him in Myra and informs him of her desire to return to Iconium. The presbyter relates that when Thecla arrived in Iconium, she went to the house of Onesiphorus and "threw herself down on to the ground on which Paul had sat (as he) taught the word of God" (*AThe* 42).

Traditions about the remainder of Thecla's life vary. Some manuscripts describe how Thecla withdrew to a mountain and resided in a cave, living an ascetic life and practicing a ministry of healing. At the end of her days she

> entered into the rock alive and went underground. And she departed to Rome to see Paul, and found that he had fallen asleep. And after staying there no long time, she rested in a glorious sleep; and she is buried about two or three stadia from the tomb of her master Paul.[21]

Concerning Paul's attitude towards Thecla, comparatively little is mentioned. When Thecla visits Paul by night in the prison, the presbyter relates, "Paul did not fear anything, but conducted himself in the confidence of God" (*AThe* 18). On hearing that Thecla is condemned to be burned to death, Paul demonstrates his concern by fasting for many days. When Paul sees Thecla again, he offers a fervent thanksgiving to God. Together with Onesiphorus and his family, he rejoices with Thecla, and "there was great love" (*AThe* 25). However Paul refuses Thecla's offer to become his disciple, although he does permit her to travel with him to Antioch. When Alexander seeks Paul's permission to marry Thecla, Paul protests, "I do not know the woman of whom you speak, nor is she mine" (*AThe* 26). Paul is evidently not present when Thecla is thrown to the wild beasts; in fact, he has left no word of his whereabouts. He does not hear about her "baptism" until later, although he had previously exhorted her, "Thecla, be patient, and you will receive the water" (*AThe* 25). When the two are reunited, Paul takes Thecla by the hand and brings her to the house of Hermias. There he talks and prays with her. Although Paul then commissions Thecla, "Go and teach the word of God" (*AThe* 41), it is only after she has announced to him her plans. At the end of the story, Thecla gives to Paul money and clothing, which he is to distribute to the poor.

It seems clear that Thecla's attitude towards Paul was one of intense love and reverence, verging almost on worship. She regarded him as her strong support in time of trouble, sought him out after each miraculous deliverance, and clung with devotion to the memories she had of special times spent in his presence. Paul, on the other hand, is represented as being much less involved with Thecla than she with him. Though he fasted and prayed for her deliverance from the fire, he apparently was not to be found when she was abandoned to the wild beasts. His commissioning of Thecla to teach the word of God seems to confirm her own decision, rather than to prompt it. In the matter of

clothing and gold to be given to the poor, Paul has become the recipient
and Thecla the benefactress.

IV. Thecla and Christian Ministry

Thecla's admiration for Paul produces within her a strong desire to
participate in Christian ministry. Her initial request to accompany Paul
on his travels carries with it the promise that Thecla will cut her hair after
the fashion of a man. "And Thecla said to Paul, 'I will cut my hair and I
will follow you wherever you may go'" (AThe 25). Later, when Thecla
sets off to search for Paul in Myra, the presbyter informs us that, "taking
young men and maidens, she girded herself, and sewing her tunic into a
coat styled like that of a man, she set off for Myra" (AThe 40). It is
possible that Thecla assumed the appearance of a man in order to protect
herself as she travelled. Perhaps a man on a journey would be less likely
to attract attention or be attacked than a woman in similar circumstances. However, in the second instance mentioned above, it is clearly
stated that Thecla was accompanied by "young men and maidens," and
there is no suggestion that all of the women masqueraded as men. It
therefore seems probable that Thecla wore manly attire so that she might
participate in a ministry of preaching and teaching, on the assumption
that Paul permitted such a ministry only to men. The cutting of the hair
is intended as a bargaining point; Thecla will do this in order to make her
offer of a joint ministry more acceptable to Paul.[22] The wearing of male
attire precedes Thecla's announcement to Paul that she is travelling to
Iconium, where she intends to pursue a ministry of teaching.[23]

Thecla's assumption of male attire relates also to the expression of
her sexuality. That sexual advances are a problem is shown by the story
of Thecla's experience in Antioch, where Alexander fell in love with her.
Paul's objection to accepting Thecla as a fellow-worker was made on this
basis, "the times are shameful and you are beautiful," he said. "May no
other temptation worse than the first overtake you" (AThe 25). Evidently
Paul did not consider the short-cropped hair sufficient disguise of Thecla's femininity. Having successfully resisted the first temptation by re-
fusing to marry Thamyris, Thecla might nevertheless succumb to
another offer of marriage. In her now enlightened state, this would in
fact prove to be a more serious test. At the time when she agreed to
become betrothed to Thamyris, she did not know the "new teaching" of
the Christians. Now she is fully aware of it, and would be acting in
rebellion. Thecla is therefore discouraged from assuming the rôle of
itinerant teacher on the basis that this would expose her to temptation of
a sexual nature. So Thecla's masculine attire represents not only her
assumption of the male rôle which would thus validate her right to

teach, but also a denial of her sexual nature which might otherwise lure her into temptation. The context clearly indicates that to indulge such appetites would exclude Thecla from any meaningful rôle as a Christian teacher.

Thecla's teaching ministry is mentioned only briefly. Before the governor she presents her message:

> God alone is the compass of salvation and the reality of eternal life; for he is a refuge for the storm-tossed, relief for those oppressed, protection for those in despair . . . if a person does not believe in him, he will not live but die for ever (AThe 37).

This is a strangely negative witness and does not contain any specifically Christian feature. For eight days Thecla instructs Tryphaena and her maidservants in the word of God, and many believe her message (AThe 39). Returning to Iconium, Thecla preaches to her mother, Theocleia, and then goes on to Seleucia where she "enlightens many with the word of God" (AThe 43). Other manuscripts add that arriving in Seleucia, Thecla found herself afraid of the people. She therefore withdrew to a mountain and resided in a cave. The text continues:

> And some of the well-born women, having learned about the virgin Thecla, went to her, and learned the oracles of God. And many of them bade adieu to the world, and lived an ascetic life with her.[24]

The people of the city who visited her came because they heard that she had power to heal, and so great did that power prove to be, that "before they came near the door they were speedily released from whatever disease they were afflicted by."[25] This way of life Thecla continued until her death at ninety years of age.

Thecla's ministry of baptism is even more limited. The only baptism that she is reported as performing is that of herself. Her baptism takes place publicly, in the arena where Thecla is to be thrown to the wild animals.

> She turned and saw a large trench full of water, and she said, 'Now is the time for me to be washed.' And she threw herself in saying, 'In the name of Jesus Christ I baptize myself on the last day' (AThe 34).

But the issue of baptism is raised on more than one occasion. When Paul cautions Thecla, "May no other temptation . . . overtake you" (AThe 25), Thecla's response is, "Only give to me the seal in Christ, and temptation will not touch me."[26] Paul's reply is, "Be patient, Thecla, and you will receive the water" (AThe 25). When Paul meets Thecla in Myra, thinking that she has succumbed to temptation, Thecla reassures him with the words, "I have received the baptism, Paul, for the one who worked along with you for the gospel has also worked along with me for baptism" (*AThe* 40). The association of baptism with abstention from sexual activity is found prior to this in the benedictions with which the document opens. "The ones who have preserved the baptism" are "the virgins," "the ones who have kept the flesh pure," "those who exercise self-control" (*AThe* 5–6). But for Thecla, baptism is not only an indication that the person baptized is vowing to abstain from sexual activity; it is also a guarantee (or seal) that places the baptized person outside the realm of sexual temptation. Thecla assumes that this will be added assurance to Paul that she is a fit person to follow the way of life of a Christian minister.

The writer of this document thus clearly links the issue of sexuality with that of the appointment of a person to the office of itinerant preacher and teacher. Paul is at first reluctant to accept and commission Thecla to such a ministry because she is a woman. It is necessary for Thecla to convince Paul that she can, to some degree, conceal her femininity, and that she is able to repress and deny the expression of the sexual side of her nature. Only in this way may she aspire to such an office in the early church. The office which she does finally achieve is somewhat limited in scope, and Thecla's ministry is largely directed towards women.

V. Response

In the *Acts of Paul and Thecla*, Paul is represented as a strong proponent of the encratite viewpoint. Married people are to refrain from sexual intercourse, and unmarried people are to refrain from marriage. Sexual activity is categorized as "defilement," "impurity," "sin"; the expression of sexuality must therefore be restrained. To what extent does this decidedly negative viewpoint derive from the canonical literature relating to Paul?

Within the New Testament, Paul condemns sexual expression only when it involves the *abuse* of sexual powers. Paul describes homosexuality as a "dishonorable passion," "unnatural," "shameless" (Rom. 1:26–27). He condemns an incestuous relationship: it is immoral, and the man concerned is to be excluded from the church community (1 Cor. 5:1–2). Consorting with prostitutes must not be indulged in by Christians: ". . . shall I take the members of Christ, and make them members of a prostitute? Never!" (1 Cor. 6:15).[27] Adultery is named as a sin which would exclude a person from the kingdom of God (1 Cor. 6:9–10). But when sexual intercourse within marriage is under consideration, Paul's comments are affirmative. Confronted by an ascetic element within the Corinthian church, Paul is immediately aware of danger. The slogan, "It is well for a man not to touch a woman," was being used by some to suggest that married people should not indulge in physical union.[28] Paul views this apparently "super-spiritual" stance as being unrealistic. Such restraint is contrary to nature, and in fact exposes the Christian community to all manner of sexual temptation. If for no other reason than this, such a viewpoint should be discouraged.[29] Marriage not only provides a framework within which sexual intercourse is permissible; it is a state in which this should be encouraged. Indeed, abstention from such must be only by mutual consent and of limited duration.

In the Corinthian correspondence, Paul also confronts the issue of celibacy. In this connection, the slogan the Corinthians were seeking to popularize appears to have been, "It is well for the unmarried to remain single," the example of Paul being cited to give substance to the validity of this viewpoint.[30] Paul does not deny that for him the celibate state is preferable to marriage, but he refuses to draw from his own situation the conclusion that Christians in general should not marry. Indeed, Paul cites several reasons why this would not be good advice, among them the significant fact that the Lord assigns to each Christian the particular way of life to which he is suited. In espousing a way of life to which he is basically alien, a Christian would be courting danger.[31] When Paul does recommend celibacy as a state preferable to marriage, it is within the context of eschatological thought. The impending end of the age, with its foreboding of doom, casts a shadow over the family unit. Persecution and distress will only be multiplied to those who have family responsibilities. And the resultant urgency of the missionary task heightens the necessity for undivided allegiance to the Lord.[32]

Thus Paul's approach to the issue of sexuality and its expression within marriage is realistic and affirmative. The contracting of a marriage provides opportunity for the fulfilment of sexual desire. For most people, this is a way of life assigned by God, just as for some, celibacy is a way of life assigned by God. The question at issue is not which state is preferable, ontologically speaking, but which state is most satisfactory for a particular individual. The ascetic way of life is not an end in itself, and no useful purpose is served by imposing it as a norm upon the Christian community. To do so would be harmful. There are no special rewards promised to the celibate, nor are there special honours reserved for those who marry. The issue in itself is morally neutral. Where abstention from marriage is suggested, the reason given does not in any way imply that the purpose of such is to avoid any "corruption" or "sin" which might be associated with the act of sexual intercourse.[33] Such an issue does not even arise in Paul's treatment of the subject. The canonical Paul certainly speaks of "self-control." But for him ἐγϰϱάτεια does not imply sexual abstinence.[34] Rather it is a disciplined way of life which enables a person to fulfil the task to which he is commissioned by

God.[35] For the canonical Paul, ἐγκράτεια is not a way of salvation,[36] nor is it a means of attaining to resurrection.[37]

Another issue raised in the *Acts of Paul and Thecla* is that of Thecla's attitude towards Paul. The love Thecla once had for Thamyris is gone, and in its place is found another kind of devotion, this time devotion directed towards Paul. Although Paul is not physically attractive, Thecla finds herself bound to him in affection; he is ever uppermost in her mind, and his influence pervades her life. Thecla does not touch Paul, but she kisses his chains and rolls herself on the floor where Paul once stood. In the place of physical communication of love, there comes about an intense desire on Thecla's part to identify with Paul by participating in the same calling, that of a Christian minister. Thecla must gain Paul's acceptance and approval in order to fulfil this rôle. Even after his death, Paul's influence over Thecla is strong, and ultimately her body is laid to rest not far from his.

The canonical material parallels the *Acts of Paul and Thecla* in its suggestion that Paul's personal appearance was not outstandingly attractive, although the evidence is sometimes slight and open to other interpretation. In the *Acts of the Apostles* we read that at Lystra Paul was identified with Hermes, the short, stocky, winged messenger of the gods, rather than with the commanding figure of Zeus.[38] The Corinthian church rumoured that "his letters are weighty and strong, but his bodily presence is weak, and his speech of no account."[39] Paul himself refers to a "bodily ailment"[40] which might have hampered his preaching; and the "large letters" written with his own hand have been thought by some to indicate his shortsightedness, or some other eye problem.[41] Nevertheless, there was something about his person and activity which led some to indulge in a cult of personal devotion to the Apostle. The Lycaonians, impressed with a miraculous healing performed by Paul, wanted to worship him as though he were a god.[42] The Corinthian church was divided into factions, one of which was grouped around Paul and avowed its allegiance to him.[43] In both instances Paul firmly denounces such attitudes. The Lycaonians are directed to the one true God; the Corinthians are reminded that they were baptized into Christ and that he is to be the object of their undivided allegiance.[44] There is certainly no indication in the canonical material that the women with whom Paul worked were personal devotees of the Apostle. They are spoken of as "fellow-workers,"[45] and they move quite naturally in and out of the narrative, independently involved in their own respective ministries. The presbyter who wrote the *Acts of Paul and Thecla* wrote it, Tertullian claims, out of "love of Paul." His document reflects as its basic theme the extension of Paul's influence through his devotee, Thecla. Although personal devotion to the Apostle might have been a widespread phenomenon in the early centuries, it did not meet with Paul's approval. The Apostle strongly discouraged the existence of such personal influence within the Christian community, whether it related to him or to anyone else. Paul would have been unlikely to commission to Christian ministry either a man or a woman whose call was motivated by anything less than undivided allegiance to Christ.

A third issue raised in the *Acts of Paul and Thecla* is that of Thecla's rôle as a woman and a Christian minister. The apocryphal work strongly suggests that the woman is assuming a male rôle when she aspires to be an itinerant teacher. In order to be accepted in such a rôle, she must efface her femininity and must dress like a man. Even so, it is with reluctance that Paul commissions Thecla to her work, and the sphere of ministry she at last assumes is one which relates largely to women.

The canonical Paul handles the issue from a very different perspective. In the Corinthian correspondence, Paul assumes that women will be exercising leadership rôles in the church. If he did not assume this, his argument in 1 Cor. 11:2–6 would be meaningless.[46] The matter under discussion here is not whether a woman should pray and speak publicly in mixed gatherings of the church, but rather how she should be dressed when exercising these functions. Two points are made very clearly: (1) A woman leading congregational worship must preserve her sexual identity *as a woman*. As a woman, she will dress in a manner different from that of a man; and the man is reminded that he too should maintain this differentiation. The nature of these differences will be dictated by what seems proper to the group concerned. "Judge for yourselves," the Apostly advises, thus laying the situation open for divergent opinions. The application may vary, but the principle is to be adhered to—men and women are different because God has made them so, and being "one in Christ"[47] does not obliterate this difference. (2) A woman leading congregational worship does so by virtue of her relationship to Christ, not by virtue of her relationship to a man. She does not stand before the congregation as representative of her rôle in the created order, as the glory of man, but rather as representative of her rôle in the redemptive order, in the image of God. In covering her hair and shoulders, the woman demonstrates to the congregation that now in Christ she is restored to the original dignity and equality intended by God when he created "man" male and female.[48] No longer in subjection to man, she stands before the congregation in relation to God, as does the male. Thus the veil symbolizes her "authority" (verse 10) to stand and speak as man's equal before God.[49]

These two complementary ideas must be held in balance. In the light of the Corinthian correspondence, it is clear that Paul did not intend the manifesto, "In Christ Jesus there is neither male nor female,"[50] to be interpreted as a dictum which would de-emphasize the essential differences between man and woman. On the contrary, these are to be clearly maintained as an affirmation of the creative activity of God. But the Christ-event has brought about a radical change in the respective status of men and women. In Christ, men and women now stand side by side as equals, and this is to be reflected in the organization and worship of the local church. The canonical Paul shows no reluctance in affirming the leadership positions held by women in the Christian community. Women are spoken of as "fellow-workers" with the Apostle. Phoebe is recognized as a "deacon" and is to be accorded the same honours as any man in a similar ministry.[51] Prisca works alongside her husband in a joint ministry.[52] Tryphaena and Tryphosa and other women are listed along with various men who are commended for their Christian witness. There is no suggestion that the women are involved in any ministry other than that basic to the early church, in which each person worked for the common good.[53]

VI. Conclusion

Tertullian is right in assuming that the *Acts of Paul and Thecla* is out of harmony with Paul's attitudes and teaching, but he is wrong in his evaluation of the issues. Rather than presenting a viewpoint more liberal than that of Paul, the *Acts of Paul and Thecla* presents a viewpoint which is more restrictive. If we look to this document for an exalted portrayal of the liberated woman, who in the face of negative social pressures affirms her call to full-time ministry, and as a woman fulfils the rôle for which she is destined by God, we are in fact headed for disappointment. Thecla is but a pale reflection of such a figure. Her avenue to the stated destiny is shadowed by the denial of all within her that is essentially female. She must deny herself the fulfilment of marriage, and must cut her hair and wear her clothes as though she were a man. This alone will permit her to be accounted worthy of such a leadership position. Ever in the background of her story is Paul, causing her to be enamoured of his teaching, inspiring in her personal devotion to himself, giving or withholding his permission for her baptism or her ministry, and even in his absence and after his death, proving to be the lodestar of her being. Tertullian's analysis is convincing when he states that the writer of the *Acts of Paul and Thecla* wrote, "augmenting Paul's fame," for although the leading character of the story is Thecla, she exists only as an extension of Paul's influence and personality, and she acts only in the strength which the memory of him gives her, and in undying devotion to his cause. The document marks a retreat from the affirmation of womanhood into the byways of self-abnegation, and from the positive development of a woman's potential in leadership, to the acceptance of artificially structured rôles.

Notes

1. Ed. by J. E. Grabe in *Spicilegium* (Oxford, 1698); by C. Tischendorf in *Acta Apocrypha* (Leipzig, 1857); and by R. A. Lipsius in *Acta Apostolorum Apocrypha* (Leipzig, 1891–1903; Vols. I, II, reprinted 1959). Unless stated otherwise, the Lipsius edition has been used as a basis for translation of *AThe* in this essay. English translations are available in E. Hennecke, *New Testament Apocrypha*, Vol. II, ed. W. Schneemelcher (E.T., ed. R. McL. Wilson [Philadelphia, Westminster, 1965]) and in *The Ante-Nicene Fathers*, Vol. VIII, eds. A. Roberts and J. Donaldson (revised and supplemented ed. by A. C. Coxe [Grand Rapids, Eerdmans, 1967]).

2. *On Baptism* XVII, 19–21.

3. K[ατά]. See W. Schneemelcher, *New Testament Apocrypha*, II, 323.

4. III Cor. 3:1.

5. *De Princip.* I.2.3, ed. Koetschau, GCS 22, 30; *Com. Jn.* XX.12, ed. E. Preuschen, GCS 10, 342. See W. Schneemelcher, *New Testament Apocrypha*, II, 324 for an evaluation of this evidence.

6. *Com. Dan.* III.29.

7. *Hist. Eccles.* III.25, 4. Also listed under this heading are: the Shepherd of Hermas, the Apocalypse of Peter, the Epistle of Barnabas, the Didache, the Apocalypse of John, and the Epistle to the Hebrews.

8. Codices 181 and 460, 2 Tim. 4:19, add "Lectra, his wife, and Simaeas and Zeno, his sons," identifying the household of Onesiphorus. Codex 181, 2 Tim. 3:11, adds "which he suffered on account of Thecla", accounting for Paul's problems in Antioch.

9. *On Baptism* XVII, 19–21.

10. See A. F. Findlay, *Byways in Early Christian Literature* (Edinburgh, T. and T. Clark, 1923), 241–244.

11. *On Baptism* XVII, 21–23, citing 1 Cor. 14:34–35. Tertullian expresses a similar sentiment concerning women elsewhere in his writings: "The very women of these heretics, how wanton they are! For they are bold enough to teach, to dispute, to enact exorcisms, to undertake cures—it may be even to baptize" (*Contra Haer.* XLI.13–14).

12. Cf. Acts 13:51–14:6.

13. Cf. 2 Tim. 1:16–18; 4:19. These texts suggest that Onesiphorus was a resident of Asia, but the tradition that his home was in Iconium has survived only in *AThe*.

14. Cf. 1 Cor. 7:29.

15. Cf. J. M. Ford, "The Meaning of Virgin," *NTS* 12 (1965–66), 293–299. Ford offers evidence that the concept of virginity in the early Christian era was wider than is generally acknowledged. It could include, for example, people married only once. This does not apply in *AThe*. Thecla must break her betrothal if she is to respond fully to Paul's teaching.

16. W. Grundmann, ἐγκράτεια, *TDNT* 2 (1964), 339–342.

17. Cf. W. L. Lane, "I Tim. iv.1–3. An Early Instance of Over-realized Eschatology?" *NTS* 11 (1964–65), 164–167. Lane suggests (on the basis of 2 Tim. 2:18 and 1 Tim. 4:1–3) that the false teachers referred to here were theologically

motivated in forbidding marriage. They believed that the "age to come" had come, because the resurrection of Jesus was an event of the past. Jesus' statement, "in the resurrection they neither marry nor are given in marriage" (Matt. 22:30), was therefore applied by these teachers to the present age of the church. This differs from the situation in *AThe*, but forms an interesting parallel in the relationship between celibacy and resurrection.

18. Cf. 2 Tim. 4:10, 1:15, where Demas and Hermogenes are mentioned among those who had once been Paul's supporters but who later discontinued their association with the Apostle. Here they are introduced as hostile to Paul and in disagreement with his message from the start.

19. E. Hennecke, *New Testament Apocrypha*, II, 354. This unflattering description of Paul may be influenced by the canonical writings (e.g., 2 Cor. 10:10; Gal. 4:13–14). A. F. Findlay cites a more attractive description of Paul in the Ethiopian *Contendings of the Apostles* (Budge, ii.531): "He was a vigorous man of fine upright stature, and his countenance was ruddy with the ruddiness of the stem of the pomegranate; his complexion was clear, and his cheeks were full and bearded and of the colour of a rose" (*Byways in Early Christian Literature*, 336). Cf. the description of Socrates in F. Thilly, *A History of Philosophy*, 3rd ed., rev. by Ledger Wood (New York, Holt, Rinehart and Winston, 1966), 63: "In personal appearance Socrates was not prepossessing. He was short, stocky, and stout, blear eyed and snub nosed; he had a large mouth and thick lips and was careless in his dress, clumsy and uncouth.... But all these peculiarities were forgotten when he began to speak, so great were his personal charm and the effect of his brilliant conversation." Cf. Plato, *Symposium* 215b, 221b; Aristophanes, *Clouds* 362.

20. Cf. Chrysostom, *Hom. Ac. Ap.* 25, "Hear about the blessed Thecla. She gave her gold that she might see Paul, but you, that you may see Christ, do not give a single obol"; cited by Findlay, 335.

21. ANF, 491.

22. Cf. Acts 16:3. Timothy underwent circumcision in order to be counted worthy to accompany Paul as a fellow-worker.

23. Whether Thecla's clothing was exclusively male is open to question. The longer ending in some mss. describes how "lawless men" who approached the cave caught hold of Thecla's veil and were able to tear off a part before the rock opened up to rescue her. ANF, 492.

24. ANF, 491–492.

25. ANF, 492.

26. Cf. *Herm. Sim.* IX.xvi.3–7, xvii.4.

27. H. von Campenhausen, *Tradition and Life in the Church* (London, Collins, 1968), 110.

28. 1 Cor. 7:1. Cf. J. C. Hurd, *The Origin of 1 Corinthians* (London, SPCK, 1965), 158–169.

29. 1 Cor. 7:2–7. Cf. F. F. Bruce, *Paul: Apostle of the Free Spirit* (Exeter, Paternoster Press, 1977; Grand Rapids, Eerdmans, 1977), 226–267.

30. 1 Cor. 7:8–9. Cf. J. C. Hurd, *Origin of 1 Corinthians*, 165–167.

31. 1 Cor. 7:7, 9, 17.

32. 1 Cor. 7:25–35. Cf. F. F. Bruce, *1 and 2 Corinthians* (Greenwood, S.C., Attic Press, 1971), 73–76.

33. Cf. C. K. Barrett, *First Epistle to the Corinthians* (New York, Harper and Row, 1968), 255. Barrett observes that the comment, "all things come from God" (1 Cor. 11:12), clearly indicates Paul's stance in this matter. God is the source of

sexual differentiation and sexual function. In no sense, therefore, can these be considered evil.

34. 1 Cor. 7:9.

35. 1 Cor. 9:24-27. Cf. *TDNT* 2 (1964), 341-342.

36. Rom. 3:28. Cf. F. F. Bruce, *The Epistle of Paul to the Romans* (London, Tyndale, 1963), 108-109.

37. 1 Cor. 15:22.

38. Acts 14:12. Cf. W. S. Fox, *The Mythology of All Races*, I, *Greek and Roman Mythology* (New York, Cooper Square, 1964), where Zeus is described as "a fully developed man standing or seated in an attitude of serene dignity and undisputed power," whereas later representations of Hermes depict him as "a youth, nude or scantily garbed, shod with the winged sandals" (163, 195). Luke, however, comments that Paul was identified with Hermes because he acted as spokesman. J. Munck (*The Acts of the Apostles* [New York, Doubleday, 1967], 131-132) reminds us that although bearing Greek names, the two gods referred to here might well have been local deities about whose personal appearance we know nothing.

39. 2 Cor. 10:10.

40. Gal. 4:12-15.

41. Gal. 6:11. Cf. Gal. 4:15.

42. Acts 14:13. See Ovid, *Metamorphoses*, viii.626ff., and cf. F. F. Bruce, *The Acts of the Apostles* (Greek Text) (London, Tyndale, 1951), 281-282, with ref. to W. M. Calder, "New Light on Ovid's Story of Philemon and Baucis" in *Discovery*, iii (1922), 207ff.

43. 1 Cor. 1:12.

44. Cf. C. K. Barrett, *First Corinthians*, 43-49.

45. Rom. 16:3.

46. I am indebted to C. K. Barrett (*First Corinthians*, 247-258) for much of the argument of this paragraph. See also J. C. Hurd, *Origin of 1 Corinthians*, 182-184.

47. Gal. 3:28.

48. Gen. 1:27.

49. For discussion of the controversial counterpart to this passage, namely 1 Cor. 14:33-36, see C. K. Barrett, *First Corinthians*, 329-334.

50. Gal. 3:28.

51. Rom. 16:1. The word διάκονος, here translated "deacon" (RSV), is the same word as that used to describe Epaphras (Col. 1:7), Paul (Col. 1:25), and Tychicus (Col. 4:7). In the three latter instances, where men are referred to, the RSV significantly translates the word "minister."

52. Rom. 16:3; Acts 18:26.

53. 1 Cor. 12:7.

Chapter 4

THANKSGIVING WITHIN THE STRUCTURE OF PAULINE THEOLOGY

PETER T. O'BRIEN

AT THE CONCLUSION OF HIS STUDY on early Christian hymns Reinhard Deichgräber, when discussing the theology of praise and thanksgiving, aptly commented: "The praise of the church is the response to God's act of salvation . . . praise is never the first word, but always occurs in the second place . . . [it is] never *prima actio*, but always *reactio, reactio* to God's saving activity in creation and redemption, to his orderly working in nature and history."[1] The purpose of this paper, affectionately dedicated to my esteemed teacher, Professor Bruce, under whose supervision my research into the subject of Pauline thanksgiving was conducted, is to determine generally what place the theme of thanksgiving[2] had within Paul's teaching and, in particular, whether Deichgräber's comment is consistent with the texts dealing with thanksgiving in the Pauline letters.

I. Introduction

At the outset it is necessary to limit the area of inquiry. Our investigation will be restricted to the instances of the εὐχαριστέω word-group (including εὐχάριστος and εὐχαριστία), together with examples of χάρις when it has the meaning of "thanksgiving" or "thankfulness"—a total of some forty-six occurrences,[3] which are fairly evenly distributed throughout the letters of the Pauline corpus, appearing in every epistle except Galatians and Titus. But no attempt will be made to examine terms for praise (the αἰνέω and ὁμολογέω word-groups), doxology (δόξα and its cognates), blessing (εὐλογέω, εὐλογητός, etc.), boasting (καυχάομαι and kindred words), rejoicing (χαίρω and related words) and worship (προσκυνέω, etc.) where in certain contexts at least the notion of thanksgiving appears to be present.[4] Some of these examples will be noted but for reasons of space a detailed examination will not be made.

Then, too, it is not our intention to investigate the so-called hymnic passages of the Pauline letters, e.g. Eph. 1:3–14; Phil. 2:6–11; Col. 1:15–20; 1 Tim. 3:16; etc. These have been treated in some detail in recent years,[5] though it might be argued that the fruits of these stylistic and exegetical inquiries still need to be harvested within the field of Pauline theology generally, to say nothing of the theology of the New Testament. But that is another question.

Rather, it is our intention to note briefly how the language of thanksgiving was employed outside the New Testament as well as in the non-Pauline material of the New Testament before classifying the uses found in Paul.

II. The Thanksgiving Terms Outside the New Testament

Except for some isolated instances of εὐχάριστος and its cognates in the classical literature, this word-group[6] did not appear until the Hellenistic period. It was not unrelated to χάρις when the latter meant either "a *sense of favour* received," "*thankfulness*," "*gratitude*"; or "*grace*" shown toward someone.[7] The verb εὐχαριστέω appeared in the third century BC in Asia Minor and Egypt meaning "to do a good turn to" (someone), "to oblige."[8] In the following century it came to mean "to be grateful" and "to give thanks," while εὐχάριστος, the first εὐ-construction to occur, most often meant "grateful," e.g. a "grateful city" (ἡ πόλις εὐχάριστος),[9] and this continued as its usual meaning.[10] Εὐχαριστία, like χάρις with reference to grace felt on the part of the receiver, meant "gratitude" or "thankfulness," and only later came to mean "the expression of gratitude," i.e. "thanksgiving."

According to Ledogar, by the first century BC εὐχαριστέω meant "to thank," "give thanks," "return thanks" more frequently than "to be thankful," so that in the New Testament the former may be its only meanings. If so then it signifies "*the outward expression in word or deed of the interior sentiment of gratitude for a favor received.*"[11]

All three terms were found frequently in the *inscriptions* either to express gratitude to political persons, groups, etc., with an accompanying promise of loyalty, or to offer thanksgiving to the deities for favours received.[12] In the *papyri* the verb was used in a variety of ways, sometimes meaning "to oblige" or "to do a favour,"[13] but more often in the sense of "to give thanks," as an expression of gratitude for blessings received, to either the gods or men (cf. P. Lond. 42).[14]

When we turn to the LXX we note that εὐχαριστέω and εὐχαριστία are completely absent from the canonical books, in spite of the fact that the Psalter might have provided ample opportunity for their use.[15] Εὐχαριστέω appeared only slowly and tentatively in Jewish Biblical literature—in those books of the Apocrypha which betrayed the clearest Hellenistic influence.[16] Apparently, as has been suggested, these words had not come into their own even in pagan circles prior to 200 BC, while Hebrew verbs such as ברך and הודה already had εὐλογέω and ἐξομολογέομαι as Greek equivalents.[17] Of all the books in the LXX 2 Maccabees has the most frequent and widest range of uses.[18]

Philo of Alexandria used εὐχαριστέω and an unusually large number of derivatives well over one hundred times.[19] Thanksgiving obviously played an important role in his thought,[20] and this is all the more unusual when it is borne in mind that he was frequently commenting on those texts of the LXX where εὐχαριστέω and its cognate noun did not appear. Thanksgiving, according to this Alexandrian Jew, was the highest of all virtues, a work of God in man and yet a duty incumbent on both him and creation alike.

In Josephus the verb "to thank" (εὐχαριστέω) was employed to denote political gratitude (or lack of it!), e.g. with reference to Hyrcanus II and Herod the Great (J.W. 1.214), where εὐχαριστέω is contrasted with ἀχάριστος ("ungrateful"). The verb also occurs with a more general sense of "to congratulate"[21]—a meaning already present in Polybius. Even here the note of thanksgiving is not absent, as those who offer their congratulations have benefitted (or are to benefit) by what has happened (cf. J.W. 1.457).

III. The Thanksgiving Terms in the non-Pauline Material of the New Testament

As we examine the non-Pauline instances in the New Testament of the thanksgiving word-group (including χάρις when it meant "thanksgiving" or "gratitude") several interesting facts emerge. First, the occurrences in these writings are few. The noun εὐχαριστία ("thanksgiving") does not appear in the Gospels at all, and is found only in Tertullus' speech for the prosecution at Paul's trial before Felix (Acts 24:3), together with two liturgical passages of the Apocalypse (Rev. 4:9; 7:12); while, apart from the Last Supper and the Feeding of the Four Thousand (together with the Feeding of the Five Thousand at John 6:11, 23), εὐχαριστέω ("to give thanks") appears on only six occasions: Luke 17:16; 18:11; John 11:41; Acts 27:35; 28:15 and Rev. 11:17. Χάρις meaning "thanks" turns up only once outside of Paul at Heb. 12:28.[22] Second, in none of these occurrences does εὐχαριστέω have an epistolary function, i.e. to introduce and indicate the main themes of a letter. Paul, who utilized a letter-form of the day, at the same time developing and transforming it, was the only New Testament writer to have done so. This leads to a third observation, namely, that in the non-Pauline instances (apart from Acts 24:3)[23] εὐχαριστέω and εὐχαριστία apply to thanksgivings over food, or to prayers which are quoted or reported. No strictly exhortatory uses are to be found outside of Paul.

The public nature of thanksgiving is accented on several occasions. So the leper after his cleansing returns to Jesus and *exhibits his gratitude* by glorifying God (Luke 17:15) and by publicly thanking Jesus as he falls at his feet (εὐχαριστῶν αὐτῷ, verse 16). In the resurrection of Lazarus scene (John 11:41) the Fourth Evangelist presents the prayer of Jesus: "Father, I thank you (εὐχαριστῶ σοι) that you have heard me." This public acknowledgment is made because, "I knew that you always hear me, but I said this for the benefit of the people standing here, that they may believe that you sent me" (verse 42, NIV). Here the thanksgiving is designed to evoke or increase the faith of those in whose presence it is uttered (cf. Acts 27:35).

In the Synoptic accounts of the Last Supper εὐχαριστέω ("to give thanks") and εὐλογέω ("to bless, praise") appear to have been used synonymously, and any subtle distinctions *in this context* are difficult to sustain. Whether or not we explain the use of εὐχαριστέω, with Jeremias[24] as a "graecism" of the Semitic εὐλογέω or with Robinson[25] as an increasing tendency of Christians to speak of thanksgivings, in contrast to Jews who referred to blessings, the point is that the former has reference to a prayer of thanksgiving said over the bread (Luke 22:19; cf. 1 Cor. 11:24) and the cup (Mark 14:23 and parallels). It is quite possible that this was already the common word used for the blessing at table in Hellenistic Judaism.[26] It is difficult to determine the exact content of the blessing used. In Jesus' day it was probably not fixed, but we may assume with Audet, Jeremias and others that Jesus gave it a content that was proper to him. Certainly the idea of thanksgiving to God was present—that expression of gratitude for the fruits of the earth encouraged in the Old Testament (Deut. 26:10, 11) and followed by the rabbis (*m.Ber.* 6.1).

Several other instances of the verb εὐχαριστέω appear in the contexts of meals. But this does not mean we are obliged to read "Eucharistic" associations into them, even if the basic pattern of λαβὼν ἄρτον – εὐχαριστήσας – κλάσας – ἔδωκεν ("he took bread, gave thanks, broke it and gave it") reminds us of the Last Supper or even suggests the accounts were written up with this in mind (cf. Mark 8:6; Matt. 15:36; John 6:11; cf. verse 23; Acts 27:35).

At Acts 24:3 in the context of Tertullus' speech (verses 2–

8) for the prosecution at Paul's trial before Felix the expression "with all thankfulness" (μετὰ πάσης εὐχαριστίας) occurs, and it is clear that the words, composed in accordance with the conventional formal pattern for such occasions, connote polite gratitude.[27]

In the Apocalypse the verb εὐχαριστέω occurs in an ascription of praise by the twenty-four elders (Rev. 11:17). This constitutes "the first heavenly answer to the proclamation in verse 15,"[28] where the kingdom of the world is said to have become "the kingdom of our Lord and of his Christ, and he shall reign for ever and ever." God is addressed directly in the second person, "We give thanks to you (εὐχαριστοῦμέν σοι), Lord God Almighty, who is and was," while the grounds for thanksgiving are spelled out in the ὅτι-clause which immediately follows.[29] Here εὐχαριστέω which is used in the context of worship (προσεκύνησαν τῷ θεῷ, verse 16) refers to the praise of God because of his being, his reign and his judgment. Εὐχαριστία ("thanksgiving") appears twice in doxologies of the Apocalypse (Rev. 4:9; 7:12) where the glory of God is acclaimed. "Thanksgiving" is parallel to "glory" (δόξα) and "honour" (τιμή)[30] at 4:9, and one of a series of seven such terms in 7:12. In such contexts it is not possible to draw any precise distinctions between the various terms. Creation (4:11) rather than redemption is the basis for praise. In a strict sense God is not being given anything. Rather, his right to glory, honour, thanksgiving, etc. is being ratified.[31] In the context εὐχαριστία "shows very little that would specify it as thanksgiving."[32]

The non-Pauline uses of our terms in the New Testament are thus restricted, applying, in the main, to thanksgiving offered at meals or reports of prayers where the notion of gratitude, which is expressed outwardly or publicly, predominates. The "liturgical" uses in the Apocalypse are exceptions.

IV. The Thanksgiving Terms in Paul

As we move to the Pauline material from the rest of the New Testament literature in our examination of the thanksgiving terminology, we note several significant differences. While the non-Pauline occurrences of the thanksgiving terms are few in number and restricted to particular contexts, the instances in Paul's letters are considerable,[33] appearing in every epistle except Galatians and Titus. The apostle, in fact, mentions the subject of thanksgiving more frequently per page than any other Hellenistic author, pagan or Christian.[34] In addition, Paul exhibits a great degree of flexibility in using the terms, employing them in a variety of contexts, e.g. introductory paragraphs, exhortatory material, didactic contexts and the like. His expressed grounds for thanksgiving may be as specific as the good news brought by Timothy about the Thessalonian

Christians' standing firm in their faith (1 Thess. 3:9; cf. verse 6) or as wide-ranging as God's great work of salvation in Christ, beginning with election and culminating in the possession of Christ's glory on the final day (2 Thess. 2:13, 14).

Our method of approach will be to survey the instances within the different groupings, that is, in introductory paragraphs, colloquial uses, thanksgivings said over food, those in exhortatory material, instances in didactic contexts, together with short expressions for thanksgiving, drawing out points relevant to our aim. Some occurrences, such as the colloquial uses, are not particularly important; others are highly significant, and this will be indicated as we examine each classification and then draw the threads together by way of conclusion.

(a) Introductory Paragraphs: Thanksgivings for Congregations and Individuals in the Gentile Mission

By far the most significant group of references to thanksgiving in Paul's letters are the dozen or so instances in the opening paragraphs where the apostle, sometimes in conjunction with his associates, gives thanks to God for the progress in faith, love and hope of his readers within the Gentile mission (Rom. 1:8; 1 Cor. 1:4; 2 Cor. 1:11; Eph. 1:16; Phil. 1:3; Col. 1:3; cf. verse 12; 1 Thess. 1:2; cf. 2:13; 3:9; 2 Thess. 1:3; cf. 2:13; Phlm. 4). These have been treated in some detail elsewhere[35] but for the sake of convenience we shall note those points of particular relevance to this study.

Introductory thanksgivings appear in nine of Paul's letters (1 Tim. 1:12 and 2 Tim. 1:3 are considered below), addressed to a variety of Christian readers (the thanksgiving in the letter to Philemon is with réference to an individual—a colleague of Paul). We have previously argued at length that these paragraphs, which open with a statement of thanksgiving to God, have an epistolary function:[36] that is, they introduce and present the main themes of their letters, setting the tone, atmosphere, etc. Most of them have a didactic function so that either by fresh teaching or through a recall to instruction previously given the apostle sets forth theological matters he considers to be important (cf. especially Col. 1:9–14). A paraenetic or exhortatory purpose also features in several of the introductory thanksgiving periods. It is particularly clear in the petitionary prayer of Phil. 1:9–11, the wish-prayer of 1 Thess. 3:11–13 where a transition to the second half of this letter occurs, as well as the petitionary prayer of Col. 1:9–14 which introduces exhortatory themes subsequently picked up in chapters 3 and 4.

Further, Paul's opening thanksgiving periods, particularly the thanksgivings and petitions contained within them, give evidence of the apostle's deep pastoral and apostolic concern for the readers, sometimes for an individual (cf. Phlm. 3–6), but on most occasions for congregations (cf. Phil. 1:3–11 and even 1 Cor. 1:4–9).

At the same time it must be borne in mind that these paragraphs purport to record, perhaps by way of summary, *actual* thanksgivings and *actual* petitions for the readers. The apostle's prayers of thanksgiving are directed to the God of the Psalmists (τῷ θεῷ, "God," 1 Cor. 1:4; 1 Thess. 1:2; 2:13; 3:9; 2 Thess. 1:3; 2:13; or τῷ θεῷ μου, "my God," Rom. 1:8; Phil. 1:3; Phlm. 4), who is known to Paul as the Father of Jesus Christ (cf. Col. 1:3), and they are offered "always" (πάντοτε, 1 Cor. 1:4; Phil. 1:4; Col. 1:3; 1 Thess. 1:2; 2 Thess. 1:3; 2:13; Phlm. 4) or "unceasingly" (ἀδιαλείπτως, 1 Thess. 1:2; 2:13), expressions which do not refer to continual prayer but to the apostle's remembrance of them in his regular times of prayer.[37]

Those for whom Paul gives thanks to God are the readers, some of whom were well known to him (e.g. the Philippians, Corinthians and Thessalonians), others who had been converted through the ministry of a colleague (so the Colossians had become Christians through the labors of Epaphras), while others were outside the sphere of his previous ministry and yet came within his scope as apostle to the Gentiles (cf. the Roman Christians).

The grounds for Paul's thanksgivings were manifold. Frequently the early Christian triad of faith, love and hope (with some variations: 1 Thess. 1:2, 3; 2 Thess. 1:3; Col. 1:4; Phlm. 5; cf. Rom. 1:8; Eph. 1:15) was set forth as the *immediate* basis for the expression of thanks. This might appear to place an undue stress on the "achievements" of the readers as though they sprang from their own inherent resources. But to take this line is to misunderstand Paul's statements, for on closer examination we note that these were graces given in Christ Jesus. Furthermore, the prior activity of God is regularly seen as the *final* ground for thanksgiving: at 1 Thess. 1:4 it is the Thessalonians' election by God; in 2 Thess. 2:13, 14 God had chosen these same readers to be saved, an eternal choice that included not only their final salvation but also the various means by which it was to be realized, culminating in the obtaining by the Thessalonians of the glory which the Lord Jesus possesses; in Phil. 1:6 the Philippians' godly actions (verses 3, 5) were evidence of God's good work in them which he would bring to completion on the day of Christ Jesus; at 1 Cor. 1:4–9 the stress on God's amazing, gracious activity in Christ is quite marked: note the Corinthians had been given God's grace (verse 4, τῇ χάριτι τοῦ θεοῦ τῇ δοθείσῃ), they had been enriched (verse 5, ἐπλουτίσθητε), the testimony to Christ had been confirmed in their midst (verse 6, ἐβεβαιώθη), and they had been called into fellowship with God's Son by him who is utterly reliable (verse 9, πιστὸς ὁ θεὸς δι' οὗ ἐκλήθητε); and finally, at Col. 1:12–14, the Colossian Christians are to give thanks to the One who has fitted them to share in the inheritance of his people, an inheritance that involves deliverance from the tyranny of darkness, transference into a kingdom in which his beloved Son holds sway, as well as redemption and the forgiveness of sins.

What is particularly striking in this connection is the conjunction between gospel (or its equivalent) and the grounds for thanksgiving.[38] The bases for Paul's offering of thanks are inextricably linked with the gospel and its right reception. So those for whom he expresses his gratitude to God show, by the outworking of their faith, love and hope, that the gospel has come to them dynamically (1 Thess. 1:3–5; cf. 2:13 where they are said to have welcomed the word of God), that they had been called through the gospel (2 Thess. 2:14), had the testimony to Christ confirmed in their midst (1 Cor. 1:6), demonstrated their active participation in the gospel (Phil. 1:5), or received a hope that was an integral element of that gospel (Col. 1:5). Clearly God had been mightily at work through his gospel in the midst of these groups of Christians scattered around the Mediterranean world.

(b) Colloquial Uses

Three instances of εὐχαριστέω ("give thanks," Rom. 16:4; 1 Cor. 1:14; 14:18) express gratitude at a conversational level.[39] In the first example Paul states he is grateful to Priscilla and Aquila for risking their lives[40] on his account. "All the Gentile congregations" (NEB) also express their thankfulness, either because of Paul's co-workers' action on his behalf, or else for some other unknown activity for these congregations themselves.

In the second example (1 Cor. 1:14) Paul is grateful he baptized only one or two in Corinth. Certainly none was baptized *into* his name, and because he baptized only a few he does not own a group of Corinthian Christians. There is no valid reason for misunderstanding and thus he is thankful for the way in which events have turned out.

At 1 Cor. 14:18 Paul cannot be suspected of wrongly devaluing speaking in tongues on the grounds that he did not have the gift. On the contrary, he speaks in tongues more than any of the Corinthians and for this he is thankful to God.

(c) Thanksgivings Said over Food

On six occasions[41] in Paul's letters thanksgiving over food is mentioned. At Rom. 14:6 in the context of the Christian's not judging his brother, either with reference to days or food, Paul points out that the one who eats meat does so to the Lord, for over his meal he gives thanks to God. Likewise the believer who abstains from eating meat[42] says his prayer of thanksgiving to God over his meal of vegetables.⁴³ Both recognize that what they eat are the gifts of God to be enjoyed, and they express their gratitude by their prayers of thanksgiving. In 1 Cor. 10:30⁴⁴ the note of thankfulness is underlined by the cognate χάριτι ("with gratitude"), while the verb εὐχαριστέω again points to the prayer of thanksgiving (a counterpart to the Jewish blessing) which is said by the Christian who in this context acts with a good conscience, recognizing that "the earth is the Lord's and everything in it" (verse 26).⁴⁵

The cognate noun εὐχαριστία ("thanksgiving") is found in the context of the giving of thanks at meals in 1 Tim. 4:3, 4. The Christian who believes and knows the truth has special reason for acknowledging with gratitude that all material things come from above. Everything God has created is good and is to be received "with thanksgiving" (μετὰ εὐχαριστίας). The writer is referring not to gratitude in general but that expressed in grace at meals.⁴⁶ "The sentence does not claim that an additional sanctification, over and above its intrinsic goodness as God's creature, is imparted to food by saying grace."⁴⁷ The phrase "by the word of God and prayer" (διὰ λόγου θεοῦ καὶ ἐντεύξεως, verse 5) explains the preceding statement "received with thanksgiving" (μετὰ εὐχαριστίας λαμβανόμενον), and should be understood as a single idea;⁴⁸ ἔντευξις is the actual prayer of thanksgiving, while λόγος θεοῦ points to the content of the prayer, either similar to or based on the Jewish prayer and thus containing excerpts of Scripture (e.g. Ps. 24:1).

(d) Exhortations to Thanksgiving

The three cognate words for thanksgiving (εὐχαριστέω, εὐχαριστία and εὐχάριστος) appear in several paraenetic or exhortatory contexts of the Pauline letters, particularly in Colossians.⁴⁹ The apostle exhorts the readers to be given to continual thanksgiving, whether it be private or public—a thanksgiving to be offered joyfully under all circumstances. His first exhortation at 1 Thess. 5:18 draws attention to the paradoxical nature of this Christian activity, for it is not simply "always" (πάντοτε), so much as "under all circumstances" (ἐν παντί; cf. NIV). Paul reinforces the injunction by showing that, together with prayer and rejoicing, such a giving of thanks is God's will⁵⁰ for the Thessalonians.

In other contexts the comprehensive nature of thanksgiving is stressed. So the offering of thanks to God as Father is to be the accompaniment of every activity (Col. 3:17) of those called into the body of Christ. A "thankful attitude" (εὐχάριστοι, Col. 3:15) is inculcated upon those who are in this new relationship to God—an attitude that will show itself outwardly and corporately as they "sing psalms, hymns and spiritual songs with gratitude" (ἐν [τῇ] χάριτι).⁵¹ The parallel injunction in Eph. 5:20 stresses the continuity of the thanksgiving (πάντοτε), its corporate nature (cf. verse 19; though this need not be restricted to worship in church), and the fact that it is the proper outcome[52] of those who are filled with the Spirit (verse 18). At Col. 2:7 those who have received Christ Jesus as Lord for their tradition are to continue in him "abounding in thanksgiving" (περισσεύοντες ἐν εὐχαριστίᾳ). In this context firmness and strength of faith, coupled with thanksgiving, describe the Christian way of life.

As might be expected in these exhortatory contexts thanksgiving is conjoined with petitionary prayer. So the Colossian Christians (Col. 4:2) who are exhorted to persevere in this latter activity (a point stressed by προσκαρτερεῖτε, "devote yourselves," on the one hand, and γρηγοροῦντες, "being watchful," on the other), are to match it with the giving of thanks (ἐν εὐχαριστίᾳ), i.e. their petitions will be accompanied by prayers of thanksgiving. But the Philippians (4:6), who are enjoined not to be anxious about everyday matters,[53] are instead to let their requests be made known to God with thanksgiving. Their petitions are to be definite and precise (αἰτήματα), while the thanksgiving offered is not necessarily based on a knowledge that these requests have been granted. It is the prayer offered in conjunction with the petitions, and is evidence of a thankful attitude to God for past favours and present blessings.

Finally, the exhortation to thanksgiving at Eph. 5:4, "Nor should there be obscenity, foolish talk or coarse joking, which are out of place, but rather thanksgiving (εὐχαριστία)," contrasts this Christian activity with coarse vulgarity and flippancy of speech. The latter are to be avoided by those who are "imitators of God" (5:1) because they are not fitting. Tongues given to thanking God should not be used for language that dishonours his name.

So in paraenetic contexts thanksgiving to God springs from a thankful attitude and is often linked with petitionary prayer, though it is not to be restricted to this, since it ought to accompany any and every Christian activity. Such thanksgiving may be private, or public when it can be demonstrated in corporate singing of praises to God.

(e) Instances in Didactic Contexts

Seven examples of the thanksgiving word-group appear in the main bodies of Paul's letters rather than in the exhortatory sections, though they are frequently applied to the pastoral situations concerned. The ideas associated with the notion of thanksgiving thus tend to be more theological than when the terms appear in the exhortatory paragraphs.

So in Rom. 1:21 rendering thanks is parallel to giving God glory (ἐδόξασαν ἢ ηὐχαρίστησαν). The apostle assumes men possess the raw materials of the knowledge of God. And as God's *creatures* they were bound to render glory and thanksgiving to their *creator*,[54] i.e. "to recognize his lordship and live in grateful obedience." But men were destitute of that gratitude which the knowledge they possessed should have drawn forth, and which should have been expressed in thanksgiving (note the ἀχάριστοι, "ungrateful," of 2 Tim. 3:2 which describes the character of men in the last days).[55]

Thanksgiving and the glory of God are related on several occasions in 2 Corinthians. So at chapter 4:15 Paul states that all his apostolic sufferings and afflictions are for the Corinthians' sakes. The final aim of his labours is that thanksgiving will increase (cf. 1:11), and so God will be increasingly glorified.[56] Here εὐχαριστία refers to prayer which is corporate and public, though private thanksgiving is probably not to be ruled out. The notion of gratitude is not lost, but in this context thanksgiving occurs with a broad meaning. Later in the same letter (9:11, 12) the term appears twice with special reference to the expression of gratitude by the poor saints of Jerusalem who, assuming their financial needs are met by the Corinthians and they benefit from the generosity of their fellow-believers, render grateful thanksgiving to God.

At 1 Cor. 14:16–18 the words "to bless" (εὐλογέω) and "to thank" (εὐχαριστέω) appear to be used synonymously[57] and refer to a public prayer (it is at least heard by an ἰδιώτης, "a simple listener" [verse 16]) of thanksgiving spoken in a tongue.[58] The one who has not understood it, however, cannot add his "Amen" to the thanksgiving.

The notion of public prayers offered in worship is stressed (πρῶτον πάντων) in the context of 1 Tim. 2:1ff. where four terms for prayer—δέησις ("petition"), προσευχή ("prayer"), ἔντευξις ("request") and εὐχαριστία ("thanksgiving")—are used. Although it is probably precarious to press distinctions between the terms, or at least between the first three, εὐχαριστία seems to refer to prayers of thanksgiving offered by the congregation, in conjunction with their petitions (cf. Phil. 4:6) for *all*[59] men. Our term would then point to thanksgivings in words, offered as part of public worship (though it is perhaps not to be restricted to this), as an expression of gratitude to God, possibly for past kindnesses of those for whom they pray.[60]

(f) Short Expressions of Thanksgiving

The final group of passages to be examined are those short expressions of gratitude (χάρις τῷ θεῷ, "thanks be to God")[61] which occur occasionally in Paul's letters (Rom. 6:17; 7:25; 1 Cor. 15:57; 2 Cor. 2:14; 8:16; 9:15; 1 Tim. 1:12; 2 Tim. 1:3), sometimes as the spontaneous outburst of thanksgiving by the apostle for some great blessing which he or the readers have received from God. These eight instances are scattered throughout various contexts. Two examples in the Pastorals (1 Tim. 1:12; 2 Tim. 1:3 where χάριν ἔχω is employed) function as introductory thanksgivings (and are therefore similar to his use of the εὐχαριστέω-formula) while the remaining instances occur at pivotal points in the letters denoting a change in direction in the apostle's argument. So Paul brings a section to a conclusion with an outburst of thanksgiving (e.g. Rom. 7:25; 1 Cor. 15:57; 2 Cor. 9:15), or begins a new theme on such a note (2 Cor. 2:14; 8:16).

This short formula, according to Deichgräber,[62] is a mixture of Greek and Jewish elements, the former represented by the wording χάρις τῷ θεῷ which together with its equivalents occurred often enough in the papyri, etc., while the latter was discernible in the participial expression which spelled out the grounds for thanksgiving (cf. 1 Cor. 15:57; 2 Cor. 2:14; 8:16). In fact, these short expressions of gratitude are similar to another example of "declarative praise,"[63] the eulogy or berakah.

Unlike the introductory thanksgiving formulae commencing with εὐχαριστέω where Paul gives thanks for the work of God in the lives of others, namely the readers, in these short outbursts of gratitude he often includes himself as a recipient of blessing (Rom. 7:25; 1 Cor. 15:57; 2 Cor. 2:14; and note especially 1 Tim. 1:12). Once again the grounds for the offering of thanks are wide-ranging: from the personal expression of gratitude offered to Christ for showing mercy to one who had been a blasphemer and for appointing him to his service (1 Tim. 1:12), to the "victory" (note the play on νῖκος at 1 Cor. 15:54, 55, 57) over sin and death which Christ effected on behalf of his people and in which they through the agency of God's Spirit participate (cf. Rom. 8:2). Thanks are offered to God for the assurance of ultimate deliverance from the body of this death (Rom. 7:25), for the fact that the apostles are joyful participants in their commander's triumphal procession (2 Cor. 2:14), that God has given a deep zeal and pastoral concern to Titus for the Corinthians (2 Cor. 8:16), and finally for his indescribable gift—an expression that points to the gift of generosity given to the Corinthians but which, in the light of chapter 8:9 (note the play on χάρις), must point to the ultimate gift of God's Son himself (cf. Rom. 8:32).

V. Conclusions

We have observed that the apostle Paul mentioned the subject of thanksgiving more often per page than any other Hellenistic author, pagan or Christian. Further, he exhibited a greater degree of flexibility in using the terms for thanksgiving than other New Testament writers, employing them in various types of material. The number of occurrences and, more importantly, their place within the various contexts show that the theme of thanksgiving was of some significance for the apostle.

The terms we have studied consistently express the notion of gratitude. But we have also observed that this grateful attitude regularly found outward expression in thanksgiving. There is an emphasis in the Pauline letters on the public aspect of thanksgiving. By mentioning what God has graciously done in his Son other Christians are encouraged to praise him also. This is precisely what Paul does in the openings of his letters; and as thanksgivings abound, God is glorified (2 Cor. 4:15; cf. 1:11).

In the light of these remarks it is clear that Pauline thanksgiving approximates to what we normally understand by "praise." Certainly the English word "thanksgiving" is rather more limited in its range of meanings as it normally denotes the expression of gratitude for personal benefits received and is to that extent rather man-centered. But this sort of notion does not fit Paul's language for he regularly gives thanks for graces wrought in the lives of others by God, particularly those within the churches of the Gentile mission.

We return to the point at which we began and conclude, on the basis of our limited inquiry, that thanksgiving in Paul is, as Deichgräber indicated, always a *response* to God's saving activity in creation and redemption. It is never the first word, but always the second. Even on those occasions when thanksgiving is offered for something that is to be realized in the future, for example at the parousia (cf. 1 Cor. 1:8; Phil. 1:6), it is based on the faithfulness of God who has acted so wonderfully in the past.

While the grounds for the giving of thanks in Paul's letters are manifold, the great emphasis falls upon the mighty work of God in Christ bringing salvation through the gospel. God's activity in creation is, on occasion, mentioned as a basis for the expression of gratitude (cf. Rom. 1:21 and note the thanksgivings said over food). But the majority of the Pauline references are in the context of God's grace given in Christ (1 Cor. 1:4; and cf. 2 Cor. 9:15 with 8:9). Even when gratitude is expressed for the faith, love and hope of the Christian readers these are not to be understood as the inherent achievements of the believers but are regularly related to the prior work of God in leading men and women to himself through the gospel. And because Paul's apostolic labours are intimately bound up with that saving activity among Gentiles, he is able to give thanks for his calling as an apostle to them (1 Tim. 1:12).

It has been suggested that thanksgiving was almost a synonym for the Christian life. We have already observed that all men, as God's creatures, ought to render thanksgiving and glory to him (Rom. 1:21), but fail to do so. Christians, however, because of the grace given to them in Christ Jesus are to live out their lives with joyful thanksgiving. We are encouraged to be given to thanksgiving "under all circumstances" (1 Thess. 5:18); it should be offered to the Father through Jesus Christ as the accompaniment of every activity, being the appropriate response of those who are filled with God's Spirit (Eph. 5:18-20). God's action in Christ is that of grace; our response should be one of gratitude.

Notes

1. R. Deichgräber, *Gotteshymnus und Christushymnus in der frühen Christenheit* (SUNT 5; Göttingen, Vandenhoeck & Ruprecht, 1967), 201, my translation.

2. For a survey of previous research on Pauline thanksgiving, a neglected area of New Testament study, like the more general theme of prayer, see P. T. O'Brien, *Introductory Thanksgivings in the Letters of Paul* (NovTSup 49; Leiden, Brill, 1977), 4-15.

3. Εὐχαριστέω: Rom. 1:8, 21; 14:6 (twice); 16:4; 1 Cor. 1:4, 14; 10:30; 11:24; 14:17, 18; 2 Cor. 1:11; Eph. 1:16; 5:20; Phil. 1:3; Col. 1:3, 12; 3:17; 1 Thess. 1:2; 2:13; 5:18; 2 Thess. 1:3; 2:13; Phlm. 4; εὐχαριστία: 1 Cor. 14:16; 2 Cor. 4:15; 9:11, 12; Eph. 5:4; Phil. 4:6; Col. 2:7; 4:2; 1 Thess. 3:9; 1 Tim. 2:1; 4:3, 4; εὐχάριστος: Col. 3:15; χάρις: Rom. 6:17; 7:25; 1 Cor. 15:57; 2 Cor. 2:14; 8:16; 9:15; Col. 3:16; 1 Tim. 1:12; 2 Tim. 1:3.

4. For references see G. P. Wiles, *Paul's Intercessory Prayers* (SNTSMS 24; Cambridge, University Press, 1974), 297. In addition to the terms mentioned a full-scale investigation of the praise and thanksgiving themes would require us to examine those passages in Paul's letters where none of the technical terms was present but the notion itself was. An analogous example is Ps. 116:12, "What shall I render to the Lord for all his bounty to me?" which is an interrogatory way of saying "I give thanks", but where neither εὐχαριστέω nor any other related term is used. To this extent our inquiry is a limited one. For a preliminary analysis of the verbs for praise and thanksgiving in a variety of contexts, both Hellenistic and Jewish, see R. J. Ledogar, *Acknowledgment: Praise-Verbs in the Early Greek Anaphora* (Rome, Herder, 1968). In addition to the relevant *TDNT* articles see O'Brien, *Introductory Thanksgivings*, 273-86, for further bibliographical details.

5. For bibliographical information see R. P. Martin, "Approaches to New Testament Exegesis," *New Testament Interpretation*, ed. I. H. Marshall (Exeter, Paternoster, 1977), 220-51.

6. According to T. Schermann ("Εὐχαριστία und εὐχαριστεῖν in ihrem Bedeutungswandel bis 200n. Chr.," *Philologus: Zeitschrift für das klassische Altertum* 69 [Leipzig, 1910], 376) εὐχάριστος is found once in Herodotus and three times in Xenophon, while εὐχαριστία and εὐχαριστέω seem to have been used first by Hippocrates.

7. LSJ (9th ed., 1940), 1978-79.

8. MM, 267; Schermann, *ibid.*

9. Cf. Schermann, 377.

10. Ledogar, *Acknowledgment*, 91.

11. *Ibid.*, 92.

12. MM, 267–68; BAG, 328–29. For examples see P. Schubert, *Form and Function of the Pauline Thanksgivings* (BZNW 20; Berlin, Alfred Töpelmann, 1939), 145–46.

13. See MM, 267, and Schubert, *Form*, 159, for examples.

14. Schubert, *Form*, 160–62.

15. This of course does not mean that the notion of gratitude or thanksgiving, its outward expression, was absent from the Old Testament or the Psalter in particular (see note 4). Some of C. Westermann's statements in this connection, if not incorrect, are certainly misleading; *The Praise of God in the Psalms* (London, Epworth, 1966), 26, 27.

16. Correctly noted by both Schubert, *Form*, 120, and Ledogar, *Acknowledgment*, 102.

17. While αἴνεσις was frequently used to translate תודה.

18. An epistolary usage occurs at 2 Macc. 1:11, a liturgical use at 10:7 (if the reading εὐχαριστοῦν be correct, but this is doubtful), an expression of formal gratitude at 12:31, and of political gratitude at 2:27. Other references in the LXX are: εὐχάριστος, Prov. 11:16; εὐχαριστέω, Jdt. 8:25; Wis. 18:2; 3 Macc. 7:16; εὐχαριστία, Esth. 8:13; Wis. 16:28; Sir. 37:11.

19. Cf. Schubert, *Form*, 123.

20. Cf. J. Drummond, *Philo Judaeus; or The Jewish-Alexandrian Philosophy in Its Development and Completion* (2 vols.; London and Edinburgh, Williams and Norgate, 1888), 2.319: "Philo attaches special importance to thanksgiving." The full significance of this motif in Philonic thought still needs to be assessed.

21. Cf. *J.W.* 1.456 where ὑπὲρ τῆς τοῦ γαμβροῦ σωτηρίας εὐχαριστῶν is rendered by H. St. J. Thackeray as "[Archelaus, who] congratulated him on his son-in-law's acquittal" (Josephus, *The Jewish War, Books I–III* [The Loeb Classical Library, 9 vols.; London, Heinemann, 1926–65], 2.215), though rather unusually Rengstorf's concordance does not list "congratulate" as a possible meaning; K. H. Rengstorf, *A Complete Concordance to Flavius Josephus* (4 vols.; Leiden, Brill, 1973–   ), 2.248–49.

22. The rendering of ἔχωμεν χάριν (the subjunctive is to be preferred to the indicative ἔχομεν on contextual grounds) by "let us be grateful" (RSV) or even "let us . . . give thanks" (NEB) is better than the translation "let us have grace" (ASV).

23. See below.

24. J. Jeremias, *The Eucharistic Words of Jesus* (1st Eng. ed.; London, SCM, 1966), 162, 175.

25. J. M. Robinson, "Die Hodajot-Formel in Gebet und Hymnus des Frühchristentums," *Apophoreta: Festschrift für Ernst Haenchen*, eds. W. Eltester and F. H. Kettler (BZNW 30; Berlin, Alfred Töpelmann, 1964), 201–203.

26. Paul, according to Jeremias, *Words*, 175, is by accident the sole witness to this fact, although a reference in Philo (*Spec. Leg.* 2.175) does point in the same direction.

27. Schubert, *Form*, 99.

28. E. Lohmeyer, *Die Offenbarung des Johannes* (HNT 16; 2d ed. Tübingen, Mohr, 1953), 95.

29. Cf. Rom. 1:8; 1 Cor. 1:5; 1 Thess. 2:13; 2 Thess. 1:3; 2:13.

30. G. Delling, "Zum gottesdienstlichen Stil der Johannes-Apokalypse," *NovT* 3 (1959), 128, states: "with these words he clearly points to the character of the heavenly worship." For a discussion of the passage see Deichgräber, *Got-*

teshymnus, 49, 50; and K.-P. Jörns, *Das hymnische Evangelium* (SNT 5; Gütersloh, Mohn, 1971), 31–40.

31. Cf. E. Lohse, *Die Offenbarung des Johannes* (NTD 11; 8th ed.; Göttingen, Vandenhoeck & Ruprecht, 1965), 51.

32. Ledogar, *Acknowledgment*, 140.

33. See note 3.

34. Schubert, *Form*, 42.

35. O'Brien, *Introductory Thanksgivings*.

36. See especially Schubert, *Form*, for a detailed presentation of this point.

37. To speak of prayer by this and similar terms, e.g. "day and night" (1 Thess. 3:10; 2 Tim. 1:4), "at all times" (Eph. 6:18), "with perseverance" (Rom. 12:12; Col. 4:2; cf. Acts 2:42, 46; 6:4), was part and parcel of the style of ancient letters, being a Jewish practice as well as a pagan one. Cf. G. Harder, *Paulus und das Gebet* (NTF 1.10; Gütersloh, Bertelsmann, 1936), 8–19; and R. Kerkhoff, *Das unablässige Gebet: Beiträge zur Lehre vom immerwährenden Beten im Neuen Testament* (München, Zink, 1954).

38. Cf. P. T. O'Brien, "Thanksgiving and the Gospel in Paul," *NTS* 21 (1974–75), 144–55.

39. Schubert, *Form*, 83, 84.

40. This is one Pauline instance of thanksgiving to man. We do not know on what occasion they risked their lives for Paul's sake; some commentators suggest it may have been at Ephesus (Acts 19:23–40), but we cannot be sure. As P. Althaus (*Der Brief an die Römer* [NTD 6; 10th ed.; Göttingen, Vandenhoeck & Ruprecht, 1965], 150) aptly commented: "Paul was often in danger of death."

41. Εὐχαριστέω: Rom. 14:6 (twice); 1 Cor. 10:30; 11:24; εὐχαριστία: 1 Tim. 4:3, 4.

42. C. K. Barrett, *A Commentary on the Epistle to the Romans* (BNTC; London, Black, 1957), 259: "Their meals, therefore, whatever they may consist of, are eaten with reference to the Lord; they are not secular functions."

43. J. Murray (*The Epistle to the Romans* [NICNT; 2 vols.; Grand Rapids, Eerdmans, 1959–65], 2.179) notes: "this thanksgiving is likewise in his case a manifestation of his sense of indebtedness to God." The thanks he offers refer to what he does partake. Following F. A. Philippi, Murray adds that it has no reference to *what* he does not eat, which would be absurd, or *that* he does not eat, which would be Pharisaic (cf. Luke 18:11).

44. On the precise meaning of the difficult verse 29, and its relation to verse 30, see C. K. Barrett's discussion, *A Commentary on the First Epistle to the Corinthians* (BNTC; London, Black, 1968), 242–44.

45. On 1 Cor. 11:24 see the notes on the Last Supper, above.

46. J. N. D. Kelly, *The Pastoral Epistles* (BNTC; London, Black, 1963), 96; and J. Jeremias, *Die Briefe an Timotheus und Titus* (NTD 9; 10th ed.; Göttingen, Vandenhoeck & Ruprecht, 1965), 27.

47. Kelly, *The Pastoral Epistles*, 96, 97.

48. So many commentators.

49. See O'Brien, *Introductory Thanksgivings*, 62–67.

50. Many commentators think the τοῦτο ("this") of verse 18 applies to all three of the preceding injunctions, which are a unity. They are not three attitudes so much as three aspects of one attitude; cf. B. Rigaux, *Saint Paul: Les Épitres aux Thessaloniciens* (EBib; Paris and Gembloux, Gabalda and Duculot, 1956), 589; L. Morris, *The First and Second Epistles to the Thessalonians* (NICNT;

Grand Rapids, Eerdmans, 1959), 174; and A. L. Moore, *1 and 2 Thessalonians* (NCB; London, Nelson, 1969), 83.

51. The manuscript evidence is divided as to whether the definite article should be included or not, and even then the meaning is not clear; e.g. should the phrase be rendered "gratefully," "by the grace (of God)," or "in the (sphere of God's) grace"?

52. Commenting on "Be filled with the Spirit" of verse 18, F. F. Bruce (*The Epistle to the Ephesians* [London, Pickering and Inglis, 1961], 110) remarks: "Some of the symptoms of this spiritual fulness are mentioned in the following verses," i.e. 19–21.

53. Cf. J. Gnilka, *Der Philipperbrief* (HTKNT 10/3; Freiburg/Basel/Vienna, Herder, 1968), 169, 170.

54. So most commentators. Str-B, 3.43–46, draw attention (particularly in the Jewish apocalyptic literature, e.g. *Apoc. Bar.* 48:40) to "the pride and ingratitude of paganism."

55. Murray, *Romans*, 1.41, and Deichgräber, *Gotteshymnus*, 202.

56. H. Lietzmann and W. G. Kümmel, *An die Korinther I.II* (HNT 9; 5th ed.; Tübingen, Mohr, 1969), 202; cf. H. Windisch, *Der zweite Korintherbrief* (MeyerK 6; 9th ed.; Göttingen, Vandenhoeck & Ruprecht, 1924), 151.

57. So H. Conzelmann, *Der erste Brief an die Korinther* (MeyerK 6; 11th ed. = 1st ed. New Series; Göttingen, Vandenhoeck & Ruprecht, 1969), 281; cf. A. Robertson and A. Plummer, *A Critical and Exegetical Commentary on the First Epistle of St Paul to the Corinthians* (ICC; 2nd ed.; Edinburgh, Clark, 1914), 314; Ledogar (*Acknowledgment*, 125, 126), however, has suggested it is possible that the former term signifies the prayer in question is a praise-prayer, while the latter is more specific, showing it is praise for something received.

58. I.e. in the spirit *only*, and not with the mind. So many commentators.

59. Note the stress on "all" in the passage: verse 1 (twice), verse 2 (twice) and particularly verse 4: "God wishes that all men be saved and come to a knowledge of the truth."

60. W. Lock, *A Critical and Exegetical Commentary on the Pastoral Epistles* (ICC; Edinburgh, Clark, 1924), 25.

61. Deichgräber, *Gotteshymnus*, 43, 44.

62. Deichgräber, *Gotteshymnus*, 43.

63. To use Westermann's designation, *Praise*, 81–90.

Chapter 5

ADAM AND CHRIST
ACCORDING TO PAUL

SWEE-HWA QUEK

IN HIS MISSIONARY PREACHING AND TEACHING Paul found that by juxtaposing Adam and Christ in a dialectical pattern[1] he had a complete scheme for understanding the history of mankind. It was an original and profound contribution to the development of Christian thinking. We attempt here an exegesis of the two crucial passages in which he used the Adam–Christ Analogy directly, 1 Cor. 15:21–22, 45–49 and Rom. 5:12–21. It is recognized that this Analogy has wide implications in the rest of Paul's writings[2] and in other parts of the New Testament,[3] but it is not possible to treat these implications here. Nor need we develop the theological[4] and *religionsgeschichtlich*[5] aspects of the subject to which adequate attention has already been given.

In the Adam–Christ Analogy two types of reasoning àre used.[6] First, positively ("as . . . so")[7] and once negatively ("not as . . . so")[8] the similarities and differences between the two figures are clearly given. This took the form of the Semitic-hellenistic *Satzparallelismus*.[9] Words and phrases used in one *stichos* find their counterparts in a parallel *stichos*. By examining such paired-expressions it is possible to pinpoint the exact meaning intended. Less often used but nevertheless still significant, the second type of reasoning is the *argumentum a minori ad maius* ("if . . . how much more"), which is expressed in the Rabbinic קל וחמר argument.[10] The parallelism here is quite different. Since it is essentially a thought parallelism rather than a verbal one, an entire line moves synthetically into a longer and fuller statement, requiring a new method of interpretation.

Let us examine now the fourteen formulations which make use of the first type of reasoning. The first set of these formulations is introduced in an eschatological discussion of the resurrection from the dead.

FI   1 Cor. 15:21a   ἐπειδὴ γὰρ δι' ἀνθρώπου θάνατος,
                        b   καὶ   δι' ἀνθρώπου ἀνάστασις νεκρῶν·
FII   22a   ὥσπερ γὰρ ἐν τῷ 'Αδὰμ πάντες ἀποθνήσκουσιν,
                        b   οὕτως καὶ ἐν τῷ Χριστῷ πάντες ζῳοποιηθήσονται.

The analogous element in FI, the twice-occurring anarthrous prepositional phrase "through man" (not "through a man"), is in the emphatic first-position of the sentence, reference being to Adam and Christ as men. While this is true of Adam,[11] it does not describe Christ completely: the divine nature is left out of account without invalidating the Analogy.[12] The contrast and main point in FI is the thought-axis, "death... resurrection of the dead".[13] The anarthrous Θάνατος here may denote both the physical phenomenon itself as well as death as a quality of life in its un-resurrected, "soulish" (ψυχικόν) Adamic state.[14] Similarly, the corresponding anarthrous expression ἀνάστασις νεκρῶν applies to the Christian dead and may denote both the anticipated[15] bodily phenomenon (1 Cor. 15:35–58) and that quality of the resurrected life which every person "in Christ" experiences in this life: Paul calls that spiritual (πνευματικόν) life.[16] With the conservative elements of Judaism he and the early church shared a belief in a bodily resurrection.[17] The difference comes in the Christian understanding of such a resurrection as grounded in Jesus Christ.[18]

Characteristically of *Satzparallelismus* the sentences are compressed and the verbs are left out, but the sense is clear: "as through man [came] death, through man [came] also the resurrection from the dead".

FII is longer, building on FI. The analogous element is the solidarity of all in either Adam or Christ: πάντες in both *stichoi* should be linked with the prepositional phrases rather than the verbs.[19] The fact that both groups are not equal[20] does not render them incomparable. There is a double synthetic development between FI and FII: the ἄνθρωποι of verse 21a, b are now identified as Adam and Christ, and the διά- phrases give way to the pregnant Pauline expressions, ἐν τῷ 'Αδάμ... ἐν τῷ Χριστῷ. The *tertium comparationis* ἀποθνήσκουσιν... ζῳοποιηθήσονται is substantially the same in meaning with the earlier paired-concept θάνατος... ἀνάστασις νεκρῶν; the added thought here is the concept of a collective dying and a collective restoration to life.

The argument at this juncture drifts into a recital of three eschatological events (1 Cor. 15:23–34). Two rhetorical questions (15:35) relating to the fact and *modus operandi* of the resurrection from the dead are given a meticulously worded reply (15:36–58). Mention of the σῶμα ψυχικόν and σῶμα πνευματικόν (15:44) brings Paul back again thematically to the contrast of the two Adams.[21] The adjectives used anticipate the nouns ψυχή and πνεῦμα in the next verse. Notice the next set of Adam–Christ formuations:

	[Gen. 2:7b LXX	ἐγένετο ὁ	ἄνθρωπος	εἰς ψυχὴν ζῶσαν.]
FIII	1 Cor. 15:45a	ἐγένετο ὁ πρῶτος ἄνθρωπος Ἀδὰμ εἰς ψυχὴν ζῶσαν·		
	b	ὁ ἔσχατος Ἀδὰμ εἰς πνεῦμα ζῳοποιοῦν.		
FIV	47a	ὁ πρῶτος	ἄνθρωπος	ἐκ γῆς χοϊκός,
	b	ὁ δεύτερος	ἄνθρωπος	ἐξ οὐρανοῦ.
FV	48a	οἷος ὁ χοϊκός,	τοιοῦτοι καὶ οἱ χοϊκοί,	
	b	καὶ οἷος ὁ ἐπουράνιος, τοιοῦτοι καὶ οἱ ἐπουράνιοι·		
FVI	49a	καὶ καθὼς ἐφορέσαμεν τὴν εἰκόνα τοῦ χοϊκοῦ,		
	b	φορέσομεν καὶ τὴν εἰκόνα τοῦ ἐπουρανίου.		

FII and FIV concern the One and FV and FVI the Many. In FIII note that 15:45a is a quotation of Gen. 2:7b LXX and the second *stichos* 15:45b is a haggadic midrash by Paul himself.[22] The form of the quotation is tendentious: πρῶτος and Ἀδάμ were added in anticipation of ἔσχατος and Ἀδάμ. Ἄνθρωπος becomes unnecessary but is retained with regard to the Septuagintal text. It is taken up again in 15:47a, b. The total impact of FIII is breath-taking:[23] with the additional explanation Paul has hit upon an analogy which opens up a window to the entire scope of *Heilsgeschichte*.

The analogous elements in these four formulations are, first, the humanity of both figures (FIII and FIV therefore repeat the same analogical basis as in FI and FII) and, second, the observation that the Many in each solidarity bear the image of their respective representative (FIV and FV); in the latter a new basis is introduced to the Adam–Christ Analogy. FIII to FVI therefore throw light on FI and FII in this way: what causes death or life is the identical nature or image man shares with Adam or Christ. In Rom. 5:12–21 a different explanation is given: sin causes death and grace restores life to man. In 1 Corinthians 15 all the formulations concern the nature of each Adam whereas in Romans 5 it is rather the respective act of each Adam and its impact.

A series of contrasts brings out the radical difference between the two solidarities. "First" is opposed to "last" (FIII) or "second" (FIV).[24] With reference to the nature, origin and substance of each Adamic figure, we have the following paired-concept: a living soul, earthly, from the earth as opposed to a life-giving spirit, heavenly, from heaven.[25] The same holds for the Many in each solidarity.

It is significant that the *modus operandi* of each solidarity is stated vaguely: how is image-bearing to be construed? In FV it is simply assumed. Paul was not interested in developing speculatively this aspect of the problem.

We come now to Romans 5 where a different, though related, use
of the Adam–Christ Analogy is found.

FVII   Rom. 5:12   Διὰ τοῦτο
        a ὥσπερ δι᾽ ἑνὸς ἀνθρώπου ἡ ἁμαρτία εἰς τὸν κόσμον εἰσῆλθεν
        b καὶ διὰ τῆς ἁμαρτίας ὁ θάνατος,
        c καὶ οὕτως εἰς πάντας ἀνθρώπους ὁ θάνατος διῆλθεν,
        d   ἐφ᾽ ᾧ πάντες ἥμαρτον.

The comparison here is unfinished,[26] but the rest of it is not hard to
determine: one single man (εἷς ἄνθρωπος) is opposed to all the rest of
mankind (ὁ κόσμος / πάντες ἄνθρωποι) and contrasted with another
individual[27] described in greater detail in 5:18b and 19b. Ἁμαρτία is
arthrous, indicating a specific sin. Paul speaks of a collective "sin" in
Adam rather than of "sinning" in the way Adam sinned.[28] Furthermore
sin is the cause of death: διὰ τῆς ἁμαρτίας (12b) is essentially the same in
meaning as ἐφ᾽ ᾧ πάντες ἥμαρτον (12d).[29]

The two halves of Romans 5 are linked closely by διὰ τοῦτο in this
way: sin is universal (5:8) and the helplessness of man (5:6) estranged
from God (5:10) leads to the reconciling work of Christ (5:11). That is the
same message as in 5:12–21.

FVIII   Rom. 5:15   Ἀλλ᾽
        a οὐχ ὡς τὸ παράπτωμα,
        b οὕτως τὸ χάρισμα·
FIX 16a   καὶ οὐχ ὡς δι᾽ ἑνὸς ἁμαρτήσαντος τὸ δώρημα·
FX   b τὸ μὲν γὰρ κρίμα   ἐξ ἑνὸς   εἰς κατάκριμα,
       c τὸ δὲ   χάρισμα   ἐκ πολλῶν παραπτωμάτων   εἰς δικαίωμα.

Caught off-guard after the structural awkwardness of 5:12 Paul
resumes the Analogy, using compressed sentences and contrasting the
acts rather than the persons of Adam and Christ (FVIII and FIX). His
formulations are more successful. The emphasis is on the incomparabil-
ity of Adam's act, as indicated by the first-position of the various
Adamic expressions. FIX is unusual: it begins a new sentence and departs from the parallel form in which the other formulations were
couched. It states simply how the gift of righteousness was not given.[30]
How it was given—δι᾽ ἑνὸς δικαιώματος—comes in 5:18b.

A mixture of Hebrew and Hellenistic modes of thought characterizes this passage.[31] Hesitantly but confidently, Paul feels his way
through a complex series of points and counterpoints as he searches for
a complete and thoroughly satisfying formulation on Adam and Christ.
This is finally achieved in the next two formulations.

FXI   Rom. 5:18   Ἄρα οὖν
        a ὡς   δι᾽ ἑνὸς παραπτώματος   εἰς πάντας ἀνθρώπους
        b οὕτως καὶ   δι᾽ ἑνὸς δικαιώματος   εἰς πάντας ἀνθρώπους
           (18a) εἰς κατάκριμα,
           (18b) εἰς δικαίωσιν ζωῆς·

FXII   19a   ὥσπερ γὰρ   διὰ τῆς παρακοῆς   τοῦ   ἑνὸς ἀνθρώπου
       b   οὕτως καὶ   διὰ τῆς ὑπακοῆς   τοῦ   ἑνὸς
       (19a) ἁμαρτωλοὶ   κατεστάθησαν   οἱ πολλοί,
       (19b) δίκαιοι   κατασταθήσονται   οἱ πολλοί.

The exploratory stage now over and the missing dimension in 5:12 having been supplied in the preceding set of formuations, the argument proceeds smoothly with a comparison of the two acts viewed from the standpoint of their results (παράπτωμα . . . δικαίωμα) and the nature of the acts themselves (παρακοή . . . ὑπακοή). There is a further synthetic development in the particularization of πάντες ἄνθρωποι as οἱ πολλοί.[32] The two corporate groupings are boldly characterized as ἁμαρτωλοί (compare 5:12d) or δίκαιοι. But, as in FVI, the statement concerns only the *factum operandi* of each solidarity. Does κατεστάθησαν . . . κατασταθήσονται signify loosely a pattern of behaviour corresponding with the distinctive action of each representative? Or does it mean strictly that all in each group became in actual fact sinners or will become righteous on account of each representative act? The latter seems to be more consistent with the tenor of the whole passage. In ἁμαρτωλοί, therefore, there is primary reference, not to the actual sins committed by man, but to the collective lostness of mankind in Adam. The fact that men do become sinners by actual sinning is outside the scope of the Adam–Christ Analogy proper. It is however not far from Paul's thoughts as he takes this aspect up immediately from 5:20 and carries the thought into chapter 6. What is noteworthy in the two crucial passages, Romans 5 and 1 Corinthians 15, is that Paul is virtually silent on the *modus operandi* of each solidarity.

FXIII Rom. 5:20   οὐ δὲ
       b   ἐπλεόνασεν   ἡ ἁμαρτία
       c   ὑπερεπερίσσευσεν   ἡ χάρις,
FXIV   21   ἵνα
       a   ὥσπερ ἐβασίλευσεν ἡ ἁμαρτία
       b   οὕτως καὶ ἡ χάρις βασιλεύσῃ   διὰ δικαιοσύνης
       (21a) ἐν τῷ θανάτῳ,
       (21b) εἰς ζωὴν αἰώνιον διὰ Ἰησοῦ Χριστοῦ τοῦ κυρίου ἡμῶν.

The formal Analogy ended at 5:19 but Paul is not yet through. Two colossal powers are at work. He speaks of the entrance of sin (5:12), the fire for its numerical growth (5:16c, 20b) being fed by the introduction of νόμος (5:20a), not just the Mosaic Law[33] but also the governing principle behind collective lostness (or sin) in Adam. The power of sin (21a), and with it death (12c, 15c, 17a) is more than matched by another power, the "superabundant" power of grace (15d, 17b, 20c, 21b). The growth of sin is permanently checked.[34] The discussion is now complete and, quite characteristic of his reverential treatment of Biblical themes, Paul ends with a liturgical affirmation.

In FXII and FIV Paul takes up his earlier קל וחמר arguments (FXV and FXVI) and develops them. But his general argument is more or less spent and his thoughts are repetitive, adding little new to what he had already stated. But he has shown clearly where the emphasis should lie.

We come now to his last two formulations, discussed separately. because they are different in character from the rest.

FXV Rom. 5:15c Premise εἰ γὰρ τῷ τοῦ ἑνὸς παραπτώματι οἱ πολλοὶ ἀπέθανον,
        d Inference πολλῷ μᾶλλον ἡ χάρις τοῦ θεοῦ καὶ ἡ δωρεὰ ἐν χάριτι τῇ τοῦ ἑνὸς ἀνθρώπου Ἰησοῦ Χριστοῦ εἰς τοὺς πολλοὺς ἐπερίσσευσεν.
FXVI   17a Premise εἰ γὰρ τῷ τοῦ ἑνὸς παραπτώματι ὁ θάνατος ἐβασίλευσεν διὰ τοῦ ἑνός,
        b Inference πολλῷ μᾶλλον οἱ τὴν περισσείαν τῆς χάριτος καὶ τῆς δωρεᾶς τῆς δικαιοσύνης λαμβάνοντες ἐν ζωῇ βασιλεύσουσιν διὰ τοῦ ἑνὸς Ἰησοῦ Χριστοῦ.

It is important to see that the parallelism is not verbal but conceptual, otherwise it could be construed, as R. J. Scroggs does,[35] that the analogy in 15c, d is between Adam (τοῦ ἑνός) and God the Father (τοῦ θεοῦ). The whole thought in 15d is pitted against 15c, the effect of Christ's representative act against the effect of Adam's act. Note also that in both solidarities there is a clear contrast between the One and the Many. When Paul speaks of all men he does not see mankind as an undifferentiated mass, but rather selectively as in Adam or in Christ. In both premises (15c, 17a) we see a development of 5:12b. The whole statement turns on πολλῷ μᾶλλον ("all the more it is certain that...")[36] and highlights the superiority of Christ over Adam within an eschatological framework.[37]

Certain observations emerge from the foregoing exegesis. Two uses of the Analogy are found. In 1 Corinthians 15 the common factor between both representative figures is their essential humanity and the basic point of the Analogy is that death came through Adam and life through Christ. In the later passage, Romans 5, attention shifts from the "person" of each representative to their respective "work" or acts. Stress is placed not only on the contrasts between the two acts (more so than in the earlier comparison between the two "persons") and their equally different outcomes, but also on the surpassing worth of the Christ-solidarity.[38] The general argument "stops and starts" because Paul attempts to do justice to the sin problem: that all men do actually sin knowingly and culpably is a fact he could not deny; he allowed this to intrude into his argument at several points;[39] but he stuck tenaciously to the idea of a collective sin which he holds in dialectical tension with the concept of actual sinning.

If it is important for us to confine ourselves to what he has stated explicitly, it is also important to see what he leaves out if we are to represent his teaching accurately. It has been noted that certain of his expressions seem to equate Jesus with the Holy Spirit.[40] Yet a consideration of all the Adam–Christ formulations shows that the Analogy is clearly between Adam and Christ, not Adam and the Holy Spirit. "It is by no means established that Paul ever identifies the Spirit with the risen Christ." There is a double contrast in 1 Cor. 15:45: "the ultimate Adam, in contrast to the first, is 'life-giving' and not merely 'living', and is 'spirit' and not merely a mortal self.... This is by no means tantamount to equating Christ with the Holy Spirit."[41]

Furthermore Paul is silent on the question of individual responsibility for Adam's sin (or for that matter, for Christ's act of justification). In his focus on the Many he does not lose sight of the individuals which make up the sum total of each solidarity.[42] Also absent is the idea of communal responsibility. Paul's thinking moves in one direction only: what the representative did affected the rest; nothing is affirmed as to how the rest became responsible for their representative's actions. Should we then continue to speak of the underlying influence of the Hebrew conception of corporate personality here in the Adam–Christ passages?[43] Insofar as this can be used in a non-juristic sense[44] and without reading too much realism into the Pauline use of the conception,[45] we see no objection to the Hebrew idea exerting a powerful, lingering influence on Paul's mind, even though the corporate idea was alien to the spirit of his times. Paul's independent mind and spirit, which was thoroughly saturated with pious regard for his nation's past history, allowed him both to use what he could find in his own heritage as well as to strike off at the same time into new directions.

We reaffirm the importance of the Adam–Christ Analogy as a key concept in Paul's teaching. It is however not the *centrum Paulinum*.[46] The Analogy proper is used with great reserve[47] without any attempt to exploit every possible and imaginable theological significance.

Notes

1. Cf. F. F. Bruce, *The Epistle of Paul to the Romans* (Tyndale New Testament Commentaries; London, Tyndale, 1963), 125–33; *Paul: Apostle of the Free Spirit* (Exeter, Paternoster, 1977), 114, 122–23, 205, 329. See also C. K. Barrett, *From First Adam to Last* (London, Adam & Charles Black, 1962). Barrett uses a broader dialectical pattern, focussing on representative individuals who "incorporate the human race, or sections of it, within themselves" (*ibid.*, 5).

2. E.g., the antithesis ὁ παλαιὸς ἄνθρωπος / ὁ νέος (καινὸς) ἄνθρωπος (Rom. 6:6; Col. 3:9–10; Eph. 2:15; 4:22–24) together with related contrasts such as

ἡ παλαιὰ ζύμη / νέον φύραμα (1 Cor. 5:7). Also ὁ ἔξω ἄνθρωπος / ὁ ἔσω ἄνθρωπος (2 Cor. 4:16; Rom. 7:22) and other contrasts, e.g. ψυχικὸς ἄνθρωπος / ὁ πνευματικὸς (ἄνθρωπος), 1 Cor. 2:14–16; *et al*. See, further, Phil. 2:5–11 and the σῶμα passages. Note that Paul uses the Adam–Christ Analogy with great reserve: it is found only in 1 Corinthians 15 and Romans 5 (M. Black, "The Pauline Doctrine of the Second Adam," *SJT* 7 [1954], 170–79).

3. The corporate significance of Adam and Christ intersects other areas, like the Son of Man sayings in the Synoptics which relate to Dan. 7:13, the Johannine concept of abiding in Christ (e.g. John 15:5), and Abraham's relationship to Melchizedek in Hebrews (C. F. D. Moule, *The Phenomenon of the New Testament* [SBT 2/1; London, SCM, 1967], 29–39).

4. The earliest interpreters of Paul used the Analogy more or less as a germinal concept to propound dogmatic theories of their own; cf. Irenaeus, *Haer*. 3.19.6; 5.16.2; *et passim* 3–5; Methodius, *Conviv*. 3.2.4–5. With Ambrose and Augustine attention turned to the subject of Original Sin; see Augustine, *De corr. et gratia* 12; *De gratia Christi et pecc. orig*. 2.29.41; *De pecc. mer*. 1.15–16, 27; 3.11. This trend was seen in the Tridentine *Decretum de peccato originali*; J. Calvin, *Institutes of the Christian Religion*, ed. J. T. McNeill (LCC 20; 2 vols.; Philadelphia, Westminster, 1960), 1.246–55; *The Epistles of Paul the Apostle to the Romans and to the Thessalonians*, eds. D. W. Torrance and T. F. Torrance (Calvin's Commentaries; Edinburgh, Saint Andrew, 1961), 111–20; W. A. Teller, *Lehrbuch des christlichen Glaubens* (Helmstedt, C. H. Hemmerde, 1764); O. Kuss, "Röm. 5, 12–21. Die Adam-Christus-Parallele," unpubl. diss. (Breslau, 1930); J. Murray, *The Imputation of Adam's Sin* (Grand Rapids, Eerdmans, 1959).

With F. D. E. Schleiermacher (*The Christian Faith* [Edinburgh: T. & T. Clark, 1968], sections 88–89, 95) a new trend began: mankind's corporateness in either Adamic figure was considered an objective relationship transcending the limitation of time and space. On the subjective level Schleiermacher taught man's consciousness of himself and of his dependence on God. Reminiscent of Irenaeus's *recapitulatio* doctrine, stress was placed on the Christ-relation as reflecting the true nature of man. See R. Rothe, *Neuer Versuch einer Auslegung der paulinischen Stelle Römer V, 12–21* (Wittenberg, n.p., 1836); A. Dietzsch, *Adam und Christus. Röm. V, 12–21. Eine exegetische Monographie* (Bonn, A. Marcus, 1871); G. Feuerer, *Adam und Christus als Gestaltkräfte und ihr Vermächtnis an die Menschheit* (Freiburg i. B., n.p., 1939); P. Galtier, *Les Deux Adam* (Paris, n.p., 1947); K. Barth, *Christ and Adam: Man and Humanity in Rom. 5* (SJT Occasional Papers 5; Edinburgh, Oliver & Boyd, 1963) = *Christus und Adam nach Röm. 5* (Zurich, 1952). See R. Bultmann's reply to Barth in "Adam and Christ According to Romans 5," *Current Issues in New Testament Interpretation*, O. Piper Festschrift (London, SCM, 1962), 143–65 = "Adam und Christus nach Röm. 5," *ZNW* 50 (1959), 145–65; P. Lengsfeld, *Adam und Christus. Die Adam-Christus-Typologie im NT und ihre dogmatische Verwendung bei M. J. Scheeben und K. Barth* (Koinonia; Beiträge zur ökumenischen Spiritualität und Theologie 9; Essen, Ludgerus-Verlag, 1965).

5. In the last fifty years various studies have underscored Paul's originality in creating this Analogy while at the same time showing the extent of his indebtedness to his predecessors. For those that dealt with possible links with Rabbinic Judaism and other contemporary Jewish beliefs, see J. Freundorfer, *Erbsünde und Erbtod beim Apostel Paulus. Eine religionsgeschichtliche und exegetische Untersuchung*... (Neutestamentliche Abhandlungen 13; Münster i. W., Aschendorffschen Verlagsbuchhandlung, 1927); J. Jeremias, "'Ἀδάμ," *TDNT* 1

(1964), 142–43; M. Black, "The Pauline Doctrine," 179; cautiously W. D. Davies, *Paul and Rabbinic Judaism* (2d ed.; London, SPCK, 1955), 32, 52–57; R. J. Scroggs, *The Last Adam. A Study in Pauline Anthropology* (Oxford, Blackwell, 1966), xxiv, 32–58. For a wider *religionsgeschichtlich* background, see B. Murmelstein, "Adam ein Beitrag zu Messiaslehre," *WZKM* 35 (1928), 242–75; 36 (1929), 51–86; F. H. Borsch, *The Son of Man in Myth and History* (London, SCM, 1967). For the allegation that Paul adapted a pre-Christian Gnostic myth of the two Adam-*anthropoi*, see R. Bultmann, "Adam and Christ," 150, 154; E. Brandenburger, *Adam und Christus, Exegetisch-religionsgeschichtliche Untersuchung zu Röm. 5, 12–21 (1 Kor. 15)* (WMANT 7; Neukirchen, Neukirchener Verlag, 1962), 154–57 et *passim*. Brandenburger also sees indications of a late-Jewish influence, all the traditions, Christian and non-Christian, going back to a common linguistic and conceptual source. See also H. Seebass, "Adam," *The New International Dictionary of New Testament Theology* 1 (1975), 86–87; ed. Colin Brown corrects this view. The search for possible backgrounds has produced conflicting answers. Paul's originality and partial dependence on the Old Testament on this question is the most likely view; cf. C. K. Barrett, *From First Adam*, 23–24, 30; A. J. M. Wedderburn, "Adam and Christ. An Investigation into the Background of 1 Corinthians xv and Romans v.12–21," unpubl. Ph.D. thesis (Cambridge, 1970), 114–15. C. F. D. Moule (*Phenomenon*, 39–42) has an eloquent account of Paul's originality.

  6. F. Prat, *Theology of St. Paul* (2 vols.; London, Burns & Oates, 1927), 1.438–39.

  7. See ἐπειδὴ γάρ ... καί (1 Cor. 15:21); ὥσπερ, καθώς or ὡς (γάρ) ... οὕτως καί (1 Cor. 15:22; Rom. 5:12, 18, 19, 21); οἷος ... τοιοῦτοι (1 Cor. 15:48); or simply two statements joined without using any formula (1 Cor. 15:45, 47; Rom. 5:20). One concludes that Paul's fertile mind worked with ease, moulding the Analogy in any given literary situation with confidence even though he encountered important anomalies in using the Analogy at certain points in his arguments.

  8. See οὐχ ὡς ... οὕτως καί (Rom. 5:15). It is significant that while Paul could have emphasized many incomparable aspects between Adam and Christ, to him the point of the whole exercise was to show that they were comparable.

  9. See E. Norden, *Die Antike Kunstprosa* (2 vols.; Leipzig, B. G. Teubner, 1898), 2.509–10; *Agnostos Theos* (Leipzig, B. G. Teubner, 1913), 254–62, 355–64; R. Schütz, *Der parallele Bau der Satzglieder im Neuen Testamentum* (FRLANT 11; Göttingen, 1920), 6–8. Paul's Greek style is strongly Hellenistic, like that of Demetrius of Phalerius; see C. Toussaint, *L'Hellénisme et l'Apôtre Paul* (Paris, 1921), 346–47. The key to understanding his style is found in the LXX; see T. Nägeli, *Der Wortschatz des Apostel Paulus* (Göttingen, 1905), 13, 74. But it is still baffling (see Norden, *Die Antike Kunstprosa*, 2.499), for he can produce the finest examples of *Kunstprosa* (as the *isocola* in 1 Cor. 15:53–54 show). Here however in the Adam–Christ formulations he did not sacrifice precision in thinking for alliteration and balance in the length of his *stichoi* (see Rom. 5:21).

  10. This is the first of R. Hillel's Seven Middoth; cf. H. L. Strack, *Introduction to the Talmud and Midrash* (New York, Harper & Row, 1965), 93–96. The Hebrew formula is כל שכן ... מה אם or some variant. For some examples, see *B. Bat.* 9.7; *Sanh.* 6.5 and *'Abot* 1.5; also 1 Cor. 6:16–17; 2 Cor. 3:7–8, 9, 11; Rom. 5:8–9, 10; 11:12, 24. Unlike the Hellenistic *Satzparallelismus*, the parallelism here is basically conceptual rather than verbal and the inference is usually considerably longer than the premise.

  There are only two uses of this argument in the Adam–Christ passages: Rom. 5:15c, d and 17a, b. The reason for its use only in Romans is this: death and life are stark contrasts; it would be pointless to speak more of life than death; hence the argument is not employed in 1 Corinthians 15. However, in Romans 5 it is admirably suited to bring out the impact of grace vis-à-vis that of transgression. Concerning the formula εἰ γὰρ . . . πολλῷ μᾶλλον note that while εἰ γάρ clauses are virtually causal in meaning (see M. Thrall, *Greek Particles in the New Testament* [NT Tools and Studies 8; Leiden, Brill, 1962], 87) we must distinguish between "causality" in a logical sense (as we see in Romans 5) and in reality (it cannot be said that what Adam did caused Christ to act as he did).

11. Paul was probably aware of the exaltation of Adam in Jewish literature. See R. J. Scroggs, *Last Adam*, 21–28, 38–40; H. Mueller, "The Ideal Man as Portrayed by the Talmud and St. Paul," *CBQ* 28 (1966), 278–91. His "first" Adam was very different from that of Judaism.

12. H. M. Gale, *The Use of Analogy in the Letters of Paul* (Philadelphia, Westminster, 1964), 9–20. Calvin noted two jarring factors; see *Romans and Thessalonians*, 116–17.

13. Every analogy has a basic point of comparison or contrast, a third component which throws light on the two things juxtaposed. Thus in the formula "X¹ therefore Y and X² therefore Z" the analogous elements are X¹ and X² and the all-important *tertium comparationis* is the thought-axis, YZ.

14. Contrast ὁ θάνατος in 1 Cor. 15:26, 54, 56; Rom. 5:12 *bis*, 14, 17, 21.

15. See especially ζωοποιηθήσονται (1 Cor. 15:22b) and φορέσομεν (49b).

16. Perhaps the latter aspect is denoted in the arthrous expression ἡ ἀνάστασις τῶν νεκρῶν, 1 Cor. 15:42.

17. See *Sanh.* 10.1; *Ber.* 7.5. Compare Acts 4:2; 24:15; 1 Pet. 1:3.

18. For this there was recourse to the words of Jesus as reported by the Evangelists. See Matt. 22:31–33; Luke 20:34–38 (compare Exod. 3:6); John 11:25. The argument "if Christ is raised from the dead, then Christians too will be raised from the dead" appears often in the Pauline writings; see 1 Cor. 6:14; Rom. 6:5; Col. 2:12–13; 3:1; Eph. 2:1, 5–6.

19. The placement of a qualifying phrase before πάντες is attested in Paul's writings. For the examples in 1 Corinthians alone, see 7:17; 9:24; 12:13; 13:2; 15:7, 10.

20. For some indications of the limited scope of the Christ-solidarity, see ἀδελφοί (15:1, 58); ἐν ὑμῖν τινες (15:12); οἱ κοιμηθέντες ἐν Χριστῷ (15:18). Compare οὐ γὰρ πάντων ἡ πίστις (2 Thess. 3:2).

21. Compare ψυχικὸς ἄνθρωπος / ὁ πνευματικὸς (ἄνθρωπος), 1 Cor. 2:14–16; also 3:1; 9:11; 10:3–4. See also ψυχικός, Jas. 3:15; Jude 19; and πνευματικός, 1 Pet. 2:5. The antithesis is found also outside the New Testament, notably in Philo and the Hermetic Writings. But the verbal resemblance between the various uses is superficial. Paul's distinction is unique; but E. Käsemann ("Kritische Analyse von Phil. 2, 5–11," *ZTK* 47 [1950], 344; *Leib und Leib Christi* [BHT 9; Tübingen, 1933], 163) postulates a Gnostic influence.

22. F. F. Bruce speaks of this as a "targumising practice"; see "Promise and Fulfilment in Paul's Presentation of Jesus," *Promise and Fulfilment. Essays presented to Professor S. H. Hooke*, ed. F. F. Bruce (Edinburgh, T. & T. Clark, 1963), 37–38.

23. On the New Testament writers' use of the Old Testament, see C. H. Dodd, *According to the Scriptures* (London, Collins, 1965), 130. F. F. Bruce (*Biblical Exegesis in the Qumran Texts* [London, Tyndale, 1960], 88) sees distinctive use of the Old Testament in the New in which the "original meaning is not set aside but [is] caught up into something more comprehensive and far-reaching than

was foreseen before He [Jesus] came." Compare the midrashic exegesis of Ps. 143:2 in Gal. 2:16 and Rom. 3:20. E. E. Ellis (*Paul's Use of the Old Testament* [Edinburgh, Oliver & Boyd, 1957], 147–48) notes that the meaning Paul found in the Old Testament was more important to him than the words or form of the text.

24. The latter actually implies a series ("last of all") but Paul sees only two on an equal footing with each other. We may have here a case of the Hellenistic use of the superlative ἔσχατος as a comparative; see A. T. Robertson, *A Grammar of the Greek New Testament in the Light of Historical Research* (4th ed.; Nashville, Broadman, 1923), 667–69. Compare Deut. 24:3 LXX and Rev. 1:17. The words ἔσχατος and δεύτερος are therefore used by Paul in a loose way.

25. For the identification of Paul's figures with the primal and heavenly man of Hellenistic mythology, see J. M. Creed, "The Heavenly Man," *JTS* 26 (1925), 113–36; R. Reitzenstein, *Die hellenistischen Mysterienreligionen* (2d ed.; Leipzig, 1920); A. M. Hunter, *Paul and His Predecessors* (London, Nicholson & Watson, 1940), 86–88; but see H. A. A. Kennedy, "St. Paul and the Conception of the 'Heavenly Man'," *The Expositor* 7 (1914), 97–110; and L. Cerfaux, *Christ in the Theology of St. Paul* (New York, Herder & Herder, 1959), 230. For those who affirm the link with the Danielic Son of Man (Dan. 7:13), see T. W. Manson, "The Son of Man in Daniel, Enoch, and the Gospels," *BJRL* 32 (1950), 171–93; M. D. Hooker, *The Son of Man in Mark* (London, SPCK, 1967), 11–30; *et al.*

26. The formula ends with καὶ οὕτως ("and thus") rather than οὕτως καί ("so also").

27. There is a significant synthetic development: (a) the earlier statements used δι' ἀνθρώπου ("by man" *qua* human agency, 1 Cor. 15:21); (b) in Rom. 5:12 the idea is more specific: δι' ἑνὸς ἀνθρώπου ("through a single man"). Compare 5:16a δι' ἑνὸς ἁμαρτήσαντος; 16b ἐξ ἑνός; 18a δι' ἑνὸς παραπτώματος; 18b δι' ἑνὸς δικαιώματος. (c) The fullest expression, which points to the corporate idea, uses the article to point either to the person of each representative (τοῦ ἑνὸς ἀνθρώπου, 5:15d; διὰ τοῦ ἑνός, 5:17 *bis*; διὰ... τοῦ ἑνός, 5:19 *bis*) or to their acts (τῷ τοῦ ἑνὸς παραπτώματι, 5:15c and 17a). The corporate idea is reinforced by the use of the article also in οἱ πολλοί.

28. Ἐφ' ᾧ is correctly rendered "because". "In whom" may be a mistranslation but it is a "true interpretation" (see F. F. Bruce, *Romans*, 130). See also W. Beyschlag, *New Testament Theology* (2d ed.; Edinburgh, T. & T. Clark, 1899), 60; J. Cambier, "Péchés des Hommes et Péché d'Adam en Rom. v.12," *NTS* 11 (1965), 217–55; *et al.* Contrast the well-known saying of 2 Bar. 54:19, "Adam is therefore not the cause save only of his own soul, but each of us has been the Adam of his own soul."

29. Πάντες is identical with πάντας ἀνθρώπους, which denotes "the rest of mankind".

30. A poorer reading (ἁμαρτήματος) is found in the Western Text and other MSS (D *Gpc* it vgᶜˡ syᵖ). It is preferred by F. Blass and A. Debrunner, *A Greek Grammar of the New Testament and Other Early Christian Literature* (Cambridge, University Press, 1961), section 488/3.

31. For a discussion of the Hebrew modes, see FXV and FXVI below.

32. The correspondence between Rom. 5:19b and Isa. 53:11 (MT) is striking:

MT — ... בְּדַעְתּוֹ יַצְדִּיק צַדִּיק עַבְדִּי לָרַבִּים

LXX — (καὶ κύριος βούλεται...) δεῖξαι αὐτῷ φῶς καὶ πλάσαι τῇ συνέσει, δικαιῶσαι δίκαιον εὖ δουλεύοντα πολλοῖς...

Note the arthrous forms οἱ πολλοί (Rom. 5:19 bis, also 15c, d) and לָרַבִּים. The article is left out in the LXX. Paul knew of its use in the Servant Passage and applies it mutatis mutandis to the Many in Adam. Also ὑπακοῆς (Rom. 5:19b) echoes the root meaning of בְּדַעְתּוֹ, "by his knowledge (of submission)"; see L. C. Allen, "Isaiah liii.11 and its Echoes," Vox Evangelica 1 (1962), 24–28; "The Old Testament in Romans I–VIII," Vox Evangelica 3 (1964), 21; but see R. P. Martin, Carmen Christi (SNTSMS 4; Cambridge, University Press, 1967), 212. For the relation between Rom. 5:19 and Isaiah 53, see B. W. Newton, Remarks on the Revised English Version of the Greek New Testament (London, Houlston, 1881), 132–42; O. Cullmann, The Christology of the New Testament (London, SCM, 1959), 7; W. Zimmerli and J. Jeremias, The Servant of God (SBT 1/20; London, SCM, 1965), 89; F. F. Bruce, Romans, 132.

33. See M. J. Lagrange, Épître aux Romains (Paris, 1950), 112; J. Murray, The Epistle to the Romans (NICNT; Grand Rapids, Eerdmans, 1960), 1.207; E. Brandenburger, Adam und Christus, 248; R. J. Scroggs, Last Adam, 82. The function of the Mosaic Law was to deal with sin (Gal. 3:19; Rom. 7:7) but the resultant effect was the increase of sin (compare Sir. 23:3). There is no need to restrict the reference to the Mosaic Law in 5:20a.

34. In a full appreciation of grace there need be no pessimism in speaking of the calamity brought by Adam, for this is cancelled out by the final triumph made possible by Christ.

35. Last Adam, 81. The contrast is rather between two men, Adam and Christ. The Western Text had ἐν τῷ ἑνὶ παραπτώματι (17a), showing a tendency to emphasize the sin rather than the person of Adam.

36. See R. Rothe, Neuer Versuch, 78; A. Dietzsch, Adam und Christus, 19; N. A. Dahl, "Two Notes on Romans 5," ST 5 (1951–52), 45; K. Barth, Christ and Adam, 21. But some render wrongly, "how many more"; see Augustine, De civ. Dei 20.10–11, 20; De trin. 4.3; F. Godet, Commentary on St. Paul's Epistle to the Romans (2 vols.; Edinburgh, T. & T. Clark, 1890), 1.362–64.

37. Note ἐβασίλευσεν . . . βασιλεύσουσιν (17a, b) and the interplay of aorist and future tenses in the other Adam–Christ formulations (FVI and FXII). See also Rom. 5:9, 10.

38. D. M. Stanley (Christ's Resurrection in Pauline Soteriology [Analecta Biblica 13; Rome, Pontifical Biblical Institute, 1961], 177–80) noted that Romans 5 pushes attention to a point in time earlier in Christ's life. It speaks of the crucifixion, whereas 1 Corinthians 15 has reference to the resurrection. M. Thrall ("Christ Crucified Or Second Adam? A Christological Debate Between Paul and the Corinthians," Christ and Spirit in the New Testament, C. F. D. Moule Festschrift; eds. B. Lindars and S. S. Smalley [Cambridge, University Press, 1973], 156) sees in Romans 5 a further synthesis of the two themes, Christ crucified and last Adam; Romans is the happy outcome of the Corinthian "debate" with Paul. But J. D. G. Dunn ("1 Corinthians 15:45—Last Adam, Life-Giving Spirit," Christ and Spirit, 139–41) thinks "that one man" of Rom. 5:15–19 is strictly speaking not identical with the "last Adam" of 1 Cor. 15:45.

39. See Rom. 5:13–14, 16, 20–21. Does Rom. 5:12d speak of actual sin? See note 28 above.

40. J. D. G. Dunn, Christ and Spirit, 127, 139–41.

41. C. F. D. Moule, "The New Testament and the Doctrine of the Trinity: A Short Report on an Old Theme," ExpT 88 (1976), 18.

42. Not at least in 2 Cor. 5:17, εἴ τις ἐν Χριστῷ. . . .

43. The classic exposition is by H. W. Robinson, "The Hebrew Conception

of Corporate Personality," *Werden und Wesen des Alten Testaments* (BZAW 66; Berlin, A. Töpelmann, 1936), 49–62. F. F. Bruce accepts its influence on Paul; see *Romans*, 126; he has reaffirmed this view recently in *Paul*, 329, 420–21. C. F. D. Moule (*Phenomenon*, 21–42) speaks of "inclusive personality" and adds that Paul, John and the early church accepted daringly the teaching of the "Corporate Christ".

The influence of the Hebrew conception has been challenged by Mendenhall and Porter (see note 44 below); R. A. Sizemore, "Christus Victor," unpubl. Ph.D. thesis (Edinburgh, 1965), 259–60; J. W. Rogerson, "The Hebrew Conception of Corporate Personality: a Re-Examination," *JTS* 21 (1970), 1–16; and A. J. M. Wedderburn, "Adam and Christ," 173–75, 243–45. But the Hebrew conception need not be construed as undermining the importance of the individual; see H. W. Robinson, *Werden und Wesen*, 50; A. R. Johnson, *The Vitality of the Individual in the Thought of Ancient Israel* (Cardiff, University of Wales, 1949), 7.

44. G. E. Mendenhall, "The Relation of the Individual to Political Society in Ancient Israel," *Biblical Studies in Memory of H. C. Alleman*, ed. J. M. Myers *et al.* (New York, J. J. Augustin, 1960), 89–108. J. R. Porter's warning against applying the idea to aspects (especially with reference to the law) for which it is not suited should be heeded ("The Legal Aspects of the Concept of 'Corporate Personality' in the Old Testament," *VT* 15 [1965], 361–80), but one need not assume that Paul's understanding of this concept is linked necessarily with an acceptance of the principle of communal responsibility.

45. As e.g. in R. P. Shedd, *Man in Community. A Study of St. Paul's Application of Old Testament and Early Jewish Conceptions of Human Solidarity* (London, Epworth, 1958), 103, 108–9; and possibly A. R. Johnson, *One and the Many in the Israelite Conception of God* (Cardiff, University of Wales, 1942), 37. The oscillation between the One and the Many is only conceptual, not literal. On the dynamic interplay between these two aspects, see J. de Fraine, "Adam and Christ as Corporate Personalities," *TD* 10 (1962), 99–102; and the excellent, lively and clear-cut articles by W. Barclay, "Rom. 5, 12–21 (Great Themes of the New Testament)," *ExpT* 70 (1958), 132–35, 172–75.

46. J. G. Gibbs thinks it is; see *Creation and Redemption. A Study in Pauline Theology* (NovTSup 26; Leiden, Brill, 1971), 2. The history of scholarship on Adam and Christ shows unwarranted attempts to invest this Analogy with overarching significance not only for Paul's theology but also for the entire Christian Faith; see W. A. Teller, *Lehrbuch des christlichen Glaubens*; S. J. Baird, *The First Adam and the Second. The Elohim Revealed in the Creation and Redemption of Man* (Philadelphia, 1860); D. Somerville, *St. Paul's Conception of Christ or The Doctrine of the Second Adam* (Cunningham Lectures; Edinburgh, T. & T. Clark, 1897); R. G. Bandas, *The Master-Idea of Saint Paul's Epistles* (Bruges, Desclée, 1925).

47. M. Black, "The Pauline Doctrine of the Second Adam," *SJT* 7 (1954), 179.

Chapter 6

THE CHRISTIAN LIFE:
A LIFE OF TENSION?
A Consideration of the Nature of Christian Experience in Paul

DAVID WENHAM

THE QUESTION OF WHAT IS NORMAL in Christian experience is one that has interested Christians throughout the ages and that continues to interest—and also to divide—today. One particular question that has divided Christians is whether believers should expect to experience consistent victory over sin through the Spirit, or whether the Christian life will be a struggle and consistent victory will be experienced only in the life to come. In this essay our purpose is not to look at this question in general, but to re-examine Paul's teaching in particular, to see whether he gives any guidance about the subject. We make no claims to great originality, but we hope to help clarify a confused issue.

Two preliminary observations are in order. First, the question being examined is one in which personal prejudices and experience can easily cloud the issue; the present writer would incline to the more melancholy view of the Christian life as one of struggle. But such personal prejudices must not be allowed to control exegesis.

Second, it is possible that the sort of question we are asking may be unanswerable. It is certainly arguable that Paul in his letters is not interested so much in defining and describing normal Christian experience as in proclaiming and expounding the divine kerygma and its implications.[1] But, although it is wise to beware of expecting answers to questions that the biblical authors did not intend to answer, in this case it is not unreasonable to hope to find at least hints of an answer, since the questions of sin and victory over sin were very important to Paul in his writings; and his teaching is not a theoretical kerygma or didache, but is something with very definite, practical implications in experience.[2]

It may help to clarify the issues if we begin by making certain statements regarding Paul's view of Christian experience that are relatively uncontroversial. (1) To be in Christ means in some real sense release from slavery to sin and evil powers (e.g. Gal. 4; Rom. 6). (2) To be in Christ means having the Holy Spirit and his immeasurably great power at work in one's life (e.g. Romans 8; Ephesians 1). (3) The Christian is called to holiness and perfection (e.g. 2 Cor. 6:14–7:1; Phil. 3:12–14). (4) The Christian life should be a life of growth and is not a life of suddenly and finally achieved perfection (e.g. Phil. 3:12–14; Col. 1:10; Eph. 4:15, 16). (5) Satan and the forces of evil continue active in their attacks on the believer after his conversion (e.g. 1 Thess. 3:5; 2 Cor. 12:7; Rom. 16:20; Eph. 6:11, 12). (6) Our old sinful and weak nature does not disappear at conversion; it continues to be a threat to the believer (e.g. Gal. 5:16–26). (7) It is possible for the Christian to sin and indeed (to judge from the problems dealt with by Paul in his letters) it is common for Christians to sin. (8) Because of the preceding points the Christian life is a fight— against the flesh and the devil in the power of the Spirit. Vigilance and effort are called for (e.g. 1 Thess. 5:8–11; Rom. 13:12–14; Eph. 6:11–18).

What we have said so far can hardly be disputed; but there is still room for considerable difference of opinion over the nature of the Christian fight: Did Paul believe that his readers could experience consistent victory in their spiritual warfare, or did he know that their Christian lives would be up and down affairs in which they would experience defeats? The point may seem a rather fine one; but it is one that divides scholars as well as popular preachers and one that has practical and pastoral implications.

One scholar who has recently and ably defended the second view of the Christian life is J. D. G. Dunn in his *Jesus and the Spirit*,[3] and it will be useful to take his discussion of Paul as a starting point. He speaks of Paul's view of the Christian life as one of "continuing frustration, since the believer finds himself torn in two by conflicting desires and impulses".[4] The Christian, on this view, is a divided man who is frustrated by his inability to live as he would. Dunn bases his case both on particular texts, notably Gal. 5:16–26 and Romans 7 and 8, and also on general observations about Paul's view of the present as a time of eschatological tension between the old age and the new creation.

These general observations, which we will consider first, are of considerable force. Dunn cogently argues that Paul rejects the view of the gnostics and the pneumatics that the mark of the Spirit of God in the present is primarily power of word and action. Rather for Paul the true mark of the Spirit is Christ-likeness, and that means the death-resurrection pattern: the present is a time of suffering and death for the true believer, not a time of glorious victory and heavenly reign.

There is no doubt that this is a very important motif in Paul's understanding; but what is less clear is whether the death-life pattern can be applied to the area of moral struggle and experience in the same way as to the physical sphere. Paul believed in and experienced the continuing reality of Satan's work in persecution and probably in physical sickness;[5] the old age was continuing in these aspects, and it was in such situations that God's power could most strikingly be seen. But when we come to the moral and spiritual sphere, the situation is rather more complicated: God's power may be seen when Satan inflicts a physical defect on the believer, but God's power cannot be said to be seen when Satan inflicts on him a moral or spiritual defeat. The normative death-life pattern of Christ's experience may be seen when the believer suffers physical death or damage at Satan's hands, but it is not seen when the believer suffers moral defeat at Satan's hand, as Christ was without sin (2 Cor. 5:21). This is not to deny that the eschatological tension in which the Christian finds himself has any relevance in the moral and spiritual sphere; indeed we shall conclude that it does. But we cannot agree that Paul would have seen the experience of moral and spiritual frustration and defeat as an integral dimension of Christian life; indeed the argument from Christ's example would point in the opposite direction, as Christ's life was not one of sin leading to victory, but of victory over sin and weakness.

At this point it may be worth observing that Paul in his letters gives remarkably little hint that he is conscious of sin in his own life as a believer. There are, on the contrary, more and clearer indications of Paul's confidence in his own moral uprightness (seen of course entirely as the work of grace). This and the lack of exhortations to his readers to confess their sins could be taken to indicate that the spirit of penitence resulting from consciousness of sin was not nearly as important for Paul as it has been for many saints of later generations. It is an observation that would tell against Dunn's argument.

But Dunn does, of course, cite particular passages to support his interpretation. He cites a number of passages to show that the Christian after his conversion continues to be a man of σάρξ ("flesh"). The difficulty with most of the verses cited is that σάρξ is not clearly being used in a morally negative sense. There is no question that the Christian does continue "in the flesh" in some sense after conversion, but σάρξ can be used in a morally neutral sense,[6] and to establish Dunn's view it has to be shown that the Christian is being described as a man of σάρξ in the morally negative sense (which is opposed to πνεῦμα, "spirit").

The two passages which are fundamental to Dunn's case do use σάρξ in the negative sense. In Gal. 5:17-24, a passage in which Dunn rightly says that Paul is speaking to Christians about the Christian life, the contradiction between the flesh and the Spirit is spelled out very clearly, and the important sentence "these (i.e. flesh and Spirit) are opposed to each other, in order that you may not do those things that you wish" is found. This verse and the subsequent context certainly justify Dunn's view that there is a tension between the contradictory forces of the flesh and the Spirit in the Christian; but the clause "in order that (or "so that") you may not do those things that you wish" hardly proves that Paul views the Christian life as a state of frustration or moral impotence. Especially if we take ἵνα here as a final particle ("in order that")[7] and not consecutively, with Dunn, Paul may here be seen as speaking of the tendency of the tension between flesh and Spirit rather than the actual and necessary results of the tension. But quite apart from that, the whole context of Galatians 5 tells against the assumption that Paul is describing a state of moral frustration here: the context is a confident call to live by the Spirit, and the assumption is that it is possible and proper to live by the Spirit and not by the flesh.[8]

Romans 7 is such a controversial and well-debated passage that one might think it unwise to base much on a particular interpretation of it; but the passage is important for Dunn, and his arguments must be considered. He sides with those scholars who see verse 14 onwards as descriptive of normal Christian experience;[9] and if this view is correct, then it is evidently weighty evidence in favour of seeing the Christian life as a life of unresolved tension.

Dunn[10] presents at least seven arguments for his view of Romans 7:

1. His first argument—that the position of ch. 7 in the section of Romans describing the justified man (chs. 5-8) supports the post-conversion interpretation of verses 14-25—is not very compelling, unless one assumes that Paul could not allow himself a long (but relevant) digression in the argument.[11]

2. Nor does the position of 7:25b decisively favour Dunn's view. Verse 25a on any view must be considered an interjection that is not strictly part of the argument, and verse 25b simply reverts to and sums up the preceding train of thought.[12]

3. The tense of ἤδειν in 7:7 may, as Dunn argues, suggest some ongoing knowledge of sin; but this scarcely proves the struggle of 7:14-25 to be Christian experience.

4. The positive portrayal of the νοῦς in verse 25 and the earlier use of the phrase ὁ ἔσω ἄνθρωπος in verse 22 do not prove that Paul is speaking of the believer: it may be true that Paul does not normally speak so favourably of the unbeliever's νοῦς, but that does not mean that he might not do so in order to portray the moral inability of the unbeliever and the powerlessness of the law.[13] It may also be true that in 2 Cor. 4:16, 17 Paul uses ὁ ἔσω ἄνθρωπος of the believer's new life in Christ; but that does not mean that he could not have used the same dualistic terminology of a non-Christian.[14]

5. The argument that Paul nowhere else portrays his pre-conversion experience as one of anguish over indwelling sin is one that has seemed persuasive to many. The argument is that Paul's description of his past life, e.g. in Gal. 1:14; Phil. 3:4–6, suggests that as a Jew before his conversion he was conscious not of moral struggle and defeat, but rather of moral rectitude and achievement;[15] thus the experience of 7:14–25 must be his post-conversion experience. The force of this argument has evidently been felt by scholars who see 7:14–25 as pre-Christian experience, since some have explained that the passage does not give an autobiographical record of how Paul felt as a Jew, but a Christian verdict on the pre-Christian state.[16] Others have explained that this was probably Paul's pre-Christian experience shortly before his conversion, when his Pharisaic self-confidence had been upset by the challenge of the Christian gospel: his confrontation with the gospel made him realize that God requires perfection of life and purity of heart, something much more demanding than his former Pharisaism believed to be necessary.[17] This suggestion could well be correct; but whether the discrepancy between Philippians 3 and Romans 7, if both refer to pre-Christian experience, is so difficult as all these views suppose, is questionable. If the difference in context and perspective between Romans 7 and Philippians 3 is recognized, then it is possible to consider both as descriptive of Paul's pre-Christian experience even before his confrontation with the gospel. It is possible that, despite his outstanding superficial achievement (referred to in Philippians 3), he did experience inward struggle.[18] And there is no good reason to suppose that he would have failed to recognize that non-Christians (e.g. Jews with a true love of God's law) often can and do experience moral struggle.[19]

6. A further argument relates to ch. 8. At first sight ch. 8 seems to be introducing a contrary thought to ch. 7: ch. 7 describes defeat and ch. 8 victory, and it is natural to take ch. 8 as describing the solution to ch. 7. Dunn, however, argues that ch. 8 is merely elaborating the other side of the paradox of Christian life. He goes on to point out that ch. 8 describes a tension in the Christian life from verse 4 onwards and in particular in

verse 10—"The body is dead because of sin, but the Spirit is life because of righteousness." This verse sums up the paradox of Christian experience. Dunn explains: "The body is dead because the Christian is still as flesh a member of the first Adam—dead towards God, dead in sin, heading for death; the body of which Paul speaks in 8:10 is the same 'body of death' of which he spoke in 7:24...".[20]

This argument of Dunn is much more substantial than his others. If it can be established that ch. 8, which is unmistakably speaking of Christian experience, portrays the same tension as is portrayed in 7:14–25, then 7:14–25 may also plausibly be taken of Christian experience. But, although there can be no question that ch. 8 does describe a tension in the believer's life (e.g. verses 12, 13), it is not so certain that the tension of ch. 8 is the same as the radical, almost schizophrenic, experience of 7:14–25.

One of the important, but debatable, points in Dunn's argument is his interpretation of 8:10: εἰ δὲ Χριστὸς ἐν ὑμῖν, τὸ μὲν σῶμα νεκρὸν διὰ ἁμαρτίαν, τὸ δὲ πνεῦμα ζωὴ διὰ δικαιοσύνην. Dunn correctly rejects the sacramental interpretation of this verse which takes the death of the body referred to here as the believer's baptismal death with Christ referred to in ch. 6.[21] But his view that the verse describes the two sides of the Christian's divided experience—the sinful-dying-body side over against the living-Spirit side—would be disputed by many. It is possible and, according to many commentators, preferable to take the phrase "the body is dead because of sin" simply as a statement of future physical mortality—because you have sinned, your body will have to die—and not as a description of one element in man's present moral condition (i.e. his sin-affected dead body).[22] A similar division of opinion would apply to 8:23, where the groaning of the Spirit-led believer may be understood either as a groaning over the physical weakness and mortality of our present bodies, or as a groaning also over the sinfulness and moral weakness of our present existence.

The notorious difficulty of Paul's anthropological terminology means that the choice between the two interpretations in this passage is not an easy one. It is clear, on the one hand, that the σῶμα in 8:10 is not identical with the old man or the old nature, since the σῶμα is to be raised to life in the future (verse 11) and to be redeemed (verse 25). It is also clear, on the other hand, that in Romans 6–8 σῶμα is used on several occasions in a rather derogatory sense as the site where sin gains a hold over the Christian.[23] Thus 6:12 says "Let not sin reign in your mortal body to obey its desires"; here the Christian is called to resist the desires of his mortal body, and so evidently the body is or has become in a real sense an ally of sin and a moral enemy.[24] In 7:24 the frustrated man calls for someone to rescue him from "this body of death"; his meaning, as the context makes clear, is not just that he wants deliverance from mortality, but rather that he longs for someone to free him from the power of sin which is at work in the members of his body and which is seeking to drag him down to death. These two verses (6:12 and 7:24) are notable parallels to 8:10, since all three speak of the mortality of the body at the same time that they speak of the sinfulness of the body. The same thought comes out in 8:13 where Paul promises that "if by the Spirit you put to death the deeds of the body, you will live". Again the body is spoken of as a morally negative quantity.

In the light of this evidence it seems very plausible to take "the body is dead because of sin" not just to mean that the body will die because you have sinned, but that the body will die because it is a continuing ally or centre of sin in your life. It would be inaccurate to say that in verses 7–13 Paul explains the relationship of the law and sin by experience ("the body") and the new man ("the Spirit"); but the verse does point to two realities in the believer—his body, which is a dead thing (i.e. on the way to death) because it is a sin-affected entity, and the Spirit, who is life because of righteousness.[25] If this conclusion is correct, then Dunn's argument is justified at this point.

We may also agree that the groaning for the redemption of the body (8:23) is not just groaning for redemption from mortality and decay, but rather redemption from the influence and power of sin that is at work in the body.[26] Our conclusion is, then, that ch. 8 does portray the believer as a man conscious of and troubled by his sinful σῶμα, and this evidence lends weight to Dunn's view of ch. 7 as Christian experience.[27]

7. The other rather strong argument for seeing 7:14–25 as Christian experience is the present tense in this section. It is true that a present tense may be used dramatically of past experience; but in the flow of ch. 7 there is a very definite shift from the past tenses of verses 7–13 to the present tenses that follow. The simplest explanation of this is arguably that in verses 7–13 Paul explains the relationship of the law and sin by referring to the past, but then in verses 14–25 he explains the same point from a different angle by appealing to his readers' present knowledge of their own experience (especially so if "we know" in verse 14 is taken to introduce the whole section from verse 14 onwards and not only the phrase "the law is spiritual").

Before, however, this argument is taken for granted, an important question is whether the change of tense can be explained in another way. One significant point observed by K. Kertelge[28] is that there is not only a shift of tense but also a shift in the point being made. The matter being discussed in 7:7–25 is the law; Paul has spoken of its involvement with sin and of the believer being freed from it. This inevitably raises serious questions about the traditional view of the God-given nature of the law. So in 7:7 Paul asks "Is the law sin?", and he answers "By no means". But in the verses that follow he does little to defend the law; in fact he goes on in verses 7b–11 to describe the law's considerable involvement together with sin in "my" death. The question still remains as to whether the law is not a malignant influence—verse 13, "Did that which is good, then, bring death to me?" It is only from this point in verse 13 that Paul really takes up the defence of the law by proving that it was sin that was really responsible for my death. So whereas in verses 7–11 the involvement of the law was the point, from verse 13 onwards the real responsibility of sin is the point; repeatedly the blame is put on indwelling sin (verses 13, 17, 20, 23, 25).

The relevance of this observation for the question of the change of tense may not seem obvious; after all, the change in the direction of the argument takes place at verse 13 and the change of tense at verse 14. However, although verse 13 begins the indictment of sin with a direct statement of sin's responsibility, it is only in verse 14 that Paul begins to justify the statement by appeal to experience. (Note the γάϱ connection between verses 13 and 14 omitted by the RSV in translation.) Thus in verse 14 Paul begins to give evidence for the guiltlessness of the law and the responsibility of sin. The coincidence of the change of tense with the beginning of a new stage in the argument does not necessarily mean that the use of the present tense is not significant; but it does mean that the change of tense is not a wholly isolated phenomenon, and it is impossible to argue from the premise that Paul makes the same point first in the past tense and then in the present. The fact that verses 14–25 are seen to be explanatory of verse 13, which refers to the pre-conversion experience, might seem to demand that verses 14–25 also be taken in the same way. But this conclusion is not inevitable: the justification for the conclusion of verse 13 that it was sin not the law which killed me in my pre-Christian past could be found in my partially parallel present experience as a believer.[29]

On the other side the argument from the sustained and vivid use of the present tense remains powerful for the post-conversion interpretation of the passage.[30] Despite the objections it is hard to suppose that throughout this section Paul is speaking of past experience; it is easier to think of something that is a present reality in the believer's life—of the sinful body which ch. 8 proves to be a present reality in the believer and not only in the unbeliever.

The last two arguments lend support to Dunn's interpretation of 7:14–25.[31] But there are counter-arguments; and just as Dunn's strongest argument was based on ch. 8, the biggest objection to his view is also based on ch. 8, or to be more precise on the total context of Romans and especially chs. 6–8. The objection is this: the failure of the law and the way of the law contrasted with the "success" of Christ and the way of grace is a recurrent theme throughout Romans, and it comes out in the context immediately preceding 7:14–25 (i.e. 7:6) and in the immediately following context (i.e. 8:2). The almost inevitable impression is that 7:14–25 is describing the state from which we are delivered,[32] and not something that continues side by side with the life of the Spirit. This impression is reinforced when the contrasting parallelism of 7:14–25 and of ch. 8 is observed: for example, in 7:23 Paul speaks of a law "making me captive" to the law of sin in my members, and he goes on to lament this body of death; but in 8:2–4 he speaks of the law of the Spirit which "set you free" from the law of sin and death and which enabled you to fulfil the righteousness of the law that you could not fulfil according to the flesh. Paul goes on in 8:7 to speak of the "mind of the flesh which is hostile to God; it does not submit to the law of God, indeed it cannot". This reminds us of the frustration of ch. 7, and the impression is inevitable that the Spirit of ch. 8 is the antidote to the impotence of ch. 7.[33]

We find ourselves then coming to two contradictory conclusions: there seem to be arguments for seeing 7:14–25 as a Christian experience, and yet there seem to be equally good arguments for seeing 7:14–25 as a state from which believers are released. It is not surprising that scholars have ended up divided on the matter; nor is it surprising that a number of scholars have, as it were, stood near the border-line between the two opinions: on the one hand there are those who believe that 7:14–25 describe a non-Christian under Christian influence,[34] or those who believe that the passage describes a pre-Christian experience which can continue to threaten a Christian even after conversion,[35] and on the other hand there are those who see the passage as describing a Christian recently come out of unbelief or not living in the fullness of the Spirit's power or slipping back into unbelief.[36] The present writer finds it hard to choose between the view that 7:14–25 are meant to be describing a pre-Christian experience which has an echo in Christian experience and the possibly preferable view that he is describing a Christian experience that has much in common with some non-Christian experience.[37]

Certainly for Paul the Christian has a σάρξ / σῶμα nature that is a reality in his life, that pulls him down and that he longs to be rid of (as we see in chs. 6 and 8; see also Gal. 5:13; Rom. 13:14); and it may be to their knowledge of this experience that Paul is appealing in 7:14–25. This is, of course, not the whole of Christian experience; in 7:14–25 Paul is quite specifically talking about "my flesh" (verses 18, 23, 25), and he ignores the Spirit. The reason is not that he thinks that there is such a thing as a believer without the Spirit, but because he knows that even the believer experiences a σάρξ / σῶμα pull in his life leading him away from God's law, and it is this experience (not the experience of the Spirit) that is relevant in ch. 7 where he is showing how sin thwarts our good intentions to keep the law. The context of ch. 7 thus leads him to a very selective—one might say distorting—perspective on the Christian life.

But although Paul may be referring in ch. 7 to a σάρξ / σῶμα reality that his readers will recognize in their Christian experience and that doubtless Paul knows in his experience, he does not accept that this experience is something to be regarded as acceptable or necessary. Indeed in ch. 8 he makes it very clear that the Spirit is given to enable us to resist and conquer the old man. The picture in Romans 7 and 8 is thus precisely that of Galatians 5: there is a struggle in the believer and opposite tendencies, but Paul would not accept that a Christian should go on yielding to the old life, now that the Spirit has come.

Our position ends up close to that of Professor Bruce and R. N. Longenecker, with 7:14–25 taken to describe the believer living without the Spirit.[38] Whether the words αὐτὸς ἐγώ should be pressed to mean "I by myself", i.e. I without the Spirit, is debatable.[39] But we would agree that for Paul Rom. 7:14–25, though not infrequently experienced by believers, is not the life of victory that is possible through the Spirit; anyone living consistently in 7:14–25 would need urgently to learn and to appropriate for himself what is available to him in Christ.

Where does this leave us more generally on Paul's view of the Christian life? (1) Paul would never admit the inevitability of defeat in the Christian life. His conviction is clear that "with the temptation God will also make the way of escape" (1 Cor. 10:13). The power of the Spirit is the power that raised Jesus from the dead and will give us newness of life in the present as well as in the future. For Paul this is the most important reality of Christian experience, and he would not subscribe to the melancholy view that Spirit and flesh are two almost equal contestants within the believer's life.[40] Undoubtedly Paul would have subscribed to the view that the Christian life can be a life of victory, if only we will recognize and appropriate the Spirit's power.

(2) Yet Paul also knew the strength of the forces ranged against the believer. So as well as promising the way of escape from temptation, he warned, "Let him who thinks he stands take heed lest he fall" (1 Cor. 10:12). Paul was aware that the pressures on the believer were often severe (e.g. 1 Cor. 7:5): outside there were the principalities and powers, defeated by Christ and yet a fierce foe; inside was the flesh/the body with its constant tendency to sin and its constant tendency to reassert its enslaving power in the believer. The enemy for Paul was no paper tiger; probably in Rom. 7:14–25 he was speaking from personal experience.[41] He urges his readers not to get tired (e.g. Gal. 6:7–10), an injunction

necessary because the battle is one in which it is easy to grow weary. The reality and unpleasantness of the enemy is made clear by Paul's expressions of longing for future liberation—a liberation only partially realized now and fully to be enjoyed in the future.

The explanation of Paul's two-sided view lies, as Dunn rightly observes, in Paul's eschatology: he believes that the new age has broken into history in Christ, the new Adam, especially in his resurrection and in the pouring out of the Spirit. He believes that by being united to Christ in faith and baptism the believer enters into that new age, receives a new relationship with God and experiences the power of the new age in his life.[42] But he is not taken out of the old age (cf. Rom. 12:1–2; 13:11–14); he is still part of Adam's humanity. It is indeed by living the life of the new age in the old age that he becomes conformed to Christ's likeness. The old age confronts him in the world with its persecutions and also in his inmost being in the "body", and the believer has to learn to follow Christ in accepting suffering and in putting sin to death through the power of the Holy Spirit. The final victory over the old self and the old age will not be experienced until the end, and in the meantime the Christian life should be a continual process of purification and growth through the Spirit that has been given to us.

Notes

1. Stendahl has warned of the dangers of attributing to Paul the "introspective conscience of the West" in *Paul among Jews and Gentiles and other Essays* (Philadelphia, Fortress, 1976), 78–96 [= "The Apostle Paul and the Introspective Conscience of the West," *HTR* 56 (1963), 199–215].

2. J. D. G. Dunn, in his *Jesus and the Spirit* (Philadelphia, Westminster, 1975), perhaps goes too far in stressing the primacy of experience for the NT church.

3. Also in his article "Rom. 7, 14–25 in the Theology of Paul," *TZ* 31 (1975), 257–73.

4. *Jesus and the Spirit*, 313. Dunn expresses his view still more starkly in his article: "The believer is still in the flesh, still in all too real a sense a man of flesh, still experiencing the dominion of sin in an integral dimension of his present existence" ("Rom. 7, 14–25," 269). For an opposite point of view to Dunn's see R. Jewett, *Paul's Anthropological Terms. A Study of their Use in Conflict Settings* (Leiden, Brill, 1971), 106.

5. See 2 Cor. 12:7. If the thorn in the flesh is correctly identified as a physical ailment, then we see here a striking example of the eschatological tension—alongside the fact of Spirit-given healing in Paul's churches, a sign of the new age, we find the stubborn fact of disease that does not respond to powers of miraculous healing, a characteristic of the ongoing old age.

6. *Pace* Dunn, "Jesus—Flesh and Spirit: An Exposition of Romans I.3–4," *JTS* 24 (1973), 40–68.

7. See E. Schweizer (*TDNT* 6 [1968], 429); also Jewett (*Paul's Anthropological Terms*, 106–107), who points out that verse 17 is explanatory of verse 16, not a

complete description of the Christian life. The objections to taking ἵνα as a final particle do not seem decisive, especially if it is taken in a rather weak sense to refer to the tendency of the Spirit-flesh conflict (rather than to suggest that the Spirit's deliberate purpose is to frustrate the believer's desires). The flesh-Spirit antithesis is such that the believer is conscious both of conflicting desires and of conflicting forces (flesh and Spirit).

8. In Galatians 5, living in the flesh is to revert to one's pre-Christian way of life. (So H. N. Ridderbos, *Paul. An Outline of His Theology* [London, SPCK, 1977], 269–70; cf. D. M. Lloyd-Jones, *Romans: An Exposition of Chapters 7:1–8:4* [Grand Rapids, Zondervan, 1973], 230–32.) On the other hand, fleshly living is still a possibility for the Christian—to be resisted.

9. Also A. Nygren (*Commentary on Romans* [London, SCM, 1952], 284–303) and C. E. B. Cranfield (*A Critical and Exegetical Commentary on the Epistle to the Romans*, 1 [Edinburgh, Clark, 1975], 340–47).

10. See *Jesus and the Spirit*, 313–15 and "Rom. 7, 14–25," 260–64.

11. See Ridderbos, *Paul*, 143.

12. It is true that several scholars who have viewed 7:13 onwards as pre-Christian experience have postulated some textual dislocation at the end of ch. 7. But they, like Dunn and Cranfield, are in danger of assuming that Paul's development of thought must be entirely logical without digressions or interjections.

13. Cf. W. G. Kümmel, *Man in the New Testament* (2nd ed.; London, Epworth, 1963), 59. R. H. Gundry (*Sōma in Biblical Theology with Emphasis on Pauline Anthropology* [Cambridge, 1976], 140) argues that though Paul refers at times to the corruption of the unbeliever's mind yet the relevant contexts suggest that "in the beginning the mind had known and desired better".

14. See F. J. Leenhardt, *The Epistle to the Romans* (London, Lutterworth, 1961), 193–94; R. H. Gundry, *Sōma*, 135–40; R. Scroggs, *The Last Adam* (Philadelphia, Fortress, 1966), 110–11; J. Jeremias, *TDNT* 1 (1964), 365; J. Behm, *TDNT* 2 (1964), 698.

15. Professor Bruce doubts if Paul the Jew had the introspective conscience of 7:14 onwards; see *Paul: Apostle of the Free Spirit* (Exeter, Paternoster, 1977), 196.

16. Cf. E. Stauffer, *TDNT* 2 (1964), 357–62. Although there may be some truth in this suggestion, it seems more straightforward to take the passage as descriptive of an experience in which the subject is conscious of the struggle described rather than as a theological description of a trans-subjective state. This is one argument against the existentialist interpretation of Romans 7 advocated, e.g., by R. Bultmann in his essay "Romans 7 and the Anthropology of Paul" in *Existence and Faith* (London, Fontana ed., 1964), 173–85. According to this interpretation the tension in Romans 7 is not a conscious tension between good intentions and evil actions, but an existential tension in the man who hopes to achieve life and authenticity through law-keeping, but who paradoxically finds that that way leads to death. Although there is a certain attraction in this view, "my" problem in 7:14–25 is most simply understood as being that I cannot keep the law, not that I have mistakenly tried to do so. (E.g. in verse 15 the problem is trying to keep the law and failing, i.e. transgression. See also the earlier chapters of Romans where it is failure to keep the law that spells man's downfall and brings the wrath of God.) Against the existentialist interpretation see Ridderbos, *Paul*, 146 and B. C. Wintle, *The Law of Moses and the Law of Christ* (unpublished Manchester University Ph.D. thesis, 1977), 95. A summary of Dr. Wintle's argu-

ments on Romans is accessible in the *TRACI/ETS Journal* (New Delhi) 12 (1978), 26–35.

17. Cf. D. M. Davies, "Free From the Law," *Int* 7 (1953), 160–62; W. D. Davies, *Paul and Rabbinic Judaism* (2nd ed.; London, SPCK, 1955), 141; Lloyd-Jones, *Romans 7*, 256 and *passim*; Wintle, *The Law*, 98–101.

18. Since those who regard 7:14–25 as Paul's Christian experience can find very few other passages to show that Paul the Christian experienced the sort of struggle described in this passage, they cannot make too much of the argument that Paul does not refer to an experience of struggle in his pre-conversion days.

19. D. M. Davies, "Free From the Law," *Int* 7, 160–62; also W. D. Davies (*Paul*, 17–31), who notes the Rabbinic idea of two warring impulses in man, and R. N. Longenecker (*Paul: Apostle of Liberty* [New York, Harper, 1964], 115) on the Qumran community. The counter-argument that Paul elsewhere portrays unbelievers as dead in sin rather than as struggling with sin overlooks the possibility that Paul may portray different aspects of the truth in different contexts. The argument that the intensity of the struggle does not fit in with non-Christian experience is scarcely cogent, though it might possibly be accepted that Paul the Christian gives in Romans 7 a one-sided picture of pre-Christian experience (almost a caricature) in order to make his particular point in this context.

20. *Jesus and the Spirit*, 315–16.

21. So also Cranfield, *Romans*, 389; Gundry, *Sōma*, 43; against, Jewett, *Paul's Anthropological Terms*, 296–98.

22. Cf. Bruce (*Paul*, 206) who distinguishes 8:10 from 7:24 and 6:6.

23. σῶμα is used here much as σάρξ is used elsewhere in Paul, though probably not identically. On the use of σῶμα in this section see Jewett (*Paul's Anthropological Terms*, 158–60, 290–98); Gundry (*Sōma*, 37–40 and elsewhere).

24. Gundry (*Sōma*, 42) prefers the minority reading "to obey it (αὐτῇ = sin)"; but see Cranfield (*Romans*, 317). Gundry comments that even if the alternative reading is accepted, this "need not mean any more than that sin uses bodily desires to gain a bridgehead in its attack upon man". Yet "obeying the body's desires" seems equivalent to sin here, and so the body is not quite as neutral as Gundry would like.

25. The meaning of διὰ δικαιοσύνην is disputed. Although it is probably simplest to take it to mean "because of justification", it is tempting to take it to mean "because of (*not* "for the sake of") righteousness of life" (which the Spirit produces in the believer). Compare 8:4 and other verses in chs. 6–8 that connect holy living with eternal life.

26. This would be in line with Paul's redemption language elsewhere. The creation's groaning in verse 22 may also be groaning for redemption from futility (verse 20) and not just from mortality.

27. Not that the parallel between the experience of ch. 8 and that of ch. 7 necessarily means that the experience is the same, but it makes the suggestion more likely.

28. "Exegetische Überlegungen zum Verständnis der paulinischen Anthropologie nach Römer 7," *ZNW* 62 (1971), 108–109.

29. We might wish to make the connection of thought clearer by beginning verse 14, "For we know even in our experience now that, though the law is spiritual, I am carnal . . .".

30. Compare Cranfield, *Romans*, 344–45; J. I. Packer, "The 'Wretched Man' in Romans 7" (*Studia Evangelica* II [Berlin, 1964], 625), suggests that verse 25b in particular should be in the past tense if verses 14–25 speak of pre-conversion experience.

31. If certain of Dunn's arguments on 7:14–25 seem persuasive, other less decisive arguments might be brought in. We might reconsider the argument that the νοῦς of 7:14–25 sounds like the renewed mind of the believer who loves the law of God and wants to do it, or we might note the argument that verses 14–25 represent a greater intensity of struggle than that of verses 7–13, a struggle more compatible with the experience of the regenerate than of the unregenerate. But the greater intensity of struggle in verses 14–25 may simply reflect the change of point being made (see above), and neither of these arguments is at all unambiguous.

32. Wintle (*The Law,* 93, 94) endorses C. H. Dodd's view (*The Epistle of Paul to the Romans* [London, Hodder, 1932], 108) that for Paul to speak of Christian experience in the terms of 7:14–25 would be to stultify Paul's whole argument. Cranfield's comment (*Romans,* 346–47), that the failure to recognize the legitimacy of speaking of a Christian as "sold under sin" etc. reflects a failure to recognize the full seriousness of the ethical demands of God's law or the gospel, really misses the point. The question is not whether we have difficulty in applying such language to a Christian, but whether Paul's teaching elsewhere suggests that he would have spoken thus.

33. By way of reply to this point it is argued by Cranfield (*Romans,* 346) and others that the man of 7:14–25 is one who in his mind is a "slave" of the law of God (verse 25) and that such a man in Pauline terms must be a Christian having the Spirit (cf. 6:17–20; 8:7). This argument is not wholly convincing, however: both in ch. 6 and ch. 8 the Christian is not only one who has right desires towards the law of God, but he also has the power to carry them out; but in ch. 7 the wretched man is unable to do what he desires. If Paul seems a trifle inconsistent in speaking of an unbeliever "serving the law of God" with his mind, the explanation could be in terms of the different context of the remarks of ch. 7 and chs. 6 and 8. We have already argued that Paul would probably not have denied any moral striving to non-Christians.

34. See n. 17 above.

35. See Ridderbos, *Paul,* 130; also Kertelge, "Exegetische Überlegungen zum Verständnis der paulinischen Anthropologie nach Römer 7," 112.

36. See Bruce, *Paul,* 198, and also on this and other points his *Epistle of Paul to the Romans* (London, Tyndale, 1963), 150–56. Also A. M. Hunter as cited in M. Black, *Romans* (London, Oliphants, 1973), 113.

37. The valuable discussion in Longenecker's *Paul* anticipates mine in various ways. See his conclusions on p. 116: "Romans 7 . . . cannot be considered an exclusively Christian conviction. It is the human cry . . . of the spiritually sensitive. . . . It may be that Paul's Christian presentation in Romans 7 differs from his preconversion position only in the intensity of his realization and expression." Longenecker's suggestion that 7:11–13 describe Adam's fall and then 14–25 the existential Adam in each man is illuminating.

38. Nygren (*Romans,* 295) regards the idea of the Christian standing on his own legs without the Spirit as an abstraction; but Paul certainly regarded it as a practical, though not justifiable, possibility for the Christian to neglect and not walk by the Spirit.

39. Although this is one possible explanation of the otherwise redundant αὐτός, against this see Packer, "The 'Wretched Man' in Romans 7," *Studia Evangelica* II, 625 and Wintle, *The Law,* 90. We wonder if the word could have been added for no better reason than euphony.

40. Cf. Ridderbos, *Paul,* 272. Dunn himself seems to see this point, when he speaks of "I in my inner man" having to choose against "I as flesh", for he

goes on to say, "By the power of the Spirit it can be done" (*Jesus and the Spirit*, 316). But this recognition of the Spirit's superior power seems at odds with what Dunn says elsewhere about the Christian struggle.

41. 1 Cor. 9:26, 27 is striking evidence for the seriousness of Paul's struggle with indwelling sin, if the traditional interpretation of the verse is accepted (as by C. K. Barrett, *A Commentary on the First Epistle to the Corinthians* [London, Black, 1968], 218). But it has been argued that Paul is not here speaking of a personal struggle with indwelling sin, but metaphorically of his willingness to give up his rights in commending the gospel to others. The preceding context, especially verse 23, would support the view that the self-discipline being referred to here is discipline in denying himself his legitimate rights. (See Wintle, *The Law*, 264, citing V. C. Pfitzner, *Paul, the Agon Motif*, NovTSup 16 [Leiden, Brill, 1967].) But it could be that Paul's thought has moved on in verse 27 to a more general idea of self-discipline as in the traditional interpretation.

The infrequency of Pauline reference to a struggle with sin may be explained in various ways: (a) Paul was probably not a self-conscious introvert! (b) He was more interested in encouraging his converts to go on than in reflecting on the difficulties in the way or recounting his experience. (His reflection in 7:14–25 is purely to make his point about the law. See Stendahl, *Paul among Jews*, 92. But Stendahl probably goes too far in denying that ch. 7 reflects any subjective struggle of conscience. Although Paul is making a theological point, he is doing so by appealing to a conscious experience of failure.) (c) For him the gift of the powerful Holy Spirit was the thing worth talking about, not the old nature that was passing away.

42. To be exact, he experiences a foretaste of the new age and the firstfruits of its blessings, not the blessings in full.

Chapter 7

THE CHRIST-CHRISTIAN RELATIONSHIP IN PAUL AND JOHN

STEPHEN S. SMALLEY

INVESTIGATING THE RELATIONSHIP between Paul and John is no longer the fashionable academic exercise it once was. The work of such scholars as Deissmann, Schweitzer and Sanday[1] is evidence that in the earlier years of this century the precise links between Pauline and Johannine thought formed the subject of an ongoing and lively debate.[2] Today, however, this topic is seldom raised in critical circles; and the reason for this is probably that such an investigation is now regarded as an inconclusive, and therefore unfruitful, enterprise.

Why then, it may be asked, should this issue be revived in a collection of contemporary Pauline studies such as this? The answer is twofold. First must be mentioned our continuing interest in the matter.[3] Second, and more importantly, a comparative study of Paul and John is still, we believe, worth undertaking. In the course of this it is hoped that some further understanding may be gained of each writer individually, and also that the significance of any kind of common ground between them may emerge. Our trust that such an exploration may yield positive results is increased by the fact that it is intended to limit the scope of this enquiry to one theological area: namely, the personal relationship of the believer with Christ. This is on any showing a theme of fundamental importance in the writings of both Paul and John, as well as in the general life of early Christianity. It is also, of course, a central concern for the contemporary church and its individual members. It seems to us appropriate, therefore, to dedicate an essay on this crucial question to one who for so many years has combined scholarly expertise with devotion to the experience and practice, as well as to the study, of the Christian faith.[4] To Professor Bruce, valued mentor and long-standing friend, these thoughts are accordingly offered with affection and high regard.

I

Three points of delineation are required at the outset. 1. For the purposes of this article the Pauline corpus of letters is taken to include all the documents traditionally ascribed to Paul in the New Testament canon, with the exception of the Pastorals. 2. "John" here means basically the Fourth Gospel, although 1 John and even the Apocalypse will not be ignored. In neither case are any conclusions about authorship implied by the use of the name.[5] 3. It is naturally important to be constantly sensitive to the different types of document involved in this analysis: on the one hand a kerygmatic Gospel, however theological;[6] and on the other, letters written with theological sensitivity, however didactic and practical their original inspiration may have been.

II

We now proceed to an examination of ten points at which it may be claimed that there is some measure (at least) of correspondence between the Pauline and Johannine approaches to the theological motif of the Christ-Christian relationship. In each case a representative selection of references, only, will be cited for consideration. At the end of this exegetical analysis we shall submit some conclusions of a more broadly theological nature.

1. *The basis of the Christ-Christian relationship, for both Paul and John, is to be found in Jesus: in his life and death and resurrection/exaltation* (Rom. 5:8–11, cf. 4:25; and John 3:13–18).[7] These passages include primitive elements. In Rom. 4:25 (Jesus was "put to death for our trespasses and raised for our justification"), as Barrett says, Paul appears to use a traditional christological formula; however, as Barrett goes on to point out, its pre-Pauline history "must remain a matter of speculation".[8] And, despite the obviously Johannine tinting of the section in John 3, the Son of man logia in verses 13 and 14 probably belong—as with the Son of man christology generally in the Fourth Gospel—to an early, traditional theological stratum.[9] Thus it may be argued that the theology of the relation between Christ and the believer, as presented by both Paul and John, rests ultimately on a kerygmatic foundation.

2. *In both Paul and John, Jesus is presented as the (unique) way to the Father* (Col. 1:19f.,[10] but see Eph. 1:10, where the force of "uniting τὰ πάντα in Christ" may be regarded as inclusive rather than exclusive; cf.

Eph. 2:17f. and John 14:6,[11] but see John 1:9, which may be interpreted in a similarly "inclusive" manner; cf. 1 John 5:20).

3. *The means of union with Christ, for both Paul and John, is faith.* This involves a personal and conscious commitment, and leads to an individual relationship between the believer and God through Jesus Christ (Rom. 5:1f., cf. Eph. 2:8; and John 20:27-31, cf. 3:16, 18).

Two further comments may be made on this point. First, in Pauline thought the faith required of the believer is "objective" in character; that is to say, faith in the given Christ event. In Johannine terms, on the other hand, the faith in view appears to be much more "subjective"; that is to say, the believer's continuing *life* of faith.[12]

Second, union with Christ, for John as well as Paul, is associated with the sacramental life. In this connection, however, Paul's understanding of the place of the sacraments in Christian experience—both initial and continuing—is more explicit and more developed than John's. Paul does not draw out the precise link between baptism and forgiveness, any more than John does; but in Paul's view, nevertheless, baptism (with faith) is seen as the basis of a mystical or eschatological "being-in-Christ" (Rom. 6:3f.; Col. 2:12).[13] It seems also that Paul regarded the Christ-Christian relationship as sustained by the eucharist (1 Cor. 10:16;[14] cf. 11:24f.). The place of the sacraments in the Fourth Gospel is much less clear, chiefly because John is more concerned with "the sacramental" than with the rites of baptism or eucharist as such.[15] But John's Gospel does speak of rebirth through "water and the Spirit" (John 3:5), and of abiding in Christ by means of eucharistic participation (6:56); and even if the (ritual) sacramental references here are not primary, or—especially in the case of the John 6 passage—are in fact later redactions, they cannot be excluded altogether from John's theology as it now exists.[16]

4. *To be in union with Christ, according to both Paul and John, is "to have (eternal) life".* Paul's typical and distinctive description of this life-giving union, is being "in Christ". In John ἐν Χριστῷ is replaced by ἐν ἐμοί;[17] and the thought of "abiding" or "remaining" in Jesus[18] (using the verb μένειν[19]) is a characteristically Johannine extension of this idea (Rom. 8:1f., "life in Christ Jesus"; 6:23, "eternal life in Christ Jesus our Lord", cf. 1 Cor. 15:22;[20] and John 14:19f., 15:4-10,[21] cf. 1 John 5:11f.,[22] Rev. 1:9[23]).

5. *To be "in Christ", and its equivalent in John, is not only a guarantee of (eternal) life; it is also, ethically, the means of life* (that is to say, the power for living). Thus, for both writers, the concept of "Christ in you" is used interchangeably with that of "you in Christ" (Gal. 2:20, Eph. 3:17-19, cf. Col. 1:27; and John 14:20f., 15:4f.). Such "mutual abiding", according to Paul as well as John, is consistently

necessary; for one result of the total Christ-Christian relationship—"you in Christ, Christ in you"—is the establishment of a perpetual tension between "flesh" (being "of the world"[24]) and "spirit" (being "in Christ") (Gal. 5:16f., cf. Rom. 8:5; and John 3:6, cf. 6:63).[25]

6. *The resources for life in Christ are mediated by the Spirit (of Christ) as the agent of God* (Rom. 8:8f., cf. Gal. 5:25, also Titus 3:5f.; and John 14:12–17).[26] Thus, for both Paul and John, being "in Christ" and "in the Spirit"—and the reverse, "Christ in you" and "the Spirit in you"—are parallel (Eph. 2:21f.,[27] with the reverse in Rom. 8:10f.; and John 15:4–9, 4:23f.,[28] with the reverse in John 14:18–20, 16f.).

Two additional comments may be made as a development of this point. First, the Spirit of God is explicitly (and distinctively) identified by Paul as the Spirit of *Christ* (Rom. 8:9f., Phil. 1:19).[29] In the current study of the Fourth Gospel, however, it is a matter for debate whether or not John identifies the Spirit-Paraclete with the *alter ego* of Jesus.[30] In our view he does.[31]

Second, Paul describes the results of the believer's life in Christ and in the Spirit as a harvest of the "fruits" of the Spirit (Gal. 5:22f.). John, on the other hand, shows that the source of such "fruit" is ultimately Jesus himself (John 15:4f.). Theologically, of course, these two ideas are complementary rather than in conflict.

7. *Salvation in Christ, according to both John and Paul, is trinitarian in character and operation.* Both speak—although John rather more fully—of the believer in God and Christ and the Spirit, and of God and Christ and the Spirit in the believer. Thus:

You in God	Col. 3:3[32]	John 17:21[33]
You in Christ	2 Cor. 5:17	John 15:4f.[34]
You in Spirit	Rom. 8:9	John 4:23f.[35]
God in you	Phil. 2:13[36]	John 14:23[37]
Christ in you	Col. 1:27[38]	John 14:18–20[39]
Spirit in you	1 Cor. 3:16[40]	John 14:16f.[41]

8. *Salvation in Christ, for both Paul and John, is conceived in corporate as well as individual terms* (Rom. 12:4f., cf. 1 Cor. 12:12, Eph. 4:15f.;[42] and John 1:51,[43] 10:7 and 11,[44] 15:1[45]).

9. *The Christ-Christian relationship in both Pauline and Johannine thought (being "in Christ"/"in the Spirit") is (thus) the means of unity in the church* (Rom. 12:5, "one body in Christ", cf. 1 Cor. 12:27, 12f., "the body of Christ";[46] and John 10:16, 17:21–23[47]).

10. *There is an eschatological, and indeed cosmic, dimension to the Christ-Christian relationship as it appears in Paul and John.* For both, salvation is regarded as operative here *and* hereafter (Eph. 1:3–14,[48] 1 Thess.

4:16, cf. Rom. 8:17,[49] 1 Cor. 15:22;[50] and John 5:24–9, 14:3 and 18, 16:33, cf. Rev. 14:13[51]).

III

We are now in a position, on the basis of our survey so far, to draw some conclusions.

First, Paul's theology of the Christ-Christian relationship is both developed and developing. We have noticed this to be so, for example, in the case of the Pauline doctrine of baptism, as the basis of a spiritual "being-in-Christ"; and also in Paul's identification of the Spirit, who mediates the resources for Christian living, as the Spirit of Christ.[52] This development within Paul's thinking is natural, of course, given the nature and chronology of the documents which make up the Pauline corpus of letters. John's understanding of the relationship between Christ and the believer, however (appearing mostly, as it happens, in the farewell discourse), while more advanced than that of the synoptic writers,[53] is generally less explicit than Paul's, and does not appear to be in process of development.[54] We can see this from the two ideas of baptism and the Spirit which have just been cited as examples of theological progress in Paul.[54] At the same time we may note that the theologically sophisticated doctrine of "circumincession"—the Christ-Christian relationship as reflecting the relationship between Jesus and the Father—is in fact Johannine, and *not* Pauline.[56]

Second, John (especially in the farewell discourse) appears to distinguish more clearly than Paul between the believer's experience of Christ—before or after the resurrection—and his experience of the Spirit (-Paraclete).[57] For Paul, as we have seen, the Spirit is explicitly and practically experienced as the Spirit *of Christ* (cf. Rom. 8:9); whereas although it is true that for John the Paraclete is in some sense the *alter ego* of Jesus (cf. John 16:7), the theology of the Fourth Gospel (perhaps surprisingly, in view of the tension between the present and the future characteristic of its eschatology) does not appear to "run together" the relationship between the believer and Jesus on the one hand, or the believer and the Spirit on the other. Might this distinction on John's part have arisen because the tradition behind the Fourth Gospel, on which the Johannine theology rests, was close to the historical and *human* Jesus? After the exaltation, therefore, the Johannine church (responsible, I would say, for the final composition of John's Gospel[58]) may have found it difficult to express the *spiritual* relationship between Christ and the Christian in the same terms as would be used to describe this relationship before the resurrection had taken place. Paul, on the other hand, almost certainly did *not* know the human Jesus;[59] and as a result he possibly found it easier than John to express a synonymity between the Jesus of history, and Jesus as he could be known in Spirit after his exaltation.[60]

Third, an important difference exists between Paul and John, so far as their theology of the Christ-Christian relationship is concerned, in terms of their respective interpretations of the "love command". In Paul, God in Christ is described as loving *us*;[61] while the required response from the believer is to love *others* with Christ's love.[62] Rather than *loving* God or Christ,[63] the disciple (according to Paul) is called to *believe* (continuously in them).[64] In John, God and Christ are both described as loving the world of men,[65] as the Father loves the Son;[66] and believers are also summoned to love others with a Christ-like love.[67] So far these two witnesses run along roughly parallel lines. But John parts company with Paul on the question of the believer's attitude towards Christ. In several key Johannine passages the Christian is commanded not only to believe in Jesus[68] but also to *love* him;[69] and this is a thought which does not appear in the extant Pauline literature. (Oddly enough, John—like Paul—does not speak of an obligation to love *God*.[70])

Fourth, the differences between Paul and John which have been noticed, in the one major theological area considered (the Christ-Christian relationship), do not outweigh the remarkable correspondences in their thought. This need not imply that John depended directly on Paul; rather, it suggests that both were indebted—in the "underground"—to a common and primitive Christian tradition (through Ephesus?).[71] Obviously such a thesis, if accepted, will affect any consideration of the (historical) nature of John's tradition,[72] and may possibly also have implications for the final dating of the Fourth Gospel itself.[73]

Finally, despite the common ground, in terms of Pauline and Johannine theology, at this point, Paul and John are obviously individual writers. We can see this when we compare their theologies as a whole, and examine (for example) their distinctive interpretations of the work of Christ. And the fact is that we need *both* witnesses in the New Testament, which by its very nature exhibits theological diversity as well as unity.[74]

Notes

1. Cf. G. A. Deissmann, *Paul: a Study in Social and Religious History* (E.T.; London, 1926²), esp. 155, 197f.; A. Schweitzer, *The Mysticism of Paul the Apostle*

(E.T.; London, 1953³), esp. 349–72; W. Sanday, *The Criticism of the Fourth Gospel* (Oxford, 1905), 205–35.

2. Deissmann, for example, regarded the Gospel and letters of John as "the greatest monument of the most genuine understanding of Paul's mysticism" (*Paul*, 155). But this was hotly disputed by Schweitzer, who considered Johannine mysticism to be a "*Hellenization* of the Pauline" (*Mysticism*, 372, italics mine).

3. An interest maintained since we discussed it in our Tyndale Lecture for 1965. See S. S. Smalley, "New Light on the Fourth Gospel", *TynB* 17 (1966), 50–55. See also S. S. Smalley, *John: Evangelist and Interpreter* (Exeter, 1978), 155–57.

4. For a recent example of Professor Bruce's contribution to this particular area of theological study with reference to Paul, see F. F. Bruce, *Paul: Apostle of the Free Spirit* (Exeter, 1977), esp. 325–38, 427–40.

5. For our views, in the case of the Gospel, see S. S. Smalley, *John: Evangelist and Interpreter*, esp. 68–82.

6. Cf. *ibid.*, 150ff.

7. In both Paul and—although less strongly—John, this relationship seems to have its origin in the eternal purposes of God (cf. Eph. 1:4; Rom. 8:29f.; and John 1:9).

8. C. K. Barrett, *A Commentary on the Epistle to the Romans* (London, 1957), 99.

9. There are, of course, immense problems involved in the background, application and meaning of the expression "Son of man" wherever it occurs in the New Testament. For a defence of the traditional, and indeed authentic, character of the Son of man logia in John 3:13f. (their Johannine shaping notwithstanding), see S. S. Smalley, "The Johannine Son of Man Sayings", *NTS* 15 (1968–9), 278–301, esp. 289–92. See also R. Maddox, "The Function of the Son of Man in the Gospel of John", in R. J. Banks (ed.), *Reconciliation and Hope: New Testament Essays on Atonement and Eschatology* (Exeter, 1974), 186–204, esp. 187–93. Maddox rightly makes the points that "genuineness" is not the only aspect of Johannine Son of man research which should preoccupy us; and that Son of man logia in the Fourth Gospel should not be treated in isolation from each other or from their contexts. Cf. further B. Lindars, "The Son of Man in the Johannine Christology", in B. Lindars and S. S. Smalley (eds.), *Christ and Spirit in the New Testament: Studies in Honour of Charles Francis Digby Moule* (Cambridge, 1973), 43–60, esp. 43–50.

10. Col. 1:15–20 may be an adaptation of a pre-Pauline hymn. See R. P. Martin, *Colossians and Philemon* (London, 1974), 61–66, and the literature there cited.

11. The "I am" sayings of Jesus in the Fourth Gospel are distinctively Johannine, and to that extent problematic. But traditional elements (at least) are not necessarily lacking in them. See S. S. Smalley, *John: Evangelist and Interpreter*, 186ff.

12. See M. Vellanickal, *The Divine Sonship of Christians in the Johannine Writings* (Rome, 1977), esp. 69–87, 363f. However, it is equally true that in Paul's theology "faith" is a dynamic concept, and not a static one (thus Eph. 4:11–16; Phil. 3:8–14, *et al.*).

13. Cf. S. Mary (= Sister Sylvia Mary, C.S.M.V.), *Pauline and Johannine Mysticism* (London, 1964), 109f., 131; also (on "sacramentalism" in Paul) D. E. H. Whiteley, *The Theology of St. Paul* (Oxford, 1974²), 170–73. For the "eschatological" nature of faith, as expressed also in baptism, see R. Bultmann, *Theology of*

the New Testament 1 (E.T.; London, 1952), 144, 329f. Space does not permit here an examination of Paul's reference in 1 Cor. 15:29 to "baptism on behalf of the dead", and its implications for the necessity of individual faith and the place of the sacraments in salvation (cf. in this connection the references to "household baptisms" in Acts 16:15, 33). For studies of this passage see F. F. Bruce, *1 and 2 Corinthians* (London, 1971), 148f.; and D. E. H. Whiteley, *Theology of St. Paul*, 173f.

14. In this text, however, "participation" *in* the blood and body of Christ (κοινωνία τοῦ αἵματος [τοῦ σώματος] τοῦ Χριστοῦ) is mentioned without the use of the locative ἐν.

15. Cf. S. S. Smalley, *John: Evangelist and Interpreter*, 204–10.

16. On the balance between the sacramental and non-sacramental exegesis of these two Johannine passages, see R. E. Brown, *The Gospel according to John, I–XII* (London, 1971), 141–44, 284–91.

17. Cf. S. Mary, *Pauline and Johannine Mysticism*, 73.

18. For John, "remaining" in Christ is not a matter of "fusion" but of "following". So V. P. Furnish, *The Love Command in the New Testament* (London, 1973), 145.

19. For the use of μένειν ἐν in 1 John, see E. Malatesta, *Interiority and Covenant: a Study of* εἶναι ἐν *and* μένειν ἐν *in the First Letter of Saint John* (Rome, 1978).

20. It is possible that in 1 Cor. 15:21f. Paul's "last Adam" christology (cf. Rom. 5:14; 1 Cor. 15:45) is really a "Son of man" christology. So O. Cullmann, *The Christology of the New Testament* (E.T.; London, 1963²), 137–52, 166–81. But, on the other side, see R. Scroggs, *The Last Adam: a Study in Pauline Anthropology* (Philadelphia and Oxford, 1966), esp. xv–xvii.

21. For John, "remaining in Christ" is an aspect of spiritual rebirth (cf. John 3:3); and this is a Johannine but not a Pauline category. (But see the possibly related idea of resurrection to new life in Rom. 6:3–11; 1 Cor. 15:22; see also 2 Cor. 5:17; Rom. 8:15–17; Gal. 4:4–7.)

22. Note also John's reference to the believer being "in" God and Jesus *together* (John 17:21, ἐν ἡμῖν). As we shall see below, both Paul and John presuppose that to be in Christ is to be in the Father; although John's christology (Jesus is explicitly one with the Father, 10:30; cf. 17:21) is such that this presupposition emerges more clearly in his writing. Both the Gospel and first letter of John also speak of Jesus "abiding" in the believer (cf. John 15:4; 1 John 3:24).

23. Note the Greek: συγκοινωνὸς ἐν τῇ θλίψει καὶ βασιλείᾳ καὶ ὑπομονῇ ἐν Ἰησοῦ. For this section see further G. A. Deissmann, *Die neutestamentliche Formel 'in Christo Jesu'* (Marburg, 1892), esp. 99–124. For Deissmann, however, being "in Christ" (or "in the Lord") refers—mystically—to the "atmosphere" in which Christians live, rather than to an experienced relationship with Christ.

24. Cf. John 17:16, using ἐκ τοῦ κόσμου.

25. Paul's dualism, like John's, is ethical. See F. F. Bruce, *Paul: Apostle of the Free Spirit*, 203–11; also (on the character and "theological structure" of the Pauline ethic), V. P. Furnish, *Theology and Ethics in Paul* (Nashville and New York, 1968), 207–27; and S. S. Smalley, "Diversity and Development in John", *NTS* 17 (1970–71), 278f.

26. We may notice that the "spiritual" is not divorced from the "practical" in either Paul or John; both have a theology of "works" (cf. Eph. 2:10; John 14:12)!

27. Assuming that κύριος in verse 21 refers to Christ, and πνεῦμα in verse 22 refers to the (Holy) Spirit. So T. K. Abbott, *A Critical and Exegetical Commen-*

tary on the Epistles to the Ephesians and to the Colossians (Edinburgh, 1897), 75f.; cf. also C. L. Mitton, *Ephesians* (London, 1976), 115–17.

28. Worship "in spirit" in this passage refers chiefly, of course, to *man's* spirit. But presumably John does not intend to exclude from his thought at this point either the presence of *God's* Spirit (note the phrase in verse 24, πνεῦμα ὁ θεός), or the possibility of the believer living "in the Spirit". See further C. K. Barrett, *The Gospel according to St. John: an introduction with commentary and notes on the Greek text* (London, 1978²), 238f.

29. Cf. Acts 16:7.

30. For a summary of this debate, and a survey of the relevant literature (including the work of R. E. Brown, G. Johnston and O. Betz), see S. S. Smalley, *John: Evangelist and Interpreter*, 227–33.

31. *Ibid.*, 232. Cf. John 16:7; 15:26 (14:26).

32. Cf. 1 Cor. 7:24, "remain with God" (using μένειν).

33. Cf. 1 John 2:24; 4:15f.

34. Cf. 1 John 2:24.

35. Cf. John 4:23f. (see note 28); 1 John 4:2; Rev. 1:10.

36. However, the idea of the believer being "in God (the Father)"—and its correlative, "God in the believer"—is not characteristically Pauline. Cf. C. F. D. Moule, *The Origin of Christology* (Cambridge, 1977), 64. It belongs more to the Gospel, and even more to the letters, of John. See I. H. Marshall, *The Epistles of John* (Grand Rapids, Michigan, 1978), 34f.; and the table in C. F. D. Moule, *Origin of Christology*, 64f.

37. Cf. 1 John 4:15f.

38. Cf. 1 Cor. 6:13. As C. F. D. Moule points out (*Origin of Christology*, 58) it is characteristic of Paul to speak of believers as "in Christ", but "less characteristic to speak of Christ as in a believer"; "almost the reverse is true", he adds, "of Pauline phrases concerning the Spirit" (*ibid.*).

39. Cf. John 17:23; 1 John 3:24.

40. Cf. Gal. 4:6 (note the trinitarian expression, "God has sent the Spirit of his Son into our hearts"). See also note 38.

41. Cf. John 20:22; 1 John 4:13. We may notice the consistent witness of John's first letter to the theological point that salvation in Christ is fully trinitarian in its nature.

42. See, *inter alios*, J. A. T. Robinson, *The Body: a Study in Pauline Theology* (London, 1952); J. A. Ziesler, *The Meaning of Righteousness in Paul: a Linguistic and Theological Enquiry* (Cambridge, 1972), 164–71.

43. See S. S. Smalley, "Johannes 1, 51 und die Einleitung zum vierten Evangelium", in R. Pesch and R. Schnackenburg (Hrsgg.), *Jesus und der Menschensohn: für Anton Vögtle* (Freiburg im Breisgau, 1975), 300–13, esp. 308–13.

44. On the "shepherd" imagery in John 10, see M. L. Appold, *The Oneness Motif in the Fourth Gospel: Motif Analysis and Exegetical Probe into the Theology of John* (Tübingen, 1976), 254–60.

45. Cf. M. de Jonge, *Jesus—Stranger from Heaven and Son of God: Jesus Christ and the Christians in Johannine Perspective* (E.T.; Missoula, Montana, 1977), 179. On the general point, with reference to John, see C. F. D. Moule, "The Individualism of the Fourth Gospel", *NovT* 5 (1962), 171–90. T. G. A. Baker, in *Questioning Worship* (London, 1977), 53, suggests that Paul's image of the "body" is of the *horizontal* kind (its members are linked closely with each other), while John's image of the vine is of the *vertical* type (each believer is linked individually with the Lord). Even so, there are collective elements in John's imagery, just as there are individual elements in Paul's.

46. In fact Paul argues not simply for unity, but rather for diversity *in* unity! Cf. J. A. T. Robinson, *The Body*, 58-67.

47. Cf. M. de Jonge, *Jesus—Stranger from Heaven*, 159, 174; also M. L. Appold, *The Oneness Motif*, esp. 157-236. On the theology of circumincession in the John 17 passage, see above, p. 99 and n. 56.

48. The thought of "salvation in Christ" in this passage relates to the past, present *and* future. Note also the "universal" scope of verse 10.

49. Using συγκληρονόμοι Χριστοῦ.

50. The whole section 1 Cor. 15:22-28 (like Rom. 8:18-25) is emphatically cosmic: more so than anything we have in John.

51. Using ("the dead") ἐν κυρίῳ.

52. See II 3 and 6, above.

53. Interestingly enough, this advance does not appear to be matched in 1 John (presumably written later than the Gospel). For in 1 John Christians are said to be "in God" (cf. 1 John 2:5); whereas in John's Gospel this relationship is mediated precisely through Christ (cf. John 15:5). See I. H. Marshall, *The Epistles of John*, 34.

54. But see II 6 and 7, above. John locates more exactly than Paul the source of spiritual "fruit"; and the Johannine soteriology is more fully "trinitarian" than the Pauline.

55. It could be argued, also, that John's sacramentalism is less developed than Paul's; but the fourth evangelist—who is more concerned with "the sacramental" than with the sacraments as such—may have his own reasons for this. See II 3, above.

56. Cf. esp. John 17:21-23, 26; also 14:20; 15:9f. But see, on the other hand, 1 Cor. 2:11f. Paul's version of the Johannine circumincession is to be found in the less developed notion of Jesus as the obedient Son of the Father, and the requirement of Christlikeness (in this sense) from the believer. Cf. Phil. 2:5-11; also Eph. 5:2. On the general point see further C. F. D. Moule, *The Origin of Christology*, 63-5.

57. In the Fourth Gospel the tension is clear: Jesus goes, and the Paraclete comes. Cf. John 7:39; 14:16-18 (but note verse 18, ἔρχομαι πρὸς ὑμᾶς); 14:26; 16:7, 16. In this respect John's theology provides a bridge between the synoptic Gospels (Jesus goes) and Acts (the Paraclete comes). See also John 20:22.

58. See S. S. Smalley, *John: Evangelist and Interpreter*, 119-21.

59. Cf. F. F. Bruce, *Paul and Jesus* (London, 1977), 15-22, esp. 18-22.

60. See further F. F. Bruce, "Christ and Spirit in Paul", *BJRL* 59 (1977), 259-85.

61. Rom. 5:8; Eph. 3:19.

62. Phil. 2:1f. (love "in Christ/in the Spirit"); cf. the allied exhortations to "walk in him" (Rom. 6:4) and to "live in him" (Col. 2:6). See also Rom. 13:9; Gal. 5:14 (citing Lev. 19:18 without its traditional companion Deut. 6:5, as in Matt. 22:36-40). See further V. P. Furnish, *The Love Command in the New Testament*, 94f.

63. But see Rom. 8:28; 1 Cor. 2:9; 8:3; 16:22; Eph. 5:1; 2 Thess. 3:5; Phlm. 4f. In the last passage, and possibly 1 Cor. 16:22, we have two of the very few references in Paul to the command to love Jesus. In the remaining passages a reference to the believer's love for God appears, but not in an hortatory context.

64. Cf. Gal. 5:6, where "faith working through love" (for others) is advocated: although in Eph. 1:15 (cf. Col. 1:4) faith and love (for the saints) appear to be distinguished. See also Eph. 3:17f.; 6:23.

65. John 3:16; 14:21.

66. John 15:9; and also as the Son loves the Father (John 14:31).

67. John 13:34f.; 15:12, 17.

68. E.g. John 14:1.

69. John 14:15; 15:10–17; cf. 15:4 ("abide in me"); 1 John 2:5f., 27 ("abide in him").

70. But cf. 1 John 4:21.

71. Cf. W. Sanday, *The Criticism of the Fourth Gospel*, 231ff.; also H. Conzelmann, *An Outline of the Theology of the New Testament* (E.T.; London, 1969), 326–30, esp. 326.

72. In these days of the "new look" on John, it is interesting to recall the comment on the Fourth Gospel by Charles Gore, originally written in 1922: "I am not without hopes that the essentially Palestinian, and not Hellenistic, origin and character of the Gospel, and its high value as an historical witness both to the events of our Lord's life and to His teaching, may soon come to be regarded as an 'assured result' of critical enquiry" (C. Gore, *The Reconstruction of Belief*, [London, 1926²], 403 n.1).

73. J. A. T. Robinson, *Redating the New Testament* (London, 1976), 254–311, esp. 307, has now suggested a date for the final form of John's Gospel of around AD 65.

74. Cf. J. D. G. Dunn, *Unity and Diversity in the New Testament: An Enquiry into the Character of Earliest Christianity* (London, 1977), 21–32, et passim.

Chapter 8

"A REMNANT CHOSEN BY GRACE" (ROMANS 11:5):
The Old Testament Background and Origin of the Remnant Concept

RONALD E. CLEMENTS

PAUL'S THEOLOGICAL UNDERSTANDING, expressed in Romans 11:5, "So too at the present time there is a remnant, chosen by grace", provides a key feature of the apostle's apologetic regarding the fate of Judaism. Why have the majority of his fellow Jews rejected the Christian kerygma? Why have the majority of Jews not recognised in the person of Jesus of Nazareth the coming of the messiah? Does not such rejection in its own way nullify the claim of Jesus to be the messiah? The answer to all these questions is provided by an argument from the Old Testament which centres upon the claim that God is acting in the present, as he has acted in the past, by means of a remnant, and the identity and election of this remnant has been established by his grace. Far from the Jewish rejection of Jesus nullifying his claim to messianic status, it rather confirms it, once the manner of God's acting in the days of the Old Testament is understood. That only a remnant has proved faithful and believing is entirely consonant with the entire history of Israel from the days of Abraham. Faithful Israel has always partaken of the nature of a remnant.

In view of the importance of the concept of a remnant to Pauline thought, and of its centrality to the way in which the New Testament writers employ and interpret the Old Testament scriptures to provide the foundations of a Christian theology, it is worthwhile looking at the origin and development of the concept again. It may be thought particularly appropriate to do so in honor of so distinguished a teacher as F. F. Bruce, who has himself drawn attention to the topic as a basic guideline to the way in which the Old Testament is interpreted in the New.[1] However, in view of some major treatments of the theme in recent years, it may be asked what an Old Testament student has to say that is new regarding a subject that has often proved an elusive area of investigation.[2] One thing at least is clear, and this is that the New Testament exercises a considerable originality in the manner in which it interprets the Law and Prophets of the Old Testament to bring out the significance of the concept of a remnant (cf. Rom. 9:6–13, 29). It is not those passages where a remnant is explicitly mentioned which are necessarily uppermost in the Pauline apologetic. Hence it is the "theme", or "concept", of a remnant, which is in many respects more important than the particular occurrence of the term. It is this point which may be held up as something of a weakness in the exemplary and massive study of the subject by G. F. Hasel,[3] and in fact a weakness of the general tendency to approach the study of the concept in the Old Testament almost exclusively by examining the occurrence of the terms $sh^e\bar{a}r$ and $sh^e\bar{e}r\hat{i}th$. This is undoubtedly an area where the word-study method of approach may prove to be as much a hindrance as a help.[4] Undoubtedly a great many instances of these terms in the Old Testament have a relatively neutral meaning so far as the understanding of the nature of the true Israel is concerned. All the more does this apply to the many occurrences of related terms in the ancient Near East. Furthermore there are clearly indications that, so far as the New Testament writers were concerned, a great many narrative and prophetic passages were felt to display the principle of God's working through a remnant, elected by grace, even where the actual word denoting a "remnant" is not explicitly used. This is evidently the case, for example, in regard to Paul's citation of Isa. 1:9 in Rom. 9:29.

There is one very prominent theological reason why the concept of a remnant is of great importance to the biblical writers in both Testaments. This is because it serves to resolve very effectively the tension inherent in the belief in Israel's divine election with the vicissitudes and realities of Israel's history. The Old Testament, as well as the New, is very conscious of the experiences of judgement, failure and defeat which marked the actual story of the people of God. At so many points it took the form of a kind of "Unheilsgeschichte" (cf. Ezek. 20:5–31; Ps. 106), in which the repeated disobedience of Israel made it impossible for God to bring to fruition his election promises to his people (cf. Deut. 28:15–68). At the same time God's word was immutable, so it was believed that he would not ultimately fail to bring his promises to realization (cf. Deut. 4:29 with verse 26). The seeming irreconcilability of historical reality with divine intention found at more than one point a degree of resolution through the belief in the existence of a saved and saving remnant. The same tension found particular expression in the post-exilic period with the parallel emphases upon *torah*, as the divine law to be obeyed, and upon a thoroughgoing eschatological expectation, with its anticipation of the rule of God, to be established by divine grace, and for which men could only wait and pray.[5] The tug-of-war between an emphasis upon divine grace and initiative and human response and obedience, once again pointed to the existence of a remnant, who would be both the object of the divine action, and yet also the instruments through whom salvation could be brought to all Israel, and even to the Gentiles. It is not, therefore, simply the convenient existence of a ready-made concept or idea of a remnant which has provided the starting-point for the New Testament resort to the idea. Rather some very deep-seated factors in the history-writing of the Old Testament, with its particular theological emphases, and in the very structure of the Old Testament canon as a parallel juxtaposition of Law and Prophets, have given rise to this. The twin foundations of divine demand and divine promise have formed a continuing basis of theological interaction in both Jewish and Christian approaches to the Old Testament literature.

The present essay ventures to point to two facets of recent study of the Old Testament as offering some further contribution to a better understanding of the term, and towards a better grasp of the reason for the formation of the Pauline apologetic. The first of these concerns the origin of the concept as a special way of understanding the true nature of Israel as the people of God, and the second relates to the lifting of the idea from being an *ad hoc* interpretation of a unique historical situation to the status of a principle, or *theologoumenon*, of how God continually acts in his world.

So far as the first question is concerned there can be no doubt that the foundation text from which the entire concept has been built up is to be found in Isa. 7:3, with its reference to the first of Isaiah's children to be given a mysterious sign-name, Shear-jashub. An immense variety of interpretations, and would-be interpretations, has been attached to this text, and it can be of little help to summarize them here.[6] Nevertheless a clear interpretation can be deduced for it, first by examining the interpretation which the prophet himself gives to it in the prophecy that follows in Isa. 7:7–9 (verse 8b is rightly and widely recognised to be a gloss). Secondly, a careful study of the two parallel sign-names, with their respective interpretations, in Isa. 7:14–17 and 8:1–4 shows so closely related a development that it is evident that we have to do here with a trilogy of sign-names, with an ascending pattern of interpretation. Each adds something to what has gone before.[7] Bearing this in mind we can return to the interpretation of the name Shear-jashub in Isa. 7:7–9. This reads:

> Thus says Yahweh God:
> "It shall not stand,
>   and it shall not come to pass.
> For the head of Syria is Damascus.
>   and the head of Damascus is Rezin.
>
>   . . . .
>   . . . . . .
> And the head of Ephraim is Samaria,
>   and the head of Samaria is the son of Remaliah.
> If you will not believe,
>   surely you shall not be established."
>   (Isa. 7:7–9)

The message, in spite of the complex circumlocutions so beloved by Isaiah, is not so very difficult to understand. The threat that faces Ahaz from the Syro-Ephraimite coalition will come to nothing—"it shall not come to pass". The reason is that behind such a threat there are simply the plans of men, which cannot, by implication, thwart the purposes of God. The name Shear-jashub therefore, which is interpreted by this saying, contains a message of re-assurance to Ahaz, but only on condition that he shows faith in God. Since the idea of a "remnant" of an army indicates that some kind of defeat has overtaken it, we can readily see how the name Shear-jashub is to be understood in this context. The armies (of the Aramaeans and Israelites) which threatened Ahaz and Jerusalem were to suffer a defeat which would frustrate their purpose of deposing the king of Judah and of replacing him by "the son of Tabeel" (verse 6).[8] Although the idea of a "remnant" therefore contains a veiled hint of disaster and defeat, it is not in reference to the army of Judah that Isaiah intended it here. The interpretations that are given of the other two sign-names fall precisely in line with that given to the first (7:16; 8:4). The idea of a "remnant" of Judah does not properly arise in this prophecy, neither does that of a "specially preserved remnant" of Israel, meaning the Northern Kingdom, except in a rather derivative fashion. Furthermore, at this juncture the concept of a "remnant", in accordance with its proper context and meaning, is basically an indication of coming judgement, although, because it points to a judgement upon those who threatened Judah, it occurs in a prophecy which conveys a message of assurance to the king of Judah in this crisis.

It is not until we come to examine how this name of Shear-jashub has been taken up and developed in the formation of a sequence of further prophecies that we come to see how the idea of a remnant, in the sense in which it was later understood, came to emerge. What we are faced with here is a phenomenon that is particularly prominent in regard

to the prophecies of Isaiah, but is, in some measure, to be found in all
the prophetic literature. One initial prophecy has become the basis for a
whole sequence of further prophecies, since it has been understood as a
"living" word from God, fraught with the possibility of more than one
meaning.[9] Until we have looked at these further prophecies of a remnant in the book of Isaiah, we cannot properly consider the question of
their authorship and time of origin. It is sufficient at this point to note
that they are derivative from an initial prophecy, and in this sense secondary.

The first of these derivative "remnant" prophecies is to be found in
Isa. 10:20–23:

> In that day the remnant of Israel and the survivors of the house of Jacob
> will no more lean upon him that smote them, but will lean upon Yahweh,
> the Holy One of Israel, in truth. A remnant will return, the remnant of
> Jacob, to the mighty God. For though your people Israel be as the sand of
> the sea, only a remnant of them will return. Destruction is decreed, over-
> flowing with righteousness. For Yahweh, Yahweh of hosts, will make a
> full end, as decreed, in the midst of all the earth.   (Isa. 10:20–23)

The direct interpretation of the name Shear-jashub—a Remnant
Will Return—in verses 21 and 22 leaves us in no doubt that we are
dealing here with a further interpretation, or rather series of interpretations, of the child's name Shear-jashub from Isa. 7:3. The general import
of the various sayings is quite clear, although a good deal of debate and
uncertainty surrounds their time of origin, which carries, by a necessary
implication, a great deal of weight regarding their true relevance. Several recent commentators have taken the view that the reference is to the
broader hope of a return of exiled Jews to their homeland in the post-
exilic period, so that the time of origin of this development is relatively
late, perhaps as late as the second century.[10] Yet we must question
whether this is really as probable as has frequently been assumed. If we
accept that the phrases "remnant of Isarel" and "survivors of the house
of Jacob" refer to the peoples of the Northern Kingdom of Israel who
had suffered the ravaging of their land and a widespread compulsory
deportation and migration since the fall of Samaria in 722, it makes
perfectly good sense. It would then far more plausibly be of pre-exilic
date. This too accords with the assurance that they "will no more lean
upon him that smote them", which refers to the treaty of vassaldom to
Assyria which had been forced upon Israel since the end of the Syro-
Ephraimite war in 732. Such a reference would have little meaning after
the exile, but fits very appropriately in the latter half of the seventh
century when the time of Assyrian domination was coming to an end. In
this case we have a very convincing situation of origin for the saying,
almost certainly during the period of Josiah's reign (640–609). In spite of
the ancient promise that the descendants of Jacob will become as nu-

merous as the sand on the seashore (Gen. 22:17; 32:12; cf. Josh. 11:4; Judg. 7:12), only a small remnant of them will return to take part in the restoration of the nation. This restoration was looked for under the reign of Josiah, in whose time the end of Assyrian domination could be hoped for (cf. Isa. 10:24–27).

In this case the interpretation given to the name Shear-jashub, which originated with the Isaianic prophecy of Isa. 7:3, is quite intelligible. The significance of the remnant idea is still understood almost entirely negatively as a sign of threat that "only a remnant will return." Furthermore the application is to the Northern Kingdom of Israel, as it had been, at least in part, in its original application to the Syro-Ephraimite alliance which threatened Jerusalem. In this respect therefore the development of the concept of a remnant in Isa. 10:20–23 marks the first real beginning of the "doctrine" of the remnant. Although the concept is based upon the Isaianic prophecy of Isa. 7:3, it was not until political catastrophe had overtaken the Northern Kingdom at the hands of the Assyrians that the concept could be extended to provide a model, or pattern, of expectation for Israel's future. In the strict sense therefore we can scarcely claim that the doctrine of the remnant derives from Isaiah himself, although it was his use of the sign-name Shear-jashub, and the political situation to which it was addressed, which established the basis for such a doctrine. Although attempts can therefore be made to trace a concept of a remnant in Isaiah's own preaching, this appears only in a very circumstantial way in such passages as Isa. 1:9. It was not until the political disasters had taken place which could be regarded as providing the fulfilment of Isaiah's threats, that the idea of a remnant began to take on even a marginally hopeful connotation. This is what we find in Isa. 10:20–23, and a very convincing case would appear to be available for ascribing it to the age of Josiah.

A considerable development in the interpretation of the nature, identity and purpose of the remnant is then to be found in a passage which marks chronologically the next stage in its growth. This is to be found in the prophecy ascribed to Isaiah (2 Kings 19:30–31 = Isa. 37:31–32), and incorporated into the narrative account of Jerusalem's deliverance from Sennacherib in 701 BC (2 Kings 18:17–19:37 = Isa. 36:1–37:38). The prophecy shows every sign of expansion, since it now appears in three parts: verses 21–28 are addressed to Sennacherib, verse 29 to Hezekiah, while verses 30–31 are formulated impersonally. It would appear therefore that verses 30–31, which contains the prophecy concerning the remnant with which we are concerned, has been the latest part of the text to have been added.[11] However this in itself is a somewhat relative and limited observation. From its contents we shall see that it must evidently be placed in a time later than that of the composition of Isa. 10:20–23. At the same time it seems highly improbable that additions of this nature have been made to the Deuteronomic History very much after 550 BC, since there is an almost complete lack of allusion to the kind of hope that emerged for the future of Israel after that time. Given these broader limits the contents themselves quickly establish the most convincing setting for its significance and time of origin:

> "And the surviving remnant of the house of Judah shall again take root downward, and bear fruit upward; for out of Jerusalem shall go forth a remnant, and out of Mount Zion a band of survivors. The zeal of Yahweh will do this."
>
> (2 Kings 19:30–31 = Isa. 37:31–32)

Some points are immediately striking about this prophecy. In the first place it clearly assumes the existence of a remnant in the future as a point that can be taken for granted. Yet this is to be a remnant of Judah, and is to go out from Jerusalem. If the author had a specific Isaianic prophecy in mind it would certainly appear to have been that of Isa. 1:9. Judah, however, had already suffered defeat and judgement so that it was reduced to a remnant. Yet the belief in the remnant's existence and rôle is undoubtedly a sign of hope for the restoration of Israel in the future. Two major developments have taken place therefore: the identity of the remnant has been narrowed to Judah, primarily Jerusalem, and the remnant has become a sign of hope. A great deal of importance attaches in consequence to locating the situation of origin of the saying if we are to trace a developing concept of a remnant. Many commentators have, understandably, ascribed the saying to the post-exilic age, and related it most closely to the eschatological hope which came to centre upon the restored community in Jerusalem and Judah.[12] Yet there are reasons for doubting whether this can be satisfactorily maintained. At this period of time it is evident that the predominating understanding of the remnant was that it referred to a remnant of the Israel which had been dispersed among the nations who would return to their homeland. Furthermore it is far from clear that after the middle of the sixth century the hoped-for community in Jerusalem and Judah could properly be termed a "remnant out of Jerusalem". The eschatological hope that emerged after that time came to focus exclusively upon a return of the exiles who had been taken to Babylon. In every way therefore it is much more likely that we should look to an earlier date for the emergence of the prophecy of 2 Kings 19:30–31. This accords with the general likelihood that the entire Deuteronomic History was virtually in the form which we now have by the middle of the sixth century, apart, of course, from the separation of its introduction in the book of Deuteronomy itself.

If then a date before 550 is probable for the prophecy, it must also be later than 598 BC for the awareness that Judah has also suffered severe judgement to have arisen.[13] Hence a date between 598 and 550 is most plausible. Since the sorely chastened Jerusalem is to be the source of the remnant, it seems probable that we can narrow the time of origin down yet more to the period of Zedekiah's reign, since it is shortly after 587 that virtually all hope for Jerusalem and its survivors was abandoned and attention turned to the Babylonian exiles (cf. Jer. 24:4-7; 29:10-14; Ezek. 33:23-29). This would accord well with the fact that this period must be that in which the narrative of the Babylonian emissaries to Hezekiah originated (2 Kings 20:12-19 = Isa. 39:1-8).[14] In fact the period of Zedekiah's fateful rule in Jerusalem provides a very convincing background for the emergence of the kind of hope of a remnant from Jerusalem which we find in 2 Kings 19:30-31. After the destruction of the city and its temple in 587, with the removal of the last surviving Davidic king actually reigning on the throne of Judah, attention turned increasingly to the Babylonian exiles as the source of Israel's hope. From this it was only a short step to associate the idea of a remnant of Israel with the Diaspora and with the expectation of their eventual return to the homeland. Further illumination upon the development of the belief in a remnant is then to be found in 2 Kings 21:14, which forms a part of the long editorial note (2 Kings 21:10-15) which relates to the evil reign of Manasseh.

This note is of special importance because it is the clearest and fullest indication to be found in the Deuteronomic History, prior to the recording of the event itself, that a fearful destruction awaited Jerusalem comparable to that which had overtaken Samaria. F. M. Cross has rightly recognized that it forms a part of the revision of that History made after 587.[15] The reviser was concerned to draw the reader's attention to features in the earlier life of Judah which served to explain the extent and horror of the catastrophe which took place in that year.

Our immediate concern is with a single verse of this section, 2 Kings 21:14, which is of special interest because it appears already to presuppose the interpretation of the identity and significance of the remnant which we have found in 2 Kings 19:30-31. It is taken for granted that the remnant is to be found in Judah, but asserts that now even they will be abandoned to the power and destruction of their enemies:

> "And I will cast off the remnant of my heritage, and give them into the hand of their enemies, and they shall become a prey and a spoil to all their enemies."
>
> (2 Kings 21:14)

The remnant that is assumed to be known to exist in Jerusalem and Judah is here threatened with being entirely cast off by Yahweh, so that they will no longer effectively provide a basis of hope for the future. For them there is to be no future. The use of the term in this instance therefore presupposes the interpretation of 2 Kings 19:30–31, in which the remnant is formed from the inhabitants of Jerusalem, but goes considerably beyond it. No longer is there any positive note of hope for the remnant, but rather one of total hopelessness in their being abandoned to their enemies. The event that is in mind, and which we must presume to have taken place by the time that this editorial note was made, was that of the destruction of Jerusalem in 587. So far as the development of the belief that the remnant of Israel was to be provided by Judah and Jerusalem is concerned, a belief that almost certainly goes back to Josiah's time or shortly thereafter, it marks the end of the road. Judah can no longer provide the remnant of Israel, from whom the restoration of a new nation and people of Israel could emerge. They too have suffered a similar fate to that which had overtaken the Northern Kingdom.

There would appear to be a strong case from the study of the passages which we have considered for arguing that we are presented here with a connected and traceable development. This was initiated by the prophecy in Isa. 7:3 concerning the name of Isaiah's son Shear-jashub. No doubt also there has been some influence from the prophecy of Isa. 1:9, and more broadly from the historical perspective provided by the section Isa. 1:4–9, which must date from shortly after the time of Sennacherib's invasion in 701. In view of the development of the idea of a remnant in the book of Isaiah by the secondary interpretation and elaboration of the name of the prophet's son in Isa. 7:3, this connection is intelligible as a part of the redactional growth and development of the prophetic book. However, in view of its further appearance in the Deuteronomic History in two passages of key importance for the interpretation of the last days of Judah, its influence upon the wider Deuteronomic movement can be established. That some connection existed between the collection and transmission of Isaiah's prophecies and this movement is a view that has come increasingly to commend itself to scholars. It is in any case rendered highly probable in view of the prominent place given to the work of Isaiah in the key chapters of 2 Kings 18–20, which serve to show why Judah had been spared at the time when the Northern Kingdom was destroyed.

What we have with this development of the remnant theme is not so much a fully rounded "concept", or "idea", of a remnant, but rather a prophetic catchphrase, or seminal prophecy.[16] Although the original phrase goes back to Isaiah, the roots of the idea which it was used to develop are more loosely to be found in the passage Isa. 1:4–9, where the word "remnant" is not itself used. The original prophecy containing the name Shear-jashub was related in a perfectly meaningful way to the political crisis of the Syro-Ephraimite war (735–732 BC). Subsequently events had occurred which were felt to shed a new light on the mysterious name and its meaning, once the Northern Kingdom had been overthrown and dismembered by its absorption into the Assyrian provincial system (Isa. 10:20–23). By the time of Josiah's rule the power of Assyria was weakening, and we can see from the rise of the great reform movement in this king's reign that the minds of men in Judah turned towards the hope of restoring and rebuilding a great and united kingdom of Israel once again, taking their pattern from the tradition of the Davidic-Solomonic era. It is from this situation that the developed interpretation of Isaiah's prophecy has come.[17] At this stage the notion of the remnant was still applied to the Northern Kingdom, but its "returning" was understood to be a returning to Yahweh (and to the house of David; cf. also Hos. 3:5).

After Josiah's untimely death in 609 BC, events quickly overtook Judah, and the high optimism of Josiah's reign proved to be ill-founded. With the passing of the Assyrians, Judah encountered a new enemy, this time the Babylonians. The overthrow of Jerusalem, which appeared to have been averted by a miracle in 701 BC in the face of Sennacherib's armies, now occurred in 598 with Nebuchadnezzar's forces. Yet, while Judah had suffered much, and Jerusalem had been compelled to surrender, there still appeared to be hope for the city, with its temple and its royal dynasty. The house of Yahweh still stood intact and the descendant of David in the person of Zedekiah still ruled from Jerusalem. At this stage the catchphrase of "the Remnant that Returns" was invested with a yet further meaning. We have noted the significance of the transition from the interpretation found in Isa. 10:20–23 to that in 2 Kings 19:30–3 when the concept was applied to "the house of Judah" and to "Jerusalem". A yet further stage in this intriguing chain of development is then to be seen in the terse and sharp reference in 2 Kings 21:14, which asserts that even this remnant is to be cast off. By this stage evidently the "Isaianic" prophecy had become a part of the conceptual world of the exilic Deuteronomic school in Jerusalem. In a sense their final comment regarding the eventual "casting off" of the remnant should have marked the end-stage of this complex sequence of prophecies, all stemming from the mysterious sign-name given to Isaiah's son.

However the historical and political situation which arose after the overthrow of the Babylonian empire, with the gradual return of a number of Judean exiles from Babylon to Jerusalem, gave rise to a new interest in the term. It is at this point that we can introduce the second of our major points regarding some recent lines of Old Testament research which have a significant bearing on the concept of a remnant. This concerns the great change in the understanding of "Israel" as the elect people of Yahweh during the period of the Babylonian exile and its aftermath.[18] It is a commonplace of historical study to recognize that the concept of "exile" (*gōlâ*) passed almost imperceptibly into that of a Diaspora. Already in the period after the fall of Samaria in 722 BC the identity of "Israel" had undergone a change, for there is no doubt that the term quickly came to be claimed by Judah, and provided a central feature in the expectation of a restoration of the greater Israel of Josiah's age, which we have already noted. Now after the experience of the Babylonian exile there grew up a consciousness that Israel was no longer a nation, but was scattered among many nations. Thus even the ancient and central promise to Abraham that his offspring would become a great nation, could be extended to embrace the idea that they would become several nations (cf. Gen. 12:2 J with Gen. 17:5–6 P). No longer in fact could it be readily assumed that Israel was in any sense a "nation" (Heb. *gôy*) at all, but rather a "religious community" (Heb. *'ēdâh, qāhāl*).[19] In a surprising and dramatic way a much larger concept of Israel emerged than that which had formerly thought of Israel as a single nation, or even as a nation divided between the two "houses" of Judah and Israel. Already we see something of this complex and extended understanding of the nature and identity of Israel in the work of the Chronicler.[20] On the one hand it clearly became important to retain an understanding that those who had been scattered into Egypt, Assyria, Babylon and the many other lands beyond these (cf. Isa. 11:11) were still a part of "Israel" and were therefore still children of Abraham and heirs of the promises to him and his descendants. Yet on the other hand it was not possible to lose sight of those features of Israel's life as Yahweh's people which focussed more directly on the national dimension of their existence. Here particularly we must think of the "land"—the *'eretz Israel*—which had been promised to the patriarchs, but also of Jerusalem, with its unique spiritual significance as "Zion", and also of the Davidic kingship with all the promises which attached to it (cf. Isa. 55:3–5). To have endorsed a concept of "Israel" which accepted the Diaspora as a permanent condition, and was content to include all the scattered descendants of those who had been taken to Assyria, to Egypt, or Babylon, would have been to abandon several of those features which were felt to belong inseparably to the true nature of Israel as the people of Yahweh. On the other hand, to have made the occupation of the land promised to Abraham, or participation in the life of such institutions as the temple of Jerusalem and a Davidic monarchy, essential to the *Verus Israel*—the authentic people of God—would have been to designate the entire Diaspora as apostate. Indeed the issue of the monarchy posed a serious question, since the failure to restore it after the time of the Babylonian exile marked the frustration of a major feature of the hope that had flourished during and immediately after the exile (cf. Hag. 2:23).

That a concept of Israel emerged which quite openly and explicitly included all the scattered survivors who had been dispersed among the nations is shown very clearly by the prayer attributed to Daniel in Dan. 9:3–19. In verse 7 there is a very noteworthy interpretation of who was to be included in the understanding of Israel:

> "To thee, O Yahweh, belongs righteousness, but to us confusion of face, as at this day, to the men of Judah, to the inhabitants of Jerusalem, and to all Israel, those that are near and those that are far away, in all the lands to which thou hast driven them, because of the treachery which they have committed against thee."
>
> (Daniel 9:7)

The designations used—men of Judah, inhabitants of Jerusalem and all Israel—show very clearly that the concept of Israel is here understood in much more than a national context and embraces the entire Diaspora in its compass. It is in a very real measure this extension, and in some measure break-up, of the concept of a clearly defined and definable "Israel" which has injected new life and meaning into the notion of a "remnant". In the first place the importance of the recovery of a foothold in Jerusalem, of the rebuilding of its temple, and the establishing under Nehemiah of a viable regional government for "Jerusalem and Judah", meant that this small Jerusalem community could come to be regarded as a "remnant" (cf. Hag. 1:12, 14; 2:2). In this way the earlier belief that the "remnant" would come from Jerusalem and from Mount Zion was re-activated. The community which had striven to rebuild the temple and to recover that part of the "land" which the political exigencies of Persian rule made possible could claim in a very real sense to have laid a foundation on which a new nation could one day be built. In this measure it can be seen how important the life and welfare of this small Jerusalem enclave of pious Jews were during the periods of Persian and Hellenistic domination. Their importance for keeping alive the eschatological hopes of Jews throughout the Diaspora was immense. They bore witness to the belief that the true Israel, as the promises of God to the patriarchs had affirmed that it would one day become, was a community with a land, a temple and its own independent government. Certainly this was how the great exilic prophets, Ezekiel and Deutero-Isaiah, had envisaged it, and this was how the growing eschatological hope of the Persian and Hellenistic eras continued to look for its realisation. It is, in a very large measure, the great fluidity that entered into the concept of Israel in the post-exilic age that re-invigorated the earlier idea of a remnant.

Already we have seen how, in the prophecies of Haggai, the small sixth-century community in Jerusalem could regard itself as forming such a remnant (cf. also Jer. 40:11, 15; 42:2, 15; 43:5; 44:12, 14, 28). Quite a different perspective on the nature and identity of the remnant is to be found elsewhere in the book of Jeremiah (Jer. 23:3; 31:7). In these two instances the word refers to the scattered survivors of the Northern Kingdom of Israel, as well as the exiles from Judah, suggesting that it represents a fresh interpretation of the meaning of the name Shear-jashub—A Remnant Will Return. This is undoubtedly the case in the secondary passage Isa. 11:10–16.[21] The hidden promise of the name which means "A Remnant Will Return" has come to be understood as a divine pledge that the peoples of the now defunct kingdoms of Israel and Judah who had been dispersed would be brought back to their homeland. The return of the remnant became an image and model of Jewish hope, and thereby the concept of a remnant entered into a central position in Jewish eschatological hope.

However, to speak of a "doctrine", or fixed concept, of the remnant would certainly be to go too far. Rather we can see that the fluid and loosely defined condition of Israel in the era of the Diaspora gave to the ancient prophetic sign-name a constantly renewed relevance as a divine promise for the future of Israel as Yahweh's people. As in the case of the comparable belief in a coming messiah, so in that of the remnant, there was no rounded doctrine by which the belief could be more narrowly defined and identified. Rather it was a vital image, or guideline, by which a great variety of scripture passages could be understood and related to the later condition of Judaism. We see this very clearly in regard to the way in which later Jewish interpreters searched the scriptures to learn about the coming of the messiah.[22] So, similarly, was a considerable variety of passages evidently open for examination to discover the nature and rôle of the remnant.

We have earlier referred to the fact that the motif of a remnant served, at least in part, to resolve some of the tensions between the historical reality of the Israelite-Judean political experience and the theology that underlies the conviction that Israel was a divinely elect people. The awareness of the continued existence of a remnant, however this was more precisely identified, averted the situation in which the belief in the significance of such a divine election was thrust altogether into the realm of eschatology. It is in line with this that an inevitable, and in many ways fruitful, tension arose between the notion of Israel as a covenant people, responsive to the Law (Torah), and Israel as an eschatological community who would one day inherit the earth. The inwardness of the demand for obedience to the Law clashed with the political realism of the expectation of Israel's destined greatness. How was the belief in the remnant to be understood in relation to these two very different conceptions of the people of God? It is here that the Pauline use of the theme brings out its greatest originality, and where we may hope to see something of the freshness of Paul's understanding.

From the perspective of Jewish apocalyptic writings the political aspirations of the remnant and their close association with the land—the *'eretz Israel*—appear to have been uppermost (cf. IV Esdras 9:7; 12:31–34; 13:48). Yet in the emergent stream of rabbinic-Amoraic interpretation the prime demand upon Israel was for obedience to the *Torah*, so that there could be no true Israel, or remnant of Israel, which was not established through the Law. Paul's interpretation in Romans 9–11 asserts very emphatically that the selection and identification of the remnant is solely a matter of divine grace. His exposition of the age of the patriarchs and of Moses in Rom. 9:6–18 asserts the sovereign freedom of God in choosing and selecting his people, thereby affirming the principle that God acts through grace, and not through any merit of obedience. Yet such an understanding appears to leave more open and indefinite than ever the question of who it is who constitute the remnant. It is here that we can see the value of going back to the seminal text from which the entire sequence of interpretations of the identity and role of the remnant has arisen in Isa. 7:3. In the interpretation of this name addressed to Ahaz, which we have seen to be so important a part of understanding its original meaning, there occurs the significant admonition:

"If you will not believe,
surely you shall not be established."
(Isa. 7:9)

May we not see in this instance a case where scripture has been allowed to interpret scripture, so that it is this admonition which for Paul has been allowed to determine the identity of the remnant? It is those who "believe" who are thereby "established" to have a share in the life of the remnant. Faith becomes the way by which the divine grace which chooses the remnant becomes effective. This would certainly imply that the Pauline interpretation of the identity of the remnant is a strikingly fresh and original creation from Paul's own mind. Yet it would also make clear that its underlying assumptions, and the manner of its appeal to the Old Testament, are wholly in line with a far older series of scripture interpretations about the remnant. These ultimately stem from the mysterious name of Isaiah's son mentioned in Isa. 7:3, and the promise that was felt to be contained within it that one day a remnant of the shattered and dispersed people of Israel would return to God.

Notes

1. F. F. Bruce, *This is That* (Exeter, 1976), 57–59.
2. Recent treatments of the theme are to be found in G. F. Hasel, *The Remnant: The History and Theology of the Remnant Idea from Genesis to Isaiah* (*AUSS* 5; Berrien Springs, 1974[2]); cf. also *idem*, "Remnant", *IDBSup* (1975), 735a–736b;

H. Wildberger, "*š'r*, übrig sein," *ThHwAT*, II (Munich, 1975), cols. 844–855; R. de Vaux, "Le reste d'Israel d'après les prophètes", *Bible et Orient* (Paris, 1967), 25–39, originally published in *RB* 42 (1933), 526–539. For the usage in Isaiah particularly, cf. also U. Stegemann, "Der Restgedanke bei Isaias", *BZ* n.f. 13 (1969), 161–186.

3. G. F. Hasel, *The Remnant*, 135ff.

4. Cf. J. Barr, *The Semantics of Biblical Language* (Oxford, 1961), 263ff.

5. Cf. D. Rössler, *Gesetz und Geschichte: Untersuchungen zur Theologie der jüdischen Apokalyptik und der pharisäischen Orthodoxie* (WMANT 3; Neukirchen-Vluyn, 1960), 45ff.

6. Cf. H. Wildberger, *Jesaja I–XII* (BKAT X, 1; Neukirchen-Vluyn, 1972), 277f.; S. Herrmann, *Die prophetischen Heilserwartungen im Alten Testament: Ursprung und Gestaltwandel* (BWANT V:5; Stuttgart, 1965), 129f.

7. For the interpretation of the three names as belonging to three children of the prophet, cf. H. Donner, *Israel unter den Völkern* (VTSup 11; Leiden, 1964), 7ff.

8. The identity of this "ben Tabeel" is still obscure. W. F. Albright ("The Son of Tabeel", *BASOR* 140 [1955], 34–35) has argued that he was a native Davidide, but against this cf. H. Donner, *Israel*, 12, n.; A. Vanel ("Tabe'el en Is. vii 6 et le roi Tubail de Tyr", *Studies on Prophecy: A Collection of Twelve Papers* [VTSup 26; Leiden, 1974], 17–24), has argued that he was a Tyrian prince.

9. For such a conception of prophecy as a "living" word from God, from which a variety of meanings could be derived, cf. P. R. Ackroyd, "The Vitality of the Word of God in the Old Testament: A Contribution to the Transmission and Exposition of the Old Testament Material", *Annual of the Swedish Theological Institute*, I (1962), 7–23; H. W. Hertzberg, "Die nachgeschichte alttestamentlicher Texte innerhalb des Alten Testaments," *Beiträge zur Traditionsgeschichte und Theologie des Alten Testaments* (Göttingen, 1962), 69–80; originally published in *Werden und Wesen des Alten Testaments* (BZAW 66; Berlin, 1936), 110–121. Cf. also U. Stegemann, "Der Restgedanke bei Isaias", 176ff.

10. Cf. H. Barth, *Die Jesaja-Worte in der Josiazeit* (WMANT 48; Neu-kirchen-Vluyn, 1978), 40f., who does not rule out a time in the Seleucid era, citing also B. Duhm, G. B. Gray and W. Eichrodt.

11. O. Kaiser, *Isaiah 13–39. A Commentary* (E.T. by R. A. Wilson; London, 1974), 376, 395f., who suggests that 2 Kings 19:30–31 = Isa. 37:31–32 may have been added after the preceding verses of the prophecy.

12. Cf. *ibid.*, 396f.

13. The question of whether the prophecy of 2 Kings 19:30–31 presupposes that Judah had already suffered a severe defeat must remain open. Set against the perspective of the fall of both kingdoms, Judah and Israel, at the hands of the Assyrians, it would not have been inappropriate to describe Judah and Jerusalem as forming a Remnant before the defeat of 598. In this case, the inclusion of the prophecy in the narrative of Sennacherib's failure to take the city (2 Kings 18:17–19:37) could be placed earlier. However, since the story of the Babylonian emissaries in 2 Kings 20:12–19 undoubtedly presupposes that the events of 598 had already taken place when it was composed, it seems probable that this is true also of the prophecy ascribed to Isaiah in 2 Kings 19:30–31. For the broader problem of the date and purpose of the account of the Babylonian emissaries see further my article "The Isaiah Narrative of 2 Kings 20:12–19 and the Date of the Deuteronomic History", *Studies in Ancient Narrative and Historiography* (I. L. Seeligmann Anniversary Volume), eds. A. Rofe and Y. Zakovitch (Jerusalem, 1978).

14. Cf. my article cited in the preceding note.

15. F. M. Cross, *Canaanite Myth and Hebrew Epic* (Cambridge, Mass., 1973), 285ff.

16. Cf. U. Stegemann, "Der Restgedanke bei Isaias", 176ff.

17. Cf. H. Barth, *Die Jesaja-Worte in der Josiazeit*, passim.

18. Cf. N. A. Dahl, *Das Volk Gottes. Eine Untersuchung zum Kirchenbewusstsein des Urchristentums* (Oslo, 1941; rep. Darmstadt, 1962), 51ff.; P. Richardson, *Israel in the Apostolic Church* (Cambridge, 1969); B. F. Meyer, "Jesus and the Remnant of Israel", *JBL* 84 (1965), 123–130; V. Herntrich and G. Schrenk, "λεῖμμα", *TDNT*, IV (1967), 194–214; S. Sandmel, "Israel, Conceptions of", *IDBSup* (1975), 461–463.

19. Cf. my article *"góy"*, *TDOT*, II (1975), 426–433.

20. Cf. H. G. M. Williamson, *Israel in the Books of Chronicles* (Cambridge, 1977), 87ff.

21. That these verses are of post-exilic derivation must be regarded as certain. Cf. H. Wildberger, *Jesaja I–XII*, 458ff., 466f. They provide yet a further indication of the developed interpretation of the notion of the remnant, first adumbrated in Isa. 7:3.

22. Cf. my book, *Old Testament Theology: A Fresh Approach* (London, 1978), 146f.

Chapter 9

PROCESS THEOLOGY AND THE PAULINE DOCTRINE OF THE INCARNATION

BRUCE A. DEMAREST

I. The Current Theological Challenge

NO MOVEMENT PROMISES to exert more influence on theological studies during the last quarter of the twentieth century than Anglo-American process theology. Behind the burgeoning interest in evolutionary theology lies the process thought of A. N. Whitehead (1861–1947), the Cambridge mathematician and philosopher who rounded out his career at Harvard. Whitehead insisted that reality is constituted not by static concepts of being or substance but by the dynamic concept of becoming.[1] Charles Hartshorne, an assistant to Whitehead later associated with the Universities of Chicago and Texas, developed his mentor's vision into a systematic philosophy of religion.[2]

If Whitehead is the acknowledged father of process philosophy and Hartshorne the father of process theology, Norman Pittenger, a Canadian Anglican who lectured at General Theological Seminary in New York and latterly at King's College, Cambridge, has produced the most complete and readable synthesis of process thought and theological studies.[3] In addition to the Chicago scholars H. N. Wieman, Bernard Loomer and Schubert Ogden, other Whiteheadians such as Daniel Day Williams, John Cobb and David Griffin probe the frontiers of process thought on the American scene. British scholars such as J. A. T. Robinson, Peter Hamilton and David Pailin have developed process approaches to theology in the old world.

In developing the thought of Whitehead and Hartshorne, process theologians have rejected traditional theism, neo-orthodoxy and contemporary existentialism. The immutable God of theism is said to suffer

122

the same deficiencies as Aristotle's Unmoved Mover. So static and unresponsive a being as the god of Greek philosophy proves irrelevant to the world of men. The attempt to establish a metaphysics of static perfection, together with the postulate of a God who creates, wills and cares, involves a hopeless contradiction.[4] In any case, empirical science has proven that the God-talk of theism proves meaningless in the modern world. Whitehead sums up matters by describing classical theism as a "scandalous failure."[5]

Neo-orthodoxy's postulate of the infinite qualitative difference between God and man is the very antithesis of the process vision of reality. A God who is radically Other is incomprehensible to finite man. Moreover, empiricism and positivism have shown that the non-verifiable propositions of neo-orthodoxy lack any meaning. Their irrationality dooms them to oblivion. The fate of the new "biblical" theology is more perilous than that of traditional theism.

Process theology allows that existential interests such as engagement and decision, or, in Whitehead's language, awareness of a subjective aim, contribute to human authenticity. Yet existentialism is rejected as an adequate philosophical representation of reality. After the Bultmannians have completed their demythologizing work, one is still left with a creator God beyond nature who confronts man as sovereign lord and judge. As Pittenger observes, "We still have God who in some fashion moulds and moves nature, history and man, and who can and will achieve his purposes, both in time and over time."[6] Moreover, Whiteheadians insist that the chief concerns in today's world are not primarily existential but societal and global. Problems of racism and ecological ruin, it is argued, prove more amenable to process rather than to existentialist solutions. The process rejection of contemporary alternatives requires that we briefly survey the Whiteheadian representation of reality.

II. A Brief Overview of Process Thought

Process metaphysics postulates the dynamic or processive character of reality. Far from being static and unchanging, the "stuff" of the universe consists of an unremitting process of becoming and perishing, with new becomings emerging from that which has perished. Thus the becoming of the cosmos constitutes its being. On this showing Whitehead's foundational work, *Process and Reality*, could well have borne the title *Process Is Reality*.

The ultimate "stuff" of the cosmos, then, is not an aggregate of substantial entities, but a series of sub-atomic societal energies which Whitehead termed "actual occasions." These basic units of reality are drops or moments of experience. Thus God, man, or the smallest puff of life constitutes a richly variegated organic unity which we may think of as a focus of experiences. Whatever *is* may be considered as an energy-event caught up in creative advance towards genuine novelty.

But the Whiteheadian scheme is not only dynamic, it is inter-relational in character. Everything in the universe profoundly affects everything else. Nothing exists in isolation, but each entity is part of a larger whole. The dynamics of the interrelationship simplify as follows. Each actual occasion "prehends" or feels entities antecedent to itself, incorporating the previous moments of experience into its own universe, thus forming a creative and novel synthesis. In turn, the new occasion serves as an experience to be prehended by succeeding actual occasions. The former experience perishes, yet is immortalized in the process of the creative advance to novelty.

Process theology postulates a dipolar deity in the sense that God has both primordial and consequent aspects. On one hand, God is abstract; on the other, concrete. God is necessary yet contingent; eternal yet temporal; transcendent yet immanent; absolute yet relative. On the primordial side God is above the process as the ground of actuality. God is the principle of limitation and the *telos* of the cosmic process. God is infinite but not absolutely unlimited. Comments Pittenger, "his nature, the purpose which he is accomplishing in the world, the love which is his supreme characteristic, must in some sense limit him."[7]

The consequent or concrete nature describes what God is at any moment in the emergent process. R. C. Miller of Yale explains God's consequent nature:

> We identify God with the creative order of the world, a process which transforms human beings, brings values from a potential to an actual state, and works to overcome evil with good. God is that process by which we are made new, strengthened, directed, comforted, forgiven, saved, and by which we are lured into feelings of wonder, awe and reverence.[8]

Clearly the God of process theology is brought into closest relation with the process of transformation immanent in nature. As Whitehead has said, "the actuality of God must also be understood as a multiplicity of actual components in process of creation."[9] By bringing potentiality to actuality, by moving the world by his love, God evolves along with the world. Thus God in his consequent nature is not a God of static perfection. God suffers, experiences pleasure, in short, undergoes change.

Pittenger concedes that "the distinction between 'abstract' and 'concrete' or 'primordial' and 'consequent' . . . is only for the purpose of analysis and discussion. The *real* God—by which is meant God as he is actually known—is the concrete, active, dynamic reality who does this or that."[10] God on the primordial side is a philosophical abstraction. The real God is the relative, immanent reality which is identified with the creative process in nature.

Process theology defines the relation between God and the world as "panentheism." God is not the world (pantheism), nor is God a discrete entity separate from the world (classical theism). According to Hartshorne, "God literally contains the universe,"[11] so that every part of it exists in him. Panentheism thus signifies that "God is in all and all is in God." The panentheist model is championed because it avoids the difficulty of regarding Christ as an intruder from another realm. It ensures that God is continuously and profoundly related to the world while not being lost in the natural order.

III. The Process Vision of the Incarnation

The incarnation of God in Christ is the central datum, the Archimedean point, of Christian theology. Karl Rahner insists that the incarnation is not only the foundational statement of Christology, but "the fundamental dogma of Christianity."[12] Thus as we evaluate the process interpretation of the incarnation in the light of the Pauline development, we are dealing with an issue of central importance to the Christian faith.

Charles Hartshorne has concentrated on probing the concept of God within natural theology. Yet Hartshorne does make a summary statement of Christ and the incarnation:

> I have no Christology to offer, beyond the simple suggestion that Jesus appears to be the supreme symbol furnished to us by history of the notion of God genuinely and literally 'sympathetic' (inconceivably *more* literally than any man ever is), receiving into his own experience the sufferings as well as the joys of the world.[13]

The man Jesus is the decisive symbol of the God who loves and suffers with the world. Far from being Deity in an ontological sense, Jesus is the most profound human exemplification of the divine life. Jesus' "uniqueness" resides in the fact that the living God is imaged in him with a clarity and specialty not found in other men. Although statements such as "Jesus was God" are ambiguous and misleading, nevertheless the doctrine of the incarnation "enshrined important religious truth."[14] So defined, the incarnation involves an ineffable mystery, the reality of which can be experienced but not formally defined.

John B. Cobb, Jr., of the Claremont School of Theology, argues that the traditional view which perceived Jesus as the transcendent, omnipotent ruler of the universe who visited earth in human form must be abandoned. Common sense dictates that two objects, like a stone and a table, cannot occupy the same space at the same time. The substantialist model of the incarnation must give way to an experiential relation in which societies of past events or experiences merge in creative synthesis.

Cobb defines the Logos as the impersonal power of creative transformation latent in the universe:

> The Logos is the cosmic principle of order, the ground of meaning, and the source of purpose. Whitehead called this transcendent source of the aim at the new the principle of concretion, the principle of limitation, the organ of novelty, the lure for feeling, the eternal urge of desire, the divine Eros, and God in his primodial nature.[15]

Christ, Cobb contends, is the power of creative transformation immanent in the man Jesus.[16] Indeed the Logos is incarnate in all men, religious traditions, and the whole of creation. Yet Jesus exemplified the fullest indwelling of the immanent Logos. "In Jesus there is a distinctive incarnation because his very selfhood was constituted by the Logos."[17] To say that Jesus' "I" was structured by the indwelling Logos is to acknowledge that the Nazarene possessed a unique structure of existence—which is to say that Jesus was the Christ.

Such a construction avoids the alleged fallacy of identifying Jesus with God. Immanence, Cobb notes, does not mean identity. The name Christ "does not designate deity as such but refers to deity as graciously incarnate in the world."[18] In sum, then, Jesus was a man in whom the power of creative transformation was so completely immanent as to co-constitute the very structure of his existence. Other great religious figures may have possessed an existence-structure similar to that of Jesus. Herein lies the possibility of an authentic religious pluralism.

Schubert Ogden, a former student of Hartshorne, is associated with the Divinity School of the University of Chicago. In *The Reality of God* (1966), Ogden argues that God is related to the world as the human self is related to the body. But since the self is also related to a society of other beings, God is genuinely temporal and social, hence radically different from the timeless and unrelated Absolute attributed to classical theism. To understand Jesus' relation to God one must differentiate between acts of God, special acts, and God's decisive act.

Assuming that a human act is that by which the human self is constituted a self, an act of God refers to "the act whereby, in each new present, he constitutes himself as God."[19] In this act God responds to the previous stage of the world and, by thus constituting himself, lays the foundation for the next stage of the creative process.[20] Given this definition of an act of God, God's act in Jesus is identical with the way in which God acts in any other event. Jesus thus differs from other men in degree not in kind.

A "special" act is a characteristic action in which the person is uniquely re-presented or revealed to others. God's act in Jesus is "special" in that God's being and action are given peculiarly apt expression in him. On the other hand, a "decisive" act of God is one in which the reality of God is re-presented or revealed in a way that is normative. Since Jesus' every word and deed were grounded in the reality of God, he re-presents God's being and action in a decisive or normative fashion. That is, whereas God has not acted differently in Jesus than elsewhere in the world, the man from Nazareth was remarkably transparent to the reality of God. In precisely this sense we are to understand the "incarnation" of God in Christ.

David Pailin of Manchester University postulates the continuity between the actuality of God and the world. God is inextricably related to the world as its ground and end. Thus there is a high degree of probability that the "active actuality" of God will find expression in a human life. By God's "active actuality" Pailin means not the metaphysical qualities of God's structure of existence (aseity, eternity, infinity), but such personal qualities as love, mercy and respect for others. Continues Pailin:

> If God called the man Jesus to act according to his will in every situation and if Jesus through unbroken relationship with God, completely grasped the character of that will and expression, would it not be valid to claim that in Jesus' acts we perceive the active actuality of God within the limits imposed by human life? The mode of the incarnation is thus interpreted as a vocation for Jesus to be perfectly at one with God and a vocation which he perfectly fulfilled.[21]

Thus in the sense that the man Jesus responded fully to God's call to a servant vocation, it may be said that he "incarnated" God's active actuality. Jesus' uniqueness *vis-à-vis* other men is twofold. First, he was called to express God's actuality in ways that others were not called. And second, through unbroken fellowship with God, Jesus discharged his calling to perfection.

Professor Norman Pittenger argues that a God who is so remote and unrelated that he can only intrude into the creation from without amounts to a deistical concept. Contrary to postulates of a chasm between God and the world, Pittenger insists that God is continually incarnating himself in nature and history, thereby energizing the cosmic process:

> If God is himself related to everything else, and is affected or influenced by everything else . . . , then there is always and everywhere an interpenetrative activity between God and the creation. Not in Jesus only, but throughout the cosmos, there is an 'incarnating movement'—God comes to us as he acts in that which is not himself.[22]

The catastrophic intrusion model called for by the traditional doctrines of the virgin birth and incarnation disrupts the regular workings of nature and thus must be rejected.[23] Consistent with the modern evolutionary world view, the incarnation must be brought into closest relation to the cosmic process.

Jesus' becoming, or the realization of his selfhood, was shaped by a whole constellation of environmental and relational factors ("occasions") in the flow of history. Selfhood "is a specific . . . routing or series of occasions in which there is a continuity which includes the memory of the past, the relationships of the present, and the projective aim toward the future."[24] That is, Jesus cannot be abstracted from his cultural and historical milieu, otherwise he would not be the carpenter from Nazareth, the Son of Joseph and Mary.

The incarnation of God in Christ must be interpreted as the actualization in a human life of God's revelatory activity. Jesus was a man so transparent to Deity that he became the personal agent through whom God could act.[25]

> At every point in the existence of Jesus, the divine activity is operative, not in contradiction of the humanity nor in rejection of any part of it but in and through it all—in teaching, preaching, healing, comforting, acting, dying, rising again. . . . He is indeed the personalized instrument for the Self-Expressive Activity of God.[26]

Pittenger proceeds to define the hypostatic union more precisely. "The unity of the divinity and manhood in him is the *coincidence* of the divine and human acts, the act of God and the act of man."[27] Plainly, what the church traditionally called Christ's "divinity" is God active in Jesus releasing to the world a new stream of energy.

Plainly Jesus differed from the rest of humanity in degree only. If Jesus were dissimilar in kind his solidarity with the race would be compromised. Pittenger prefers to speak of the decisiveness, the "onceness," the specialty of Jesus. "For us, the uniqueness of Jesus Christ can only be seen in his specialty, his supreme and decisive expression of that which God always and everywhere is 'up to' in his world."[28]

The theological works of J. A. T. Robinson incorporate the evolutionary insights of scholars such as Teilhard de Chardin and Pittenger. In his Christological essay, *The Human Face of God*, Robinson insists that Jesus was a true man, a member of the species *homo sapiens*, divinely raised up to represent man before God. Yet as "a genuine product of the evolutionary process,"[29] Jesus has been in development from the beginning. Argues Robinson:

> We know enough at any rate to say that to be a member of the species *homo sapiens* includes having genes shaped by millions of years of evolu-

tion. No one can just *become* a man out of the blue: a genuine man (as opposed to a replica) can only come out of the process, not into it.[30]

But how does Robinson explicate the incarnation? Clearly, "God become man" is not to be viewed as a "bolt from the blue" or a "Christ comet" where a celestial visitor lands on planet earth, stays for a while, and then takes off after completing his mission. Such, Robinson says, is the language of mythology. Nor can we employ the old model of the union of two substances, which would make Jesus out to be a kind of "centaur" or "bat-man."

If Jesus is not the "God-man," he may be thought of as "God-in-man."[31] Adopting a historical and functional approach, Robinson argues that Jesus "is not a divine or semi-divine being who comes from the other side. He is a human figure raised up from among his brothers to be the instrument of God's decisive work."[32] Jesus is distinctive (not unique or final) in that he emerged from the historical process as the exemplary vehicle of God's self-expression.

IV. The Pauline Interpretation of the Incarnation

1. Galatians 4:4, 5

We now turn to the biblical record to explicate the Apostle Paul's understanding of the incarnation and to compare it with the process interpretation. Assuming the validity of the South Galatian hypothesis, the letter to the Galatians represents the earliest canonical document from the pen of Paul. In the context of the discussion that law-keeping leads to slavery but faith results in adoption as sons, Paul writes, "when the time had fully come, God sent forth his Son, born of woman, born under the law, to redeem those who were under the law" (Gal. 4:4, 5).

The phrase ὅτε δὲ ἦλθεν τὸ πλήρωμα τοῦ χρόνου suggests that the divinely ordained educatory work of the law had achieved its purpose. A heightened sense of sin had been wrought and the inability of all other systems to save had been pointed up. The arrival of the χρόνος was precipitated by the realization of man's hopeless servitude under the law. The text plainly suggests that God is not unresponsive and unrelated to the world. Rather, God is envisaged as brooding over the creation, personally attentive to the human drama as he weighs man's moral response to the demands of the law. Paul thus conceives of God as living, dynamic, related and loving—a God profoundly operative in the flow of history, wooing individuals to himself. Paul's God is the antithesis of the Unmoved Mover or the deistical Creator, for the text implies that the actively involved God is working to an established plan (cf. Gal. 4:2; Eph. 1:10).

Paul continues that when the time was ripe "God sent forth (ἐξαπέστειλεν) his Son." The verb can hardly be restricted to the inauguration of Jesus' public ministry (cf. John 1:6) following the silent years of private life.[33] The parallel teaching of God sending the Spirit into the hearts of believers (verse 6) suggests that the act in view is the sending forth of the pre-existent Son into the space-time world on a redemptive mission (cf. Rom. 8:3). Even if the interpretation is expanded to include the whole of Jesus' ministry on earth, it can hardly be gainsaid that Paul regards the pre-existent, divine Son as One sent forth from God. A. M. Hunter agrees: "Then 'God sent forth his Son,' Paul says, clearly conceiving Christ as a divine Being, filially related to the Almighty, existing with him before he appeared in time."[34] From the Pauline perspective the ordered historical continuum was perforated by a mighty act of God's initiative. Whereas the apostle contemplates no arbitrary intrusion, he does teach a divine intervention *ab extra* which is supremely purposeful. Paul's God is not limited to the processive operations of nature.

We find no justification in Gal. 4:4 that Paul understood Jesus as a "routing of occasions" in the process sense. But the apostle does portray Jesus in his mission of saving mercy as One "routed" from heaven by the Father's Love. Ostensibly Paul had no bias against ontology, for he explicates a perfect balance between the incarnate *person* of Christ (verse 4) and his redemptive function or *work* (verse 5).

2. 2 Corinthians 5:19

In 2 Cor. 5:11–20 Paul urges the Corinthian believers to pursue a ministry of reconciliation among men on the grounds that "God was in Christ reconciling the world to himself" (2 Cor. 5:19). From a process perspective Pittenger translates θεὸς ἦν ἐν Χριστῷ κόσμον καταλλάσσων ἑαυτῷ as, "In Christ God was reconciling the world unto himself." That is, Jesus Christ was the human vehicle through which the Self-Expressive Activity of God was instrumentally operative. Comments Pittenger:

> God is *doing something* there, in that historical and human event. The Pauline text is not so much concerned with the *how* of God's 'presence' as it is with the *what* of God's activity. Thus we have here a clear instance of the general scriptural stress upon God's energizing in the historical process.[35]

From the process point of view God's presence ἐν Χριστῷ denotes God's immanent energizing Activity. Thus the incarnation is seen as the union of human and divine activity at a decisive moment in the long history of the universe's emergence.

Admittedly, a significant exegetical tradition (Alford, Denney,

Plummer, Barrett, Bruce) links ἦν with καταλλάσσων in a periphrastic construction and interprets ἐν Χριστῷ instrumentally (cf. verse 18). On this showing the statement "God was in (or, through) Christ reconciling the world to himself," points to the complex of events, especially the cross, by which atonement was made for sin. Yet the traditional interpretation (Luther, Calvin, Calov, Bengel, Neander, Westcott, Lenski, Hughes) appears preferable on several counts. First, θεὸς ἦν ἐν Χριστῷ constitutes the logical unit of meaning. On this assumption, the assertion "God was in Christ" is modified by two present, durative participles, καταλλάσσων and μὴ λογιζόμενος. The fact that καταλλάσσων is separated from ἦν by both ἐν Χριστῷ and κόσμον suggests that ἦν naturally is linked to ἐν Χριστῷ.

Second, contra Denney, the statement that "God was in Christ" as a real ontological presence is fully congruous with Paul's teaching in Col. 1:19, "in him all the fulness of God was pleased to dwell," and in Col. 2:9, "in him the whole fulness of deity dwells bodily." Moreover, it is strictly paralleled by our Lord's own saying in John 10:38, "the Father is in me and I am in the Father." The presence of God in Christ cannot be restricted to immanent activity (note the Jews' angered response to Jesus' teaching), but involves a unity of being as well as of purpose and work.

One detects in the text Paul's response to the charge that there was nothing more ultimate in Jesus' life and death than the man himself. Paul responds by asserting that the saving refreshment of Jesus' life flowed from his real and vital union with God. For Paul, then, "God was in Christ" in the sense that the Father was united with him in being and action. As Hughes puts it, "the unanimity of Father and Son flows from their eternal unity."[36]

3. 2 Corinthians 8:9

In 2 Corinthians 8 and 9 Paul exhorted the church at Corinth to contribute to the relief of impoverished Jewish-Christians in Jerusalem. Instinctively Paul's mind turned to Christ as the ultimate paradigm of liberality. Thus in 2 Cor. 8:9, at the heart of his ethical discourse on Christian giving, the apostle interjects a remarkably succinct statement on the incarnation—what R. P. C. Hanson calls "a manual of compressed dogma":[37] "you know the grace of our Lord Jesus Christ, that though he was rich yet for your sake he became poor, so that by his poverty you might become rich."

The full title, "Lord Jesus Christ," denotes the Saviour's heavenly dignity, human reality and vocation as God's Anointed. The pregnant phrase πλούσιος ὤν can only signify the Son's eternal existence clothed with the glory of the Godhead (1 Cor. 2:8; 2 Thess. 2:14; John 1:14; 17:5).

Hanson strikes at the heart of the matter with the comment that "the verse serves to make clear St. Paul's conviction that Jesus Christ was not a man specially gifted or favored by God, but a Being who had existed before he took human form among us."[38] Paul then had no hesitation in representing Jesus Christ (through the symbolism of unparalleled wealth) as ontologically one with God the Father.

The phrase δι' ὑμᾶς ἐπτώχευσεν points to our Lord's transition to the state of humiliation at the incarnation. Christ entered this abject condition when he laid aside the wealth of heaven's glory and identified with our lowly estate. The poverty symbolism is scarcely exhausted by the simple, uncluttered life lived by the Galilean preacher (Luke 9:58). The ingressive aorist ἐπτώχευσεν refers to the historical moment when the Lord Christ became man.

In that which follows—"so that by his poverty you might become rich"—Paul inextricably links Christ's incarnation with the atonement. Again we detect the apostle's conviction that Christ's person and work constitute an indissoluble whole. Paul's consciousness, then, of the reality of Jesus Christ is clear. He is "the Son who was *sent,* the One who *came* into the world, the Word who *became* flesh, the Lord who for our sakes *impoverished* himself."[39]

4. Romans 8:3

In Romans 8, against the backdrop of the impotence of the law, Paul teaches that sin and death have been vanquished through Christ and the Spirit. Thus in Rom. 8:3 the apostle writes of God's decisively new intervention: "sending his own Son in the likeness of sinful flesh and for sin, he condemned sin in the flesh."

Robinson interprets this text from a process perspective. "The picture is not of a divine being arriving to look like a man, but a man born like the rest of us, from within the nexus of the flesh, law and sin, who nevertheless embodied the divine initiative and saving presence so completely that he was declared... to be everything God himself was."[40]

The title God's "own Son" is crucial to a right interpretation of the passage. The expression τὸν ἑαυτοῦ υἱόν, where ἑαυτοῦ is emphatic, is equivalent to the Johannine μονογενὴς υἱός (John 1:18; 3:16 *et al.*) or ἴδιος υἱός (Rom. 8:32). Ostensibly the Son's relation to the Father is one of profound personal union. No mere adoptionist sonship is in view, rather an eternal oneness of being and perfections.

In affirming that God sent (πέμψας) his Son, Paul captured in a single glance the enfleshment of our Lord and the inauguration of His earthly mission. Bengel makes the pithy deduction from the aorist participle that πέμψας "denotes a sort of separation, as it were, or estrangement of the Son from the Father, that He might be the Mediator."[41]

Anders Nygren adds, "It is true of God's own intervention by which God's own Son came 'in flesh.' It is true of the incarnation of the Son—that and nothing else."[42] Paul's language strongly suggests that the Son had a real existence with the Father prior to his manifestation in the space-time world. His selfhood transcends the causal nexus of the temporal realm.

Process theologians frequently insist that if Christ were genuinely man he must have participated in the human experience of sin.[43] Yet Paul argues that Jesus appeared ἐν ὁμοιώματι σαρκὸς ἁμαρτίας. While insisting that God authentically became man in Jesus of Nazareth, Paul chose his words carefully so as to avoid identifying Jesus with the fallen human condition. Does Jesus' freedom from the taint of sin negate his true humanity or compromise his solidarity with the race? Not at all. Scripture views fallen man as sub-human, in the sense that the *imago Dei* has been marred by sin. Only the sinless Jesus was authentically human as the paradigm of unspoilt humanity (2 Cor. 5:21).

5. Colossians 1:19

In two related Colossians texts Paul paints a rich portrait of the incarnate Lord. Extolling Christ as a unique redemptive revelation of God, Paul makes the claim, "God was pleased to have all his fulness dwell in him" (Col. 1:19). The proto-Gnostic teachers commonly understood πλήρωμα as the plenitude of divine emanations and energies which filled the void between the spiritual and material worlds. Since the divine powers were distributed among the numerous aeons, it was claimed that Deity was only marginally present in Jesus. As an aside we note that the proto-Gnostic schema, whereby Christ was but one among many mediators, bears some resemblance to the process claim that the divine immanence is operative in many religious leaders, including Gautama and Mohammed.

Paul's understanding of πᾶν τὸ πλήρωμα was shaped by his theistic world-view derived from Judaism and refined by his encounter with Jesus Christ. The phrase denotes the totality of the divine being and attributes.[44] Far from being parcelled out among many intermediaries, God in all his fulness has made his abode, Paul insists, in Jesus of Nazareth.[45] The aorist κατοικῆσαι underscores the fact that the full indwelling of God in Jesus is of permanent rather than fleeting duration. The context which follows again suggests that Paul viewed Christ from the balanced perspective of person and work, ontology and function.

6. Colossians 2:9

In the parallel Col. 2:9 text the apostle makes two significant additions. First he utilizes the fuller expression πᾶν τὸ πλήρωμα τῆς θεότητος. The abstract noun θεότης—only here in the NT—denotes the essence, or spirit-being of God, as opposed to the divine qualities or attributes (θειότης, Rom. 1:20). Paul, then, teaches not that the divine workings were displayed in Christ, but that God himself in his spirit-reality had co-joined with the man Jesus.

Second, the apostle adds that "in him the whole fulness of Deity dwells σωματικῶς." Lightfoot and Moule argue that σωματικῶς points to the historic moment of the incarnation, whereas Martin allows that such an interpretation is possible.[46] Even if the word should mean "wholly," or "actually" (Augustine, Bengel, Ridderbos, Bruce), the context suggests that Paul contemplated Jesus Christ in his historical manifestation. In him the plenitude of Deity was co-joined with humanity in vital, ontological union. As an aside, Paul establishes in Col. 2:9, 10 a parallelism between the indwelling of God in Christ and the union of Christ and the believer. As the latter is a real, vital and organic union, so the union between God and Christ must be more than a mere moral or instrumental relation. Hence the process interpretation of the incarnation again fails to square with the Pauline witness.

7. Philippians 2:6–11

The crowning jewel of the NT christological passages is Phil. 2:6–11.[47] Robinson's process interpretation challenges the traditional incarnational focus of the text.

> Jesus was not, I believe, for Paul, as he became for later dogmatics, a divine being veiled in flesh or one who stripped himself of superhuman attributes to become human; he was a man who by total surrender of his own gain or glory was able to reveal or unveil the glory of God as utterly gracious, self-giving love.[48]

Linguistic and conceptual considerations suggest that Paul appropriated an extant hymn in praise of Christ and reshaped it when he wrote to the church at Philippi. Just as an earlier ethical exhortation to sacrificial giving led Paul to reflect on Christ's voluntary impoverishment (2 Cor. 8:9), so also here the apostle's enjoinder to humility and self-forgetfulness prompted recollection of Christ's incomparable renunciation for us.[49]

Far from regarding Jesus as a man in whom the divine working was most fully actualized, Paul contemplated four epochal stages in the existence of the church's Lord: his pre-existent condition (verse 6), his incarnation (verse 7), his humiliation and death (verse 8), and his triumphant exaltation to the heavenly world (verses 9–11).[50]

The hymn's opening assertion on behalf of Christ is simply but powerfully put: ὃς ἐν μορφῇ θεοῦ ὑπάρχων. Whatever else we might wish to say, the participle ὑπάρχων ("existing," or "subsisting") certainly asserts Christ's existence prior to his historical manifestation. Lightfoot, Vincent, H. C. G. Moule and others rightly observe that the participle suggests a time focus which is both past and present.[51]

But Paul claims for Christ a timeless existence ἐν μορφῇ θεοῦ. One leading exegetical tradition (Augustine, Lightfoot, Vincent, Gifford, Foulkes) identifies μορφή with οὐσία or φύσις, thus affirming that prior to becoming man Christ possessed the divine essence or nature.[52] Others such as Behm, Schweizer and Martin argue that μορφὴ θεοῦ signifies the divine glory (John 17:5), the visible manifestation of our Lord's intrinsic reality. It is preferable to interpret the phrase as including both the intrinsic reality and its outward manifestation. Thus μορφὴ θεοῦ denotes the spirit-being which underlies the divine attributes, as well as the attendant glory which properly belonged to the pre-existent Christ.[53] Robinson's argument that the expression refers to Jesus constituted in the image of God as the ideal Adam ostensibly finds little support in the text.

The hymn continues that the pre-existent Lord "counted not the being on an equality with God (τὸ εἶναι ἴσα θεῷ) a thing to be grasped" (ASV). That is, he chose not to regard existence-in-a-manner-of-equality-with-God (i.e., the heavenly environment of majesty and glory) a treasure to be greedily hoarded.[54] Instead he stripped himself (ἐκένωσεν) of his prerogatives as the divine Son (his God-equal existence) by "taking the form of a servant"—namely, by taking the form and exhibiting the condition of a common slave. While renouncing participation in the heavenly glory, Christ retained the divine form.

The hymn explicates further the dynamics of the incarnation of the heavenly Lord—"he was born in the likeness (ὁμοίωμα) of men." Christ's resemblance to other men was real. Yet the relation was one of "likeness," for in his intrinsic being he was more than a man. Because of his ontological identity with God, Jesus Christ was both God and man.

Lest anyone be misled in a docetic direction from the preceding "likeness" relation, the hymn quickly adds that as to outward appearance (σχῆμα) Jesus was regarded by all as a true man. The One who from eternity possessed the reality and the glory of God and who in an act of supreme self-renunciation assumed the existence of a lowly servant, was in word, bearing and action an authentic man among men.

Thus, far from affirming that God was merely instrumentally immanent in Jesus, the hymn fragment adopted by Paul sets forth a patent scheme of humiliation followed by exaltation, of descensus followed by ascensus. Paul's perspective thus diverges radically from the process model in its underlying assumption.

8. 1 Timothy 3:16

After citing the spiritual qualifications required of bishops and deacons (1 Tim. 3:1–13), Paul pauses to define the Gospel as a "mystery" disclosed to those who possess the spirit of piety. Thus the apostle writes in 1 Tim. 3:16, "By common consent great indeed is the mystery of our religion." The six balanced and rhythmic lines which follow— excerpted from a primitive creedal hymn—explicate the heart of the Christian mystery, namely, the person and history of Jesus Christ (Col. 1:27; 2:2).

The structure and interpretation of the hymn-fragment have been widely debated. The relative ὅς, which introduces the quotation, has as its antecedent τὸ τῆς εὐσεβείας μυστήριον. Barrett holds that the six strophes form a strict chronological progression attesting the incarnation, resurrection, ascension, preaching of the Gospel, response thereto, and Christ's final victory.[55] E. F. Scott sees in the hymn two strophes of three lines each. According to this structuring, lines one and two describe Christ's life on earth, lines four and five the response to Gospel preaching, whereas lines three and six serve as appropriate refrains.[56] Robert H. Gundry argues that the hymn moves from the incarnation to ascension in three couplets which highlight, respectively, the revelation, proclamation and reception of Christ.[57] Gundry's overall analysis of the hymn fragment proves convincing, although one might differ with his interpretation of one or two lines within the hymn.

Nevertheless it is clear that line one of the hymnodic piece ὅς ἐφανερώθη ἐν σαρκί points to Christ's manifestation on earth as man, with possible secondary reference to his temporal ministry. The verb φανερόω is employed in the technical sense of incarnation by Paul (Rom. 3:21; 2 Tim. 1:10), by the writer of Hebrews (Heb. 9:26), by Peter (1 Pet. 1:20), and by John (1 John 1:2; 3:5, 8). Moreover, the passive form of the verb implies the prior existence of the one who subsequently was revealed in the space-time continuum. Thus Scott comments that Jesus' earthly life should be regarded as the revelation in visible form of one who in essence was divine.[58]

The phrase ἐν σαρκί denotes the human manner of Christ's appearing, a usage well attested in Paul (Rom. 8:3; Eph. 2:15; Col. 1:22) and elsewhere in the NT (John 1:14; Heb. 5:7; 1 Pet. 3:18). Calvin discovers in the text evidence of Christ's two natures (the divine Christ "was manifest in the flesh") and the unity of his person—an inference which we judge to be valid.

The creedal hymn, with its concise historical allusions to Jesus' redemptive experience, reflects the church's early consciousness of its Lord. The text provides no occasion for regarding Jesus as a profound exemplification of the divine life, or as the man in whom the power of creative transformation was immanent. Taken at face value, the hymn witnesses to Christ's pre-existence and his historical manifestation as Jesus of Nazareth.

V. A Concluding Assessment

The purpose of this paper precludes a full philosophical critique of process theology as a system.[59] In affirming that Jesus Christ was a mere man in whom the power of creative transformation was most fully actualized, process theology has been guided less by the teachings of Scripture than by the philosophy of Whitehead, which bears certain similarities to Stoic and Gnostic thought. Admittedly, process advocates such as Pittenger and Robinson do not dismiss Scripture lightly. Yet ultimately the Christology of the school is derived philosophically rather than inductively from the data of special revelation. Process scholars insist that the NT portrait of Christ was couched in myths so that the apostolic testimony possesses little cash value in the formulation of a modern Christology.[60]

But it may be questioned whether the apostolic representation of reality has in fact distorted the primitive Gospel as the Bultmannians claim. To be sure, in describing the world as it appeared to the human eye the biblical authors wrote from a phenomenal rather than from a strictly scientific perspective. But a description of reality from the human vantage point (e.g., that Christ "came down" from heaven) does not of itself vitiate the truth intended (e.g., that the Lord of the universe invaded the earthly scene). Moreover, the NT writers spoke of God and his relation to the world human-wise via metaphors and analogies. But the use of analogical language to describe God does not constitute mythological talk. Paul would have agreed that the very purpose of revelation was to facilitate an authentic objectification of God in terms meaningful to finite man.

In addition, the Bultmannian claim that the world is a closed system governed by fixed natural laws no longer can be sustained. Thus supernatural intervention from without cannot be summarily dismissed as a distortion of the way things are. Contemporary psychic and occult phenomena confirm that the cozy, predictable world of the closed system is open to serious challenge. What modern science recently considered mythical now accords to a high degree of probability with reality. Indeed, Macquarrie takes Bultmann to task for being "still obsessed with a pseudo-scientific view of a closed universe that was popular half a century ago."[61]

Moreover, it is highly unlikely that the NT writers would have formulated the truth of Christ in the myths of Jewish apocalyptic and the Hellenistic mystery cults given their stated aversion to the fantasies of the Oriental world. The apostles Paul (1 Tim. 1:4; 2 Tim. 4:4; Titus 1:14) and Peter (2 Pet. 1:16) sternly warned that such myths and fables lead away from the truth of God.

Consistent with its total view of reality, process theology postulates that its primary epistemological datum is prehension or sense perception. At heart Whitehead was a radical empiricist.[62] Knowledge of God emerges from insights gained through exceptional moments of immediate experience. Thus Hartshorne claims that all theological knowledge is rooted in the total experience of being a man.

Paul, however, insists that analysis of one's sensory experience yields a knowledge of God which is at best partial (1 Cor. 2:6–10). Authentic knowledge of God is acquired through the faith reception of intelligible special revelation. After Peter's confession of Jesus as the Anointed Messiah and Son of God, the Lord replied with the saying, "You did not learn this from mortal man; it was revealed to you by my heavenly Father" (Matt. 16:17, NEB). Jesus' retort proves that an authentic estimate of Christ is possible only on the basis of what God has revealed. Paul undoubtedly was of one mind with Jesus who remarked to skeptical Pharisees, "You have no idea where I came from or where I am going. You judge by human standards" (John 8:14, NIV).

Furthermore, process Christology is characterized by vigorous logical coherence within a non-supernaturalist framework. When one starts with Greek concepts of being as static and changeless, the traditional view of the incarnation is as absurd as the claim that two billiard balls can occupy one spot. It is the Greek concept of being as static and unrelated that leads to contradiction when one postulates the union of an inactive divine nature with an active human nature. But the Hebrew tradition does not start there but with a living, active being working in the ordinary events of nature and the supernatural display of miracles. The God of the Jewish-Christian tradition is changeless in attributes and purposes but He is supremely active, responsive and related vis-à-vis nature, man and history.

Nevertheless, after reason has done its proper work the enfleshment of the living creator and sustainer of the universe remains a spiritual mystery (1 Tim. 3:16; Col. 2:2). While resisting assertions of sheer paradox or contradiction as groundless, Christian theology does not purport to set forth a comprehensive explication of the union of godhead and manhood in Jesus of Nazareth. The Christian is not offended by the mystery but rests on the teaching of revelation which receives ample confirmation from historical and experiential evidences.

Although the orthodox view of the incarnation defies complete formal analysis, the doctrine proves consistent with our knowledge of the God of the Bible. Paul himself taught, "No one can say 'Jesus is Lord,' except by the Holy Spirit" (1 Cor. 12:3).

In addition, process Christology has bought into the modern embargo on ontology.[63] All process theologians operate on the premise that God cannot be objectified as a static existent or a substantial self. Hence it is impossible to establish any ontological link between Jesus and God. God's changing activities rather than his being and attributes constitute the sole focus of interest. But surely it is reasonable to insist that the God who acts and who may be experienced is the very God who *is*. Geisler rightly concludes that for the process theologian "there is a moving without anything moving; becoming but no being that comes to be."[64] If a meaningful Christology is sought, the ontological foundation upon which the soteriological edifice is built must be retained. Far from being peculiarly Aristotelian, ontological affirmations constitute the very warp and woof of the inspired NT testimony to Christ (John 10:30; 2 Cor. 8:9; Col. 2:9; Heb. 2:14).[65]

From our study of the relevant Pauline literature it is clear that the apostle's estimate of Jesus Christ diverges at crucial points from the process model.[66] Our Lord is more than the supreme symbol of God immanent and operative in a human life. Paul regarded Jesus as the second Person of the eternal Godhead who left the Father's presence to become man. The mystery of the incarnation resides in the fact that the eternal Son, the Christ, who assumed our humanity never relinquished his deity. Paul's Jesus is co-equal with the Father in being, purpose and action.

It is irresponsible to dismiss the Pauline testimony with the shibboleth, "whether we like it or not, things are different nowadays."[67] Committed to the timeless truth of revelation, orthodoxy is concerned that the eternally changeless yet relevant person of Jesus Christ is not relativized to suit the whims of the current philosophical fad.[68] From our study of the Pauline consciousness we have no reason to doubt that the apostle was one with later Christians who proclaimed their Lord's humanity, deity and redemptive work by means of the acrostic symbol ΙΧΘΥΣ—"Jesus Christ, Son of God, Saviour."

Notes

1. Whitehead's basic concepts are marked out in *Science in the Modern World* (New York, Macmillan, 1925), *Process and Reality: An Essay in Cosmology* (New York, Macmillan, 1929), and *Adventures of Ideas* (New York, Macmillan, 1933).

2. Hartshorne's seminal works include *The Divine Relativity: A Social Conception of God* (New Haven, Yale University, 1948), and *Reality as Social Process: Studies in Metaphysics and Religion* (Boston, Beacon, 1953).

3. For the first Whiteheadian Christology see *The Word Incarnate: A Study in the Doctrine of the Person of Christ* (New York, Harper, 1959). See also *God in Process* (London, SCM, 1967), and *Christology Reconsidered* (London, SCM, 1970).

4. Cf. David Pailin: "The word 'God' is traditionally defined as being the direct opposite of 'man' so that each strictly excludes the other. Then to say that 'Christ is man' and that 'Christ is God' is to make mutually contradictory statements which cancel out each other's usefulness." "The Incarnation as a Continuing Reality," *RelS* 6 (1970), 318.

5. Cited by Hartshorne, "Whitehead's Idea of God," in *The Philosophy of Alfred North Whitehead*, ed. Paul A. Schilpp (Evanston, Northwestern University, 1941), 515.

6. *Word Incarnate*, 36.

7. *God in Process*, 15.

8. "Empiricism and Process Theology," *Christian Century* 93 (Mar. 24, 1976), 286.

9. *Process and Reality*, 532.

10. *Alfred North Whitehead* (Richmond, John Knox, 1969), 35.

11. *Divine Relativity*, 90.

12. *A Rahner Reader*, ed. Gerald A. McCool (New York, Seabury, 1975), 169.

13. *Reality as Social Process*, 24.

14. *Ibid.*, 152.

15. *Christ in a Pluralistic Age* (Philadelphia, Westminster, 1975), 71.

16. *Ibid.*, 107.

17. *Ibid.*, 139.

18. *Ibid.*, 66.

19. *The Reality of God and Other Essays* (New York, Harper and Row, 1966), 177.

20. *Ibid.*, 179.

21. "The Incarnation as a Continuing Reality," 319, 320.

22. "The Incarnation in Process Theology," *RevExp* 71 (1974), 49.

23. *Christology Reconsidered*, 28.

24. *Ibid.*, 79.

25. "Bernard E. Meland, Process Thought and the Significance of Christ," *Process Theology*, ed. E. H. Cousins (New York, Newman, 1971), 210.

26. "The Incarnation in Process Theology," 52, 53.

27. *Word Incarnate*, 181.

28. "Meland, Process Thought and the Significance of Christ," 214.

29. *The Human Face of God* (London, SCM, 1973), 148.

30. *Ibid.*, 43.

31. *Ibid.*, 115.

32. *Ibid.*, 184.

33. As proposed by Ernest De Witt Burton, *The Epistle to the Galatians*, ICC (Edinburgh, T. & T. Clark, 1921), 216, 217.

34. "The Letter of Paul to the Galatians," *Layman's Bible Commentary* (Richmond, John Knox, 1958), XXII, 32. Cf. Calvin: "The Son, who was sent, must have existed before He was sent; and this proves His eternal Godhead. Christ, therefore, is the Son of God, sent from heaven." *Commentaries on the Epistles of Paul to the Galatians and Ephesians* (Grand Rapids, Eerdmans, 1957), 118.

35. "The Incarnation in Process Theology," 48.

36. Paul's Second Epistle to the Corinthians, NICNT (Grand Rapids, Eerdmans, 1962), 208.

37. II Corinthians, Torch Bible Commentaries (London, SCM, 1954), 71.

38. Ibid., 301.

39. Hughes, Second Corinthians, 301.

40. Human Face, 161, 162.

41. Gnomon of the New Testament (5 vols.; Edinburgh, T. & T. Clark, 1863), III, 98.

42. Commentary on Romans (Philadelphia, Muhlenberg, 1949), 314.

43. So Cobb, Pluralistic Age, 130; Robinson, Human Face, 88–98.

44. Cf. the NEB translation of πλήρωμα in Col. 1:19: "the complete being of God." J. Schneider in NIDNTT, II, 83 defines the term as "the fulness of the being of God and Christ." J. B. Lightfoot in St. Paul's Epistles to the Colossians and to Philemon (London, Macmillan, 1875), 225, 328, and C. F. D. Moule, The Epistles of Paul the Apostle to the Colossians and to Philemon (Cambridge, CUP, 1958), 166, interpret πλήρωμα as the totality of the divine powers and attributes.

45. So F. F. Bruce, Commentary on the Epistles to the Ephesians and the Colossians (Grand Rapids, Eerdmans, 1957), 207. Cf. C. F. D. Moule, Colossians and Philemon, 169: "it appears that Christ is thought of as containing, representing, all that God is."

46. Colossians and Philemon, New Century Bible (London, Marshall, Morgan and Scott, 1974), 80.

47. Ralph P. Martin in his exhaustive study on this text comments that it expresses "the quintessence of Pauline thought on the Person of Christ." Carmen Christi (Cambridge, C.U.P., 1967), 21.

48. Human Face, 166.

49. C. F. D. Moule concurs with the ethical model interpretation and renders τοῦτο φρονεῖτε ἐν ὑμῖν κτλ. as "adopt towards one another, in your mutual relations, the same attitude which man found in Christ Jesus." "Further Reflections on Philippians 2:5–11," Apostolic History and the Gospel, eds. W. Ward Gasque and Ralph P. Martin (Exeter, Paternoster, 1970), 265.

50. So also F. W. Beare, A Commentary on the Epistle to the Philippians (London: Black, 1959), 78, and Martin, Carmen Christi, 295.

51. G. Braumann (NIDNTT, I, 706) translates ὑπάρχων as "being essentially" and adds: "It is said of this divine mode of existence that Christ existed in it in the past. . . . It refers to his pre-existence prior to the incarnation."

52. Most versions of the NT reflect this ontological interpretation. E.g., "He who has always been God by nature" (Phillips); "His nature is, from the first, divine" (Knox).

53. Cf. H. A. W. Meyer's claim that μορφή denotes the "form of being corresponding to the essence, . . . and exhibiting the condition so that μορφὴ θεοῦ finds its exhaustive explanation in Heb. 1:3." The Epistles to the Philippians and Colossians and to Philemon (New York, Funk & Wagnalls, 1885), 68.

54. C. F. D. Moule argues for the active sense of ἁρπαγμός, i.e., "the act of snatching" (raptus). The text would then read, "Jesus did not reckon equality with God in terms of snatching." "Further Reflections," 266–268, 271–276. Moule adopts a purely static or ethical interpretation of the text, although in our judgment Paul contemplates a dynamic and ontological perspective.

55. The Pastoral Epistles, The New Clarendon Bible (Oxford, Clarendon, 1963), 64, 65.

56. *The Pastoral Epistles* (London, Hodder & Stoughton, 1936), 42.

57. "The Form, Meaning and Background of the Hymn Quoted in 1 Tim. 3:16," *Apostolic History and the Gospel*, 203–222.

58. *Pastoral Epistles*, 41.

59. Norman L. Geisler has undertaken this task admirably in "Process Theology," *Tensions in Contemporary Theology*, eds. Stanley N. Gundry and Alan F. Johnson (Chicago, Moody, 1976), 237–284.

60. So, for example, Bernard E. Meland, in "The New Creation," *Process Theology*, ed. E. H. Cousins, 195: "I am persuaded by the judgment of NT scholars who say we cannot go back of the picture which the Gospel writers present to us. Yet the reality of the historical life is acknowledged."

61. *An Existentialist Theology* (London, SCM, 1955), 168.

62. "Nothing can be omitted, experience drunk and experience sober, experience sleeping and experience waking, experience drowsy and experience wide awake, experience self-conscious and experience self-forgetful, experience anxious and experience care-free, experience anticipatory and experience retrospective, experience happy and experience grieving." Whitehead, *Adventures of Ideas*, 290, 291.

63. Cf. J. A. T. Robinson: "the ontic beam to which classical theology has been fastened appears to have gotten the worm." *Human Face*, 23.

64. "Process Theology," 280.

65. Gerald Bray argues convincingly that it was Jesus himself, rather than the disciples or the early church, who made the shift from a Jewish functional Christology to an ontological Christology. "Can We Dispense With Chalcedon?" *Themelios*, n.s. 3.2 (1978), 4.

66. C. F. H. Henry notes that "this theory is so intricate and complex that God could have disclosed himself only to twentieth-century metaphysicians to make his existence intelligible." "The Reality and Identity of God," *CT* 13 (Mar. 28, 1969), 584.

67. Pittenger, *Christology Reconsidered*, 14.

68. Cf. the caution of Kenneth Hamilton: "The disadvantage of founding a theology upon relevance is that it may suddenly become irrelevant and die." *Revolt Against Heaven* (Grand Rapids, Eerdmans, 1965), 91.

Chapter 10

PAUL IN MODERN JEWISH THOUGHT

DONALD A. HAGNER

In HIS RECENT BOOK ON PAUL, Professor Bruce writes:

> Although [Paul] was rabbinically trained, his reappraisal of the whole
> spirit and content of his earlier training was so radical that many Jewish
> scholars have had difficulty in recognizing him as the product of a rabbini-
> cal education. They have found it easier to appreciate the Prophet of
> Nazareth (who, indeed, was not rabbinically trained) than the apostle to
> the Gentiles. Paul presents an enigma with which they cannot readily
> come to terms.[1]

Our century has indeed witnessed the amazing phenomenon of
the Jewish reclamation[2] of Jesus. Jewish writing on Jesus continues to
increase,[3] with the conclusion concerning Jesus' Jewishness gaining ever
more forcefulness.[4] Building upon the results of radical Protestant Christian scholarship, Jewish writers argue that the Jesus of the Gospels is to
a very large extent the product of the faith of the later Church. The actual
Jesus of history, on the other hand, is regarded as belonging with
Judaism rather than Christianity. The real Jesus is a reformer of Judaism,
a new Amos or Isaiah who calls his people back to the faith of their
fathers, a loyal Jew from whose mind nothing was further than the idea
of a new religion with himself at the centre. For modern Jews, Jesus has
indeed come home.

But what of Paul? He is, of course, regarded as the founder of the
new religion, the person largely responsible for turning Jesus, the pro-
claimer of the kingdom, into the one who is himself proclaimed as Lord,
and finally, as the person who takes this new message to the Gentiles of
the Mediterranean world with an astonishing degree of success. But to
say all this is not to account for Paul. How in fact did this amazing Jew,
who so strongly emphasizes his Jewish (indeed Pharisaic) background,

143

come to such apparently bizarre conclusions? Jewish scholars have no small fascination for Saul of Tarsus, who became the Christian Paul. He is somehow at the root of the difference between Judaism and Christianity, it is believed, and thus he demands Jewish analysis. If Jesus has been brought home, Paul has remained a stranger. Therefore several Jewish scholars (e.g. Montefiore, Klausner, Ben-Chorin), having written about Jesus, subsequently turned to write about Paul. The number of Jewish writers on Paul has increased in the last few decades[5] and will continue to increase in the future. Can there be a Jewish reclamation of Paul, even if partial, paralleling the Jewish reclamation of Jesus? What are the ingredients of the enigma which Paul presents to Jewish scholars?

The purpose of the present essay is to examine the direction taken by Jewish writers in accounting for Paul. In particular the focus of attention is on Paul's background since above all this is regarded as the ultimate source of his idiosyncratic views in such crucial areas as the Law, soteriology, christology, sacraments and mysticism. Paul's views are fairly well agreed upon; it is rather the explanation of how Paul the Jew could come to such views that interests Jewish scholars. In Paul's background and experience must lie the key that accounts for the origin of Pauline Christianity.

Before we begin our review, however, we must note the silence of Jews on the subject of Paul until the modern period.[6] Two main factors, not of equal importance, account for this silence. First, Jews at the beginning had little reason to concern themselves with Paul, this eccentric heresiarch so important to the development of Christian theology. His views were not only wrong, but also patently dangerous, as the success of his missionary endeavors made abundantly clear. It seemed the best course of action for Jews to ignore Paul as they did Christianity and even Jesus, although with less success in the last instance.[7] Far more important, however, in explaining the silence was the precarious situation of the Jews under a Christian tyranny that existed from the fourth century to the nineteenth-century Emancipation—the ultimate, but slowly realized, fruit of the Enlightenment. As long as this oppression continued, Jews were unable to speak publicly and objectively about Jesus, Paul or Christianity. Thus the history of the Jewish study of Paul is closely parallel to the history of the Jewish study of Jesus. With the new climate of freedom produced by the gradual acceptance of Jews into European society came the first scholarly assessments of Jesus and Paul from Jewish writers. A pioneer in this early scholarship was the historian Heinrich Graetz who in the second half of the nineteenth century authored the first comprehensive history of the Jews[8] and who in many ways anticipated the direction future Jewish scholarship was to take concerning both Jesus and Paul. Paul is regarded as the founder of the new religion Christianity, which he was able to create by virtue of his Hellenistic background and his consequent unfamiliarity with authentic Judaism. Indeed, were it not for Paul's transformation of the faith of the early messianic movement into Christianity, that movement would have come to its end like other messianic movements before and after. Already with Graetz it becomes apparent that Paul is more difficult to explain and more alien to Judaism than Jesus.

In the twentieth century important Jewish writings on Paul have appeared from such scholars as Claude Goldsmid Montefiore,[9] Kaufmann Kohler,[10] Joseph Klausner,[11] Martin Buber,[12] Leo Baeck,[13] Samuel Sandmel,[14] Hans Joachim Schoeps,[15] Schalom Ben-Chorin,[16] and Richard L. Rubenstein.[17] Despite certain differences between these writers, there is perhaps enough basic agreement among them to enable us to recognize an emerging modern Jewish perspective on Paul.[18]

Although the issue takes on a special importance for Jewish scholars, since for them particularly Paul's relation to Judaism demands explanation, the struggle over the question of Paul's background is of course shared by New Testament scholarship generally. Because it is important to the initial formation of a Jewish perspective on Paul, we begin with a brief review of the modern discussion of the problem.

In the first decades of our century, NT scholarship largely came under the domination of *Religionsgeschichte*, a discipline which saw Christianity as one among many religions in the Hellenistic world and which in "strictly historical" fashion attempted to account for similarities by arguing for primitive Christianity's dependence upon these Hellenistic religions. A most impressive scholarly tradition emerged, including such noteworthy names as Pfleiderer, Heitmüller, Gunkel, Reitzenstein, Bousset and Bultmann.[19] Inevitably their attention was focused on Paul, for it was above all he among the NT writers who exhibited Hellenistic influence. The Mystery Religions and Gnosticism provided a rich source of striking parallels to Paul's theology and much energy was expended in combing through literary remains, such as the Hermetic and Mandaic corpora, in search of similarities. The widespread conclusion drawn from this approach was that Paul had combined Jewish and Hellenistic ideas, with a preponderance of the latter, into a new syncretism and had thereby created a new religion. He had borrowed freely from a variety of Hellenistic sources; his sacramental views, his mysticism, his christology and soteriology and more, were fundamentally derived from the Mystery Religions, the *kyrios* cult, and Gnosticism (particularly the myth of the cosmological redeemer). In this hellenization of Christianity Jesus thus became another mystery-god and Paul perhaps the greatest of all the Gnostics.[20]

Together with this new explanation of Paul came the emphatic conclusion that Paul's religion was a radical departure from what Jesus had preached. The differences between Jesus and Paul had of course been noted much earlier. The modern debate of this problem goes back to F. C. Baur, who regarded Paul as an innovator and who was followed in this by others among whom Wendt, Goguel, Wrede and Bultmann deserve special mention.[21] These scholars drew the contrast between Jesus and Paul much more sharply than had Baur, and their viewpoint continues to have influence.[22] The newer knowledge of Hellenistic religion brought by the early twentieth century served to widen the chasm that already existed between Jesus and Paul.

Thus from Christian writers with massive scholarly erudition came conclusions that Jews had long felt to be true. Paul, importing Greek notions intrinsically foreign to Judaism, had invented a new religion quite out of sympathy with the intent of Jesus. Whereas Jesus had come to reform Judaism, Paul had subverted it; Jesus, more than ever, seemed to belong on the side of Judaism against Paul who belonged on the side of Christianity. To have such views uttered not out of a context of religious polemics or apologetics, but from what could be claimed to be "objective," "scientific" Christian scholarship was indeed a boon to the Jewish perspective.

Jewish scholars were not slow to make use of these conclusions in their own evaluation of Paul. At the same time, Jews are too aware of an authentic Jewishness in Paul amidst all that seems unfamiliar to be satisfied to account for him solely on the basis of Hellenism. It is particularly to a Hellenistic Judaism that they have in large measure resorted in seeking to explain Paul. But Paul the Hellenist remains Paul the Jew, and the most recent writers, as we shall see, stress Paul's Jewishness more than ever.

We begin with the influential writer of the early part of this century, Claude Goldsmid **Montefiore,** whose writings on Paul have as a major purpose to demonstrate that Paul's Judaism was vastly different from Rabbinic Judaism. From Montefiore's point of view, the difference is a key to understanding Paul. As he puts it repeatedly, "there is much in Paul which, while dealing *with* Judaism, is inexplicable *by* Judaism."[23] When Solomon Schechter began his sympathetic study of Rabbinic theology, he admitted that the results would not square with Paul's account of the same subject, and that this would make the Apostle to the Gentiles seem "quite unintelligible."[24] Montefiore avoids this dilemma by denying that Paul ever knew an authentic Rabbinic Judaism.[25] Paul was not, as Wellhausen had described him, "the great pathologist of Judaism."[26] On the contrary, the Judaism Paul knew was markedly different from Rabbinic Judaism and, moreover, his thinking had been affected by alien, non-Jewish influences.[27]

Montefiore's earlier essay on Paul is to a large extent a refutation of certain Christian statements bearing on Jewish theology and more particularly the book of the Christian scholar Ferdinand Weber, entitled *Jüdische Theologie auf Grund des Talmud und verwandter Schriften.*[28] It is especially the distortion of the Rabbinic teaching on the Law that Montefiore seeks to correct. Here, as well as in his later essay, Montefiore draws a sharp contrast between the Rabbinic Judaism of AD 500 (which he regards as not essentially different from that of AD 50) and the Judaism which Paul attacks in his epistles. The radical discrepancy between the two suggests to Montefiore that either Paul "was never a Rabbinic Jew at all, or he has quite forgotten what Rabbinic Judaism was and is."[29]

In his most forceful presentation of these differences, Montefiore explores eight areas of Paul's theology which are impossible to explain on the basis of Rabbinic Judaism.[30] According to Montefiore, the first two of these, Paul's view of Christ as a divine being and his commitment to the mission to the Gentiles, although not paralleled in the Rabbinic Judaism of AD 500, can be explained from first-century Jewish (even Palestinian) backgrounds without difficulty—the former on the basis of expectations of Jewish apocalyptic, the latter as a reflection of an active Jewish proselytism. But in the remaining six items Paul departs altogether from Rabbinic Judaism (whether of 500 or 50): his pessimism, his theory of Law (as in Romans), his neglect of the idea of repentance, his peculiar mysticism, soteriology and religious psychology.

Montefiore is content to stress these differences and to assert the unrabbinic character of Paul's theology. He offers no constructive account of Paul other than to designate Paul's Jewish background as a "particular sort of cheap and poor Hellenistic Judaism."[31] Diaspora Judaism is regarded by Montefiore as decidedly inferior; its religion was "colder and more sombre"; its God was more remote and less approachable than the Rabbis' God; its outlook was gloomy, anxious and defensive; it saw the Law negatively rather than positively; it became concerned with sin and salvation; it was theoretical and systematic.[32] Here it appears that Montefiore attributes to Diaspora Judaism every quality of Paul he dislikes.

It is obvious for Montefiore that Paul's Diaspora background is the key to understanding his theology. As for NT data which could be taken as referring to Paul's contact with Palestinian Judaism, Montefiore follows the critical opinion of some Christian scholars that Acts is not to be trusted as history (he cites Loisy); he does not accept the reference in

22:3 where Paul refers to being brought up in Jerusalem and educated at the feet of Gamaliel.[33] According to Montefiore the reference in Phil. 3:5–6 concerning Paul's Pharisaic background and his blamelessness according to the righteousness under the Law could have been spoken by a Hellenistic Jew as easily as a Palestinian Jew, although he adds that the passage has "no genuine Jewish ring."[34]

Montefiore was by no means the first Jewish scholar to explain Paul by appealing to the Hellenistic Judaism of the Diaspora, nor of course was he the last to do so. Kaufmann **Kohler** was one of the earliest and most forceful proponents of Paul's Hellenism in his influential article in the *Jewish Encyclopedia*. Despite Paul's own claims about his Jewishness, from his epistles Kohler can only conclude that he was "entirely a Hellenist in thought and sentiment."[35] There is no indication of rabbinic influence in Paul's writing or argumentation, according to Kohler. Therefore it is impossible that Paul could ever have been a disciple of Gamaliel; rather, the source of his theology is to be found in the literature of Hellenistic Judaism and the influence of Greek mystery cults. An additional factor in accounting for Paul's strange doctrines is his susceptibility to ecstatic visions (caused by epilepsy) and the accompanying mental paroxysms, to which may be attributed certain irrational and pathological elements in his writings.[36] All of this, argues Kohler, contributes to the decidedly un-Jewish character of Paul: "The conception of a new faith, half pagan and half Jewish, such as Paul preached, and susceptibility to its influences, were altogether foreign to the nature of Jewish life and thought."[37] Paul's christology and his view of the Law are regarded as influenced by Gnosticism; his mysticism and sacramentalism are traced to Hellenistic Mystery Religions. Yet for all of Paul's dependence upon Hellenism, he himself remained recognizably Jewish.

When Joseph **Klausner** turned his attention to Paul, he too stressed the significance of Hellenistic influence upon Paul. The primary datum is that Paul was born, raised, and lived almost all of his life, in a Hellenistic environment. Klausner does not deny that Paul had been at one time a student of Gamaliel in Jerusalem and that he therefore had some knowledge of Palestinian Judaism. But this was not sufficient to overcome Paul's basic orientation. Paul's soul, according to Klausner, was in fact "torn between Palestinian Pharisaism . . . and Jewish Hellenism—and in a certain measure also pagan Hellenism."[38] It was this divided loyalty that ultimately brought about the betrayal of Judaism by Paul.

The message which Paul proclaimed involved a world-view "completely foreign to Palestinian Jews."[39] Appealing to the abundant parallels to Paul discovered by the *Religionsgeschichte* school, Klausner argued that the un-Jewish character of Paul's teaching was the result of his religious syncretism.[40] It was indeed just this accommodation to and adaptation of pagan ideas that enabled Paul to produce a Christianity that became a world religion. There was a kind of Christianity before Paul, but only in its Pauline metamorphosis could it conquer the pagan world.[41]

Paul's message is not only new and un-Jewish, for Klausner, but fundamentally an "anti-Judaism, the complete antithesis of Judaism."[42] Paradoxically, however, Klausner can also say "that there is nothing in the teaching of Paul—not even the most mystical elements in it—that did not come to him from authentic Judaism."[43] This last statement seems incompatible with the dominant argument of the book that Paul's religion is the result of his Diaspora background with its pagan influences wherein "he was detached from the *authentic, living Judaism* which was rooted in its own cultural soil."[44] But this is a tension frequently encountered in Jewish writing on Paul.

In the work of Martin **Buber** we again find the familiar polarization between Judaism, the Pharisees and Jesus[45] on the one hand, and Paul, Hellenistic Judaism and Christianity on the other. Buber sees here two different types of faith: the former represented by *Emunah*, an existential trust wherein the person finds himself in association with community (i.e. nation); the latter represented by *Pistis*, an intellectual assent to truth whereby an individual is converted.[46] Paul must be regarded as "the real originator of the Christian conception of faith," which he arrived at through the transformation of Israel's original notion of faith.[47] Paul's new faith arises "from a Greek attitude."[48]

Buber accounts for Paul's departure from classical Judaism by the Greek influence which he received through Hellenistic Judaism. At the outset of his book, Buber rejects Schweitzer's assessment that Paul's roots lie in the Jewish rather than the Greek world, adding that he "can connect the Pauline doctrine of faith . . . only with a peripheral Judaism, which was actually 'Hellenistic'."[49] Buber does not go into detail concerning Paul's Hellenistic-Jewish background or the degree to which Paul was influenced by it. In discussing Paul's theology, however, he does refer to "the Gnostic nature of the essential features," viz., belief in powers which rule the world, the enslavement of man and the cosmos, and the consequent need of liberation.[50] Buber argues that the idea of the resurrection of Jesus found its preparation in Hellenism's Mystery Religions with their doctrine of dying and rising gods.[51] The perception of Jesus as deity was in turn made possible through "the crystallizing of the mythical element lying ready in the hearts of those influenced by Hellenism . . . until the new binitarian God-image was present."[52] When Buber contemplates Paul's theology, and in particular his doctrine of God, he writes "I no longer recognize the God of Jesus, nor his world in this world of Paul's [sic]."[53]

Paul's view, in short, is a "Gnostic view of the world."[54] At a key point, in the notion of the fatalistic domination of this world by evil powers, Paul was under the influence of "hellenistic Judaism of a popular variety."[55] It is particularly this notion of "demonocracy" with its stress on fate and the concomitant need for a mediator and redeemer that is seen by Buber to be the essence of Paulinism. Christian history, indeed, is classifiable according to the degree of influence of this Paulinism which by its very nature is antithetical to the perspective of Pharisaic Judaism.[56]

Without question Samuel **Sandmel** is the most prolific representative of the view that the key to understanding Paul is to be found in his Greek background. The Greek environment in which he lived "had worked on him intensely,"[57] indeed to the extent that Pauline Christianity can be described as "a completely Grecian phenomenon."[58] Sandmel repeatedly compares Paul to Philo, another Hellenistic Jew— that is, one for whom "the purpose, perplexities, quests, and sense of achievement of Greek religion were accepted, harmonized, and assimilated."[59] Paul's Hellenistic ideas are said to "have as much or as little a Jewish matrix as Philo's own thought."[60]

At the same time, Sandmel stresses that Paul always thought of himself as a loyal Jew and his message as the purest Judaism.[61] He *was* loyal to his Hellenistic Judaism; yet, argues Sandmel, "the content of his Judaism, like that of other Greek Jews, had undergone a subtle, but radical shift," involving not merely new definitions of old words but "a change in the fabric of religious suppositions and in the goal of the religious quest."[62] Sandmel, who more than any other of the Jewish writers discussed in this essay employs the methodology of radical biblical criticism, regards the Acts of the Apostles as possessing little historical value and denies that Paul had any contact with the Pharisaic Judaism of Palestine.[63] Fundamental to Sandmel's perspective is his insistence that "Pauline Christianity and rabbinic Judaism share little more than a common point of departure, the Bible."[64] Indeed, the two are antithetical and this is ultimately due to the fact that Hellenistic Judaism, adapting to the Greek world, is itself "the blending of antitheses."[65]

While not going into detail, Sandmel refers to the specifically Hellenistic influence in Paul's doctrine through the pagan cults, philosophy and mythology of his environment. Like Buber, he finds of basic importance Paul's Greek notion of the individual human predicament and the necessity of escape from the body.[66] With a background common to Philo and the Stoics, Paul finds the solution in mystical experience, especially union with God resulting in the possibility of becoming a divine man, the transformation of a material being into a spiritual one.[67]

This is the content through which Paul transmuted the comparatively Jewish Christianity which preceded him into a "gentilized Christianity" which itself made the Gentile mission a possibility and a success.[68] In Sandmel's view, Paul in this way recreated Christianity; it did not begin with him, but through him received new impulse sufficient to be regarded as a second beginning.[69]

Note may finally be made of Sandmel's Montefiore Lecture of 1969, "Paul Reconsidered."[70] Here Sandmel suggests that Goodenough's work on Philo's Judaism provides a key for the positive explanation of Paul which Montefiore did not attempt. Sandmel, while still finding Hellenistic Judaism the best background against which to understand Paul, does not believe this enables him to account for the genesis of Paul's religion. Unlike the majority of Jewish writers on Paul, Sandmel regards the background of Paul as "unimportant"; Paul is "so individualistic that conceivably he could have come from any kind of a background."[71]

We may turn next to Leo **Baeck,** who more than any scholar thus far considered stresses Paul's Jewishness. Baeck does not for a moment deny the influence of Hellenistic ideas upon Paul; what he does do, however, is to point out the large extent to which these ideas were at home in the genuinely Jewish Diaspora. The fundamental shift from the horizontal perspective of the prophets (future oriented) to the vertical perspective of apocalyptic (the disclosure of the "above" in the present) that was crucial to Christianity and Paul (cf. his vision of Christ) had already found expression in Jewish apocalyptic (e.g. Daniel) influenced by Alexandrian Greek philosophy.[72] Paul found much that was appealing in Hellenism; but, as Baeck puts it, since much of it was reminiscent of Jewish wisdom speculation, "no Jew could resist such aspects of Hellenism."[73] Paul's Hellenism is easily traceable; his sacramental teaching especially is influenced by the mystery cults. But much of his Greek, Stoic philosophical terminology may also be seen to be "within the Jewish compass."[74] Paul should not be regarded as a "Hellenist" at all since "his approach to the Hellenistic world was the same as that of some Palestinian teachers."[75] To be sure, Paul was "captivated by the analogies" offered by the mystery cults to the Christ-centered faith he proclaimed. Indeed analogy is basic to Paul's whole theological method.[76] Paul did not, however, create a new type of mystery religion. Rather, he saw and took advantage of the abundant means available in the Hellenistic world in order to carry out the essentially Jewish mission of gathering in the Gentiles.[77] In his missionary task and in his theology, Paul never wavered in his basic Jewish loyalty, down to and including the special election of the Jewish people.

Thus while affirming Paul's Hellenism, Baeck also emphasizes

Paul's Jewishness, and in this regard Baeck serves as an appropriate transition to the most recent Jewish trend in explaining Paul's background. Here it is argued that Paul's Judaism is indeed to be understood as a Palestinian Judaism.

Hans Joachim **Schoeps'** lengthy monograph on Paul is in some respects the most impressive of Jewish works devoted to Paul yet to appear. At the beginning of his book, Schoeps gives a full summary of Pauline research, reviewing in turn Hellenistic, Hellenistic-Judaistic, Palestinian-Judaic, and Eschatological approaches to the understanding of Paul. Regarding the Hellenistic-Judaistic approach, and in response particularly to Montefiore's structuring of the problem of Paul, Schoeps cautions that the rabbinism even of Palestine contained some exponents of Hellenistic ideas and that apocalypticism (neglected by Montefiore) also flourished in Palestine. Our present state of knowledge, moreover, "does not justify us in concluding that there was an irreconcilable opposition between Hellenistic and rabbinic Judaism."[78] There were, of course, differences between the two;[79] nevertheless, there was also considerable overlap between the two.

What is remarkable in Schoeps' portrayal of Paul is his insistence upon Paul's contacts with Palestinian Judaism. He accepts the account in Acts concerning Paul's discipleship under Gamaliel, and takes note also that Paul was able to speak Aramaic when the occasion demanded it (Acts 21:40).[80] Indeed, only from Paul's contact with Pharisaic Judaism can the general character of Paul's thought be explained, and more especially his rabbinic argumentation and exegesis.[81] "The fact that Paul was a 'rabbinist,' that his religion is to be approached as a 'radicalized Pharisaism' . . . may be accepted without further discussion."[82] Further, writes Schoeps, "rabbinic connections and parallels may be discovered for most of Paul's doctrines and expressions of faith, without its being necessary to exploit in a prejudiced way the criterion of 'Hellenistic Judaism.' "[83] Even more striking is Schoeps' insistence that in ascertaining the derivation of Paul's thought "every explanation proceeding from rabbinism deserves *a limine* preference over all other explanation."[84]

This is not to say that Schoeps finds the problem of Paul easy[85] or that he is oblivious to the reality of Hellenistic influence on Paul, or to those aspects of Paul that seem particularly non-Jewish (e.g. what he regards as sacramental mysticism).[86] In his summarizing remarks, Schoeps says that all of the schools of interpreting Paul "are relatively right."[87] Nevertheless it remains true that Schoeps is at odds with the Jewish scholars previously discussed,[88] and that he stresses Paul's authentic Jewishness even as measured by the standards of Palestinian Rabbinism. In keeping with this viewpoint, Schoeps argues for continuity between pre-Pauline Palestinian Christianity and Paul's Christianity: "The talk of Paul's acute Hellenization of Christianity which has sprung up in consequence of the Tübingen school must, however, be rejected."[89]

A recent full-length Jewish book on Paul is the very interesting contribution of Schalom **Ben-Chorin**. The burden of Ben-Chorin's book is found in his repeated insistence that Paul was and remained a Jew. Paul's argumentation, his exegesis, theology (even christology) are essentially Jewish—indeed at many points Pharisaic.[90] Paul is repeatedly dependent upon rabbinic teaching materials, as Ben-Chorin points out in the major chapter of his book, where he examines the theology of Paul's letters seriatim.[91] He disagrees with Buber's argument that Paul's concept of faith excluded the Hebrew notion of *Emunah*, siding rather with Schweitzer's opinion that "Paulus in der jüdischen, nicht in der griechischen Gedankenwelt wurzelt."[92] Even when Paul's teaching is in opposition to the views of Judaism, "er kann gar nicht anders denken, sprechen und schreiben als jüdisch, denn er ist und bleibt 'ein Pharisäer von Pharisäern.'"[93]

Paul's fundamental Jewishness traces back to his youth, to the days of his tutelage under Gamaliel. Unlike some of the Jewish scholars already discussed, Ben-Chorin accepts and affirms as of first importance Paul's time in Jerusalem at the feet of Gamaliel.[94] The young Paul was a "Talmid-Chacham," a "Jeschiva-Schüler," and the later Paul sounds again and again like a man who could not forget his earlier training.[95] The persistent Jewishness of his thought and speech, his deeply Jewish soul can only be explained by a firm rootage in Pharisaic Judaism in the days of his formal training—and only in the light of these can Paul be truly understood.

Yet Paul was also undoubtedly a Diaspora Jew in the fullest sense. Like other Diaspora Jews, he had drunk deeply of Hellenism. Paul indeed is best described as a "wanderer between two worlds"; it was his goal—and proved in no small measure his success—to be "a Jew to the Jews and a Greek to the Greeks" (1 Cor. 9:20). It is here that Ben-Chorin finds the explanation of Paul. Far from downplaying the Hellenistic dimension in Paul, Ben-Chorin calls attention to it again and again. Thus, like many of the scholars considered above, Ben-Chorin contrasts Paul the Diaspora Jew with Jesus' Palestinian Jewishness, and Paul with the original disciples.[96] Paul's transformation of Jesus and his theology in general are so Hellenistic that the original disciples could not understand him.[97] In his christology Paul employs the apocalyptic tradition of Hellenistic Judaism; for his concept of baptism he is dependent on the mystery cults.[98] His world is abstract and also dualistic (e.g. flesh and spirit).[99] For his preaching, in short, he has "das unendliche Reservoir der Heidenwelt vor sich."[100]

Paul is the prototype of the assimilated Jew who in speech and thought conforms to his Diaspora environment, but who though he appears to repress his Judaism, actually mediates it to his environment.[101] Paul indeed may be said to have had another teacher in Philo. Like Philo from whom he is said directly to have derived his allegorical interpretation of the Bible, he attempted to synthesize Jewish and Greek ideas.[102] Paul, like Philo, in the last analysis can only be understood in terms of Hellenistic Judaism.

For Ben-Chorin, then, both Palestinian and Hellenistic Judaism are vitally important to the understanding of Paul. The blend is the result of Paul's understanding of his mission to the Gentiles, itself the outworking of a Jewish universalism. What he took to them was fundamentally Jewish, but Hellenized for the sake of the mission. Inevitably Paul was misunderstood and became a tragic figure. Contrary to Paul's best intention, the Jew perceived him as a lawless, pagan Greek, and the Greek perceived him as a strange Pharisaic rabbi.[103] In attempting to bring Judaism to the Gentiles by means of Christianity, he experienced rejection both from Judaism and from early Christianity.[104] Thus without denying Paul's Hellenism, Ben-Chorin has given one of the strongest affirmations of Paul's Jewishness, insisting especially on Paul's deep rootage in Pharisaic Judaism.

Ben-Chorin was able to entitle his book on Jesus, *Bruder Jesus;*[105] now Richard L. **Rubenstein** has given us a book entitled *My Brother Paul.* In this interesting and unusual book, Rubenstein studies Paul primarily from the perspective of Freudian psychology, attempting to demonstrate the extent to which Pauline insights parallel and anticipate those of Freud. In the course of reaching this goal, however, Rubenstein engages in biblical and theological analysis important and insightful in its own right and this is the subject matter which we focus upon, to the neglect of the major purpose of the book.

Rubenstein stresses Paul's Jewishness and Pharisaic background.[106] He is of course aware of Hellenistic influence on Paul,[107] but regards this influence as minimal. He points to the influence of Hellenism upon first-century Judaism and the great difficulty of distinguishing between the Hellenistic and Jewish influence upon early Christianity.[108] He is therefore pessimistic about resolving the question of Paul's background; yet he writes "I have come to believe that Paul's thought and religious life were far more Jewish than Greek."[109]

Paul always thought of himself as a faithful Jew, loyal to the religion of his fathers.[110] Rubenstein takes "most emphatic exception" to the opinion that "no one misunderstood Judaism more profoundly than Paul."[111] Rubenstein, like several other Jewish scholars, refers to Paul's plight vis-à-vis his Jewish brethren as a "tragedy."[112] The root of the

disagreement concerned Jewish messianic expectation: for Paul fulfilment had begun. It was as a result of his Jewishness and his conviction
of the dawning of fulfilment that Paul turned to the Gentile mission.
"Nowhere is Paul more prototypically Jewish" than in this enterprise,
which he saw as the necessary precondition of the eventual consummation of God's purposes for Israel.[113]

Nevertheless, in his message of Christ crucified and risen, as in his
sacramentalism, Paul "understood clearly how profoundly Judaism had
been 'stood on its head.'"[114] More than anyone, "Paul of Tarsus stood at
the crossroads of rabbinic Judaism and Christianity."[115] But the surprise
is that Rubenstein rejects the widespread view of Jewish scholars that
Paul is the virtual creator of Christianity: "In reality it was not Paul
but Jesus who instituted the irreparable breach with established
Judaism."[116] Rubenstein also denies that there was a radical disagreement between the views of Paul and those of the primitive Jerusalem
church.[117]

The unusual character of much of Rubenstein's perspective is no
doubt to be explained by his own relativism. He rejects both Judaism
and Christianity as normative solutions to the problem of mankind.[118] In
the last analysis, when Rubenstein refers to Paul as his brother, he
affirms not Paul's religious heritage, but Paul's existential humanness.
He has empathy with Paul's conflicts and their eventual resolution
through the authority of a personal experience.[119] With this in mind,
one may question the fairness of representing Rubenstein, the self-
proclaimed "psychological man,"[120] as truly Jewish in outlook.

The above survey shows that Jewish scholars have increasingly
stressed Paul's authentic Jewishness. The trend is to locate Paul's background not primarily in Hellenistic and Diaspora Judaism as Montefiore
had done,[121] but in Rabbinic and Palestinian Judaism.[122] This trend of
course is consonant with the recent realization of some scholars that it is
no longer possible to make a facile dichotomy between Hellenism and
Judaism and thus between Diaspora and Palestinian Judaism.[123] Even
the Judaism of Palestine was subject to a high degree of Hellenistic
influence, and thus much that was previously described as Hellenistic
and alien may now be designated as Rabbinic.

It is nevertheless to be noted that despite the new willingness to
perceive Paul as a Rabbinic Jew, at key junctures Jewish scholars still
appeal to Hellenistic influence upon Paul. That is, when Paul as a Rabbinic Jew draws conclusions that do not fit the preconceived model of
Rabbinic Judaism, his position is explained by appealing to something
external to that Judaism. W. D. Davies has thus criticized Schoeps for
presenting a Paul who is a "split personality" in whose mind Jewish and

Hellenistic concepts "never come to terms," and who therefore may be "psychologically incredible."[124] Ben-Chorin, who also has recourse to the Hellenistic explanation of Paul at the most important points, indicates his awareness of the difficulty when he deliberately describes Paul as a "wanderer between two worlds."[125]

The key areas are obvious: Paul's view of the Law, his soteriology and christology, his mysticism and doctrine of sacraments. What explanation of Paul's background is most compatible with Paul's teaching on these subjects? This is the quandary of Jewish writers on Paul.

Paul's view of the Law is widely regarded by Jewish scholars as unacceptable even within the Hellenistic Judaism of the Diaspora (Montefiore, Klausner) and as indeed attributable to Gnostic (Kohler, Buber) or more generally Diaspora (Friedländer,[126] Sandmel) influence. In his important essay Leo Baeck argues that Paul's attitude toward the Law was authentically Rabbinic and is to be explained by his conviction that the eschatological age was already present because the Messiah had appeared, and therefore that the aeon of Torah was at an end.[127] This explanation of Paul's view of the Law is accepted by Schoeps who regards Paul as adhering to an aeon-theology although he still finds it necessary to see much of Paul's perspective in this area as essentially Hellenistic, especially where Paul reveals a legalistic or moralizing view of the Law.[128] Only Ben-Chorin does not appeal to Hellenistic influence in explaining Paul's view of the Law. For him the notion of suffering under the burdensome yoke of Torah is conceivable within Pharisaic Judaism[129] and hence Paul's personal frustration need not be attributed to Hellenistic influence. Paul's attitude toward the Law, according to Ben-Chorin, is paradoxical but "keinen Ausbruch aus den Judentum darstellt."[130]

Jewish scholars thus stress as far as they can Paul's Jewishness in his view of the Law. All agree in pointing out that Paul himself remained an observer of the Law and encouraged other Jewish Christians to do so; that even when Paul spoke about freedom from the Law, he did not mean the moral Law; and that it was exactly this attitude of freedom toward the ceremonial and purity laws that made possible the mission to the Gentiles to which Paul felt called, and which itself is rightly regarded as a Jewish enterprise.

The apparent necessity of the appeal to Hellenistic influence upon Paul's theology is of course even more obvious when it comes to the areas of christology, soteriology, mysticism and sacraments. Here even those who most stress Paul's Palestinian Jewishness (such as Schoeps and Ben-Chorin) turn to Hellenistic influence whether direct or indirect, via Hellenistic Judaism, to explain Paul. Yet with due recognition of Paul's appropriation of Hellenistic vocabulary for his own purposes, his theology is capable of being explained as a whole on the basis of what was available to him within Palestinian Judaism[131]—that is, if we are able to add his experience of Christ on the Damascus road as the dynamic responsible for his theology.

The irony is that the more Jewish Paul is seen to be, the more difficult it becomes to explain him when one denies the truth of his major premise, viz. that the crucified, risen Jesus is Lord of all, the fulfilment of the promises of God. If Paul is basically a syncretist, combining Hellenistic ideas derived from the Mystery Religions or Gnosticism with ideas from Judaism, then Paul may properly be regarded as the creator of a new religion, something neither Jewish nor Greek. But if, on the other hand, Paul is an exponent of fundamentally Jewish ideas, then his theology can at least conceivably reflect, as he says it does, the fulfilment of the Old Testament.

If a consistently Jewish explanation of Paul is undertaken, as in the trend of Jewish scholarship, what must be faced is Paul's major premise, which for him in turn depends upon his experience on the Damascus road. The reality of that experience as well as its central importance is affirmed by Jewish scholars (especially Baeck, Schoeps and Ben-Chorin). It is admitted that only an objective reality of some kind is able to account for the dramatic transformation of Paul and the christocentric character of his theology.[132] Damascus is clearly the watershed that is responsible for the work and thought of the Apostle.[133] What the experience actually was is not so clear. The older view that Paul was an epileptic (e.g. Kohler, Klausner) is strongly rejected by Sandmel and Ben-Chorin,[134] as is any suggestion of mere hallucination. The virtually unanimous Jewish explanation is that Paul experienced some kind of vision analogous to the psychic phenomena referred to in 2 Cor. 12:2–4, 7. Because of indications of Paul's mystic and ecstatic bent (1 Cor. 14:6, 18), he is regarded as having been especially susceptible to extraordinary visions. Several Jewish authors (Kohler, Buber, Baeck, Ben-Chorin) also refer to a Hellenistic context or influence as pertinent to understanding Paul's experience. Thus the Damascus experience of Paul is not regarded as a fabrication, but as an objective event to be explained naturalistically on the basis of Paul's psychic personality.[135] What actually happened on the Damascus road, as Ben-Chorin puts it, "bleibt letzlich das Geheimnis der Seele des Paulus."[136]

We may now make some general summarizing comments about the modern Jewish study of Paul. (1) Jewish scholars are making a genuine effort to understand Paul. They evidence a new openness to Paul and a repudiation of the old stereotypes. (2) There is a conscious attempt to bring Paul within the sphere of Judaism as far as this is possible. Explanation of Paul on the basis of Hellenism, or even Hellenistic Judaism, is giving way to the assertion of Palestinian Judaism as

Paul's background. This Jewish reclamation of Paul, however, is still hindered at important points by the appeal to Hellenism to explain what is regarded as non-Jewish. (3) From the Jewish perspective Paul's teaching is eccentric but nevertheless it is attributed ultimately to his Jewishness in that it is the result of his great burden for the Gentiles and his desire to make Judaism a truly universal religion. He thus may be said to have created a Judaism for Gentiles. Even Kohler, who minimizes Paul's Jewishness and regards him as an out-and-out Hellenist, is able to write: "He was an instrument in the hand of Divine Providence to win the heathen nations for Israel's God of righteousness."[137] That Paul remained loyal to Israel and thus never finally abandoned his Jewishness, despite this preoccupation with the Gentiles, is noted by frequent appreciative reference to Romans 9–11. (4) Jewish writers are able to speak admiringly of Paul as a great and influential theologian. Insofar as Paul is regarded as authentically Jewish he is praised.[138] A distinction of course is generally made between Paul and Paulinism. The latter is regarded as the exaggeration of certain of Paul's insights and the neglect of others, resulting in the opposite of what Paul actually held. It is Paulinism that is responsible for the widespread distortion of Paul which has concealed his true and abiding Jewishness. (5) Despite all the energy expended by Jewish scholars to uncover Paul's authentic Jewishness and to approach him positively and appreciatively, it is all the more remarkable that his theology is rejected in toto. His christology, his view of the Law, his soteriology with its pessimism concerning man's moral capability, his doctrine of sacraments, and many of his social and ethical teachings are considered objectionable.

It must be said then that although Paul's Jewishness is increasingly seen and appreciated, Jewish scholarship has not been able to reclaim Paul. The impasse that confronts Jewish scholarship at this point, though more formidable, is not dissimilar to that which is met in the Jewish reclamation of Jesus: Whence the undeniable newness, the strange, the unexpected? If the source of that newness in Paul is alien to the authentic religion of the Jews, and stems from Gnosticism or the Mystery Religions, then the Jewish argument stands and Paul the syncretist is properly regarded as the creator of Christianity. If, on the other hand, that newness is, so to speak, a Jewish newness, the result of the initial fulfilment of the promises of the Old Testament to Israel, then Paul is the recipient of truth and the rejection of Paul's theology by Jewish scholars is unwarranted. If Paul on the Damascus road really received a revelation from the resurrected Christ, then we have the dynamic that can explain Paul's theology with its newness within a fully Jewish framework, viz. as the culmination of the history of Israel and the inaugurated consummation of the Old Testament tradition.

Certain trends in Jewish scholarship on Paul seem to suggest the propriety if not the plausibility of the latter interpretation: that Paul exhibits thorough (Palestinian) Jewishness (contra the Hellenistic explanation); that Paul himself viewed his theology as nothing other than the true Judaism (and not something alien); that Paul stands in a degree of continuity with the Jerusalem apostles (rather than in total discontinuity);[139] and that Paul's Damascus road experience is to be understood as an objectively real event (not hallucination or deliberate fraud). All of this can be accounted for, and the whole of Paul's theology can be integrated satisfactorily into a fully Jewish framework, when the truth of his gospel is accepted. If the promised messianic age is somehow present in and through the crucified, risen Jesus, the surprising, required newness that even Paul had to learn before he gave it expression can be conceived. But if this possibility—the key to Paul's theology, as is correctly recognized by many Jewish scholars—is denied from the beginning, then Paul can only remain an enigma. There is much to appreciate in the stress on Paul's Jewishness in recent Jewish scholarship, but the extent of Paul's true Jewishness—its depth, its joy, and its vision—is grasped only when Paul's central premise is accepted—that "all the promises of God find their Yes in him [Christ] and that is why we utter the Amen through him, to the glory of God" (2 Cor. 1:20).

Notes

1. *Paul: Apostle of the Free Spirit* (Exeter/Grand Rapids, Paternoster/ Eerdmans, 1977), 462.
2. See the essay by Harry A. Wolfson, "How the Jews Will Reclaim Jesus," *The Menorah Journal* (1962), 25–31, reprinted in *Judaism and Christianity* (ed. J. B. Agus; New York, Arno, 1973). Wolfson's answer is: as a rabbi among rabbis, as a part of Israel's literary heritage.
3. The best survey of this research, G. Lindeskog, *Die Jesusfrage im Neuzeitlichen Judentum* (Uppsala, 1938), has now been reprinted with an epilogue on more recent Jewish study of Jesus (Darmstadt, Wissenschaftliche Buchgesellschaft, 1973). See also Pinchas E. Lapide, "Jesus in Israeli Literature," *Christian Century* 87 (1970), 1248–53; Schalom Ben-Chorin, "The Image of Jesus in Modern Judaism," *JES* 11 (1974), 401–30.
4. The following important works may be noted: C. G. Montefiore, *Some Elements of the Religious Teaching of Jesus According to the Synoptic Gospels* (London, Macmillan, 1910) and *Rabbinic Literature and Gospel Teachings* (London, Macmillan, 1930); J. Klausner, *Jesus of Nazareth*, trans. H. Danby (New York, Macmillan, 1925); S. Sandmel, *We Jews and Jesus* (New York, Oxford University Press, 1965); S. Ben-Chorin, *Bruder Jesus* (München, Paul List, 1967); D. Flusser, *Jesus*, trans. R. Walls (New York, Herder and Herder, 1969); G. Vermes, *Jesus the Jew* (New York, Macmillan, 1973); P. E. Lapide, *Der Rabbi von Nazaret* (Trier, Spee, 1974).
5. For surveys of this research, see Halvor Ronning, "Some Jewish Views of Paul," *Judaica* 24 (1968), 82–97; Wolfgang Wiefel, "Paulus in jüdischer Sicht," *Judaica* 31 (1975), 109–15, 151–72; J. Blank, *Paulus und Jesus*, SANT 18 (München, Kosel, 1968), 106–23.

6. For the possibility that Paul is alluded to by R. Eleazar in the Mishna (*Abot* 3.12), see G. Kittel, "Paulus im Talmud" in *Rabbinica*, Arbeiten zur Religionsgeschichte des Urchristentums 1, 3 (Leipzig, 1920). The passage refers to one who "profanes the Hallowed Things and despises the set feasts and puts his fellow to shame publicly and makes void the covenant of Abraham our father, and discloses meanings in the Law which are not according to the *Halakah.*" *The Mishnah*, trans. Herbert Danby (Oxford, University Press, 1933), 451. A further possible reference is found in *b. Šabb.* 30b where a pupil of Gamaliel is said to have exhibited "impudence in matters of learning." Klausner accepts the view that the pupil is Paul. *From Jesus to Paul*, 311.

7. See H. Laible, "Jesus Christ in the Talmud" in G. Dalman, *Jesus Christ in the Talmud, Midrash, Zohar, and the Liturgy of the Synagogue* (Cambridge, 1893; reprinted, New York, Arno, 1973), 1–98; R. Travers Herford, *Christianity in Talmud and Midrash* (London, 1903; reprinted, Clifton, New Jersey, Reference Book Publishers, 1966), summarized in Hastings' *Dictionary of Christ and the Gospels* II, 877–78; cf. also J. Klausner, *Jesus of Nazareth*, 18–47.

8. *Geschichte der Juden von den ältesten Zeiten bis zur Gegenwart*, 11 vols. (Leipzig, 1853–1870). A condensation of this work was published in English in six volumes, *History of the Jews* (Philadelphia, Jewish Publication Society, 1891–95). A section of volume three of the original work, on the subject of Jesus and Christian origins, appeared as a separate monograph in French translation, *Sinai et Golgotha* (Paris, 1867).

9. *Judaism and St. Paul: Two Essays* (London, Max Goschen, 1914; reprinted, New York, Arno, 1973); "Rabbinic Judaism and the Epistles of Paul," *JQR* 13 (1901), 162–217, reprinted in *Judaism and Christianity*, ed. Jacob B. Agus (New York, Arno, 1973).

10. "Saul of Tarsus," *JE* 11 [1905], 79–87; *The Origins of the Synagogue and the Church* (New York, Macmillan, 1929; reprinted, New York, Arno, 1973), 260–70.

11. *From Jesus to Paul*, trans. from Hebrew original of 1939 by W. F. Stinespring (London, Macmillan, 1943; reprinted, Boston, Beacon, 1961).

12. *Two Types of Faith*, trans. N. P. Goldhawk (London, Routledge and Kegan Paul, 1951).

13. "The Faith of Paul," *JJS* 3 (1952), 93–110; the essay appears also in German translation in *Paulus, die Pharisäer und das Neue Testament* (Frankfurt am Main, Ner-Tamid, 1961), 7–37.

14. *The Genius of Paul: A Study in History* (New York, Farrar, Straus & Cudahy, 1958; reprinted with new introduction, New York, Schocken, 1970); "Paul Reconsidered" in S. Sandmel, *Two Living Traditions* (Detroit, Wayne State University Press, 1972), 195–211; "Judaism, Jesus, and Paul: Some Problems of Method in Scholarly Research" in *Vanderbilt Studies in the Humanities*, vol. 1 (Nashville, 1951), 220–48, reprinted in *Two Living Traditions*; see also *A Jewish Understanding of the New Testament* (Cincinnati, Hebrew Union College Press, 1956), reprinted in "augmented edition," New York, KTAV/Anti-Defamation League of B'nai B'rith, 1974, 37–104; and *Judaism and Christian Beginnings* (New York, Oxford University Press, 1978), 308–36.

15. *Paul: The Theology of the Apostle in the Light of Jewish Religious History*, trans. from German original of 1959 by Harold Knight (Philadelphia, Westminster, 1961).

16. *Paulus: Der Völkerapostel in jüdischer Sicht* (München, Paul List, 1970), with annotated bibliography, 223–30.

17. *My Brother Paul* (New York, Harper and Row, 1972).

18. Note should also be taken of D. Flusser, "Paul of Tarsus" in *Encyclopedia Judaica* 13 [1971], cols. 190–92; E. I. Jacob, "Paul" in *The Universal Jewish Encyclopedia* 8 [1939–43], 415–17; and H. J. Schonfield, *The Jew of Tarsus: An Unorthodox Portrait of Paul* (London, MacDonald & Co., 1946).

19. A convenient survey of the History-of-Religions School may be found in W. G. Kümmel, *The New Testament: The History of the Investigation of Its Problems*, trans. S. M. Gilmour and H. C. Kee, from German original of 1970 (Nashville, Abingdon, 1972), 206–25, 245–80.

20. So R. Reitzenstein, *Die hellenistischen Mysterienreligionen* (Leipzig, 1910), 55–56. The quotation is found in Kümmel, *op. cit.*, p. 270.

21. For a thorough survey, see V. P. Furnish, "The Jesus-Paul Debate: From Baur to Bultmann," *BJRL* 47 (1965), 342–81.

22. The debate, however, is hardly at an end. Cf. F. F. Bruce's recent defence of Paul as a faithful interpreter of Jesus in *Paul and Jesus* (Grand Rapids, Baker, 1974).

23. "Rabbinic Judaism and the Epistles of St. Paul," 167, 207.

24. *Aspects of Rabbinic Theology* (New York, Macmillan, 1909; reprinted, New York, Schocken, 1961), 18.

25. *Judaism and St. Paul*, 12, 17.

26. *Prolegomena to the History of Ancient Israel*, trans. of second German edition (Berlin, 1883; reprint, Cleveland, World, 1957), 425. See "Rabbinic Judaism and the Epistles of St. Paul," 167 and *Judaism and St. Paul*, 21. Montefiore allows that Jesus may legitimately be called a pathologist of Judaism.

27. *Judaism and St. Paul*, 18.

28. For a contemporary refutation of the same book, see E. P. Sanders, *Paul and Palestinian Judaism* (Philadelphia, Fortress, 1977).

29. "Rabbinic Judaism and the Epistles of St. Paul," 206.

30. *Judaism and St. Paul*, 58–60.

31. *Ibid.*, 153, cf. 164. Montefiore never undertook a detailed study of how Hellenistic Paul's Judaism actually was. Cf. his avoidance of this question in "Rabbinic Judaism and the Epistles of St. Paul," 174.

32. *Judaism and St. Paul*, 93–101. The quoted words are on p. 94.

33. *Ibid.*, 90. Montefiore shows his acquaintance with critical scholarship at several points. It may also be noted here that in an appendix (pp. 221–240) he has quoted a number of passages from Loisy (on Paul's dependence upon the Mystery Religions) drawn from the *Revue d'histoire et de littérature religieuses*, 3 (1912), 556–67; 573–74; 4 (1913), 477–80; 486.

34. *Ibid.*, 94.

35. "Saul of Tarsus," 79; cf. *Origins*, 261.

36. *Ibid.*, 79, 82.

37. *Ibid.*, 79.

38. *From Jesus to Paul*, 312.

39. *Ibid.*, 354.

40. *Ibid.*, 461. "In place of a dying and rising *god*, such as was common in the various pagan religions of that time, he added to this attenuated Judaism a dying and rising *Messiah*" (449).

41. *Ibid.*, 580–81, 590.

42. *Ibid.*, 443; cf. 591.

43. *Ibid.*, 466. He describes this as "a deep conviction" arrived at through "intensive research over many years," and refers to personal letters from G. F. Moore in agreement with this view. Cf. Klausner's statement that Paul "was firmly rooted in Pharisaic Judaism in spite of himself" (606).

44. *Ibid.*, 465.

45. Buber poignantly writes "From my youth onwards I have found in Jesus my great brother." *Two Types of Faith*, 12.

46. *Ibid.*, 7–11; 170–74.

47. *Ibid.*, 44, 48f.

48. *Ibid.*, 172.

49. *Ibid.*, 14.

50. *Ibid.*, 83.

51. *Ibid.*, 100. Buber stresses that the resurrection of an individual person "does not belong to the realm of ideas of the Jewish world" (128).

52. *Ibid.*, 109.

53. *Ibid.*, 89.

54. *Ibid.*, 148.

55. *Ibid.*, 140. Hellenistic Judaism is characterized by Buber as "an eclecticism from an attenuated Biblical tradition and a not less attenuated Stoic philosophy" (145).

56. *Ibid.*, 162, 149–54. Buber finds this Paulinism outside Christianity, for example in the pessimism of Kafka (162–69).

57. *The Genius of Paul*, xvi.

58. *A Jewish Understanding of the New Testament*, 104. "Paul is a Greek Jew, remote in thought and feeling from Palestinian Jews of his time." *Ibid.*, xxxiii (from the 1974 preface).

59. *The Genius of Paul*, 23.

60. *Ibid.*, 70.

61. *Ibid.*, xvi, 15, 21.

62. *Ibid.*, 15.

63. *Ibid.*, 12–15. Cf. *A Jewish Understanding of the New Testament*, xxxiii.

64. *The Genius of Paul*, 59. So far as religious experience is concerned, "Paul and rabbinic Judaism are poles apart" (60).

65. *Ibid.*, 9.

66. *Ibid.*, 22, 80, 89.

67. *Ibid.*, 84, 92, 97. Cf. *Jewish Understanding*, 51, 99; *Judaism and Christian Beginnings* (New York, Oxford University Press, 1978), 335.

68. *Genius*, 114–16. In Paul's Hellenism there is "a resounding echo of popular philosophy, popular religion, and both the attitudes and the sense of arrival which characterized the Greek mysteries" (114).

69. *Genius*, 97, 113, 116. *Understanding*, 104.

70. In *Two Living Traditions*.

71. *Ibid.*, 210. See also *The First Christian Century in Judaism and Christianity: Certainties and Uncertainties* (New York, Oxford, 1969), 127–28.

72. "The Faith of Paul," 98.

73. *Ibid.*, 101.

74. *Ibid.*

75. *Ibid.*

76. *Ibid.*, 104, 109.

77. "Nor did Paul, by stressing his apostolate to the Gentiles, deviate from the genuine Jewish creed." *Ibid.*, 108.

78. *Paul*, 26. Montefiore's procedure was an attempt "to replace one unknown quantity—the theology of Saul—by another unknown quantity, the theology of the Pharisaic Diaspora" (*ibid.*).

79. Hellenistic Judaism for example possessed a heightened conscious-

ness of a missionary purpose, tended to ethicize Judaism, and viewed the Torah as a pedagogical book for all of humanity. *Paul*, 28–32.

80. *Ibid.*, 36–37.

81. *Ibid.*; 37–40. Paul, it is pointed out, was familiar with the seven hermeneutical rules of Hillel. Further, "as an allegorizing midrashist Paul became great among his contemporary rabbis" (39).

82. *Ibid.*, 37–38.

83. *Ibid.*, 40.

84. *Ibid.*

85. Schoeps describes the problem as "uncommonly difficult to solve" (*ibid.*, 47). He also indicates the need for great caution when he writes of Pauline doctrine that "no sure genealogies . . . can be established" (43).

86. *Ibid.*, 42.

87. *Ibid.*, 47.

88. Cf. his criticism of Klausner for neglecting the eschatological dimension in Paul (*ibid.*, 47f.). See also his criticism of Montefiore, 25f.

89. *Ibid.*, 48. Cf. also the following: "ideas of faith cherished and taught by the Jerusalem church were taken over by the neophyte Paul and are reflected in his letters" (62). In these passages Schoeps takes a deliberate stance against the Tübingen school, otherwise so influential upon Jewish scholars (e.g. Montefiore and Sandmel).

90. *Paulus*, 9.

91. "Theologie in Briefen," 106–81; cf. 39.

92. *Paulus*, 13.

93. *Ibid.*, 168; cf. 174, 179.

94. As an aid to understanding Paul, Ben-Chorin devotes an entire chapter to Gamaliel as "Die Lehrer des Paulus," 189–203.

95. *Ibid.*, 121, 152, 178.

96. *Ibid.*, 43, 48.

97. "Er ist nicht einfach ein hellenistisch assimilierter Jude, sondern er benutzt Elemente des Hellenismus zur Darstellung des Judentums, *seines* Judentums, aber dieses Judentum ist wiederum so hellenistisch durchsetzt, dass es Gedankengänge und Gedankenreihen enthält, die die Jünger Jesu . . . nicht verstehen konnten" (*ibid.*, 56; cf. 48).

98. *Ibid.*, 48, 52.

99. *Ibid.*, 49, 52.

100. *Ibid.*, 52.

101. *Ibid.*, 100.

102. The fundamental difference between the two is that while Paul wanted to be a Jew to the Jew and a Greek to the Greek, Philo tried to be a Greek to the Jew and a Jew to the Greek. *Ibid.*, 198.

103. *Ibid.*, 213.

104. *Ibid.*, 209.

105. See above, n. 4. To be fair to Ben-Chorin, he does refer to "der brüderlichen Gestalt des Juden Paulus" (*ibid.*, 217). But it is significant that he did not entitle his book "Bruder Paulus."

106. Paul derived the training necessary for his mission, his interpretive skills and methodology from the Pharisees (*My Brother Paul*, 141).

107. *Ibid.*, 90, 105, 156.

108. *Ibid.*, 19, 145.

109. *Ibid.*, 19. In a bibliographical note he mentions his conviction that

"contemporary interpretations of Paul must build largely upon the foundations laid by Davies" (in the latter's book *Paul and Rabbinic Judaism* [London, SPCK, 1955²]).

110. *Ibid.*, 6, 114.

111. *Ibid.*, 198. The words expressing the opinion (wrongly attributed to Loewe by Rubenstein) are C. G. Montefiore's in *A Rabbinic Anthology*, eds. C. G. Montefiore and H. Loewe (New York, Schocken, 1974), xiii.

112. *Ibid.*, 127. "Rejection of Pharisaism was not equivalent to rejection of Judaism" (117).

113. *Ibid.*, 129.

114. *Ibid.*, 103.

115. *Ibid.*, 23.

116. *Ibid.*, 121, following Johannes Munck, *Paul and the Salvation of Mankind*. Rubenstein notes the "watchword of much of the thoughtful Jewish New Testament scholarship in modern times"—"Jesus, yes; Paul, never!"—adding that "I have never been able to share that judgment" (114).

117. *Ibid.*, 122–23.

118. *Ibid.*, 20, 138.

119. *Ibid.*, 4–6.

120. *Ibid.*, 21.

121. Sandmel is the most notable exception to this statement. He still regards Paul as a Hellenistic Jew but without alleging that this can account for the genesis of Paul's religion. "Paul Reconsidered," 210.

122. To the scholars discussed above we may add David Flusser, who also identifies Paul's Judaism as Pharisaic in form. "Paul of Tarsus," 190–92.

123. See M. Hengel, *Judaism and Hellenism*, 2 vols., trans. J. Bowden (London, SCM, 1974); W. D. Davies, *Paul and Rabbinic Judaism*, 1–16. For a criticism of this dichotomizing as applied to the study of early Christianity, see H. Marshall, *NTS* 19 (1973), 271–87.

124. In his review of Schoeps' book on Paul in *NTS* 10 (1963–64), 293–304.

125. The title of chapter five in *Paulus*.

126. "The 'Pauline' Emancipation From the Law: A Product of the Pre-Christian Jewish Diaspora," *JQR* 14 (1902), 265–302, reprinted in *Judaism and Christianity*, ed. Jacob B. Agus (New York, Arno, 1973).

127. "The Faith of Paul," 106. (Baeck, it will be recalled, does not deny a degree of Hellenistic influence upon Paul.) See the full discussion of this subject in W. D. Davies, *Torah in the Messianic Age and/or the Age to Come*, SBLMS 7 (Philadelphia, SBL, 1952).

128. Thus on the one hand Schoeps can write: "we have here in Paul's abolition of the Law a purely Jewish problem of saving history, not a Hellenistic one" (*Paul*, 173); but on the other: "Paul succumbed to a characteristic distortion of vision which had its antecedents in the spiritual outlook of Judaic Hellenism" (213), so that "the Christian church has received a completely distorted view of the Jewish law at the hands of a Diaspora Jew" (261–62).

129. He likens Saul the Pharisee to zealous Yeshiva students in modern Jerusalem. *Paulus*, 66.

130. *Ibid.*, 69.

131. See especially W. D. Davies, *Paul and Rabbinic Judaism*; cf. E. P. Sanders, *Paul and Palestinian Judaism*; and more generally H. Ridderbos, *Paul: An Outline of His Theology*, trans. J. R. DeWitt (Grand Rapids, Eerdmans, 1975) and F. F. Bruce, *Paul: Apostle of the Free Spirit*.

132. "If we wish to understand what happened at this point in the life of the apostle, and what were its consequences, then we must accept fully the real objectivity of the encounter as it is testified in the letters and in Acts." Schoeps, *Paul*, 55.

133. "Was Paulus formte, lag vor Damaskus, was ihn unformte, erfolgte in Damaskus, in der Vision vor den Toren der Stadt." Ben-Chorin, *Paulus*, 178–79.

134. Ben-Chorin refers to a refutation of this idea in a paper read by a Jewish physician (Dr. Arthur Stern) at a neurology congress in Jerusalem in 1955 entitled "Zum Problem der Epilepsie des Paulus," later published in "Psychiatria et Neurologia," 133.5 (Basel, 1957).

135. Rubenstein explains Paul's Damascus experience in Freudian terminology as the result of Paul's yearning to regain the infant's feeling of omnipotence. *My Brother Paul*, 50.

136. *Paulus*, 37.

137. "Saul of Tarsus," 86.

138. Sometimes this appreciation can be very individualistic. Thus, for example, Montefiore admires Paul to the extent that Paul supports the perspective of Liberal Judaism; Ben-Chorin as a Diaspora Jew who has lived in Jerusalem identifies with Paul in his attempt to find a bridge between two worlds of existence; Rubenstein, on the other hand, finds psychological empathy with Paul as one who opts for the authority of his own experience over against the tradition in which he stands.

139. Of the items mentioned here, admittedly this has the weakest support from Jewish scholars. But despite dissenters, support is found in Klausner (limited), Schoeps and Rubenstein.

Part Two:

LITERARY AND EXEGETICAL STUDIES
WITHIN THE PAULINE CORPUS

Chapter 11

COLOSSIANS 1:15-20:
An Early Christian Hymn Celebrating the Lordship of Christ

PAUL BEASLEY-MURRAY

ONE OF PROFESSOR BRUCE'S EARLY WORKS was a commentary on Paul's Epistle to the Colossians.[1] It seems therefore appropriate that in this Festschrift one of his students should take a closer look at the jewel which it enshrines, Colossians 1:15–20, the hymn to the cosmic Christ. Here we find what has been described as "the summit" of Pauline Christology.[2] Here the implications of Christ's lordship over the world are spelled out in an unparalleled way.

I. The Form of the Hymn

By general consent we are here dealing with an early Christian hymn. Thus apart from the use of the introductory pronoun ὅς—a "tell-tale mark of liturgica"[3]—the hymnic character of this passage is evidenced above all by the striking parallelisms both of ideas and of form. It is this *parallelismus membrorum* which forces us to the conclusion that these lines resulted from no spontaneous lyrical outburst: rather they betray "the hand of an exacting composer."[4]

As regards the precise form of the hymn, many diverse analyses have been made. For our own part we believe that we have here a hymn composed of two basic strophes celebrating Christ as lord of creation (verses 15, 16) and redemption (verses 18b–20) respectively. These two strophes are held together by an intermediary verse (verses 17–18a) which binds together the twin ideas of creation and redemption. The central pivot of the hymn is verse 17b: both in the sphere of creation and in the sphere of redemption all things find their unity in Christ.

Into this hymn a number of insertions have been made—all of which have the Colossian syncretists in mind, all of which disturb the basic *parallelismus membrorum:* thus the expansion of "all things" in verses 16a–c and 20c emphasizes the universality of Christ's reign with particular reference to the powers; verse 18c likewise stresses Christ's lordship over all things (cf. Col. 2:10, 15); while verse 20b emphasises that the Cross was a necessary stage in Christ's reconciling work (cf. Col. 1:22; 2:14).

(A) ὅς ἐστιν εἰκὼν τοῦ θεοῦ τοῦ ἀοράτου
     πρωτότοκος πάσης κτίσεως
     ὅτι ἐν αὐτῷ ἐκτίσθη τὰ πάντα
     τὰ πάντα δι' αὐτοῦ καὶ εἰς αὐτὸν ἔκτισται

(B) καὶ αὐτός ἐστιν πρὸ πάντων
     καὶ τὰ πάντα ἐν αὐτῷ συνέστηκεν
     καὶ αὐτός ἐστιν ἡ κεφαλὴ τοῦ σώματος τῆς ἐκκλησίας

(C) ὅς ἐστιν ἀρχή
     πρωτότοκος ἐκ τῶν νεκρῶν
     ὅτι ἐν αὐτῷ εὐδόκησεν πᾶν τὸ πλήρωμα κατοικῆσαι
     καὶ δι' αὐτοῦ ἀποκαταλλάξαι τὰ πάντα εἰς αὐτόν.

II. An Exegesis of the Hymn

(A) Strophe 1: Lord of Creation

verse 15a: ὅς ἐστιν εἰκὼν τοῦ θεοῦ τοῦ ἀοράτου

Traditionally this opening line has been understood as part of Paul's Wisdom Christology, and attention has been drawn to such passages as Wis. 7:26 and Philo, *Leg. All.* i.43 where the Divine Wisdom is thus predicated. The phrase is then interpreted in terms of "representation" and "manifestation": as the image of the invisible God, Christ reveals God to men (cf. 2 Cor. 4:4).

However, while we need not deny this allusion to Wisdom, another equally possible allusion is to Gen. 1:26f. If this is so, then the hymn begins with an assertion of the lordship of Christ. For in Gen. 1:26, 28 Adam is created in God's image and given dominion over the rest of creation. There the idea of dominion cannot well be separated from "image": dominion is not only the consequence of being in the image of God, it may also be termed a constitutive part of the image. Thus it is not without significance that in Jewish speculation the glorification of Adam is frequently expressed in terms of kingship: cf. *Jub.* 2:14; *2 Enoch* 30:12; *2 Esdr.* 6:53ff.; *Apoc. Mos.* 24:4. Further, in early Christian thought Christ is sometimes described both in Adamic and lordship terms (cf. 1 Cor. 15:21ff. and Phil. 2:6–11), as if the two concepts are closely related. We seem to have a similar situation here in Col. 1:15–20. As the image of the invisible God, Christ has dominion over the whole creation.

verse 15b: πρωτότοκος πάσης κτίσεως

Taken quite literally, and interpreted without reference to the context, the line under review could quite possibly be given the Arian sense of Christ's being included amongst the created things. But such an interpretation is inconsistent with verse 16, where we find not τὰ ἄλλα or τὰ λοίπα but τὰ πάντα ἐκτίσθη. Christ is not to be included amongst the created things. πάσης κτίσεως is not a partitive genitive, but should rather be understood in a comparative sense: as first-born Christ is before all things (cf. John 1:15, 30 and 15:18).

But is the hymn first and foremost concerned with Christ's temporal priority? We believe not. The author of the hymn is more concerned to assert the lordship of Christ over all things. Christ's pre-existence is primarily a symbol of his pre-eminence. It was in this sense, for instance, that pre-existence was ascribed to the law.[5] It is very likely that the author of the hymn in describing Jesus as the "first-born" was mindful of the term's Jewish associations with the birthright and with the double share of the inheritance: cf. Gen. 25:29–34; 27; Deut. 21:17. It may not be without significance that, although Manasseh was the eldest, Jacob gave the blessing of the first-born to Ephraim because he was later said to be the "greater" (Gen. 48:19). If this line of thought is pursued, then we may conclude that Christ as the "first-born of all creation" is the one who has authority over all creation. The term "first-born" is certainly used in this sense in Ps. 89:27: "I will make him the first-born, the highest of the kings of the earth". Similarly in Heb. 1:6ff. the angels worship the "first-born".

It has been suggested that πρωτότοκος has here lost all sense of temporal association.[6] Certainly this is true in Exod. 4:22 and the variant reading in Sir. 36:11, where Israel is termed God's "first-born" without any suggestion that other nations were also God's sons. Likewise in 2 Esdr. 6:58 Israel is not only called God's "first-born", but also his "only one". In fact from *Pss. Sol.* 18:4 it would appear that πρωτότοκος and μονογενής could be used synonymously. However, we are not convinced that here in the Colossian hymn all reference to time has been eliminated. The corresponding phrase in the second main strophe (πρωτότοκος ἐκ τῶν νεκρῶν) makes it probable that interpretations both of temporal priority and of lordship should be combined, with the stress being laid on the latter: he is "Sovereign Lord over all creation by virtue of primogeniture".[7]

verse 16a: ὅτι ἐν αὐτῷ ἐκτίσθη τὰ πάντα

Christ's lordship is not founded simply on the fact of his being the "first-born". According to the hymn his lordship is above all associated with his involvement in creation. He is the image of the invisible God, the first-born of all creation, "for ἐν αὐτῷ all things were created".

What precisely does the hymn mean by saying that all things were created ἐν αὐτῷ? Not infrequently it is suggested that this phrase be understood in a local sense corresponding to Philo's view of the logos in creation: i.e. Christ is the τόπος where the eternal ideas, the νοητὸς κόσμος, had their abode.[8]

But the following objections must be raised to this Philonic interpretation. Firstly, this exegesis is inconsistent with the verb ἐκτίσθη. As A. S. Peake justly remarked, "If the Son was from eternity the archetype of the universe, then ἐκτίσθη ἐν αὐτῷ ought not to have been used, both because the aorist points to a definite time and because the idea of creation is in itself inapplicable".[9] Secondly, at the most only the κόσμος νοητός, i.e. the world of ideas, not τὰ πάντα ... τὰ ὁρατά was created. Thirdly, if Christ is here viewed as the *idea omnium rerum*, then this should have been expressed by ἐξ αὐτοῦ instead of by ἐν αὐτῷ. Lastly, in contrast to the Divine Wisdom of the LXX, the Philonic Logos is less truly personal—this is particularly so as regards creation (cf. *Som.* ii. 45; *Cher.* 127). But the Christ of the Colossian hymn is more than a 'tool' of God the Father: he is the lord of creation!

It is more probable that we should see in Col. 1:16a a local sense, which can be best compared with the 'in Christ' formula referring to the new creation. Thus F. F. Bruce makes a comparison with Eph. 1:4: "God's creation, like his election, takes place 'in Christ' and not apart from him".[10] This view is especially attractive if in verse 20 we see Christ as in some sense restoring the universe to its primeval state in his rôle of Second Adam.

verse 16b–c: (τὰ πάντα) ἐν τοῖς οὐρανοῖς καὶ ἐπὶ τῆς γῆς,
τὰ ὁρατὰ καὶ τὰ ἀόρατα,
εἴτε θρόνοι εἴτε κυριότητες
εἴτε ἀρχαὶ εἴτε ἐξουσίαι·

As we have already shown in our form analysis of the hymn, these lines did not originally belong to the hymn. They were probably added to make explicit the fact that "all things" includes the angelic powers. In view of the Colossian tendency to indulge in angel-worship (cf. 2:18), this affirmation was far from irrelevant. For if angelic beings owe their origin to Christ, then surely it was their Creator and not the created to whom worship is due.

verse 16d: τὰ πάντα δι᾽ αὐτοῦ καὶ εἰς αὐτὸν ἔκτισται

This final line of the first strophe carries the thought of Christ's lordship over creation a stage further. For not only is he the mediator of God's work in creation (cf. 1 Cor. 8:6; also John 1:3; Heb. 1:2; 2:10), but he is also the goal of creation. All things were created to find their focal point in him (cf. Eph. 1:10). This necessarily implies an acceptance of his lordship over all.

A parallel is occasionally drawn with TB Sanhedrin 98b, which records the opinion of R. Yochanan (died AD 279) that the world was created with a view to the Messiah. However, in the same passage this claim is also made for others: e.g. Rab (died 247) said: "The world was created only for David". Samuel (died 254) said, "for Moses". It would seem from this that these sayings did not carry the same deep content as εἰς αὐτόν did for the author of the Colossian hymn: "they may mean no more than that David, Moses or the Messiah is the turning point in human history".[11] But here in Col. 1:16 Christ forms the creation's objective.

This affirmation of Christ as the goal of all things (cf. Rev. 22:13) is, with the possible exception of Eph. 1:10, unique in Paul. Thus in Rom. 11:36 and 1 Cor. 8:6 God the Father is the goal of all things (cf. also Heb. 2:10). However, it is quite possible that ἔκτισται is a reverential passive, implying that it was by God the Father that Christ was appointed the "goal". In this way no necessary contradiction is involved with Pauline thought: cf. 1 Cor. 15:26ff.

Before we leave this line, a word should be said concerning the tense of the verb. It will be seen that the perfect tense, ἔκτισται, is used, as opposed to the aorist form of verse 16a, ἐκτίσθη. Rather than seeing here a reference to a creatio continua, we prefer to see the perfect tense implying that the creation has a permanent and indissoluble relationship to Christ, a relationship which ever seeks to find fulfilment in him.

(B) Intermediary Verse: Lord of Creation and Redemption

verse 17a: καὶ αὐτός ἐστιν πρὸ πάντων

The first line of this intermediary verse begins with the assertion that "Christ is before all things". As with the phrase πρωτότοκος πάσης κτίσεως, this is no mere assertion of temporal priority—supremacy is above all involved. As Reicke rightly says, "the pre-existence of Christ here is not a speculative theologoumenon, but a dynamic expression of the unrestricted world dominion of Him to whom the Church is subject in its world mission".[12] The emphasis on the lordship of Christ explains the present tense (ἐστίν), for otherwise an imperfect might have been expected: cf. John 1:1f. and 1 John 1:2. As the one before all things, Christ is the Lord over all things.

verse 17b: καὶ τὰ πάντα ἐν αὐτῷ συνέστηκεν

Here the hymn borrows from popular philosophy and interprets Christ's role in terms of the *anima mundi*. For although the verb συνίστημι is never found used in a cosmic sense in the LXX (but cf. Sir. 43:26), it was often used by the Stoics to describe the "binding together" of the universe.[13] Through this borrowing the author of the hymn is able to describe Christ as "the innermost, animating, cohesive principle of power" in the universe.[14]

However, this line says more than that Christ sustains the life of the universe. The prefix σύν- must be given its full force: Christ gives unity to the cosmos and so exercises his lordship. We take ἐν to be instrumental: all things are given unity by him. He is lord of creation.

But even more is involved. We like the suggestion that συνέστηκεν implies not only the holding together but also the putting together of sundered parts.[15] If this is so, we also have in this "pivotal" line a reference to Christ's work of reconciling and restoring the universe. The suitability of this interpretation is supported by our analysis of the hymn, whereby this line refers not just to Christ's work in creation but also to his work in redemption. The sovereign power which holds together the universe is active both in creation and redemption!

verse 18a: καὶ αὐτός ἐστιν ἡ κεφαλὴ τοῦ σώματος τῆς ἐκκλησίας

Balancing the assertion of the first line of this verse, comes the last line: Christ is not only lord of creation, he is also head of his church.

In view of the fact that the head's sphere of influence is the body, it is tempting to consider the nature of this headship in physiological terms, whereby the body's head is "the seat of the brain which controls and unifies the organism".[16] However, although the directional function of the brain had been advocated as long ago as the fifth century BC by Alcmaeon of Croton, as indeed later by Hippocrates, and had even been accepted by Plato, it would appear that this understanding of the head had been obscured by Aristotle and the Stoics, for whom the heart was the seat of intelligence. The same was true of Hebrew thinking.[17] We must therefore conclude that, according to popular first-century psychology—both Greek and Hebrew—a man reasoned and purposed not with his head but with his heart. Christ's headship over the church cannot be considered in physiological terms!

A more fruitful approach is to interpret κεφαλή in terms of its LXX usage. There we find that κεφαλή is commonly used to translate ראש in the sense of "chief", "leader": e.g. Judg. 10:18; 11:8, 9, 11; 2 Sam. 22:44; Ps. 17 (18):43; Isa. 7:8f. In none of these examples is ראש linked with the picture of a body. Thus, as distinct from secular Greek which normally used ἄρχων, the idea of leadership could be expressed in the LXX by the term κεφαλή.

S. Bedale has drawn attention to the possibility that κεφαλή may bear the sense of "beginning", "origin".[18] Support for this is found from the fact that the Hebrew ראש, which, as we have just seen, frequently has the meaning of "chief among" or "head over men", is connected, not with the controlling influence of the head over the limbs, but with the idea of priority: e.g. in Exod. 6:14; Num. 7:2; Josh. 22:14; 1 Chr. 5:24; 7:7, 9, ראש is used of the head of a family. Indeed in 1 Chr. 12:9 ראש is explicitly combined with the idea of first in a series. Further, in our comments on verse 18b we shall see that ראש in the sense of "chief" or "ruler" is sometimes rendered by ἀρχή. The connection between κεφαλή and the sense of "beginning", "origin", seems well established, even though it is true that in none of the examples given is κεφαλή used to translate ראש—ἀρχηγοί and ἄρχοντες are used instead.

If κεφαλή is used in the sense proposed by Bedale, we must then translate: Christ is the "beginning" of the church. But we would stress that this interpretation of Christ as the "beginning" need not displace, but rather supplements, the idea of lordship. As the "beginning" of the church—as its source of life, in effect—Christ is lord of the church.

(C) Strophe 2: Lord of Redemption

verse 18b: ὅς ἐστιν ἀρχή

Christ is the "beginning". The fact that this line is to be found in the second main strophe, which deals with Christ's role in redemption, indicates that ἀρχή refers to Christ's relationship with the church rather than with the world in general (cf. Rev. 3:14). In other words, the hymn affirms Christ as the beginning of the new order. He it is who initiates the redemptive process: cf. 1 Cor. 15:20, 23; Acts 3:15; 5:31; 26:23.

But the hymn does more than assert Christ's temporal priority within the new creation. The LXX usage of the term ἀρχή makes it probable that the idea of supremacy is also involved: cf. Gen. 40:13, 20; 1 Chr. 26:10. This double meaning of ἀρχή can partly be traced back to the fact that its Hebrew equivalent ראשית stems from the same root as that of ראש, which apart from its purely physical meaning could also refer to lordship. In places ἀρχή is even used to translate רֹאשׁ: e.g. Gen. 2:10; 40:13, 20; Exod. 6:25; 12:2; Num. 1:2; 4:22; 26:2; Judg. 7:16, 19f. Of particular interest is the fact that ἀρχή, when translating רֹאשׁ, can lose all temporal meaning: e.g. Ps. 118 (119):160 and Hos. 1:2 (2:2). From this we conclude that this line describes Christ as the one who initiates a process of which he is the lord.

verse 18b: πρωτότοκος ἐκ τῶν νεκρῶν

Christ is not only the "first-born of all creation", he is also the "first-born from the dead". As in the first instance of πρωτότοκος, so also here, the affirmation of Christ's temporal priority involves the idea of sovereignty. Christ is lord by virtue of his resurrection from the dead (cf. Rom. 1:4; 14:9).

verse 18c: ἵνα γένηται ἐν πᾶσιν αὐτὸς πρωτεύων

On our analysis of the hymn Paul develops the thought of the previous line by inserting this particular line (verse 18c). Christ rose as the first-born from the dead in order that he—and he alone (αὐτός)—might be supreme.

verse 19: ὅτι ἐν αὐτῷ εὐδόκησεν πᾶν τὸ πλήρωμα κατοικῆσαι

Christ's superiority in the new creation is founded upon the fact that "in him all the fulness (πλήρωμα) came to dwell". The question at once arises as to what the hymn meant by the term πλήρωμα. A variety of possibilities has been postulated.

It has often been thought that the author of the hymn is here picking up and reinterpreting a technical word used by the Colossian syncretists. However, it is quite conceivable that instead of the author's borrowing from the Colossian syncretists, the later heretics, who did come to use πλήρωμα as a *terminus technicus*, borrowed it from Paul. Indeed, the later Gnostic use of this term was different in two important respects from the use under review: firstly, for the Gnostics, the "pleroma" did not include God the Father, but rather may be said to have stood over against him (Hippolytus, *A Refutation of All Heresies* VI. 19.5f.); secondly, the Gnostic Redeemer left the "pleroma" at his descent and only returned to it on his ascent (Irenaeus, *Against the Heresies* III.11.1). This being so, we are not at all convinced that the key to πλήρωμα is to be found in some incipient Gnostic heresy.

Another school of thought would have us see here a technical Stoic term. On this view, πλήρωμα refers to the cosmos, which according to the Stoic way of thinking was "filled with God".[19] If this were the case, then the hymn affirms that "the cosmos in its totality was pleased to dwell in Christ". But apart from the difficulty of accommodating this line of thinking with Col. 2:9, where πλήρωμα again appears, there is an even more basic objection: nowhere is πλήρωμα used by the Stoics in a cosmic sense! The embarrassment of the proponents of this Stoic interpretation is well illustrated by Dupont, who cites a usage of πλήρωμα by Proclus, a fifth-century (AD) writer, only to admit that even there πλήρωμα is not found used in a cosmological sense.[20] πλήρωμα in a cosmic sense is also missing from Philo. It is found used in a cosmic sense in the *Corpus Hermeticum* (VI.4; IX.7; XII.15; XVI.3), but is never used as a *terminus technicus*.[21] We conclude that, although the thought of the universe as "filled" by God may be Stoic, πλήρωμα never became a technical term to express this thought. It is thus highly unlikely that either Paul or the original author of the Colossian hymn understood this line as signifying the inclusion of the cosmos in Christ.

In our opinion too much attention has been placed on the actual term πλήρωμα to the detriment of the line as a whole. If notice is taken of the terminology of the line as a whole, then it becomes evident that Christ is portrayed as fulfilling the role assigned to the Temple in the Old Testament. Thus in Ps. 67 (68):17 LXX we read: εὐδόκησεν ὁ θεὸς κατοικεῖν ἐν αὐτῷ (i.e. Mount Zion). The parallel is more than a matter of vocabulary. In Ps. 67 the Jerusalem Temple is the dwelling place of God: but in Hellenistic Jewish thinking the Logos was conceived of as the true temple of God (Philo, *Spec. Leg.* i.66f.; *Som.* i.62–75). The hymn develops this insofar as God chooses to dwell in Christ. πλήρωμα refers to the divine fulness—and as we shall show below, it refers in particular to the divine "fulness of power".

The question arises as to when this divine fulness came to dwell in Christ. For as the aorist εὐδόκησεν indicates, this fulness was bestowed at a particular moment in time.

Needless to say, if we accept that there was a time when Christ did not possess all the divine "fulness", this does not mean that there was a time when Christ was not fully divine. πλήρωμα should here be taken in a functional rather than in an ontological sense. As Dodd aptly puts it, the divine πλήρωμα is "God himself regarded in his attributes rather than in his personal identity".[22] This functional sense makes it also easier to conceive of an increase in the divine πλήρωμα, an increase indicated by the stress on the totality of the divine fulness (πᾶν τὸ πλήρωμα) dwelling in Christ.

What then are the possibilities as regards the time when the divine fulness came to dwell in Christ? There seem to us to be basically two. On the one hand verse 19 can be taken as an incarnational-soteriological statement. In which case we may paraphrase: "the fulness of the essence of the God of love" came to dwell in Christ. In favour of this interpretation is verse 20, with its emphasis on the Cross. But on our form-analysis the reference to the Cross is a later insertion! In view of the dependence of verse 19 (ὅτι) on verse 18, where the resurrection is to the fore, we prefer to adopt the second possibility, which takes verse 19 as referring—at least originally—to Christ's elevation at the right hand of God. The moment of resurrection-ascension is the moment when the totality of the divine fulness finds its dwelling place in Christ. In other words πᾶν τὸ πλήρωμα is a "lordship" term. For the time when "God in all the fulness of his power" chose to dwell in Christ was the time when he was given "the name above every name" (Phil. 2:5-11), when he became Son of God "in power" (Rom. 1:4).

verse 20a: καὶ δι' αὐτοῦ ἀποκαταλλάξαι τὰ πάντα εἰς αὐτόν

This last line of the original hymn works out the consequences of the divine "filling with power". Unfortunately these consequences are not as clear as we would like, for difficulties have been caused by the almost inevitable mention of τὰ πάντα.

The great difficulty concerns the hymn's apparent universalism. At first sight verse 20 appears to envisage the reconciliation of all things, men and powers alike—for as the later addition makes quite clear, τὰ πάντα includes both things on earth and things in heaven. But such an interpretation runs counter to the teaching of Paul in Colossians (cf. 2:15)—let alone in any other of his letters. One way out of this difficulty is to assume that this idea of the reconciliation of all things was an idea peculiar to the author of the hymn, not shared by Paul. But if this were so, it might well be asked why Paul expanded the reference to "all things" to include "things in heaven" as well as "things on earth". Further, it is a moot point whether Paul would have quoted something with which he basically disagreed. Surely another solution to the problem must be found.

Not infrequently scholars appear to have given ἀποκαταλλάξαι two senses: on the one hand, the powers are said to be "defeated" (or "pacified"), while mankind is saved and not overcome.[23] However, there is nothing in the word itself nor in the immediate context which can justify this dual interpretation.

An attractive suggestion is that in all the furore concerning the use of τὰ πάντα we have lost sight of the author's original stress on δι' αὐτοῦ.[24] In other words, it is being suggested that the author seeks to emphasize—perhaps over against the Colossian syncretists—that every act of reconciliation has proceeded through Christ and through him alone. But such an interpretation, which really wishes to assert that the redemption of man is primary, runs contrary to the spirit of the hymn, in which τὰ πάντα nowhere else receives such a limitation (cf. the parallel line in verse 16). Furthermore, in the original pre-Pauline hymn, the number of occurrences of forms of πάντα (seven times) is only two less than those of forms of αὐτός (nine times).

In our opinion the solution to the problem lies not in the limitation of τὰ πάντα, but in an awareness of the particular verb used. The prepositional prefix ἀπο- should be given its full due and be seen to be pointing to a "restoration of a good relation that has been lost".[25] We may fittingly compare Acts 3:21 where the preposition ἀπό plays a similar role: ἀποκατάστασις πάντων refers to the re-establishing of all things. We believe that the preposition ἀνά in Eph. 1:10 bears a similar force: the creation *again* comes under the headship of Christ. If these parallels be correct, then here in verse 20 Christ is portrayed as the Second Adam, whose salvific acts involve not only mankind but also the whole creation.

> verse 20 b–c: εἰρηνοποιήσας διὰ τοῦ αἵματος τοῦ σταυροῦ αὐτοῦ,
> δι᾽ αὐτοῦ εἴτε τὰ ἐπὶ τῆς γῆς εἴτε τὰ ἐν τοῖς οὐρανοῖς.

These lines do not call for comment. We have already stated our opinion that they are a later Pauline addition (cf. Phil. 2:9).

(D) Christ the Cosmic Lord

Jesus Christ is Lord—Lord over all. This is the theme of the Colossian hymn.

As the image of the invisible God, he has dominion over the whole creation. As the first-born he is sovereign lord over all creation. All things owe their origin to him. All things find their focal point in him. He is lord of all!

He is lord of his church—for he has initiated the redemptive process, he is the first-born from the dead. The fulness of the divine power became his at the moment of resurrection. Through him the whole universe will be restored.

These affirmations regarding his lordship over the world and his lordship over the church are bound together by the intermediary verse. His sovereign power holds the whole universe together in unity. Jesus Christ is Lord!

(E) An Extended Note on Colossians 1:18a

In our treatment of Col. 1:18a we assumed that the body of which Christ is the head is the church. This indeed is mentioned explicitly to be the case, and in our analysis of the hymn we saw no reason to believe *Contra Lohse* that the reference to the church (τῆς ἐκκλησίας) is a later Pauline addition. However, it is a fact that in much modern treatment of the hymn it is almost an unquestioned item of dogma that originally Col. 1:18a referred to Christ as the cosmic head of the world body.[26] This being so, we feel it incumbent to go into some detail in our treatment of this assumption. Hence this extended note.

Frequently it is asserted that the alleged disorder of the present structure of the hymn points to τῆς ἐκκλησίας being a later addition. But, in the form analysis of the hymn, we have seen that this is not necessarily the case. Indeed, on our analysis a reference to the church is essential if the *parallelismus membrorum* is to be preserved.

Of more interest to us at this point is the argument that on *a priori* grounds a reference to a world body here is very possible. E. Schweizer wrote: "If we remember how widely spread the idea of the world as a body permeated and held together by a divine spirit, was in Hellenistic times, we understand that it was almost inevitable that Hellenistic men would interpret Paul's concept of the body of Christ in this way".[27] But is this in fact so? It seems to us that this fundamental assumption may well be questioned. Thus Percy points out that "the existence of the conception of the universe as 'Macroanthropos' does not necessarily mean that σῶμα in itself was a common expression for the universe".[28] For while it is true that the word σῶμα is used of the universe, in practically every case it occurs in an extended allegory: e.g. Plato, *Timaeus* 32; *Philebus* 29–30; Philo, *Fug.* 108–113; *Som.* i.144. Nowhere is σῶμα—in the sense of world body—used in such an abrupt manner as is alleged to be the case in Col. 1:18a.

Another important fact, frequently overlooked, is that the standard contrast was always between the cosmic body and the divine soul (e.g. Plato, *Timaeus* 34–36; *Philebus* 30; *Zeus Hymn to Cleanthes*, fragment 537; Alexander Aphrodisiensis, *De Mixtione* 12.609) or between the cosmic body and the divine reason (e.g. Xenophon, *Memorabilia Socratis* I.4; IX.14; Aristotle, *De Anima* I.5), not between the head and the body. Thus in the *Timaeus*, although Plato allots supremacy to the head in men, he explicitly rejects an anthropomorphic body for the universe (33B–34B). In men the perfect controlling circles are in the head, but in the universe, which has no organs, they are represented by the (supposed) rotation of the universe around the centre of the earth. Reason is fused through all, and is not concentrated in one particular spot.[29]

What is even more relevant is that God is nowhere expressly termed "head" of the cosmic body—at least, this is not the case in the evidence so far brought forward to support such a view. For instance, Schweizer's only "secular" parallel is the Orphic fragment 168, whose second line runs:

Ζεὺς κεφαλή, Ζεὺς μέσσα, Διὸς δι᾽ ἐκ πάντα τέτυκται[30]

However, it is far from clear that κεφαλή should here be taken in the sense of "head". Thus the variant reading, ἀρχή, suggests that κεφαλή should be taken in the sense of "source" or "origin". Further, such a line appears to have been a common formula for expressing the identity of God with the whole cosmos.[31] That is to say, even if κεφαλή be taken here to mean "head", the "head" in this context is not contrasted with the body: the emphasis is upon the fact that together the whole cosmic body is God. This is borne out by the rest of the Orphic fragments: e.g.

ἐν δὲ δέμας βασίλειον ἐν ᾧ τάδε πάντα κυκλεῖται
πάντα γὰρ ἐν Ζηνὸς μεγάλῳ τάδε σώματα κεῖται

This surely has little in common with the point of view of the Colossian hymn, where the creation stands over against God.

Schweizer's two parallels from Philo (Qu.Ex. ii.17 and Som. i.144) likewise fail to convince that God could be termed the cosmic head. It would no doubt be otherwise if the relevant section in Qu.Ex. ii.17 were not included in the section bracketed by R. Marcus in the Loeb edition as a Christian revision. Although opinion is divided as to where this Christian revision begins, it seems to us that the whole passage bracketed by Marcus represents a real diversion from the point being discussed by Philo: for previous to this, the High Priest's hyacinthine stole has been the subject of discussion. Indeed, this section runs counter to the trend of Philo's thought as a whole: for Philo the parts of the High Priest's robe normally represent the universe rather than the members of his body (e.g. Mos. ii.109–135; Spec. Leg. i.84–97; Qu.Ex. ii.107–124). For Philo the Logos is not the head but rather the immanent soul of the cosmos (cf. Fug. 110).

Yet even if this passage in Qu.Ex. ii were to be regarded as genuine—a supposition we consider most unlikely—we would not necessarily be forced to agree with the general interpretation of Schweizer. For as Dupont remarks: "Philo has just interpreted allegorically the breastplate which the High Priest carried in the exercises of his duties: it signified the heavenly spaces; but if the breast represented the heavens, what meaning would the head have? The word head is thus imposed by the context".[32] In other words, we can draw no general conclusions from this passage.

Unfortunately the only other passage upon which Schweizer can draw is that found in Som. i.144: ὥστε βάσιν μὲν καὶ ῥίζαν ἀῆρος εἶναι γῆν, κεφαλὴν δὲ οὐρανῶν. But even here the notion of control or rule is, despite Schweizer's protestations, not at all evident. Nor do we find any explicit reference to "the body" as such.

The general bankruptcy of this "cosmic body" position is illustrated by Lohse, who has to adduce remote Iranian parallels to support the hypothesis.[33] We conclude therefore that not only is the actual structure of the Colossian hymn against our understanding κεφαλή in a cosmic sense, but also Greek usage does not favour such an interpretation. Any attempt to discern an earlier form of the hymn, in which the cosmos was termed Christ's body, we must with Bruce label as an "unwarranted exercise of the imagination".[34] Both in the pre-Pauline and the Pauline form of the hymn, the church is the body of Christ.

Notes

1. F. F. Bruce, *The Epistle to the Colossians*, New London Commentary (London, 1957).

2. A. Feuillet, *La Christ Sagesse de Dieu d'après les Epîtres Pauliniennes*, Études Bibliques (Paris, 1966), 271.

3. So R. P. Martin, "An Early Christian Hymn (Col. 1:15–20)", *EQ* 36 (1964), 197, following the monumental researches of E. Norden, *Agnostos Theos. Untersuchungen zur Formgeschichte religiöser Rede* (4th ed.; Stuttgart, 1956).

4. A. M. Hunter, *Paul and His Predecessors* (2nd ed.; London, 1961), 125. See further P. Beasley-Murray, *The Lordship of Christ over the World in the Corpus Paulinum* (unpublished dissertation; Manchester, 1970), 74–146.

5. See D. E. H. Whiteley, *The Theology of St. Paul* (Oxford, 1964), 110; and *Kommentar zum Neuen Testament aus Talmud und Midrasch* III, eds. H. L. Strack and P. Billerbeck (Munich, 1926), 256ff.

6. So A. Hockel, *Christus der Erstgeborene. Zur Geschichte der Exegese von Kol 1.15* (Düsseldorf, 1965), 129; N. Kehl, *Der Christushymnus im Kolosserbrief*, SBM 1 (Stuttgart, 1967), 82ff.

7. J. B. Lightfoot, *St. Paul's Epistles to the Colossians and to Philemon* (London, 1876), 147.

8. So, for example, E. Best, *One Body in Christ. A Study in the Relationship of the Church to Christ in the Epistles of the Apostle Paul* (London, 1955), 6f.

9. A. S. Peake, "The Epistle to the Colossians," *The Expositor's Greek Testament*, ed. W. Robertson Nicoll, 3 (London, 1903), 504.

10. Bruce, *Colossians*, 197.

11. So A. W. Wainwright, *The Trinity in the New Testament* (London, 1962), 151.

12. B. Reicke, *TDNT* 6 (1968), 687.

13. Cf. J. von Arnim, *Stoicorum veterum Fragmenta* II (Leipzig, 1921), 136.8; Pseudo-Aristotle, *De Mundo* 6.

14. J. Weiss, *The History of Primitive Christianity* (E.T.; London, 1937), 465. We reject, however, his further remark that "the fixed outlines of the personality had been softened and dissolved and replaced by the idea of a formless impersonal all-penetrating body". For here the author is adapting Stoic terminology to his Christology rather than vice-versa.

15. C. K. Barrett, *From First Adam to Last. A Study in Pauline Theology* (London, 1962), 86 n. 4.

16. So J. A. Robinson, *St. Paul's Epistle to the Ephesians* (2nd ed.; London, 1909), 103.

17. See W. K. C. Guthrie, *History of Greek Philosophy* I (Cambridge, 1962), 348; S. Tromp, "Caput influit sensum et motum", *Greg* 39 (1958), 353–366; Plato, *Timaeus* 44D; 69F; Aristotle, *De Partibus Animalium* 2.10; S. Bedale, "The Meaning of κεφαλή in the Pauline Epistles", *JTS* n.s. 5 (1954), 212.

18. Bedale, *JTS* n.s. 5 (1954), 212.

19. See J. Dupont, *Gnosis. La Connaissance Religieuse dans les Épîtres de S.Paul* (Paris, 1949), 461ff.

20. Dupont, *Gnosis*, 467 n.2.

21. Certainly it is never used in the sense of "the world in so far as it is 'filled' with life" (*pace* Dupont, *Gnosis*, 454). The impossibility of this is shown by *CH* VI.4: ὁ γὰρ κόσμος πλήρωμα ἐστι τῆς κακίας, ὁ δὲ θεὸς τοῦ ἀγαθοῦ, for on Dupont's argument this would have to mean: "for the cosmos is the cosmos filled by wickedness, but God (is the cosmos) filled by goodness"!

22. C. H. Dodd, "Colossians" in *Abingdon Bible Commentary* (New York/Nashville, 1929), 1254.

23. So, for instance, Bruce, *Colossians*, 210.

24. F. Mussner, *Christus, das All und die Kirche. Studien zur Theologie des Epheserbriefes* (2nd ed.; Trier, 1968), 69.

25. F. W. Beare, *The Epistle to the Colossians, IB* (New York/Nashville, 1955), 172f.

26. See, for instance, E. Lohse, *Die Briefe an die Kolosser und an Philemon*, Kritisch-Exegetischer Kommentar über das Neue Testament (Göttingen, 1968), 93ff.

27. E. Schweizer, *The Church as the Body of Christ* (E.T.; London, 1965), 65.

28. E. Percy, "Zu den Problemen des Kolosser- und Epheserbriefes", *ZNW* 43 (1950–51), 184.

29. See J. B. Skemp, *Theory of Motion in Plato's Later Dialogues* (Cambridge, 1947).

30. E. Schweizer, *TDNT* 7 (1971), 1037. The text of the fragment is to be found in *Orphicorum Fragmenta*, ed. O. Kern (2nd ed.; Berlin, 1963), 201.

31. So Dupont, *Gnosis*, 443 and Kehl, *Christushymnus*, 94f. Cf. also Plato, *Laws* IV.175e.

32. Dupont, *Gnosis*, 443.

33. Lohse, *Kolosser*, 93.

34. F. F. Bruce, "St. Paul in Rome. 3: The Epistle to the Colossians", *BJRL* 48 (1965–66), 280.

Chapter 12

THE PAULINE STYLE AS LEXICAL CHOICE:
ΓΙΝΩΣΚΕΙΝ and Related Verbs

MOISES SILVA

EVERYONE, I SUPPOSE, WHO HAS PURSUED A DEGREE under Professor Bruce remembers hearing, at some point, that biblical scholars would be well advised to spend twenty years studying Greek before venturing into New Testament theology. My twenty years are not up, and I am thus content to offer this modest linguistic contribution in his honour.[1]

Introduction: Purpose, Assumptions and Method

Linguistic stylistics. The attempt to shed some light on Paul's style needs hardly any justification—one would be hard pressed to find a work of biblical scholarship that does not, in one way or another, invoke the concept of style. On the other hand, students of the subject not infrequently become suspicious about particular stylistic treatments or even about the discipline in general.

To begin with, one finds that most descriptions of individual styles are characterized by relatively vague, impressionistic terminology. How much do we really learn, for example, to read that Paul's Greek is clumsy, flowing "straight out of the heart with impetuous bubbling"?[2] For an extreme example, we may consider a certain writer who described Jonathan Swift's style as "hard, round, crystalline."[3] Subjective formulations and intuitive judgments, to be sure, often prove both valid and useful; indeed, we can hardly dispense with them in scientific research. But the intuitions of respectable scholars may lead to opposing conclusions. Might not linguistic science (itself hardly a panacea) provide certain objective checks?

184

Unsatisfactory descriptions, however, account for only part of the problem. Sooner or later one becomes aware that the very *concept* of style is surrounded by considerable ambiguity. The word has become so vague that a certain author decided to use it, he tells us, precisely because it would not bind him to a specific task![4] One is then not altogether surprised to find writers who wish to deny the existence of style itself.[5]

Rather than attempt a new definition, I should like first to make clear what this article does *not* seek to accomplish. Broad rhetorical issues, such as Paul's method of argumentation; aesthetic judgments on the artistic level of the Apostle's writing, its forcefulness, etc.; questions of authorship—all of these lie outside the primary focus of this article (though the data presented here, as we shall see later on, could presumably be used for any of these purposes).

The purpose of *this* contribution is, quite simply, to propose a method for the investigation of linguistic, specifically lexical, patterns with a view to determining their relevance for exegetical decisions. Every biblical exegete—indeed, the interpreter of any type of literature— assumes the existence of linguistic patterns that differentiate one individual writer from other writers (or one group of writers from other groups). He also assumes, whether consciously or not, that he can identify a style when he sees one. The method itself is not at all invalid. On the contrary, we may be sure that a large number of exegetical decisions can only be made on the basis of such an identification.

Thus, for example, a commentator who decides that Gal. 2:4 is an anacolouthon has previously decided, perhaps unwittingly, whether and even in what circumstances Paul may be expected to have expressed himself in such a way. Needless to emphasize, stylistic considerations themselves do not provide the answer to an exegetical question. Still, these considerations play a crucial role in the interpretive process.[6] One wonders how often we allow them to play that role at the subconscious level. If, however, we can develop a method that lets us establish an author's linguistic patterns on a reliable basis and enables us to present the data in a clear and accessible form, we should then be able to make our exegetical decisions with greater confidence and responsibility.

Now linguistic patterns can be detected at all levels of expression. Following Stephen Ullmann,[7] we may distinguish between phonological,[8] lexical and syntactical[9] stylistics; to these we should now add "discourse stylistics."[10] Although the boundaries between these levels are not always clear-cut (our own discussion cannot avoid treating syntax), this article is concerned with the second level, lexical stylistics: it attempts to discover patterns in Paul's vocabulary.

It is necessary, however, to stress the word *patterns* and to make explicit what it implies. Traditionally, descriptions of an author's vocab-

ulary have consisted of inventory lists, and we may well doubt whether
determining quantities of lexical items tells us anything really significant.[11] We should note that a modern phonologist is hardly satisfied to
know how many individual sounds make up the inventory of a particular language; in comparing English and Arabic, for example, he would
make very little progress by simply identifying the sound *b* in both
languages. What he wishes to know is what kind of role that sound
plays within the whole system of phonemes. Indeed, a "structural"
examination reveals that the phoneme *b* in English and the phoneme *b*
in Arabic are very different phenomena. Similar structural considerations must be applied to the vocabulary if we wish to establish lexical
patterns of expression. We may further clarify these assumptions by
explaining the use of the word "choice" in the title of our paper.

Lexical choice.   Modern treatments of style, particularly by writers
with some background in linguistics, make frequent use of the concept
of choice.[12] To be sure, even ancient Greek writers were not ignorant of
the role played by ἐκλογὴ ὀνομάτων in rhetoric. What characterizes recent treatments, however, is the use they have made of certain investigations in the area of communication (or information) theory. According
to Warren Weaver's popularization, *information* is regarded as a measure
of one's freedom of choice when selecting a message; indeed, it is a
measure of uncertainty.[13] If there is no uncertainty whatever—if the
message is totally predictable—there is no choice in the selection of the
message and thus the message carries no information. To be more specific, information is said to vary inversely with probability.

It is not yet perfectly clear, in my judgment, just how far and under
what circumstances we may transfer these results from communication
engineering to the human linguistic system, but there can be no denying
that some fundamental analogies are present. Thus one prominent lin-
guist states bluntly that "the more predictable a unit, the less meaning it
has."[14] We may illustrate quite simply the principle by making reference
to cliches: these are generally considered stylistically weak (they carry
less "information" or "mean" less) precisely because they are frequent
and relatively predictable. On the other hand, unpredictable terms can
be used rather powerfully, as when a reviewer for *Time* magazine once
said of a certain film that its producer "does not merely present truth—
he inflicts it."

The reader will appreciate that although the term "inflict" is common enough, the particular combination (or collocation) in that sentence,
that is with "truth" as its object, is quite unusual, probably unique. We
can therefore understand why an analysis of lexical items, particularly
for purposes of stylistic evaluation, must pay special attention to syntactical combinations or, in "structural" terminology, *syntagmatic relations*.

Now in the course of speaking or writing we are constantly faced with lexical choices, most of which we make without conscious deliberation. For example, we may begin thus: "The man is walking toward the _____." While we must *choose* a word to end the sentence, the choice is greatly restricted by the context: a verb, for instance, will not do.[15] After the various restrictions imposed by the whole situational context are taken into account, the nouns which remain available to fill that slot in the sentence consist of more or less closely related terms, such as "building," "house," etc. These terms, which form semantic fields, are in *opposition* to each other, and we may refer to such oppositions as *paradigmatic relations.*[16]

Paradigmatic relations alert us to the potential for lexical expression in a particular language;[17] they are the expressive resources available to the writer. Syntagmatic relations, on the other hand, play the determinative role, for the potential becomes "actualized" only when words are in fact combined with one another by a specific writer to form sentences.[18] What we intend to do in this article is to take the semantic field of "to know"; we shall inquire into the paradigmatic resources available to Paul and determine the syntagmatic patterns that appear in his writings.

Procedure.   Most studies of specific semantic fields limit their inquiry to a handful of very closely related terms.[19] One should not assume, of course, that all researchers have identical goals; the limitations which they set for themselves may be quite appropriate for certain purposes. Generally speaking, however, a broader sample of the material, particularly one that includes antonyms as well as synonyms, would enhance these investigations.

One can hardly doubt, at any rate, that the particular goals set for this article demand a much more extensive survey of the material than is usual. But how do we go about collecting the data? The tools with which we are familiar prove inadequate for the task. Our various lexica and concordances can of course supplement the work and alleviate some of the problems involved, but in the final analysis only a careful reading and re-reading of the text can alert us to important usages undetected by these reference tools. In particular, the method suggested here requires detailed attention to the context, but by context we mean the whole paragraph where each occurrence is found. Obviously, no concordance in book form could handle so much material; even computer print-outs might prove unmanageable.[20]

Perhaps the most difficult question faced in this process is determining the boundaries of the semantic field. The vocabulary itself has no clear-cut divisions, so that in the very nature of the case *any decision must be arbitrary.* Thus, for instance, we might have quite naturally included δοκεῖν and closely related terms, and such an inclusion would have no doubt proved profitable. However, one has to stop somewhere, and since the semantic range of this verb is contiguous to, rather than overlapping with,[21] the semantic "core" of γινώσκειν, I decided to exclude it. Again, the verb γνωρίζειν (except for the occurrence in Phil. 1:22) has been excluded, since the idea of "to make known" would demand further consideration of a host of other verbs, such as ἀγγέλλειν, διδάσκειν, λέγειν, etc.

Even with these and similar restrictions, some readers may be surprised at what *has* been included. Can we, for example, justify a consideration of ἰδεῖν? Most occurrences of this verb, to be sure, have a purely physical reference and these have not been listed. Occasionally, however, the notion "to perceive" is clearly present and it seemed unwise to exclude that usage.[22] (I should add that it was the parallelism of ἰδόντες with γνόντες in Gal. 2:7, 9 that alerted me to this particular semantic relationship.) The same can be said of ἀκούειν (note Rom. 10:18–19), though the decision in individual cases proved quite difficult. For example, ἰδεῖν and ἀκούειν appear together in Phil. 1:27 and again in verse 30; after some reflection, I decided to include the latter verb in both instances, but the former only in verse 30 (and I do not anticipate unanimous agreement with this decision!). I might also note the special problem of δοκιμάζειν and some related verbs: most occurrences do not approach closely the meaning "to know," but a few of them do (note especially the presence of ἐπιγινώσκειν in 2 Cor. 13:5), and since one could hardly exclude the expression καρδίας ἐραυνᾶν (Rom. 8:27), it seemed reasonable to include the related expressions as well.

Once all promising occurrences have been noted, one must search for significant syntagmatic patterns. Now it is certainly not realistic to attempt a classification of all the syntactical patterns observed; even if that could be done in a manageable form, much of the resulting data would have little, if any, value. Subjective decisions, therefore, enter in inevitably (though not so much, I trust, as to render hopeless the search for "objective checks" mentioned earlier).[23] To note the clearest example: it is quite common to find verbal uses classified on the basis of whether the direct object is human or divine, animate or inanimate, etc. My examination of the material, however, did not make it at all obvious that such a distinction would prove helpful in this particular case: to introduce it would have the effect of cluttering the presentation. I have therefore brought all examples of verb + object together, while at the same time noting one or two interesting subpatterns.

Two notations have been used to accompany the references, an asterisk and a question mark, both of which advise the reader to examine the passage so marked. The asterisk calls attention to the fact that the context—including one whole verse preceding and following the reference—contains data that may be useful or even necessary before drawing inferences. Most of these asterisked passages contain closely related terms which may have affected the use of the verb under consideration.

The question mark, on the other hand, alerts the user to the possibility that the reference does not really belong where it is listed. For example, it may be that the syntagmatic combination can be interpreted in more than one way; in such cases, the references have been usually listed under more than one heading (e.g. when the verb both rules a direct object and is followed by ὅτι). Again, it may be that the particular occurrence of the verb suggests a meaning too far from "to know." And so on. It seemed best to err on the side of fulness of information, since the user would find it easier to omit consideration of a verse than to search out what he is interested in verifying.

For similar reasons, all of the epistles which bear Paul's name have been included. The references are listed according to their order in the New Testament; scholars who wish to exclude the material from any epistle for whatever reason can do so without difficulty. Finally, many cross-references of various types have been included to make the lists as serviceable as possible.

The Semantic Field "To Know" in Paul

I. Ruling a Direct Object

Note: Included here, in addition to the obvious references, are (a) passages where the verb is ruling a relative clause and (b) examples of apparent absolute uses where the object is explicit in the immediate context (cf. τὰ τοῦ πνεύματος γνῶναι in 2 Cor. 2:14; some of the decisions may be debatable).

ἀγνοεῖν

> Rom. 10:3*; 11:25 (+ ὅτι)
> 1 Cor. 14:38* a, b (variant reading)
> 2 Cor. 2:11*

ἀκούειν

> Rom. 10:14 a (cf. verses 18f.)
> 1 Cor. 2:9* (Isa. 64:4); 14:2?
> Gal. 1:13; 4:21
> Eph. 1:13, 15; 3:2*; 4:21*
> Phil. 1:27, 30*; 4:9*
> Col. 1:4, (5 προακούειν), 6*, 9*, 23
> 2 Thess. 3:11 (acc. ptc. = ind. discourse)
> 2 Tim. 1:13*; 2:2; 4:17?
> Phlm. 5

ἀνακρίνειν

> 1 Cor. 2:15*; 4:3*, 4*

ἀρνεῖσθαι?

    Titus 1:16* (opp. ὁμολογοῦσιν εἰδέναι)

αὐγάζειν

    2 Cor. 4:4*

ἀφιδεῖν

    Phil. 2:23* (nuance "find out")

βλέπειν

    Rom. 7:23* (cf. verse 21)
    1 Cor. 1:26? (+ ὅτι); 10:18?
    2 Cor. 10:7*?
    Col. 2:5; 4:17?

γινώσκειν

    Rom. 1:21*; 3:17 (Isa. 59:8); 6:6 (+ ὅτι); 7:1*, 7*, 15*; 11:34* (Isa. 40:13)
    1 Cor. 2:8* a, b, 11*, 14*, 16* (Isa. 40:13); 3:20* (+ ὅτι; Ps. 94:11); 4:19; 8:2*a
    2 Cor. 5:16* a, b, 21; 8:9 (+ ὅτι)
    Gal. 2:9 (cf. verse 7); 4:9*
    Eph. 3:19*
    Phil. 2:22*; 3:10
    2 Tim. 1:18; 2:19 (Num. 16:5); 3:1 (+ ὅτι)

    ἔγραψα + ἵνα γνῶ(τε) + dir. obj., or analogous construction (= "find out")
        2 Cor. 2:4*, 9
        Eph. 6:22*
        Phil. 2:19? (cf. construction in verse 28)
        Col. 4:8*
        1 Thess. 3:5*

δέχεσθαι?

    1 Cor. 2:14* (cf. 2 Cor. 6:1; 1 Thess. 1:6*; 2:13; 2 Thess. 2:10)

διακρίνειν?

    1 Cor. 4:7*; 11:29*, 31

δοκιμάζειν

    Rom. 2:18*; 14:22*?
    1 Cor. 11:28*
    2 Cor. 13:5*
    Phil. 1:10*
    1 Thess. 2:4* b

εἰδέναι

    Rom. 7:7*; 8:26*?; 13:11 (+ ὅτι)
    1 Cor. 2:2, 11*, 12*; 13:2*; 14:11; 16:15 (+ ὅτι)
    2 Cor. 5:16*; 9:2; 12:2* a, 3* a (+ ὅτι, verse 4)
    Gal. 4:8*
    Eph. 5:5* (+ ὅτι?); 6:21* (nuance "find out")
    1 Thess. 1:4 (+ ὅτι, verse 5?); 2:1* (+ ὅτι); 4:5*; 5:12*
    2 Thess. 1:8*; 2:6*
    1 Tim. 1:9* (+ ὅτι)
    2 Tim. 1:12*, 15 (+ ὅτι)
    Titus 1:16*

ἐπιγινώσκειν

> Rom. 1:32 (+ ὅτι)
> 1 Cor. 14:37* (+ ὅτι); 16:18?
> 2 Cor. 1:13* a, 14* (+ ὅτι?); 13:5* (+ ὅτι)
> Col. 1:6*
> 1 Tim. 4:3

ἐπίστασθαι

> 1 Tim. 6:4*

ἐραυνᾶν

> Rom. 8:27*
> 1 Cor. 2:10*

εὑρίσκειν

> Rom. 7:21 (cf. verse 23)
> 2 Cor. 9:4; 12:20 a

ἰδεῖν

> Rom. 11:22
> 1 Cor. 2:9* (Isa. 64:4)
> Phil. 1:30*; 4:9*

καταλαμβάνειν?

> Phil. 3:12 a, 13 (cf. Gal. 4:8f.)

καταλαμβάνεσθαι

> Eph. 3:18*

κατανοεῖν

> Rom. 4:19?

κρίνειν?

> 2 Cor. 5:14 (+ ὅτι)

μανθάνειν

> 1 Cor. 4:6*
> Gal. 3:2*
> Eph. 4:20*
> Phil. 4:9
> Col. 1:7*
> 2 Tim. 3:14 a, b

μιμνήσκεσθαι

> 2 Tim. 1:4 (cf. εἰδὼς ὅτι)

μνημονεύειν

> 1 Thess. 1:3*; 2:9*

νοεῖν

> Eph. 3:4* (nuance "find out"; προέγραψα, verse 3), 20*
> 1 Tim. 1:7*
> 2 Tim. 2:7?

παρακολουθεῖν

> 1 Tim. 4:6
> 2 Tim. 3:10*

παραλαμβάνεσθαι?

    Phil. 4:9* (cf. 1 Cor. 11:23; 15:1, 3; Gal. 1:9, 12; 1 Thess. 2:13; 4:1*; 2 Thess. 3:6*)

πεποιθέναι

    Phil. 1:6 (+ ὅτι), 25*
    Phlm. 21*

πειράζειν?

    2 Cor. 13:5*

προακούειν

    Col. 1:5*

προγινώσκειν

    Rom. 8:29; 11:2* (opp. ἀπωθεῖν)

συνειδέναι

    1 Cor. 4:4

συνιέναι

    Rom. 3:11? (cf. LXX Ps. 13:2 = 52:2, where verb rules τὸν θεόν)

II. Passive Constructions

ἀγνοεῖσθαι

    1 Cor. 14:38* b (variant reading)
    2 Cor. 6:9*
    Gal. 1:22

ἀκούεσθαι

    1 Cor. 5:1

ἀνακρίνεσθαι

    1 Cor. 2:14*, 15* b; 4:3*

γινώσκεσθαι

    1 Cor. 8:3*; 14:7*, 9
    2 Cor. 3:2
    Gal. 4:9*
    Phil. 4:5

δοκιμάζεσθαι

    1 Tim. 3:10

ἐπιγινώσκεσθαι

    1 Cor. 13:12* b
    2 Cor. 6:9*

εὑρίσκεσθαι

    Rom. 7:10; 10:20 (Isa. 65:1)
    1 Cor. 4:2*; 15:15
    2 Cor. 5:3?; 11:12; 12:20 b
    Gal. 2:17
    Phil. 2:7?; 3:9*?

καθορᾶσθαι
Rom. 1:20*
μωραίνεσθαι
Rom. 1:22*
νοεῖσθαι
Rom. 1:20*
τυφοῦσθαι
1 Tim. 6:4*? (cf. 3:6 and 2 Tim. 3:4)

III. Ruling a Clause
(relative clauses excluded)

(1) clause introduced by ὅτι

ἀγνοεῖν
(a) οὐ θέλω (-ομεν) ὑμᾶς ἀγνοεῖν, ἀδελφοί, ὅτι (cf. 1 Cor. 12:1; 1 Thess. 4:13)
Rom. 1:13; 11:25*?
1 Cor. 10:1
2 Cor. 1:8*
(b) ἢ ἀγνοεῖτε ὅτι;
Rom. 6:3; 7:1*
(c) ἀγνοῶν ὅτι
Rom. 2:4

ἀκούειν
Gal. 1:23*?
Phil. 2:26

βλέπειν
2 Cor. 7:8

γινώσκειν
(a) finite verb + ὅτι
1 Cor. 3:20? (Ps. 94:11)
2 Cor. 8:9?; 13:6*
Gal. 3:7
2 Tim. 3:1?
(b) γινώσκειν ὑμᾶς βούλομαι, ἀδελφοί, ὅτι
Phil. 1:12
(c) γινώσκοντες ὅτι
Rom. 6:6?
Eph. 5:5*

εἰδέναι
(a) finite verb + ὅτι
Rom. 2:2; 3:19; 7:14, 18; 8:22, 28*; 14:14*; 15:29
1 Cor. 8:1*, 4*; 12:2*; 16:15?
2 Cor. 5:1; 11:11?, 31; 12:3–4? (οἶδα ... ἄνθρωπον ... ὅτι ἡρπάγη)
Gal. 4:13

Phil. 1:19, 25*; 4:15
1 Thess. 2:1*?; 3:3*; 5:2
1 Tim. 1:8*
2 Tim. 1:15?
(b) οὐκ οἴδατε ὅτι; (cf. Rom. 11:2)
Rom. 6:16
1 Cor. 3:16; 5:6; 6:2, 3, 9, 15, 16, 19; 9:13, 24
(c) θέλω ὑμᾶς εἰδέναι ὅτι
1 Cor. 11:3 (cf. Col. 2:1)
(d) εἰδότες ὅτι
Rom. 5:3; 6:9; 13:11?
1 Cor. 15:58
2 Cor. 1:7*; 4:14; 5:6
Gal. 2:16
Eph. 6:8, 9
Phil. 1:16
Col. 3:24; 4:1
1 Thess. 1:4*? (ὅτι in verse 5)
(e) εἰδὼς ὅτι (cf. 2 Tim. 1:4, μεμνημένος)
1 Tim. 1:9*?
2 Tim. 2:23; 3:14 (ὅτι in verse 15)
Titus 3:11
Phlm. 21*

ἐπιγινώσκειν
Rom. 1:32?
1 Cor. 14:37*?
2 Cor. 1:13* b (ὅτι in verse 14), 14?; 13:5*?

ἰδεῖν
Gal. 2:7 (ἰδόντες ὅτι, cf. verse 9), 14?

κρίνειν?
2 Cor. 5:14? (κρίναντος τοῦτο, ὅτι)

μνημονεύειν
2 Thess. 2:5 (οὐ μνημονεύετε ὅτι;)

πεπεῖσθαι/πεποιθέναι
Rom. 8:38; 14:14*; 15:14*
2 Cor. 2:3?
Gal. 5:10?
Phil. 1:6?; 2:24
2 Thess. 3:4?
2 Tim. 1:5*, 12*

προϊδεῖν
Gal. 3:8?

(2) *clause introduced by* τί(ς)

γνωρίζειν
Phil. 1:22

δοκιμάζειν
    Rom. 12:2*
    Eph. 5:10

εἰδέναι
    Rom. 8:26?, 27*; 11:2
    1 Cor. 7:16 a, b; 14:16
    Eph. 1:18–19*
    1 Thess. 4:2

εὑρίσκειν
    Rom. 4:1?

καταλαμβάνεσθαι
    Eph. 3:18*

συνιέναι
    Eph. 5:17*

(3) miscellaneous

ἀγνοεῖν
    οὐ θέλω ὑμᾶς ἀγνοεῖν περί
        1 Cor. 12:1*
        1 Thess. 4:13 (cf. 5:1f.)

ἀκούειν
    1 Cor. 11:18
    2 Thess. 3:11? (acc. ptc. = ind. discourse)

βλέπειν
    1 Cor. 3:10

γινώσκειν
    1 Cor. 13:9*, 12*

εἰδέναι
    1 Cor. 1:16
    2 Cor. 13:2 b, c, d, 3 b, c
    Phil. 4:12 a, b
    Col. 2:1 (θέλω ὑμᾶς εἰδέναι ἡλίκον, cf. 1 Cor. 11:3); 4:6
    1 Thess. 1:5; 4:4
    2 Thess. 3:7
    1 Tim. 3:5, 15
    2 Tim. 3:14* (+ ὅτι, verse 15)

μανθάνειν
    Phil. 4:11*
    1 Tim. 5:4, 13
    Titus 3:14

μυεῖσθαι
    Phil. 4:12*

νοεῖν
    1 Tim. 1:7

πειράζειν?
2 Cor. 13:5*?

IV. Absolute Uses

ἀγνοεῖν
1 Tim. 1:13

ἀκούειν
Rom. 10:14 b, 18*; 11:8* (Isa. 6:10?); 15:21* (Isa. 52:15)
1 Cor. 14:2?
2 Tim. 4:17?

βλέπειν/ὄψεσθαι
Rom. 11:8* (Isa. 29:10), 10* (Ps. 69:23); 15:21* (Isa. 52:15)
1 Cor. 13:12*

γινώσκειν
Rom. 10:19*
1 Cor. 8:2 b, c

εἰδέναι
2 Cor. 11:11?; 12:2 d?, 3 c?
καθὼς οἴδατε
1 Thess. 2:2*, 5*, 11 (καθάπερ); 3:4* (cf. 1:5)
ἐπιγινώσκειν
1 Cor. 13:12* a

μανθάνειν
1 Cor. 14:31, 35
1 Tim. 2:11

συνιέναι
Rom. 3:11 (cf. LXX Ps. 13:2 = 52:2, where verb rules τὸν θεόν); 15:21* (Isa. 52:15)
2 Cor. 10:12

V. Fuller Verbal Expressions

(roughly equivalent to absolute uses of simple verb)

(1) *positive expressions*
γνῶσις ἔν τινι [εἶναι] 1 Cor. 8:7
γνῶσιν ἔχειν 1 Cor. 8:1*, 10
μόρφωσιν γνώσεως ἔχειν Rom. 2:20*
ἐν γνώσει πλουτίζεσθαι 1 Cor. 1:5
ἐν (ἐπι)γνώσει (κ. αἰσθήσει) περισσεύειν 2 Cor. 8:7; Phil. 1:9*
ἐν ἐπιγνώσει ἔχειν Rom. 1:28
εἰς ἐπίγνωσιν ἀνακαινοῦσθαι Col. 3:10
εἰς ἐπίγνωσιν ἀληθείας ἔρχεσθαι 1 Tim. 2:4; 2 Tim. 3:7 (cf. 2:25)
εἰς ἑνότητα ἐπιγνώσεως καταντᾶν Eph. 4:13
νοῦν ἔχειν 1 Cor. 2:16*

σοφὸς εἶναι Rom. 1:22*; 1 Cor. 3:18*
σοφὸς γίνεσθαι 1 Cor. 3:18*
ὑπόμνησιν λαμβάνειν 2 Tim. 1:5*
φρεσὶν τέλειος γίνεσθαι 1 Cor. 14:20*
φρόνιμος γίνεσθαι Rom. 12:16 (cf. LXX Prov. 3:7)
φρόνιμος εἶναι 2 Cor. 11:19*
[Note also Col. 2:2]

(2) *negative expressions*

ἀγνωσίαν ἔχειν 1 Cor. 15:34
ἄφρων γίνεσθαι 2 Cor. 12:11; Eph. 5:17*
ἄφρων εἶναι 2 Cor. 11:16*; 12:6
ἐν διαλογισμοῖς ματαιοῦσθαι Rom. 1:21*
ἐσκοτωμένος τῇ διανοίᾳ εἶναι Eph. 4:18* (papyrus 49 has colon after διανοίᾳ)
μωρὸς γίνεσθαι 1 Cor. 3:18*
ἐν ματαιότητι νοὸς περιπατεῖν Eph. 4:17*
πωροῦσθαι (subj. νοήματα) 2 Cor. 3:14
σκοτίζεσθαι (subj. καρδία) Rom. 1:21*
σκοτίζεσθαι (subj. ὀφθαλμοί) Rom. 11:10* (Ps. 69:23)
φθείρεσθαι (subj. νοήματα) 2 Cor. 11:3

[For the notion, "to make (someone) ignorant," cf. 1 Cor. 1:19f.; 2 Cor. 4:4]

Analysis

Within the confines of this article we cannot attempt a thorough analysis of the lists. Even if such an analysis were attempted, the conclusions would prove rather tenuous in view of the very limited portion of the vocabulary here examined. Ideally, we should require parallel studies of other parts of speech within the same semantic range. Then the semantic range itself should be extended to cover *all* items in Paul's vocabulary which can be used with reference to the mental faculties. Finally, we should seek to compare our results with similar surveys of other writers, both biblical and non-biblical.[24] To recognize this ideal is to begin to appreciate the very tentative and programmatic character of the present work. Nevertheless, some preliminary comments may be in order, since even the sample presented here can demonstrate the value of the proposed method.

General. The most basic point to be stressed is the ease with which a scholar, by using these lists, can identify structural relations within the vocabulary. The lexicographical tools available to us do not, of course, altogether ignore the significance of these relations. Our better concordances point out to the user some of the more important syntactical combinations. Bauer's *Lexicon* often breaks down occurrences of a word, not only on the basis of different acceptations, but also of syntagmatic relations; occasionally, it even calls attention to paradigmatic data, especially when a contrasting term is found in the context, although the material is both very selective and inconsistently presented (as a careful comparison of various articles readily shows).

Even if all the material were available in these tools, however, any attempt at a systematic inquiry into semantically related terms would prove extremely laborious. The lists presented above reveal almost at a glance all the terms used by Paul—and thus *the minimum number of terms available to him*—in specific contexts. What is of more fundamental importance, the scholar is prevented from using the material atomistically, as though each lexical item had linguistic existence in isolation from the rest of the vocabulary. The practical significance of this point will become clear presently.

Authorship. Stylistic inquiries undertaken with a view to establishing authorship would, presumably, find in these lists much more dependable evidence for that purpose, precisely because these lists may reveal "unconscious" choices[25] made by Paul due to personal (or group) patterns. No stylistic researches known to me make full use of paradigmatic evidence, and many of them, as suggested earlier, remain content wīth presenting evidence which amounts to nothing more than inventory lists. To be sure, extensive lists of that sort may create a cumulative effect of some significance, but even this may be illusory, due to the small sample of material available to us. Thus, for instance, we find that questions introduced by οὐκ οἴδατε ὅτι occur eleven times in Paul, ten of them in 1 Corinthians and one in Romans. Statistically considered, these proportions are substantially more significant than most of the data usually brought to bear on the question of authorship, yet no one has argued, for obvious reasons, that 1 Corinthians is the only certainly Pauline letter, with a slight possibility that Romans is too.

Now the fact that I have caricatured the usual procedure—some recent investigations are very sophisticated indeed—should not obscure the need for a more scientific evaluation of the principles that are at work in an individual's vocabulary. Unfortunately, our own sample is too small to demonstrate anything. It does suggest what we already know, namely, that the style of Ephesians and that of the Pastorals are somewhat different from what we find in the other epistles. For example, Paul's tendency to use the participle εἰδότες with ὅτι suggests an anomaly at Eph. 5:5, γινώσκοντες ὅτι.[26] Although even here the occurrence may be explained by the presence of ἴστε, the example remains striking. On the other hand, the presence of εἰδὼς (rather than εἰδότες) ὅτι in the Pastorals is doubtless to be explained by the personal nature of these letters, as Phlm. 21 suggests.

Stylistic comparison. A preliminary reading of Book I of Epictetus' *Discourses* permits us to make some tentative comments. Since Arrian attempted, apparently with considerable success, to preserve the colloquial style of his teacher, this material is largely free of literary affectation; and since, in addition, the contents and argumentative method of the discourses come relatively close to Paul's writings, they provide us with some ideal material for purposes of comparison.

Keeping in mind that Book I contains approximately half as much material as the Pauline Corpus, we find that γινώσκειν and εἰδέναι are not as frequent as in Paul and that the distribution of these terms differs markedly. Ruling a direct object, these verbs are found only three or four times each. Further, we find that εἰδέναι + ὅτι occurs four times (2.24 a, b; 23.5; 27.17 b), but so does γινώσκειν + ὅτι (3.2; 4.28; 18.12; 26.15). In addition, οὐκ οἶδας (not οἴδατε) ὅτι; occurs three times (4.16; 12.12; 19.5). I found no instance of εἰδώς/εἰδότες ὅτι nor of γινώσκοντες ὅτι. I found six instances of εἰδέναι, and two of γινώσκειν, ruling some other type of clause.

Among the other terms, I found five occurrences of ἀγνοεῖν, whereas Paul uses this verb 16 times (out of 21 times in the New Testament). Another striking difference is the use of such terms as αἰσθάνεσθαι (five times in Epictetus, none in Paul) and παρακολουθεῖν (seven times in Epictetus, twice in the Pastorals). Very frequent in Epictetus, but not in Paul, is μιμνήσκεσθαι: more than ten times with an object, six times in the clause μέμνησο ὅτι (24.1; 30.1, etc.; this seems more or less equivalent to the Pauline οἴδαμεν ὅτι), and once the participle with ὅτι (24.15; cf. Paul's εἰδότες ὅτι). I found no instance of πεποιθέναι or πεπεῖσθαι. Epictetus uses two verbs in the passive, καταμανθάνεσθαι (17.8) and ἀποσοφοῦσθαι (18.11). Finally, in sharp contrast to the large number of fuller verbal expressions in Paul, I noted only ἀναίσθητος εἶναι (9.32) and νοῦν ἔχειν (16.15).

It appears, even from this very limited examination of the material, that the method holds promise for the description of stylistic differences at the lexical level.

Synonymy. Of greatest interest, in my judgment, is the value of our evidence for semantic and lexicographic purposes, particularly as it may provide objective criteria for distinguishing between synonyms, an issue which lies at the root of stylistic studies.[27] For example, numerous biblical scholars have offered their opinions as to whether γινώσκειν and εἰδέναι in the New Testament preserve their Attic distinctions. One cannot help but be perplexed, and even amused, at the diametrically opposed conclusions drawn by capable scholars, and even more at the great confidence with which they express their views. Perhaps our lists, and the principles which underlie them, will throw some light on this disagreement.

It will be convenient to take as a base for our discussion a recent and sober summary by Donald W. Burdick.[28] Burdick examined all occurrences of these two words in Paul, taking special note of passages where the verbs are used in close proximity and of pairs of syntagmatically similar passages. The author begins with the assumption (which we will grant for our purposes) that classical writers used εἰδέναι of knowledge that is grasped directly or intuitively, or of knowledge characterized by assurance, or of common knowledge of facts; whereas γινώσκειν draws attention to the acquisition of knowledge (the process of knowledge obtained by experience, instruction, etc.) rather than to its possession.[29] He concludes in his article that

> of the 103 occurrences of οἶδα in the Pauline epistles, 90 were used with the classical meaning, 5 were judged to be equivocal, and 8 were used with the same meaning as the classical γινώσκω. Of the 50 occurrences of γινώσκω, 32 were used with the classical meaning, 8 were judged to be equivocal, and 10 were used with the same meaning as classical οἶδα.

In his judgment, then, "there is no room to question" the view "that Paul normally followed the classical pattern," though he adds that each occurrence must be evaluated on its own merits.[30]

We may begin by making a general observation about discussions of synonymy. When a writer states that "x and y are (or are not) synonymous," he implies (and is generally taken to mean) that in the linguistic system as such, more or less independently of actual occurrences, these terms are (or are not) synonymous. In other words, even though a writer may grant in principle that exceptions could be found, one seldom finds a recognition that semantic relationships are "established for particular contexts or sets of context."[31] Semantic distinctions which are drawn on the basis of convincing examples must not be generalized, as is usually done, without paying due attention to the possibility of semantic *neutralization*.[32]

•An instructive example from English style may be noted in the summary by Thayer, quoted below in note 29. In that passage Thayer uses the words *denotes*, *signifies*, *expresses* and *implies* respectively when summarizing the distinctive meanings of the four Greek words. Now we all know, and Thayer knew, that these four English words "mean different things"; but it is also quite clear that at least the first three could have been interchanged by him with no semantic loss whatever. We may also suspect that even the fourth term, *implies*, was not intended by Thayer to suggest that his description of συνιέναι dealt with a different aspect of meaning.[33]

Fransisco Rodríguez Adrados[34] argues that neutralization is an "omnipresent phenomenon" of the most fundamental significance and that a failure to recognize it is responsible for one of the main defects of traditional dictionaries (that is, giving definitions that do not apply in some specific contexts). Archbishop Trench's famous work on *Synonyms of the New Testament*, in spite of its obvious and enduring value, is vitiated by the same failure.[35] No scholar, of course, not even Trench, absolutizes all distinctions; Burdick himself shows commendable caution in his article. I hope to show, however, that we need considerably more sensitivity to, and a deeper understanding of, the issue at stake.

Perhaps the first pattern that strikes the reader while perusing our lists is the predominance of εἰδέναι in Section III, especially subsection (1), the verb followed by ὅτι. Perhaps a better way to appreciate the significance of this fact is to note that even though this verb occurs over twice as many times as γινώσκειν when all the sections are considered, it occurs *less* frequently in Section I, ruling a direct object: 23 times over against 33 for γινώσκειν. Probably the difference is even greater than that, since in eight of those instances (as opposed to three for γινώσκειν) εἰδέναι is followed by ὅτι as well.[36] The inference seems inescapable that the combination εἰδέναι ὅτι, being largely predictable, should not be pressed. This simple syntactic factor, however, has not played a role in modern discussions. Thus, Burdick uses Rom. 8:28 (οἴδαμεν δὲ ὅτι τοῖς ἀγαπῶσιν τὸν θεὸν πάντα συνεργεῖ εἰς ἀγαθόν), and 1 Cor. 15:58 (ἑδραῖοι γίνεσθε . . . , εἰδότες ὅτι ὁ κόπος ὑμῶν οὐκ ἔστιν κενὸς ἐν κυρίῳ) as evidence that Paul uses εἰδέναι in the classical sense of knowledge characterized by assurance. It seems more reasonable to suggest that the choice of the verb in these and similar cases was dictated by stylistic, rather than semantic, reasons.[37] In any case, the note of assurance is really provided by the whole context in these verses, as Burdick himself seems to recognize; but if so, the context is no proof that the verb itself (in contrast to, say, πεποιθέναι) conveys that nuance.[38]

One may also argue that the tendency to use εἰδέναι with ὅτι has misled scholars to view this verb as denoting knowledge of facts. Note that although in English we can say, "I know the fact" (that is, using verb + direct object), we normally *describe* the fact, for which indirect discourse becomes the pattern: "I know (the fact) *that* he went to the park." Similarly, it appears that the parallel *structure* in Greek, not the semantic distinctiveness of εἰδέναι, accounts for the use under consideration.

But now, if εἰδέναι + ὅτι should never be pressed as carrying a distinctive meaning, we should certainly pay attention to breaks in the pattern, for these deviations[39] may suggest (though even here not necessarily) the presence of semantic motivation. For example, we find eight instances of γινώσκειν + ὅτι. How shall we explain them? To begin with, four of these instances (Rom. 6:6; 1 Cor. 3:20; 2 Cor. 8:9; 2 Tim. 3:1) do not strictly belong here, since in them the verb is ruling a direct object as well. Incidentally, the first of those references (Rom. 6:6) is particularly interesting, for Burdick, who notes the use of εἰδότες in verse 9, can find "no adequate reason for the change from one term to the other."[40] But the reason appears to be, quite simply and unsensationally, the presence of τοῦτο in verse 6.[41] A fifth passage, Eph. 5:5, was mentioned earlier when commenting on the matter of authorship; we may account for it by noting the presence of ἴστε or by reminding ourselves of the distinctive style of this epistle. The other three passages, however, should probably be interpreted on semantic grounds (2 Cor. 13:6; Gal. 3:7; Phil. 1:12). In all three of them Paul wants his readers to know something they did not know before. Although εἰδέναι can be used this way,[42] we notice a decided preference for γινώσκειν with the nuance "find out." Burdick's treatment of this aspect is more satisfactory.

Finally, we may comment briefly on Section II, passive constructions, which reminds us that εἰδέναι occurs only in the active voice.[43] One wonders whether this grammatical fact can be linked to the relative infrequency of this verb ruling a direct object. At any rate, this bit of information can help us in certain situations. Take, for example, Gal. 4:8–9: τότε μὲν οὐκ εἰδότες θεὸν... ·νῦν δὲ γνόντες θεόν, μᾶλλον δὲ γνωσθέντες ὑπὸ θεοῦ. One may argue that the change from εἰδότες to γνόντες, rather than being a mere stylistic variation, is semantically motivated insofar as the latter verb is often used when speaking of someone or something not known before.[44] This is not to say that the verb necessarily means "to acquire knowledge," for in Rom. 1:21 it is used of the pre-Christian stage, just as εἰδότες is used in the Galatians passage. Still, we may grant the appropriateness of Paul's language in verse 9. But now, how about the following γνωσθέντες? Burdick wonders why, if God knows directly without the process of observation, Paul should employ this verb when referring to divine knowledge. The question is almost meaningless, however, since εἰδέναι, not being used in the passive, was not a choice available to Paul.[45]

In conclusion, we should perhaps underscore again that our presentation is only one possibility among many. The classification used here was partially determined by a desire to show as clearly as possible the potential of the proposed method. No doubt, some of its features will not stand the tests of a rigorous scientific description. Considerable refinement is needed by scholars with different interests before the procedure can be used for more definitive purposes, whether stylistic or purely lexicographic. One can hardly doubt, however, that the principles illustrated here invite further exploration in the interests of responsible exegesis.'

Notes

1. This article has close affinities with my doctoral thesis, *Semantic Change and Semitic Influence in the Greek Bible* (University of Manchester, 1972), which included a lexicographical study of the semantic field of "mind" in the LXX, the New Testament and Epictetus. Some of the material in the present article formed part of two papers: "Linguistic Choice: Key to the Mystery of Style?" (an interdisciplinary lecture sponsored by Phi Kappa Phi at Westmont College, October, 1977) and "Lexical Choice and the Pauline Style" (delivered at the Society of Biblical Literature Annual Meeting, December 1977).

2. This statement comes from that towering classicist, Ulrich von Wilamowitz-Moellendorff, in his contribution to *Die griechische und lateinische Literatur und Sprache*, 2nd ed. (Die Kultur der Gegenwart, I.8; Berlin, B. G. Teubner, 1907), 159. I would not for a minute, however, unfairly cast doubts on the value of the judgments of this master, and so I quote the fuller context:

... dass dieses Griechisch mit gar keiner Schule, gar keinem Vorbilde etwas zu tun hat, sondern unbeholfen in überstürztem Gesprudel direkt aus dem Herzen strömt und doch eben Griechisch ist, kein übersetztes Aramäisch (wie die Sprüche Jesu), macht ihn zu einem klassiker des Hellenismus. Endlich, endlich redet wieder einer auf griechisch von einer frischen inneren Lebenserfahrung....

3. W. D. Taylor, as quoted by Louis T. Milic, *A Quantitative Approach to the Style of Jonathan Swift* (Studies in English Literature 23; The Hague, Mouton, 1967), 30.

4. George M. Ridenour, *The Style of Don Juan*, quoted in Milic, *Quantitative Approach*, 40.

5. For example, Bennison Gray, *Style: The Problem and Its Solution* (De proprietatibus litteratum, series maior 3; The Hague, Mouton, 1969). Cf. also her article, "Stylistics: The End of a Tradition," in *Journal of Aesthetics and Art Criticism* 31 (1973), 501–512; and her major work, *The Phenomenon of Literature* (The Hague, Mouton, 1975), 33: "Style then is an empty concept employed to fill the obvious linguistic gap between verse and prose." I have dealt at length with her criticisms in my unpublished Phi Kappa Phi lecture (see above, n. 1). I can only state here that her comments, though valid at a few points, reveal in general a misconception of linguistic science; one may note her misunderstanding of the term "predictability" and her rather confused discussion of synonymy (*Style*, 102, 105ff.), both of which concepts are discussed in the present article. Note also the criticisms of Gray by Nils Erik Enkvist, *Linguistic Stylistics* (Janua linguarum, series critica 5; The Hague, Mouton, 1973), 11ff. Enkvist's book is a superb survey of the state of the art and includes a comprehensive bibliography through 1970.

6. Note the article by E. D. Hirsch, Jr., "Stylistics and Synonymity," reprinted in *The Aims of Interpretation* (Chicago, The University of Chicago Press, 1976), esp. 72: Although stylistic analysis "cannot be a reliable method of determining meaning," it "may indeed provide clues that help induce interpretive guesses, and may indeed provide evidence that helps shift the weight of probability from one interpretation to another. Of course, in that sense, all interpretive arguments employ some of the tools of stylistics, whether or not they call themselves stylistics."

7. Stephen Ullmann, *Style in the French Novel* (Cambridge, C.U.P., 1957), 10. Ullmann here is indebted to a classification of linguistic structure suggested

by J. Ries in 1927. Although the system has not found favor among contemporary linguists, it appears to me both coherent and strikingly useful, especially for pedagogical purposes.

8. This level has little relevance for most examples of prose. Note also the term "phonostylistics," proposed by N. S. Trubetzkoy, *Principles of Phonology*, tr. Christiane A. M. Baltaxe (Berkeley, California University Press, 1969), 24.

9. More often than not, *style* is restricted to the syntactical level. Cf. Nigel Turner's recent contribution to J. H. Moulton, *A Grammar of New Testament Greek*, IV: Style (Edinburgh, T. & T. Clark, 1976), 1: " . . . style, in our view, involves the same considerations as syntax." This statement suggests what is confirmed by the body of the work, namely, a regrettable isolation from the broader, but inextricably related, discussions in contemporary linguistics. I may add that the principles and methods suggested in the present article could probably be put to good use in the area of syntax.

10. On discourse analysis, see Joseph E. Grimes, *The Thread of Discourse* (Janua linguarum, series minor, 207; The Hague, Mouton, 1975).

11. Of course, thorough and cautious treatments of this type are not to be despised. One thinks of the model discussion by Henry J. Cadbury, *The Style and Literary Method of Luke* (Harvard Theological Studies VI; Cambridge, Harvard University Press, 1920), Part I. Note his sober use of the evidence on p. 38.

12. "The pivot of the whole theory of expressiveness is the concept of *choice*. There can be no question of style unless the speaker or writer has the possibility of choosing between alternative forms of expression" (Ullmann, *Style*, 6). Note also Ullmann's article, "Choice and Expressiveness," in *Language and Style: Collected Papers* (N.Y., Barnes and Noble, 1964), 132–153. G. W. Turner, in *Stylistics* (Harmondsworth, Penguin Books, 1973), 21, argues that the set of grammatical rules "is prior to style. It is given by the language, leaving no choice, and, though it does not appear in all definitions, an element of choice seems to be basic to all conceptions of style."

13. Claude E. Shannon and Warren Weaver, *The Mathematical Theory of Communication* (Urbana, University of Illinois Press, 1949), 8f., 19.

14. John Lyons, *Introduction to Theoretical Linguistics* (Cambridge, C.U.P., 1969), 89. For a fuller and more refined discussion of the subject, see now his *Semantics*, I (Cambridge, C.U.P., 1977), chap. 2.

15. J. R. Firth argued that, in the course of a conversation, "whatever is said is a determining condition for what, in any reasonable expectation, may follow. What you say raises the threshold against most of the language of your companion, and leaves only a limited opening for a certain likely range of responses. This sort of thing is an aspect of . . . contextual elimination." See his *Papers in Linguistics, 1934–1951* (Oxford, O.U.P., 1957), 31f. One need not subscribe to Firth's controversial context theory of meaning to appreciate that some of its basic features are both valid and extremely useful.

16. The concept of opposition was first thoroughly exploited by the Prague school of phonology; cf. Trubetzkoy, *Principles*, 31ff. The transferal of this notion to semantic theory is by now fairly common. See especially Lyons, *Semantics*, I, chap. 8. In my judgment, the most fruitful system is that of Eugenio Coseriu; note the summary of his views by Horst Geckeler in *Current Trends in Linguistics*, 12 (The Hague, Mouton, 1974), esp. 148ff.

17. Since a writer is not likely to be familiar with all of the resources in his language, one needs to restrict the discussion to those resources available in a particular dialect, at a specific stylistic "register," etc. In our attempt to identify

the style of an individual writer, we are seeking to define his "idiolect." For these concepts, cf. Turner, *Stylistics*, 165ff., and the thorough study by David Crystal and Derek Davy, *Investigating English Style* (London, Longmans, Green and Co., 1969).

18. Such a formulation, which admittedly is lacking in precision, seems to bring together, rather smoothly, the two competing approaches to style suggested by Bally and Spitzer; see Ullmann, *Style*, 4f. Note also the views of V. V. Vinogradov, reported by Enkvist, *Linguistic Stylistics*, 38.

19. Among the few exceptions is the work of Kenneth Lee Burres, *Structural Semantics in the Study of the Pauline Understanding of Revelation*, Ph.D. dissertation, Northwestern University, 1970.

20. For a survey of the many uses of the computer for stylistic and related purposes, see A. J. Aitken *et al.* (eds.), *The Computer and Literary Studies* (Edinburgh, University Press, 1973); the article by G. L. M. Berry-Rogghe, "The Computation of Collocations and Their Relevance in Lexical Studies" (103–112), has particular affinities with the present work. Note also Peggy I. Haskel, "Collocations as a Measure of Stylistic Variety," 159–168 in R. A. Wisbey (ed.), *The Computer in Literary and Linguistic Research* (Cambridge, C.U.P., 1971).

21. For this terminology cf. Eugene A. Nida, *Componential Analysis of Meaning: an Introduction to Semantic Structures* (Approaches to Semiotics 57; The Hague, Mouton, 1975), 16–18.

22. Of course, ἰδεῖν and εἰδέναι are etymologically related, but such a (diachronic) consideration is irrelevant as a criterion for including or excluding a term.

23. On the dangers of mishandling evidence, note the interesting article (itself possibly an example of the topic covered!), "The Finagle Factor," by Stephen Jay Gould, in *Human Nature* 1 (1978), 80–87.

24. D. R. Tallentire, in "Towards an Archive of Lexical Norms. A Proposal" (*The Computer and Literary Studies*, 39–60; see n. 20, above), speaks of the paramount need "to make comparisons between the lexical domains of various writers" and quotes P. Boyde (*Dante's Style in His Lyric Poetry* [1971], 18): "*any interpretation of stylistic phenomena depends on comparison and contrast. The facts about an author's style are to be sought in his work. The meaning of those facts is to be sought in the work of other authors*" (39f.).

25. I have used quotation marks because of the important objections that can be raised against a facile distinction between conscious and unconscious choice (cf. Ullmann, *Language and Style*, 132f.). The striking significance of regularity—as opposed to conscious, deliberate choices—in communication is explored by Gustav Herdan, *The Advanced Theory of Language as Choice and Chance* (Kommunikation und Kybernetik in Einzeldarstellungen 4; N.Y., Springer-Verlag, 1966); note esp. 14f., 70ff. On "stylostatistics," see the survey of research in Enkvist, *Linguistic Stylistics*, 127ff.

26. Rom. 6:6 is only an apparent violation, as we shall note below.

27. Ullmann, *Style*, 6.

28. "Οἶδα and Γινώσκω in the Pauline Epistles," in Richard N. Longenecker and Merrill C. Tenney (eds.), *New Dimensions in New Testament Study* (Grand Rapids, Zondervan, 1974), 344–56.

29. Cf. also J. H. Thayer's note in *A Greek-English Lexicon of the New Testament* (N.Y., American Book Co., 1889), s.v. γινώσκω: "γινώσκειν ... denotes a discriminating apprehension of external impressions, a knowledge grounded in personal experience. εἰδέναι ... signifies a clear and purely mental

perception, in contrast both to conjecture and to knowledge derived from others. ἐπίστασθαι primarily expresses the knowledge obtained by proximity to the things known . . . ; then knowledge viewed as the result of prolonged practice, in opposition to the process of learning on the one hand, and to the uncertain knowledge of a dilettante on the other. συνιέναι . . . implies native insight. . . ."

30. Burdick, "Οἶδα and Γινώσκω," 354.

31. John Lyons, *Structural Semantics: An Analysis of Part of the Vocabulary of Plato* (Publications of the Philological Society 20; Oxford, B. Blackwell, 1963), 80. In *Introduction*, 452, Lyons argues that synonymy in particular is *context-dependent*. It may be that Lyons has taken his position a bit too far; cf. the exaggerated criticisms of Fransisco Rodríguez Adrados in *Estudios de lingüística general* (Barcelona, Editorial Planeta, 1969), 42, and the technical discussion by Roy Harris, *Synonymy and Linguistic Analysis* (Oxford, B. Blackwell, 1973), 123ff. Possibly F. de Saussure's well-known distinction between *langue* and *parole* can shed some light on this problem (cf. Enkvist, *Linguistic Stylistics*, 36ff.). We should note, incidentally, that Gustaf Stern long ago questioned the exclusive concern of linguistics with *langue*; see his *Meaning and Change of Meaning, with Special Reference to the English Language* (Göteborg, Elanders Boktryckei, 1931), 17. Contemporary linguistics, insofar as it stresses the sociological dimension, has been paying more attention to *parole*; note William Labov, *Sociolinguistic Patterns* (Philadelphia, University of Pennsylvania, 1972), 185f. There is probably some correlation between such a move and the fresh interest in stylistics among linguists, since style implies individual (or group) *variation*; note Turner, *Stylistics*, 7ff.

32. The term is borrowed from phonology: the opposition between voiced and unvoiced stops in some languages, for example, is said to become neutralized in final position (German *Rad* and *Rat* are both pronounced with a final *t*).

33. For a persuasive discussion by a literary critic, note Hirsch, *Aims* (see above, n. 6), who argues that even the lexical units *bachelors* and *unmarried men*, which in isolation are certainly perceived as semantically distinct, may become completely interchangeable in a club charter (60f.).

34. *Estudios* (see above, n. 31), 52.

35. In defence of Trench one could argue that much of his work was an attempt to refute the exaggerated denials that semantic distinctions might be present, even occasionally. Further, Trench recognized from time to time the possibility of neutralization. Nevertheless, the practical effect of the book has been to mislead its users, who normally look up his discussion and apply it to whatever passage they are considering. For an instructive discussion of Trench's method, particularly his excessive regard for etymology, note his popular book, *On the Study of Words* (N.Y., Macmillan, 1888 [orig., 1851]), esp. Lecture VII.

36. In an additional seven instances γινώσκειν happens to be present in the context and one wonders how that factor may have influenced the choice of one term over the other. Cf. also the use of οἶδ᾽ ὅτι = *surely* in classical writers; see H. W. Smyth's *Greek Grammar*, par. 2585.

37. The terms "stylistic" and "semantic" are here contrasted purely for the sake of convenience; I do not intend to deny the view that style is a component of meaning, an issue which is plagued by terminological confusion.

38. In other words, even if the syntax were not a factor in these two passages, we could only say that the verb is more often or more naturally found in contexts of assurance. Note also Burdick's view that γινώσκειν with the

nuance "acquisition of knowledge" is confirmed by 1 Cor. 1:21, even though that nuance is rather found in the accompanying phrase, διὰ τῆς σοφίας (348); similarly, the idea of "thorough knowledge" is borne by ἀκριβῶς, not by the verb, in 1 Thess. 5:2 (354). Of some relevance for this discussion may be Hirsch's suggestions concerning "meaning-probabilities" (*Aims*, 62).

39. For this topic, cf. more generally Enkvist, *Linguistic Stylistics*, 24–26, 98ff.

40. Burdick, "Οἶδα and Γινώσκω," 350.

41. Perhaps this is also the reason for the κρίναντος τοῦτο of 2 Cor. 5:14. I suspect that very few scholars would be happy with the view that κρίνειν = εἰδέναι in this passage. Maybe not. But is it possible that we are not sufficiently sensitive to the phenomenon of neutralization?

42. 1 Cor. 2:12; 11:3; Eph. 1:18; 6:21; Col. 2:1. (According to Smyth's *Grammar*, par. 795, the verb-stem itself means "find out," but this has nothing to do with the point being made here.) Note also the references under ἐπιγινώσκειν + ὅτι: with the apparent exception of 2 Cor. 1:13 b (and even this instance can be understood differently) the references include a direct object.

43. It may be worthwhile to note that among verbs used in the passive εὑρίσκεσθαι heads the list in number of occurrences (10), even though this verb occurs only a total of 17 times in Paul. The verb was included in this study because γινώσκειν often suggests the idea of "find out"; further, εὑρίσκειν may acquire the nuance "to perceive" (cf. Rom. 7:21, parallel to verse 23; the NASB translates 2 Cor. 11:3 with "be regarded"). Note also that five of the passive occurrences (Rom. 7:10; 1 Cor. 15:15; 2 Cor. 11:12; 12:20b; Gal. 2:17) approach the sense of "appear, turn out" (a meaning regarded by some as a Hebraism) and this is very close to "to come to be known."

44. J. B. Lightfoot (*St. Paul's Epistle to the Galatians* [1866] *ad loc.*) suggests that since γινώσκειν "gives prominence either to the *attainment* or the *manifestation* of the knowledge," it is used more naturally "where there is reference to some earlier state of ignorance...." Bultmann (*TDNT* 1 [1964], 703n.) implies that we can find no distinction here between the two verbs, but possibly he is only interested in denying that one verb denotes more thorough knowledge than the other; perhaps he would not have objected to the distinction suggested by Lightfoot.

45. Burdick's own answer to the question is that Paul was describing the knowledge of persons, not of facts; however, this distinction does not seem to hold up (cf. 1 Cor. 2:2; 2 Cor. 12:2f.; 1 Thess. 5:21; Titus 1:16).

Chapter 13

WHY DID PAUL WRITE ROMANS?

JOHN W. DRANE

BY COMPARISON WITH MOST OF THE REST of the New Testament, the Epistle to the Romans is remarkably free from the kind of critical and historical questions that usually dominate the debates of New Testament scholars. It has never been seriously doubted that the author of this letter was Paul himself, or that he wrote it to the church in Rome. Nor is there any substantial difference of opinion regarding the date and immediate purpose of the letter.

This, of course, is partly due to the fact that Paul seems to make some very specific statements about his purpose in writing. In an early paragraph he informs his readers that he was eager to visit them, so that he could share in the life of their Christian fellowship, and so that he might preach his own distinctive message in Rome itself, the centre of the Gentile world (1:8–15). Then again towards the end of the letter (15:22–33) he gives more detailed information about his plans and hopes for fulfilling this lifelong ambition. With the establishment of Christian congregations at most of the important centres of population in the eastern empire, he was planning to turn his attention to the west, specifically to Spain. But to evangelise the west successfully Paul needed the full co-operation and support of the church in Rome, and so he tells his readers that though his immediate intention was to take the gifts of the Asiatic churches to the church in Jerusalem, he would make for Rome after that before beginning this new stage of his ministry.

The mention of the collection and his impending visit to Jerusalem enables us to fix more precisely the situation in which Paul found himself when he wrote this letter. It is not too difficult to equate this with the last Jerusalem visit of Acts 21:1–16, which ended in Paul's arrest and imprisonment, to be followed eventually by his appeal to Caesar in Rome and his arrival in that city as a prisoner. In Romans Paul mentions

208

a number of people with whom he is known to have been associated in Corinth, and since we know that he spent some time in Corinth just before he left on this journey to Jerusalem, the general opinion is that Paul wrote the letter while he was staying in Corinth on that occasion.

The exact date assigned to this episode depends on a number of chronological calculations, made on the one hand with reference to Gallio's proconsulship in Corinth, and on the other relating to the times when Felix and Festus were procurators of Judea. But the general consensus is that this brings us to a date of approximately AD 57 for the composition of Romans. Variations on this date have been put forward from time to time, but with the exception of Buck and Taylor, who date Romans as early as the autumn of AD 47 (on the basis of a purely internal assessment of the evidence),[1] most scholars date the epistle somewhere between AD 54 and 59.[2] Even John Robinson, in his radical redating of the New Testament, supports the general consensus when he dates Romans early in AD 57.[3]

In view of this, it does at first seem rather pointless even to ask the question posed in our title. For if Paul tells us that he wrote Romans to prepare for a visit to a church he did not know, and if most scholars are agreed on the date and general circumstances surrounding the letter's composition, what more can usefully be said on the subject?

There are, however, other important aspects of this letter which are brought into sharp focus by the relatively trivial character of this situation. For if Paul's main purpose was simply to introduce himself to a group of Christians whom he did not know, why did he send them what is arguably the most complex theological treatise he ever wrote? We know from the epistle to Philemon that Paul had no difficulty in writing a friendly, personal letter when the need arose, and surely that kind of letter would have served the purpose of a personal introduction much more satisfactorily than the kind of long, involved discourse that we now have before us? In addition, there is the curious fact that Paul chose to write this letter at a time when, by his own admission, there could be no immediate possibility of his actually fulfilling his stated intention and visiting the church at Rome. Indeed, he was about to go in the opposite direction to the eastern end of the Mediterranean on a journey that he knew would be full of danger and uncertainty. Even on the most optimistic assessment, it would be many months, if not a year or two, before Paul could hope to reach Rome. As things turned out, it was to be longer still before his wish was at last realised.

I

In the light of these observations, the question "Why did Paul write Romans?" can be seen to resolve itself into two further, more precise questions: Why did Paul write *this* letter to Rome? and Why did he write it at this point in his career? The questions, of course, are not new, and they have generally been answered in one of two ways. Some interpreters regard Romans as a kind of theological testament, written more to satisfy Paul than to comment directly on the situation in Rome. Others, however, regard Romans as analogous to the other Pauline epistles, and therefore more or less directly concerned with events and issues in the Roman church.

Those who place the emphasis on the relevance of the epistle for the church at Rome have generally tried to define its purpose not so much in terms of Paul's aspirations in relation to that church,[4] but more with reference to certain specific happenings in Rome itself. This view originated in modern times with F. C. Baur. He began, reasonably enough, by comparing Romans with the other Pauline epistles,[5] and he argued that their evidence showed quite clearly that Paul wrote letters only when he had some pressing practical problem in view, and that the content of his letters was invariably conditioned by the specific circumstances that existed among the Christians he was addressing. When we read Galatians or 1 Corinthians, we naturally assume that Paul is dealing with problems that perplexed his readers in those places. So why should we not assume that in Romans we can catch the sound of the same kind of arguments going on in that church? Baur certainly believed that he could, and in line with his general understanding of the nature of early Christianity he argued that the key to the entire epistle is to be found in chs. 9–11, which he described as "the Apostle's original conception, from which the whole organism of the Epistle was developed, as we have it especially in the first eight chapters".[6] The central feature of the letter, on Baur's view, was therefore the refutation of a Jewish Christian outlook, and this in turn led him to the conclusion that the church at Rome "consisted primarily of Jewish Christians . . . we are entitled to take it for granted that the section of the Roman Church to which the Epistle is addressed, must have been the predominating element in the Church; and if this be so, then the Church consisted mainly of Jewish Christians."[7]

Baur's detailed understanding has generally been rejected, but a considerable number of interpreters continue to look for the letter's *rationale* in the same general area of Jewish-Gentile tensions within the church at Rome. In the earlier part of this century it became fashionable in some circles to explain the polemic of the epistle by supposing that specific "parties" were in view, who are eventually characterised in chs. 14–15 as "the weak" (possibly Jewish Christians) and "the strong" (perhaps Gentiles).[8] The whole debate has been revived in recent years, with a number of scholars wishing to assert that the substance of the epistle is "a matter of settling a quarrel between a Jewish Christian group which seeks to maintain its Jewishness through legalism and a Gentile Christian group which presumably looks down on the Jews as barbarians. . . ."⁹ One recent author goes much further than this general observation and suggests that the church at Rome, torn by party divisions between Jews and Gentiles, had actually written to Paul and asked him for his opinion on the subjects in dispute: "Paul is the recognised authority on all such questions; the perplexed Christians have sent a message to him asking for guidance, and the Epistle to the Romans is the result."¹⁰

But this approach to the epistle presents considerable difficulties, and a number of questions need to be faced before we can accept that Paul was concerned with a specific set of circumstances in the church at Rome.

An important consideration is the fact that Paul does not seem to be conscious of trying to correct the beliefs and behaviour of the Roman Christians. At many points of the letter he goes out of his way to praise them, complimenting them ἡ γὰρ ὑμῶν ὑπακοὴ εἰς πάντας ἀφίκετο (16:19, cf. 1:8), and commenting that they are μεστοί . . . ἀγαθωσύνης . . . δυνάμενοι καὶ ἀλλήλους νουθετεῖν (15:14). Moreover, in outlining his own future plans for a mission to the west, he makes it clear that he expected to receive some positive help from the Roman church (1:12). Statements of this kind are quite explicit, and though they may not indicate that Paul had any real knowledge of the healthy state of the church, they certainly do not indicate that he had any information to the contrary.¹¹

Another crucial factor often overlooked in this debate is that Paul did not know the church at Rome. He was not its founder, nor was it founded under the guidance and impetus of any mission instituted by him. It is therefore quite unlike any of the other churches to which Paul wrote letters, for in the case of Rome he was writing to a church founded in complete independence of his own mission, and which was presumably under the guidance of some other apostolic figure.

This means that his direct knowledge of the church at Rome must have been minimal. Though his friends Aquila and Priscilla had probably returned to Rome just before he wrote the epistle, they can hardly have been there long enough to be in a position to report every detail of the situation back to Paul—and in any case he makes no mention of having received such a report from them, though we can see clearly enough from 1 Corinthians that when he was criticising his readers in the light of knowledge gained from a third party he was always careful to specify the source of his information. But even supposing that Paul had such information from Rome, we also have to contend with his explicit statement in 2 Corinthians 10:13ff, reaffirmed in Romans 15:20, that it was not his policy to interfere in the churches that other people had founded. As the founding apostle, he was responsible for the church at Corinth (among others), and he resented it when other people tried to interfere in its affairs by commenting about what they saw as deficiencies in the Corinthians' theology. So if Paul was offering unsolicited advice to the church at Rome we are driven to the unlikely conclusion that he was himself indulging in the very same sort of interference in another person's field that he had complained of so bitterly in writing to the Corinthians just a few months earlier.[12] This decisive difference between Rome and the other churches to which Paul wrote invalidates the methodological principle that would simply compare the style and purpose of Romans with these other letters and assume that there must be a basic consistency of intention in them all.[13]

This fact is further underlined when we compare the Roman epistle with, say, Galatians or 1 Corinthians. Though one can hardly underestimate the difficulty of comprehending the precise situations in Galatia and Corinth, it is at least clear that Paul is referring to specific people, movements and ideas. In many cases he singles out individuals for special mention, and tells us a little about their activities, while in others he draws attention to what he saw as undesirable features of church life in general. By comparison with this, however, there is no real evidence in Romans to suggest that actual individuals, or groups of people, or situations were in view. Indeed, the current debate among scholars is largely stimulated by the very vagueness of those statements that could be taken to refer to specific aspects of church life and belief. In the rhetoric of the first part of the letter, it is clear that Paul is constantly setting one side of an argument over against the other, but it is widely believed that, even though we cannot identify its precise form, this is some kind of literary device, and its use does not necessarily lead to the conclusion that Paul was dealing with two or more sets of "opponents" in the church at Rome.[14] Then in the crucial paraenetical sections of chs. 12–15, where we might expect him to be more specific about the state of affairs in the church, the statements he makes about different points of view are again so vague and generalised that at least one recent writer takes them as evidence "not for the state of affairs in Rome, but rather for Paul's scanty knowledge of the details of the situation."[15]

The observation of difficulties of this kind has led others to seek an explanation of the nature of the Roman epistle not in the state of the church at Rome, but in the state of Paul's own missionary career, or in the state of his personal theological development. Günther Bornkamm is one of the most eminent exponents of this kind of interpretation. For him, Romans is "Paul's last will and testament".[16] His basic presupposition is that "the interpretative axis for Romans is not so much the concrete situation in Rome as the Pauline gospel".[17] Bornkamm argues that to try to understand Romans by reference to alleged events and personalities in the church at Rome "gets us nowhere".[18] He points to the many ambiguities in Paul's argument, and suggests that at those points in the epistle where Paul gives the appearance of arguing against a particular viewpoint, "the objections arise out of the subject matter, or rather out of a misunderstanding of it, and not an actual historical situation".[19] Bornkamm points out that in some very important respects Romans appears to explain some of the subjects dealt with in earlier letters, though it does so in a fundamentally different way, giving a carefully measured answer to the charges often brought against Paul by Jewish Christians. Indeed he goes on to suggest that Paul wrote Romans in this form precisely because he was conscious that these were the questions he would have to answer in his impending visit to Jerusalem, and so Romans became a sort of "trial run" of the type of speech he would make in his own defence when he got to Judea and met the leaders of the Jewish church there. This could explain the note of polemic that one can find in certain sections of the letter—except that the polemic was directed not to the church at Rome but to a different situation in Jerusalem.[20]

II

It is not at all easy to choose between the various alternatives that have been put forward, and perhaps at this point in time it is not possible to reach a definitive answer to the questions raised. Nevertheless a number of points have emerged from our discussion which may usefully be examined and clarified as a preliminary stage in our quest for a satisfactory basis for the understanding of Romans and its place in the Pauline corpus. Accordingly, we must first attempt to discover something about the nature of Roman Christianity. Then we must go on to assess the nature of Romans as a piece of theological writing. Finally, we shall make a number of suggestions for a tentative answer to the question, Why did Paul write Romans?

When we look to the New Testament itself for evidence about the church at Rome, we come up against a number of unresolved problems. For example, recourse is often made to the sixteenth chapter of Romans itself. But it is difficult to see what may be proved from this. Even leaving aside the question of whether it originally formed a part of the Roman epistle,[21] it does not actually tell us much by itself. Its list of names undoubtedly indicates that the Christian community in Rome was a cosmopolitan group, while the way the list is drawn up also seems to suggest that they met together in various local groups, or "house churches" as they are often called. But we can deduce very little about the origin or nature of the Roman church purely on this basis. By itself the evidence of Romans is ambiguous, as we might expect when we remember that Paul had never visited Rome, and that at best his information about it would be secondhand through people like Aquila and Priscilla.

Nor is the rest of the New Testament any more helpful. Two further passages have often been adduced as sources of information about Roman Christianity, but neither of them is without its difficulties. One is the account of the events of the day of Pentecost in Acts 2:10f, where reference is made to οἱ ἐπιδημοῦντες Ῥωμαῖοι, Ἰουδαῖοί τε καὶ προσήλυτοι, some of whom presumably became Christians and took their new faith back home. But this account is itself full of critical and historical problems, and even if we could surmount these there is still no guarantee that Roman Jews were among those converted on that occasion, or that they then became the pioneers of a Christian mission to their own city. It is even perhaps unlikely that they did so, for as Sanday and Headlam pointed out, "it would take more than they brought away from the Day of Pentecost to lay the foundations of a Church".[22]

A connexion between Rome and Jerusalem has also been made through the "synagogue of the libertines" mentioned in Acts 6:9. This connexion depends on the likely assumption that the Greek Λιβερτινοί is a transliteration of the Latin *libertini*, meaning "freedmen", and then on a further connexion between these *libertini* and those Jews or Jewish proselytes who became involved in the scandals which surrounded the expulsion of the Jews from Rome by Tiberius in AD 19. If the "synagogue of the libertines" in Jerusalem had some connexion with other "libertines" in Rome, this would be a possible channel through which the Roman church was founded, especially in view of the apparent connexion of this synagogue and its members with the Hellenistic Christian preacher Stephen. But this argument contains too many speculative elements to be convincing. To be sure, Zahn believed that the Roman church must have been founded direct from Jerusalem through some such agency as this,[23] but Munck rightly points out that such speculations are not based on evidence so much as on the unjustified assumption that if the church was not founded by Paul it must have been founded from Jerusalem.[24]

Another observation arising from the New Testament is more circumstantial, though perhaps more useful than the specific passages to which attention has conventionally been drawn. This concerns those books of the New Testament that are commonly connected to Rome, either by virtue of their having been written there or having been sent there. For when we examine them, we discover that they seem to embrace an extraordinarily wide range of Christian understanding. Mark and Hebrews, for example, are both usually supposed to have some connexion with Roman Christianity, and yet it is hard to imagine two documents more different from one another. The one seems to be addressed to the problems of a specifically Gentile congregation, while the other is undoubtedly concerned with an obscure sect on the Jewish Christian fringe of the church. It is quite inconceivable that these documents would appeal to the same readership, and yet it seems to be beyond question that both are connected with Rome. And if we take another New Testament book with Roman connexions (e.g. 1 Peter), we seem to have a different emphasis again. The natural implication of this is that the church in Rome must have been a very strange congregation—or, perhaps, a very strange collection of congregations, for it is hard to see how one group could have embraced people of such widely different outlooks.

In the light of this, it is instructive to note the evidence drawn from other sources concerning the Jewish community in Rome. Though this again is not direct evidence about the church there, it does help to provide a plausible *Sitz im Leben* for a Roman Christian congregation, and it also supports the speculations just made on the basis of the variety of New Testament books connected with Rome.

The beginnings of the Jewish community in Rome are probably to be traced to the second century BC, though it was not until a century later with the conquests of Titus in Palestine that Jews began to migrate to Rome in any great numbers. Many of these Jews seem to have done well for themselves, and to have become a fully integrated part of Roman society. There is evidence from the Via Appia catacomb inscriptions that at least some Roman Jews gave their children Roman names, even names that were associated with the gods and goddesses of traditional Roman religion. Many pagan-style inscriptions and pictures have also been found here.[25] On the other hand, evidence from other sites gives a different picture. The Monteverde catacomb, for instance, which was used chiefly by Jews from the Transtiberine district of the city, has little evidence of Latin or pagan influence.[26]

The Jewish population of Rome was clearly not a homogeneous entity. Some Jews (perhaps the majority) laid great stress on the traditional observances of their ancestral faith, and the Old Testament food laws, the sabbath, etc., are often mentioned by Roman authors.[27] Horace even suggests that in the Augustan era such Jewish customs and practices were observed among certain classes of native-born Romans.[28] But other groups of Jews must have imbibed much of the pagan culture of their new environment. The social standing of the Roman Jews seems to have been as varied as their attitudes to religion.[29] Many of the tombs are well endowed with eloquent inscriptions, while others have no inscriptions at all, or inscriptions whose language points to a low degree of literacy among those who compiled them. References to Roman Jews in contemporary literature also mention affluent Jews, and even Jewish actors and poets[30]—though on the whole the statements made by Latin authors usually indicate that "the Jews of Rome were despised for their poverty and beggary rather than envied and hated for their wealth".[31] Leon is of the opinion that this latter group formed the majority of the Jewish community in Rome in New Testament times: "it is obvious that a distressingly large proportion of the community subsisted at a low economic level, engaged in humble pursuits, and that the lucrative mercantile activities which are associated with the Jews of later eras are not exemplified among the Jews of ancient Rome."[32]

It seems likely therefore that in the important matters of social, economic and religious class, the Jews of Rome were divided, and we may be quite sure that this led to the emergence of distinctive groupings among the Jewish population, probably organised into different synagogues according to these varied criteria.[33] This observation has an important bearing on our understanding of the development of Christianity in Rome. For however it originally arrived in the city, there can be little doubt that its claims would be a matter of interest to the Jewish community. And, given that this community was itself divided, it is likely that different synagogues would make different responses to the Christian message.

This is probably the situation that formed the background to the edict of Claudius, expelling the Jews from Rome. For according to Suetonius (*Life of Claudius* 25.4) those involved in the events leading up to the expulsion were "Jews who persisted in rioting at the instigation of Chrestus". This is usually taken to be the occasion referred to in Acts 18:2, when the Jewish Christians Aquila and Priscilla left the city and went to Corinth. But most interest has centred around the phrase "at the instigation of Chrestus" (*impulsore Chresto*). Does this refer to arguments about the Christian gospel, or does it really refer to some other incident associated with an actual person by the name of Chrestus who was stirring up trouble of a quite different sort? Chrestus was of course a common enough name at the time, but most scholars take the view that Suetonius was meaning to refer to that Chrestus whom he believed to be the founder or leader of the sect of the *Christiani*.[34]

The precise date of this incident is unclear. Suetonius himself does not date it, but Dio Cassius (*Historia Romana* 60.6.6), who also refers to a restriction of Jewish activities, places his account at the beginning of Claudius's reign, i.e. about AD 41. On the other hand, the fifth-century author Orosius (*Adv. Paganos* 7.6.15–16) places it in Claudius's ninth year, which would be AD 49—and this date is also supported by the reference to Aquila and Priscilla in Acts 18:2. The best dating therefore seems to be AD 49, which involves the assumption that Dio Cassius was referring to some earlier, less drastic measure taken by Claudius to try to contain the same problem.[35] This explanation is also supported by the fact that according to Dio the Jews were not allowed back until the beginning of Nero's reign, and whilst this is plausible if they were not expelled until AD 49, it is unlikely that Claudius could have excluded them for the whole of his period in office.

We can therefore reconstruct the situation on the following lines. Not long after the accession of Claudius (if not before), Christianity was becoming an important issue for the Jewish community in Rome. Presumably this was because of the arrival of anonymous Christian missionaries who saw (as did Paul) that the Jewish synagogue offered considerable potential for the promulgation of their message. In Rome, however, the situation was not quite so straightforward as in most of the cities Paul had visited. In Asia Minor and Greece it was more usual to find only one synagogue in each city, and sometimes (as in the case of Philippi) the Jewish population was not even large enough for that. But in Rome there were several synagogues, and significantly they were divided not merely for the practical purposes of being able to meet together in one place, but for specifically social, economic and religious reasons. So as Christian missionaries came into this situation the scene was set not only for a confrontation between Christians and Jews, but between one Jewish synagogue and another, as the Jews themselves gave different answers to the new questions introduced by the Christian claims. So serious did these debates become that they seemed even to threaten the stability of the population, and so Claudius decided to ban the Jews from Rome altogether. So far as can be seen, the ban remained in force until the beginning of Nero's reign (AD 54), and even then the Jews were probably allowed to return but not to gather publicly.

This state of affairs must obviously have had its effect not only on the Jewish community, but also on the way that the church in Rome developed at this crucial period. A number of observations can be drawn from all this:

1. If Christianity was creating so much discord among the Jewish community at this time, it is reasonable to assume that the first Christians in Rome would be Jews, or Jewish proselytes. They might have had different ideas about the relationship of Judaism to Christianity, and of both to the various elements of Roman society—but they were Jews of some kind, and not converts direct from paganism to Christianity.

2. With the expulsion of the Jews by Claudius, the scope for further evangelism among Jews must have been severely restricted. It is of course unlikely that the Jewish community disappeared from Rome entirely. For one thing, it is hard to see how Claudius's edict could be enforced in such a way that every Jew was expelled. In addition, it would have been illegal for Claudius to have done this, in view of the edicts issued at the beginning of his reign in which he affirmed the rights of the Jewish population. But he could certainly have got rid of the troublemakers—and, if they were fighting about the claims of Christian missionaries, then *ex hypothesi* they would be the ones who were likely to be most interested in what the Christians had to say. So those Jews who were left were probably numerically small, and were certainly unlikely to have any great interest in Christianity.

3. The natural implication of this fact is to suppose that once the Jewish constituency was removed, the church would find most of its converts among the Gentile population of Rome. This in turn must imply that not long after Claudius's edict the Roman church would be almost entirely Gentile.[36]

4. This would naturally mean that by the time the Jewish Christians did eventually begin to return to the city, they would be entering a situation in which they were the minority. Not perhaps a numerical minority, but no longer the dominant grouping among the Roman Christians. For the whole character and outlook of the church had probably changed dramatically during their absence.

5. It is not surprising therefore that there does not seem to have been any one unified Christian church in Rome at this period. The Jewish Christians themselves had probably never been fully united, as different synagogues reacted differently to the Christian message and evolved their own forms of Christian belief. And the Gentile outlook of those Christians whom they found when they returned from their exile can hardly have encouraged them to forget their differences and come together. They may have been banned from meeting publicly anyway, and this seems to be the kind of situation envisaged in Romans 16, where Paul appears to be sending greetings to a number of "house churches". In the light of what we can know of the situation in Rome at the time, it is perhaps not too improbable to suggest that these house churches were constituted not so much because of the physical locality in which their members lived, but rather because of the differing outlooks that existed on the one hand among the Jewish Christians themselves, and on the other between them and the Gentile Christians who had taken over the church during their enforced absence from the city.

It was probably into such a situation that Paul's letter arrived, and if we take Romans 16 as evidence for the existence of various house churches in Rome, it is of course obvious that Paul must at least have known the general outline of the situation there. Such information could have reached him through his friends Aquila and Priscilla. But since they themselves were banned from the city under the edict of Claudius, they could not have been living there for very long when Paul wrote his epistle. Indeed, 1 Corinthians 16:19 shows that they were still in Ephesus about AD 55. No doubt they reported to Paul which groups his various friends were meeting with—but it is doubtful if they described the situation in any great detail. Indeed, Paul may have heard this news from them only as he was nearing the end of his epistle, for while ch. 16 is evidence that he had some idea of what was going on in the Roman church, the rest of the epistle is evidence that he did not have any very specific knowledge of the particular incidents and personalities that may have been involved.

III

But before drawing our conclusion in any greater detail, we must come to the epistle itself. The view that the letter was not intended to be a specific comment on the situation of the Roman church has traditionally been defended on two main grounds.

First we have the claim that Paul uses a number of rhetorical devices in Romans that are similar to or identical with the Stoic-Cynic diatribes, and this is supposed to demonstrate that any "opponents" who may seem to be in view are more imaginary than real. Then there is also the assertion that the material in chs. 12–15 is of a general paraenetic nature, and is not therefore directed to a specific situation in Rome. Though these two arguments are often closely connected, from a methodological viewpoint they do not have the same status. One is based on a specific exegesis of the text in relation to other Pauline epistles, whereas the other is based on a more general impression of Paul's purpose. Moreover, the idea that Paul uses the literary devices either of the Stoic-Cynic traditions or of the Socratic tradition is far from proven, and has not been the subject of any independent investigation since the publication of Bultmann's seminal work in 1910.[37] The argument put forward by Bultmann is hardly unassailable, not least because it was based on a number of so-called Hellenistic "sources" which are not in fact extant, and so much of his argument is made by inference rather than on the basis of incontrovertible fact.[38] But this does not prevent Bornkamm from declaring that "As no other, this letter shows a plethora of examples taken from the vivid teaching form called the 'diatribe'."[39] It is, however, instructive to note that among classical scholars one looks in vain for this kind of boldness either in respect of Romans itself, or even in respect of the very existence of the so-called diatribe form. One eminent classicist describes this Stoic-Cynic diatribe as "a kind of literary counterpart to the redeemed-redeemer myth of the History of Religions school. . . . It is a ghost summoned up for lack of a more adequate explanation of what confronts us. . . . It is not at all clear that it has any claim to exist, especially at this period, but the reservations of classical scholars, and the problems of definition and evidence, are not always noticed on the New Testament side."[40]

For many reasons it is difficult to know exactly how to relate Paul to the rhetorical traditions of his day. We have little certain information about his educational background, though neither Tarsus nor Jerusalem would necessarily have given him training in the art of Hellenistic rhetoric. Indeed, certain statements in his letters could be taken to suggest that he had no such education. For example, in 2 Corinthians 11:6 he refers to himself as ἰδιώτης τῷ λόγῳ and elsewhere in the same epistle he suggests that his letters were more weighty when read out in church by trained speakers than when he spoke himself (2 Cor. 10:10).[41] At the same time, of course, these statements could themselves be rhetorical devices. But it is difficult to know, for our knowledge of the kind of rhetoric popular in the Greek cities in the first century is virtually nil.[42] It is therefore highly precarious to try to base our understanding of Romans on a comparison with rhetorical devices which may or may not have been current in the Roman empire of the first century AD.

This leaves us with the ethical exhortations of Romans 12–15. Do these have the form of a general paraenesis, or are they aimed at some specific circumstances in the Roman church? We have already seen that there are good general reasons for doubting that Paul was trying to correct the behaviour of the Roman Christians, and Dodd drew the obvious conclusion from this almost half a century ago, when he commented that it is "a waste of time to examine particular passages in detail with a view to deducing from them information regarding conditions in the Roman church"[43]—though he did allow himself the observation that the epistle shows the church to be "like most churches outside Palestine . . . of mixed Jewish and Gentile membership."[44] Others, however, have pressed on undaunted in the effort to demonstrate how every last detail of Paul's argument has its real-life counterpart in the church at Rome. The most extreme of these interpretations is that of P. S. Minear, who claims to be able to distinguish no less than five separate groups in the Roman church on the basis of the evidence in chs. 14–15.[45] Such an interpretation of the Pauline paraenesis in Romans is, however, fundamentally misguided, for when we compare it with similar passages in other epistles where Paul was undoubtedly attacking opponents, the Romans passage can be seen to be without exception vague and ambiguous, while being at the same time theologically more comprehensive than parallel passages elsewhere. Three sections of Romans support this assertion:

1. Romans 12:3–13 deals in a striking way with the same concepts as we find in 1 Corinthians 12–14, viz. Paul's understanding of the church as the Body of Christ, and the place of charismatic gifts within that context. Not only do the two passages deal with the same subject, but they do so in the same way. For in both contexts Paul's thought moves from the idea of the body itself, through the idea of specific gifts, and onto the question of love as the context in which gifts can be exercised to the edification of the church. But there the similarity ends, for while the Corinthians passage is full of detailed advice and instruction in the light of various abuses of the charismata, the Romans passage is quite lacking in such detail and deals only with the principles involved. Though Dunn writes in this connexion of "a group or faction in Rome who show at least some of the attitudes and values of the Corinthian gnostics" to such an extent that "in Rome, too, charismata may have been more of a disruptive element than a unifying factor", it is difficult to see where he gets his evidence.[46]

2. The same kind of ambiguity is evident in the discussion of "the weak" and "the strong" in chs. 14–15. It is obvious that Paul is here dealing with the same kind of issues of conscience as he had earlier dealt with in 1 Corinthians 8–10, but again it is difficult either to identify the two situations or to show that Paul is dealing with a specific problem in each instance. The problem in Corinth was obviously εἰδωλόθυτα—and Paul explicitly says so. But there are at least six possible explanations of "the weak" and "the strong" who may have been present in the church at Rome, and there is by no means a consensus as to which interpretation is correct.[47] The wide range of such explanations, from Jewish legalism through vegetarianism to the Hellenistic mystery religions, is surely strong evidence to support the contention that Paul had no specific opponents in view. Indeed, the way Paul goes beyond the approach of 1 Corinthians by neatly categorising the issue into a difference between "the weak" and "the strong" suggests that what we are dealing with here is not a direct attack on two parties, but "a generalised adaptation of a position he had earlier worked out respecting an actual, known situation in Corinth".[48]

3. Moving away from those specific sections which can be directly compared with other Pauline epistles, it is instructive to note also the

form and content of the rest of the paraenetical material here. For in both
respects it fits the general pattern of ethical instruction current in many
churches. It is what one writer calls a "bag of answers to meet recurring
problems and questions common to the members of different early
Christian communities,"[49] and as such it depends heavily on various
Jewish traditions[50] as well as the teaching preserved independently in
other circles as the Sermon on the Mount.

It seems therefore that the burden of proof lies squarely with those
who would argue that Romans is concerned with specific circumstances
in the Roman church. For though it is not possible to argue on the basis
of rhetorical forms that Romans is a generalised theological treatise, the
actual details of its paraenesis give little support to the belief that Paul
was dealing with real opponents in the church at Rome.

IV

What then was Paul doing when he wrote this letter? Our conclusions may be summed up in a series of propositions which, though they
do not constitute a full answer to the question, must nevertheless be
basic to any further attempt to define Paul's purpose more precisely.

1. The needs of the church in Rome when Paul wrote had been
conditioned by the historical situation in the city, especially as it concerned the relationship of Jews and Gentiles, and in particular the involvement of the Jewish community with Roman society in general.
Because of the initial tension between the various Jewish synagogues,
and then subsequently between different groups of Jewish Christians
and those Gentile Christians who had taken over during the expulsion
of the Jews from Rome, it is certain that the church there must have been
fragmented when Paul wrote his letter. Those who argue that Paul's
letter can be seen as a possible means of uniting the various factions are,
therefore, in an important respect correct, though it seems likely that the
situation was in reality much more complex than the straightforward
Jewish-Gentile tensions that Paul seems to be writing about.

2. It is not possible, however, to go on from this to make the
further assumption that Paul himself realised what was going on in
Rome and formulated his letter accordingly. It is striking that ch. 16 is
the only passage which provides any tangible evidence that Paul knew
anything at all about the Roman church, and even here he does not
characterise the various groups but simply mentions the names of those
people who happened to be known to him. The rest of the letter is too
vague at a number of crucial points to support the assertion that Paul
was directly countering opponents whose position he knew and understood. Manson, of course, felt that its content was so generalised that he

believed the entire letter must have been sent as a kind of circular to different churches, with ch. 16 as an appendage to the church at Ephesus.[51] The Ephesian destination of ch. 16 has been so seriously questioned as to be no longer a viable hypothesis, but the central fact remains that the body of Romans does not appear to be specifically directed to problems at Rome.

3. It is therefore far more satisfying to look for the *Sitz im Leben* of Romans not in the church at Rome, but in the events of Paul's own apostolic ministry. The letter itself was written in a period that was decisive for Paul's ministry in two respects. As Bornkamm points out, he was about to go to Jerusalem, and he needed to ascertain in advance exactly what he would say in support of his liberal gospel to those who disagreed with him there. But more important than that was what lay behind him, for he had just come through one of the most difficult periods of his whole ministry, in dealing with the complex problems of the church at Corinth. These problems had a number of different causes. On the one hand there was an unmistakable Jewish element in at least part of them. But some of the most distressing aspects of the general disarray in the Corinthian church had arisen out of a misunderstanding of Paul's own teaching by his converts there. His emphasis on the freedom of the Christian from the law had led to precisely that kind of antinomianism that the Judaizers had always said it would—indeed, it had led to even worse horrors, for Paul's distinctive ethical understanding of Christian freedom had been married to the theological outlook of some kind of incipient Gnosticism.[52]

As Paul reviewed his own position at this stage of his ministry he must have asked himself what had gone wrong. Perhaps he even wondered if he had any kind of workable theology at all, and so the question became not just a matter of what he could say in Jerusalem to justify his anti-legalism as a theological principle, but what he could say on a practical level to defend his own position. What, indeed, could he say to himself to preserve his own theological integrity? Was charismatic freedom really a viable alternative, or did it inescapably contain some kind of internal contradiction that made the whole system unworkable?

It is widely recognised that the themes of Romans are not just related to the Corinthian correspondence, but that they relate even more directly to the epistle to the Galatians which is, in Lightfoot's notable phrase, the "rough model" from which the "finished statue" of Romans was fashioned.[53] But Romans is much more than that. It is not simply a more comprehensive statement of the teaching of Galatians, but a reformulation of that teaching as Paul now saw it through the spectacles of his experiences at Corinth. What we have in this, his *magnum opus*, is therefore a conscious effort to convince himself as well as his opponents that it is possible to articulate a theology which is at once antilegalistic without also being intrinsically antinomian.

Notes

1. C. Buck & G. Taylor, *St. Paul: a Study in the Development of his Thought* (New York, 1969), 23ff, 146ff.

2. Sanday and Headlam dated Romans in the winter/spring of AD 57–58 (W. Sanday & A. C. Headlam, *A Critical and Exegetical Commentary on the Epistle to the Romans*,ICC [Edinburgh, 1902⁵]), and this dating is followed by M. Black, *Romans*, New Century Bible (London, 1973), 20. But Cranfield favours a date in the winter/spring of AD 55–56 (C. E. B. Cranfield, *A Critical and Exegetical Commentary on the Epistle to the Romans*, ICC, I [Edinburgh, 1975], 14), while C. K. Barrett (*A Commentary on the Epistle to the Romans* [London, 1957], 4f.) places it a year earlier, in spring AD 55. Dodd, on the other hand, suggests AD 59 as a more likely date, because this neatly brings the end of Paul's two-year imprisonment in Rome down to the time of Nero's persecution in AD 64. But he admits that "a year or two earlier is possible" (C. H. Dodd, *The Epistle of Paul to the Romans* [London, 1932], xxvi).

3. J. A. T. Robinson, *Redating the New Testament* (London, 1976), 55.

4. It is of course obvious that, on any view of the epistle, Paul wanted to enlist the help of the Roman church for his mission in the western empire.

5. F. C. Baur, *Paul*, I (E.T.; London, 1876²), 308–365.

6. *Ibid.*, 315. He is by no means the only one to see the key to Romans in these chapters: cf., *inter alios*, J. Munck, *Christ and Israel* (E.T.; Philadelphia, 1967).

7. *Paul*, 331. Lake agreed with him (*The Earlier Epistles of St. Paul: Their Motive and Origin* [London, 1911], 410), but the generally subjective character of such judgements becomes clear when Munck claims that the Roman church was self-evidently Gentile (*Paul and the Salvation of Mankind* [E.T.; London, 1959], 196). Even Dodd's view that the epistle shows that "like most churches outside Palestine it was of mixed Jewish and Gentile membership" (*Romans*, xxviii), is really little more than an inspired guess.

8. E.g. Lake, *Earlier Epistles*; cf. also M. Rauer, *Die Schwächen in Korinth und Rom*, Biblische Studien xxi, 2 u. 3 Heft (Freiburg, 1923).

9. The quotation is from H.-W. Bartsch, "The Historical Situation of Romans", *Encounter* 33 (1972), 335 (originally in *Communio Viatorum* 8 [1965]). The debate has been revived in a number of recent contributions to the *CBQ*: cf. R. J. Karris, "Rom. 14:1–15:13 and the Occasion of Romans", *CBQ* 35 (1973), 155–178 (who does not believe the epistle can be closely connected with affairs in the Roman church); K. P. Donfried, "False Presuppositions in the Study of Romans", *CBQ* 36 (1974), 332–355 (who takes the opposite view); W. Wuellner, "Paul's Rhetoric of Argumentation in Romans: an Alternative to the Donfried-Karris Debate Over Romans", *CBQ* 38 (1976), 330–351 (who believes their methodology to be mistaken). These studies, together with a number of other important papers, have now been collected in K. P. Donfried (ed.), *The Romans Debate* (Minneapolis, 1977). Among recent commentators, E. Käsemann takes the same view as Karris (*An die Römer*, HNT 8a [Tübingen, 1974]). Cranfield, though he refuses to take sides in his commentary (*Romans* I, 24), certainly comes down in favour of an interpretation which envisages "opponents" in the

church at Rome in his article, "Some Observations on the Interpretation of Rom. 14,1–15,13", *Communio Viatorum* 17 (1974), 193–204.

10. S. Neill, *Jesus Through Many Eyes* (London, 1976), 63.

11. Cf. J. MacRory, "The Occasion and Object of the Epistle to the Romans", *Irish Theological Quarterly* 9 (1914), 24.

12. G. Klein argues that "for Paul, Christianity in Rome still needed an apostolic foundation", and this, if true, would invalidate our argument (cf. "Paul's Purpose in Writing the Epistle to the Romans", *The Romans Debate*, 32–49; quotation from 48). But there is no real evidence to support his argument; on the contrary, there is ample evidence to support the tradition that the church in Rome was a Petrine foundation.

13. Others (e.g. Karris, "Rom. 14:1–15:13 and the Occasion of Romans," *CBQ* 35 [1973]; G. Bornkamm, "The Letter to the Romans as Paul's Last Will and Testament", *Australian Biblical Review* 11 [1963], 2–14 [now reprinted in *The Romans Debate*, 17–31 and in *Paul* (E.T.; London, 1971), 88–96]) argue that in any case the style of Romans is that of the Stoic-Cynic diatribes, and that the use of this form itself excludes any specific reference to Rome. But this is a doubtful assertion: cf. above, 219ff.

14. The argument that Paul is here using a diatribe form is very tenuous. See above, 219ff. More significant is the observation made by Lake, that "When St. Paul is at pains to discuss a point at length it is because he knew that it was disputed" (*Earlier Epistles*, 410). But of course it does not necessarily follow that it was Paul's immediate readership which was disputing it: it merely implies that Paul knew from past experience that the issues he deals with are contentious.

15. B. N. Kaye, " 'To the Romans and Others' Revisited", *NovT* 18 (1976), 45.

16. Cf. the works referred to in note 13 above.

17. R. Jewett, *Paul's Anthropological Terms* (Leiden, 1971), 48.

18. *Paul*, 93.

19. *Ibid.*, 90.

20. *Ibid.*, 96. A position also supported by Käsemann, *An die Römer*.

21. On the whole the evidence seems to favour the view that it is a part of the epistle sent to Rome. Cf. H. Gamble, *The Textual History of the Letter to the Romans* (Grand Rapids, 1977).

22. *Romans*, xxviii.

23. Th. Zahn, *Introduction to the New Testament* (E. T.; Edinburgh, 1909), I, 429.

24. J. Munck, *Paul and the Salvation of Mankind*, 208f.

25. H. J. Leon, *The Jews of Ancient Rome* (Philadelphia, 1960), 93–121, 240ff.

26. *Ibid.*, 240ff.

27. Cf. Suetonius, *Augustus* 76.2; Leon, *Jews of Ancient Rome*, 12ff, 244f.

28. Horace, *Sat.* I.9.67–72.

29. Cf. Leon, *Jews of Ancient Rome*, 233–238.

30. Martial 7.82; 11.94; cf. also Josephus, *Life* 3.16.

31. Leon, *Jews of Ancient Rome*, 234. He refers to Juvenal 3.12–16; 3.296; 6:542–547; Martial 12.57.13—commenting that though these writers are biased and critical in general, their statements must have had some basis in fact.

32. Leon, *Jews of Ancient Rome*, 238.

33. Cf. W. Wiefel, "Die jüdische Gemeinschaft im antiken Rom und die Anfänge des römischen Christentums", *Judaica* 26 (1970), 65–88 (now in E.T. in *The Romans Debate*, 100–119).

34. Cf. Leon, *Jews of Ancient Rome*, 25ff; F. F. Bruce, "Christianity under Claudius", *BJRL* 44 (1961/62), 309–326; F. F. Bruce, *Paul: Apostle of the Free Spirit* (Exeter, 1977), 379ff.

35. Cf. Bruce, "Christianity under Claudius", 314f. Leon prefers a date of AD 41 for the expulsion, because Orosius's source (and its value) is uncertain. He claims to have got the information from Josephus, though Josephus nowhere mentions it (Leon, *Jews of Ancient Rome*, 23ff).

36. Cf. J. Kinoshita, "Romans—Two Writings Combined", *NovT* 7 (1965), 259. He goes on to argue that, because Paul appears to relate to both Jewish and Gentile problems, its form can best be explained by supposing that two different writings have been combined.

37. R. Bultmann, *Der Stil der paulinischen Predigt und die Kynisch-stoische Diatribe* (Göttingen, 1910).

38. Cf. Donfried, *The Romans Debate*, 133ff (= "False Presuppositions in the Study of Romans").

39. *Paul*, 90. A claim repeated by M. Black, *Romans*, 29, 61, where he refers to Dodd, *Romans*, 148ff.

40. E. A. Judge, "St. Paul and Classical Society", *Jahrbuch für Antike und Christentum* 15 (1972), 33.

41. E. A. Judge, "Paul's Boasting in Relation to Contemporary Professional Practice", *Australian Biblical Review* 16 (1968), 37.

42. Judge, "Paul's Boasting", 41.

43. *Romans*, xxxi.

44. *Romans*, xxviii.

45. P. S. Minear, *The Obedience of Faith* (London, 1971). He traces the following groups: "the weak" who condemn "the strong"; "the strong" who condemn "the weak"; the doubters; "the weak" who do not condemn "the strong"; and "the strong" who do not condemn "the weak".

46. J. D. G. Dunn, *Jesus and the Spirit* (London, 1975), 268ff. He bases his assertion on the unjustifiable assumption that the question of *charismata* was of universal importance in the early church. But all the evidence suggests that it was a problem virtually confined to those churches which had come into contact with the Pauline doctrine of the Spirit—and that certainly excludes the Roman church at this point.

47. For an account of the various possibilities, cf. Cranfield, "Some Observations on the Interpretation of Rom. 14,1–15,13".

48. V. P. Furnish, *The Love Command in the New Testament* (London, 1973), 115.

49. D. G. Bradley, "The *topos* as a Form in the Pauline Paraenesis", *JBL* 72 (1953), 246.

50. A. T. Hanson, for example, draws attention to seven parallels between Romans 12–13 and the eleventh chapter of the Mishnah (*Studies in Paul's Technique and Theology* [London, 1974], 126–135). Daube also demonstrates that not only in their substance but even in their form some of the exhortations in Romans 12 approximate closely to the moral codes of post-biblical Judaism (*The New Testament and Rabbinic Judaism* [London, 1956], 90–91). This does not of course imply that Paul simply took over the rabbinic ideals, but it does suggest that he was here reproducing a traditional form of ethical teaching, even if, as Hanson puts it, he has passed it through "the sieve of his Christian belief" (134). Cf. also V. P. Furnish, *Theology and Ethics in Paul* (Nashville/New York, 1968), 38–42.

51. T. W. Manson, "St. Paul's Letter to the Romans and Others", *Studies in the Gospels and Epistles* (Philadelphia, 1962), 225–241; also reprinted in *The Romans Debate*, 1–16, and originally in *BJRL*.

52. Cf. J. W. Drane, *Paul: Libertine or Legalist?* (London, 1975), 109–131.

53. J. B. Lightfoot, *Saint Paul's Epistle to the Galatians* (London, 1865), 49.

Chapter 14

THE MORAL FRUSTRATION
OF PAUL BEFORE HIS CONVERSION:
Sexual Lust in Romans 7:7-25

ROBERT H. GUNDRY

DESPITE ANNOUNCEMENTS that W. G. Kümmel cut down once and for all the interpretation of Rom. 7:7–25, or at least 7:14–25, as both autobiographical of Paul and psychologically descriptive of his Christian experience,[1] that interpretation is enjoying somewhat of a revival.[2] Indeed, the honoree of this volume cautioned that Kümmel's blow was not mortal even though it was heavy.[3] I shall urge with Kümmel's critics that Paul describes an experience he himself had, but against them that he had this experience before converting to Christianity. Though it is not new, this view seems to have few advocates nowadays.

Arguments for understanding Paul as describing his *Christian* experience of moral frustration often begin with an appeal to the present tense in 7:14–25. This appeal depends on recognizing the pre-Christian orientation of 7:7–13; otherwise, the past tenses in 7:7–13 become just as problematic for Christian orientation as the present tense in 7:14–25 for pre-Christian orientation. The present tense throughout 7:14–25 "is here sustained too consistently and for too long and contrasts too strongly with the past tenses characteristic of vv. 7–13 to be at all plausibly explained as an example of the present used for the sake of vividness in describing past events which are vividly remembered."[4]

But the argument does not hold up. In Phil. 3:3–6 Paul uses the present tense to describe his Judaistic past. This use has been overlooked because it occurs in ellipses. But it is there: "For we are the circumcision, who worship by God's Spirit and boast in Christ Jesus and put no confidence in flesh, though myself having confidence even in flesh. If anyone else thinks it good to put confidence in flesh, I more [think it good to put confidence in the flesh]: with respect to circumcision, [I am] an eight-dayer; [I am] from the stock of Israel; [I am] of the tribe of Benjamin; [I am] a Hebrew of Hebrews; as to the law, [I am] a Pharisee; as to zeal, [I am] one who is persecuting the church; as to the righteousness in the law, [I am] one who has become blameless." The expressed present in verses 3–4 establishes the tense that needs supplying in the list of verses 4–6. That we instinctively resist supplying the present in the last three items only shows how vivid was Paul's recollection of his Judaistic past and therefore how easily the present tense in Rom. 7:14–25 may be taken as a similar vivid recollection. In both passages Paul sustains the present tense at some length. In both, he juxtaposes it with past tenses referring to his pre-Christian days (in Romans 7 past tenses precede in verses 7–13; in Philippians 3 the imperfect follows in verse 7). In both, the present tense concerning Paul is triggered by a preceding present tense concerning another subject (". . . the law is spiritual"—Rom. 7:14a; "If anyone else thinks it good . . ."—Phil. 3:4b). And in both, Paul uses the present tense in conjunction with ἐγώ, "I."

There is no questioning the autobiographical character of the "I" in Phil. 3:4–6. The parallels between that passage and Rom. 7:14–25 therefore create a presumption that the "I" in Rom. 7:14–25 (and, by association, in 7:7–13) is also autobiographical. That Paul *might* have used a merely rhetorical "I" Kümmel certainly established. But a rising chorus of doubt greets the claim that Paul *did* use such an "I." Representative is N. A. Dahl's statement that "the element of personal confession in vv. 24–25a (cf. 14b–15, 18b–19) makes it difficult [to] acquiesce with the interpretation of the "I"-style as being simply a rhetorical device. . . ."[5] The poignant anguish and pathetic frustration voiced by the "I" demand that Paul wrote out of his own experience. To reverse a famous comment by T. W. Manson, we may call it the biography of Everyman if we like, but here Everyman's biography is the autobiography of Paul.[6] Surely Paul puts forward his experience as typical—otherwise it would fail to carry the argument—but it remains *his*. What could be plainer than the αὐτὸς ἐγώ of emphatic self-reference in verse 25? Combined with the pathos of the preceding outcry (verse 24), a rhetorical "I myself" would be incredibly theatrical.[7] Even a vicarious experience in Adam at the Fall would leave the intensity of emotion curious, to say the least.[8] And what would a rhetorical "I" gain for solving exegetical problems? Nothing, unless it excluded Paul. But elsewhere it does *not* (see Rom. 3:7; 1 Cor. 6:12, 15; 10:29–30; 13:1–3, 11–12; 14:11, 14–15; Gal. 2:18–21).

There are other reasons to doubt that Paul means to portray the Fall of Adam under "I"—a view that has recently gained much popularity, thanks largely to the writings of S. Lyonnet.[9] To be sure, salvation-history pervades the theology of Paul, so that, other things being equal, we might easily think that Paul means to distinguish a period without law from Creation to the Fall, a period with law from the Fall to the death of Christ, and a period of grace from the death of Christ onward. The Fall has already received special notice in Rom. 5:12-21. Adam's prominence in the earlier passage suggests that he is the referent in a rhetorical "I" incorporating the whole human race (cf. 2 Esdr. 7:118; also 3:7; 2 Apoc. Bar. 48:42-43; Str-B 3.227-229). And a number of parallels may be drawn between Rom. 7:7-25 and Genesis 1-3: (1) Paul's relating the "I" to the law corresponds to Adam's being put in Eden, according to Tg. Neofiti Genesis 1-3, to keep the law rather than cultivate the garden, the tree of life even being identified with the law; (2) living apart from the law once upon a time (Rom. 7:9a) parallels Adam's life in Eden prior to the commandment not to eat from the tree of the knowledge of good and evil (Gen. 2:16-17); (3) the commandment Paul cites in Rom. 7:7b, "You shall not lust [literally, 'desire strongly'—ἐπιθυμήσεις]," is similar to the commandment not to eat from the tree of knowledge, a commandment that contains the germ of the whole law[10] and began to be broken when desire, the quintessential sin, arose; (4) in both passages a prohibiting commandment becomes an instrument of sin; (5) personified sin in Rom. 7:7-25 corresponds to the serpent in Genesis 3; (6) deception takes place in both passages (Gen. 3:13; Rom. 7:11); and (7) in both, death results from sin.

Nevertheless, Eve, not Adam, was deceived in Genesis 3 and Eve, not Adam, desired the forbidden fruit. Consequently, not only the parallel suffers, but also the supportive backdrop of Rom. 5:12-21 drops away. 2 Cor. 11:3 and 1 Tim. 2:14 show that Paul makes a clear distinction between Adam and Eve in this matter. The omission of Adam's name in Rom. 7:7-25 (contrast 5:12-21; 1 Cor. 15:22) agrees with saying that Eve rather than Adam was deceived. Furthermore, though desire led to sin in Genesis 3, the broken commandment consisted in a prohibition of eating, not in a prohibition of desiring. Paul quotes the prohibition of desiring straight out of the decalogue (Exod. 20:17 LXX; Deut. 5:21 LXX; cf. Rom. 13:9), not out of the Fall-narrative. Saying that breaking the Mosaic law has its analogue in Adam's breaking the Edenic commandment[11] does no good; for then we have a period without law lasting till the giving of the law at Sinai, whereas the Fall is supposed to launch the period of law. In fact, the whole salvation-historical approach to Rom. 7:7-25 is problematic. It started out with viewing the period without law as extending till Moses.[12] Then Lyonnet pointed out that nowhere does the Bible describe the period before Moses as one of innocence (cf. the stories of the Flood, the tower of Babel, etc.). Certainly Paul does not (cf. Rom. 1:18–32). Therefore it is hard to think he has that period in mind when writing, "For apart from the law sin is dead. And I was once alive apart from the law" (Rom. 7:8b–9a).[13]

But Lyonnet's revision—viz., cutting short the period without law at the Fall—does no better. A satisfactory revision would require a cutting short *before* the Fall, in particular at the giving of the command not to eat from the tree of knowledge. But where is the evidence for positing such a period? The command came right after the creation and setting of man in Eden: there is no hint of an interval without law (Gen. 2:15–17). If by some trick of the imagination it could be thought there was such an interval, its extreme brevity militates against Paul's making it a discrete period of salvation-history and describing life during it with an imperfect tense, which implies some duration of action (ἔζων).

Feeling these difficulties, Lyonnet suggests that Adam was without law in Eden not in the sense that God had yet to give the commandment, but in the sense that Adam looked on the commandment not as such, but as the natural state of things—thus, the period without law lasted up to the Fall, when Adam first began to regard the commandment as externally imposed rather than internally created. It takes considerable ingenuity to read a distinction between internalized and externalized law into Paul's statements. That the distinction arises out of the necessities of the interpretation rather than out of the data of the text suggests that the interpretation itself is being imposed from without. Elsewhere in Paul the internalization of the law depends on the work of the Spirit (Rom. 8:12–14; Gal. 5:16–26); but the Spirit is notably absent in Romans 7. We may also wonder how much is gained by extending the period without law up to the Fall; for the narrative in Genesis seems to indicate that the Fall occurred immediately after God put Adam and Eve in the garden. If there was a period at all, it was so short that the disproportion between it and the period from the Fall to Christ's death calls in question the interpretation which makes Paul divide history in such a way.

We have by no means reached the end of difficulties in this salvation-historical view of Rom. 7:7–25. When the commandment came, sin sprang to life. It was already dwelling within the "I." But the serpent was external to Adam and did not even confront him, but Eve. Paul recognizes that sin was not dwelling within Adam before the Fall, for he explicitly says that "sin entered the world" at the Fall (Rom. 5:12). ἀνέζησεν (Rom. 7:9) is inappropriate to the entrance of sin even though the term means "sprang to life" rather than "revived."[14] Because Paul writes that Eve rather than Adam was deceived, it does not seem to be his view that Adam was powerless to resist sin. Yet the "I" in Rom. 7:7–25 *is* so powerless. In Rom. 5:12–14 Paul's discussion depends on the giving of the law not until Moses. In Gal. 3:17–19 Paul stresses that the law was a latecomer, 430 years after Abraham. How can we think that in Rom. 7:7–25 he sees the period of law as beginning at the Fall? For *Tg. Neofiti* to support his relating Adam to the law, the tree of knowledge, not the tree of life, should have been identified with the law; for law-breaking could only be represented by eating from the tree of knowledge.[15]

If the commandment, "You shall not lust," did not come when God put Adam and Eve in Eden, when did it come? It would be natural to think of the giving of the law at Sinai except for the difficulties in treating the "I" as rhetorical rather than autobiographical and in viewing sin as dead during the pre-Mosaic period. To take Paul as referring to his attaining the status of bar mitzvah remains the best interpretation. *Indeed, we may say that Paul slips into the ἐγώ-style precisely because becoming bar mitzvah applied to him but not to most of his readers, who were Gentiles.* His Jewish experience illustrates a universal principle and establishes the inability of the law to sanctify anybody, of course; but few of his readers shared its specifics. In writing of what he *does* share with them, he uses "we," "us," and "our" (see chs. 6 and 8).

Paul's reference to becoming bar mitzvah needs qualification, however. He singles out a particular commandment to establish his autobiographical point and only then refers to an early period of freedom from the law. When sin finally springs to life, it does so in response to the particular commandment just cited. The succeeding discussion plays on Paul's confrontation with *that* commandment even though he implies the inability of the whole law to sanctify a person. Failure to pay attention to this restriction underlies the otherwise valid criticism that Jewish lads had some considerable relation to the law from circumcision onward. The commandment Paul singles out prohibits lust, the very sin which, in its sexual sense, is dead (i.e., inactive—see Jas. 2:17, 26) prior to puberty but springs to life (i.e., becomes active) in a lad about the time he becomes bar mitzvah and therefore legally and morally responsible. And lust in Paul's vocabulary often carries a sexual connotation (most clearly in Rom. 1:24; 1 Thess. 4:5). It is usually thought that Paul lops off the objects of lust in the tenth commandment—"your neighbor's house . . . wife . . . male servant, etc."—in order to make the commandment a general prohibition of all sins which grow from the seed of lust. On the contrary, the omissions probably represent a simple abbreviation, as in Rom. 13:9, where the tenth commandment is simply one among equals, all of which are subsumed under "You shall love your neighbor as yourself"; and the abbreviation serves Paul's limited purview of the awakening of sexual desire at the very time his obligation to the law matured.[16]

The medieval origin of the bar mitzvah *ceremony* does not stand against this view, for the legal shift occurring at age thirteen originated in early talmudic times.[17] Nor does instruction in the law during boyhood present an obstacle, for Paul correlates knowing sin with sin's springing to life. Not instruction alone is in view, then, but instruction accompanied by the activity of sin; and not till puberty does sin use the prohibition of lust. According to the rabbis the evil impulse, which is to be tamed by the law, is largely sexual in nature. Any sensitive bar mitzvah would be worried by the tenth commandment,[18] especially because he is catapulted into adult responsibility to keep the law at the very time his sexual urges become so active he is unable to avoid defiling seminal emissions (cf. Leviticus 15).[19] Even Lyonnet recognizes the special relation of becoming bar mitzvah and certain sexual prohibitions.[20] "Apart from the law" does not mean the absence of the law in Jewish or universal history, then, but the absence of the tenth commandment as an instrument of sin and death in Paul's prepuberal boyhood. Sin's springing to life and using that commandment define the coming of the commandment as a coming in Paul's life rather than in Jewish or world history. His consequent death cannot be physical or eternal, for it has already taken place ("I died... this commandment... was found to result in death"). Rather, the contrast with the ability of sin to carry out its design—an activity that defines sin's life—determines that Paul's death consists in his inability to carry out a contrary design. A description of this kind of death occupies the rest of the chapter.[21] By the same token, Paul's earlier living, when sin was dead, means that lust did not tyrannize over him during his boyhood. His remaining a bachelor, if so he did, would make a later unsuccessful struggle with lust (lasting till the Spirit of Christ liberated him—verse 25a and ch. 8) quite understandable. Such a struggle would also fit the terms "fleshly," "flesh," "members," and "body" very well (7:14, 18, 23, 24–25).[22]

We must now face the objection that other passages—Acts 22:3; Gal. 1:13–14; Phil. 3:4–6—show Paul to have been self-righteously content rather than upset with frustration before his conversion. First, it must be said that Paul's zeal for and advancement in Judaism does not contradict an inward struggle with sexual desire. More than one sincerely zealous and eminently successful religionist has entered that contest and lost. Second, such a struggle need not have been the decisive element in Paul's conversion, which he consistently attributes to an appearance of the risen Lord. His defeat at the one point of the tenth commandment may have prepared him for conversion, but it could hardly have turned him into a Christian. Third, confidence in the flesh need not imply a claim to perfection, but only to right ancestry and a preponderance of right conduct, so that the minority of sins are forgiven.[23] These three considerations take care of Gal. 1:13–14; Acts 22:3; and most of Phil. 3:4–6.

Only the phrase, "as to the righteousness in the law, being blameless" (Phil. 3:6), remains. But Paul writes it from the standpoint of outside observers, whereas Rom. 7:7–25 describes an invisible struggle within.[24] The preceding items on the list in Philippians 3 are all observable—circumcision, national and tribal origins, cultural identification as a Hebraist, sectarian identification as a Pharisee, persecution of the church—and provide the details behind the summarizing "blameless." Furthermore, Paul is describing himself as a whole; but in Rom. 7:7–25 he describes a narrow aspect—his confrontation with the tenth commandment. Only by making "blameless" mean sinlessly perfect could we pit the term against the pre-Christian autobiographical view of Rom. 7:7–25. The people at Qumran out-Phariseed the Pharisees; yet among them a deep sense of personal sin co-existed with the conviction that they were the righteous (see esp. 1QH, often written in the "I"-style).

If "blameless" poses a problem at all, it does so for the rhetorical "I," too. The Adamic Everyman would include Paul. Therefore the supposed contradiction would still stand. Only by excluding Paul from the "I" (a usage no one admits) could the problem be solved in a way different from one which relieves the pre-Christian autobiographical interpretation. To make Paul blameless in himself (Phil. 3:4–6) and blameworthy only in Adam (Rom. 7:7–25 understood against the backdrop of 5:12–21 and Genesis 1–3) runs up against the affirmation that all, Jews and Gentiles alike, have sinned for themselves as well as in Adam. Indeed, the necessary qualification of "blameless" by Rom. 1:18–3:23—esp. by 2:17–29; 3:9–23, dealing with Jews, like Paul—makes a knock-down argument from Phil. 3:4–6 impossible. (N.B.: in Phil. 3:6 Paul does not say he *felt* blameless, i.e., had no awareness of sin; it is Rom. 7:7–25 that deals in introspection.) The very Jews Paul describes as zealously active in establishing their own righteousness (Rom. 10:2–3) are the same as those he accuses of law-breaking (Rom. 2:17ff.). Gal. 3:10 provides an even clearer qualification: "For as many as are of the works of the law are under a curse; for it is written, 'Cursed is everyone who does not abide in all the things that are written in the book of the law by doing them.'" Since "as many as are of the works of the law" must include Paul before his conversion, he must have been under the curse for having failed to keep the law wholly.[25]

If Paul's blamelessness and defeat do not contradict each other, then, does his wretchedness in Rom. 7:14–25 contradict his pre-

Christian Pharisaism? Not necessarily. Frustration with regard to a single commandment does not tell the whole tale concerning his experience of the law; nor does the general pleasure which Pharisees took in keeping the law rule out particular frustrations over besetting sins. We get more than a hint of such frustrations in *b. Ber.* 17a, a passage that includes the element of pleasure. Like the Pharisee in Luke 18:9-13, the rich young ruler was generally self-satisfied; but one commandment—the very tenth which Paul stumbled at and Jesus led up to but left unquoted— proved his undoing (Mark 10:17-22; Matt. 19:15-22; Luke 18:18-23). Agreement with and delight in God's law (Rom. 7:16, 22) do not reflect Christian experience, which would have to include performance as well (8:4); instead, they correspond to the zeal for the law Paul attributes to his pre-Christian self and to unbelieving Jews (Acts 22:3; Rom. 10:2-3; Gal. 1:13-14; Phil. 3:4-6). Since this zeal does not preclude law-breaking, the parallel with Rom. 7:7-25 holds up. Those who delight in sin are pagans (Rom. 1:18-32). The zealous but unbelieving Jews Paul writes about do not delight in breaking the law. Though they break it, they learn it, rely on it, approve the excellent things it teaches, teach it to others, and boast in God—a description that matches agreeing with and delighting in the law (cf. Rom. 2:17-20).

The delight of OT saints in God's law included performance and therefore does not correspond to the frustrated delight in Rom. 7:14-25. Similarly, the willing of God's good pleasure in Phil. 2:13 is a willing accompanied by performance. That God is its source, therefore, does not contradict the unregenerate willing that fails to issue in performance in Rom. 7:14-25, where not the whole man but only the inner man, or mind, delights in the law.[26] The inner man is not the man in Christ, which has to do with sanctification (Eph. 2:15; 4:24; Col. 3:10), but the nonphysical part of man's constitution, which has to do with psychical feelings.[27] Likewise, the mind is not a Christian's renewed mind; for that would have transformed conduct into a demonstration of God's will (Rom. 12:1-2). Furthermore, since even the mind of a Christian has to be exhorted to renewal (Rom. 12:2), the mind as such does not imply regeneration. Even pagans recognize God's righteous edict that sinners deserve to die (Rom. 1:32); so it should not surprise us that the unrenewed mind of a nomistic Jew agrees with and delights in God's law.

Serving sin in 6:16-20 has to do with actions performed through the body (see esp. the term "members" in verse 19; cf. verses 12-14). Serving God's law in 7:25b has to do with the mind, expressly mentioned. Hence, there is no disharmony in taking both passages as descriptive of unregenerate life. In fact, 7:25b also speaks of serving the law of sin with the flesh, which, because of the interchangeability of "flesh" and "members," matches serving sin with the members in 6:16-20.

Those who oppose the pre-Christian view cite the hostility of the unregenerate mind toward God in Rom. 8:5-7 and deduce that the mind which agrees with and delights in God's law in 7:16, 22 is regenerate. But the mind of 7:14-25 is a moral monitor such as even pagans have, though it may be corrupted (again see 1:32; also 1:18-20 and perhaps 2:14-15). According to 10:2-3 the Jews, motivated by such a monitor and seeking to establish their own righteousness, "did not subject themselves to God's righteousness." The phraseology echoes 8:7: "the mind of the flesh does not subject itself to God's law." In its agreement with and delight in God's law, then, the mind stands over against sin in the flesh, members, and body. In its attempt to establish a man's own righteousness (so among the Jews) as well as in its succumbing to corruption (so among the pagans), the mind stands over against God and his righteousness. The switch from νοῦς in 7:16, 22 to φρόνημα in 8:5-7 and the qualification "of the flesh" in 8:5-7 signal the shift in connotations. But ultimately the same mind is in view.

"Mind" and "inner man" resist the notion that Paul is delineating pre-Christian experience *from a Christian point of view*, that a non-Christian would be unaware of the nature of the struggle going on within him. This way of harmonizing the self-satisfaction in Phil. 3:4-6 and the turmoil in Rom. 7:7-25 also runs up against the emotional intensity of the latter passage, an intensity that seizes on the vivid historical present, interjects the emphatic ἐγώ, lurches back and forth between confession and self-exoneration, suffers the tension of willing the good and doing the bad, takes enjoyment in God's law, and pitches into despair over inability to carry out that law. No alien analysis from a distant standpoint here! To speak the way he does, the subject must have been self-conscious at the time the warfare raged within him.[28]

His defeat at the hands of sin brings us to well-known connections and contrasts between 7:7-25 and 6:1-7:6; 8:1-39, connections and contrasts widely considered to offer the strongest evidence for taking the whole of 7:7-25 as pre-Christian. "When the commandment came, sin sprang to life and I died" (8:9b-10a) surely describes what happened before conversion. Yet Paul links this description, the whole of which occupies verses 7-13, to verses 14-25 with γάρ, "For" (14a). At this point we would have expected disjunction rather than linkage if Paul had meant to shift to Christian experience. As it is, he immediately announces that he is "fleshly" (verse 14). This announcement recalls verse 5, "For when we were in the flesh," which because of the past tense and the context of verses 1-6 clearly refers to the unregenerate state.[29] To be sure, Paul is capable of calling Christians "fleshly" (1 Cor. 3:1-3) and saying that they are "in the flesh" (2 Cor. 10:3; Gal. 2:20; Phil. 1:22, 24; Phlm. 16). But in context the latter expression has no moral connotations; it refers simply to earthly life. And the behaviour of a "fleshly" Christian calls in question the genuineness of his faith (Gal. 5:19–21). The immediate context of chs. 7–8 determines that the fleshly "I" of 7:14 is unregenerate.[30] For "those who are in Christ Jesus... do not walk according to the flesh.... For the mind of the flesh is death..., because the mind of the flesh is hostile toward God.... and those who are in the flesh cannot please God. But you are not in the flesh; rather, in the Spirit, if indeed the Spirit of God dwells in you. And if anyone does not have the Spirit of Christ, this person does not belong to him" (8:1–9, excerpts). So Paul is discussing a difference in conduct between Christians and non-Christians, not between victorious Christians and defeated Christians.

The difference cannot be evaded by limiting 7:7–25 (or 14–25) to sensitivity to sin.[31] No, sinful activity ("What I hate, this I do ... the bad which I do not want [to do], this I *practise*"—verses 15, 19) versus right conduct ("resulting in sanctification"—6:22; "walk" [a common metaphor for conduct]—8:4) spells the difference (cf. 1 Cor. 6:9–11; 2 Cor. 5:21; Eph. 2:1–3; 1 John 3:4–12). On the non-Christian side, there is extended domination by sin. Otherwise, the expressed frustration over inability to do the good and avoid the bad becomes nonsensical and the outcry in 7:24, affected. On the Christian side, possession of the Spirit makes the difference. Paul's statement that anyone who does not have the Spirit of Christ does not belong to Christ looks like a comment on the absence of the Spirit in 7:7–25.[32] The comment implies that the "I" in 7:7–25 does not belong to Christ. To this agrees the contrast between the moral defeat of the "I," which is "sold under sin" and "captive to the law of sin," and the moral victory of "those who are in Christ Jesus," who are "set free from the law of sin and of death," who fulfill "the righteous requirement of the law," and who "walk... according to the Spirit" (see also 6:17–18, 22). The law of sin and of death recalls "the passions of sins which were aroused by the law [and] worked in our members so as to bear fruit" (7:5). Since the earlier passage undoubtedly relates to those outside Christ, so also does the latter.[33]

The serving of righteousness "in newness of the Spirit" rests on believers' being "released from the law" (7:6). Yet 7:7–25 presumes being under the law: "when the commandment came,... I died.... For sin, taking opportunity through the commandment, deceived me and through it killed me... effecting my death through that which is good.... For we know that the law is spiritual.... I agree with the law, that it is good.... I delight in the law of God in the inner man, but I see a different law in my members... making me captive to the law of sin which is in my members." Paul wants not only to exonerate the law, but also to show its worse-than-inability to sanctify those who are under it—and they do *not* include Christians, as he has made plain with respect to sanctification as well as justification (6:14–7:6; cf. 8:1–4, where justification shades into sanctification[34]). The emphatic "Now then" and the back reference to release from condemnation for those who are in Christ Jesus at the start of ch. 8 (cf. 3:19–5:21) seal the exclusion: Paul is no longer talking about his pre-Christian self, captured by sin and condemned under the law, but about all those who are free from the law and justified in Christ. Thus the "I" of 7:7–25 is never said to be "in Christ." Its wretchedness (verse 24a) contrasts sharply with the assured "Abba! Father!" of those who in Christ have the Spirit.[35]

It has become quite popular to use the overlapping of the present age and the age to come as a means of making the contrasts between 7:14–25 and 6:1–7:6; 8:1–39 compatible with a Christian referent in 7:14–25. Living in both ages at the same time, Christians are simultaneously sinners and saints. It is not that they are sometimes good, sometimes bad. Rather, everything they do is conditioned by both the Spirit and sin. Thus, the Christian and his conduct may be described in seemingly contradictory ways.

Undeniably, Christians live in the ambiguity of an eschatological overlap. That they are not sinless and do die, yet are called "saints" and have eternal life, proves as much.[36] But this situation does not adequately explain the contrasts between 7:14–25 and 6:1–7:6; 8:1–39. The "I" in 7:14–25 is not merely unable to avoid a mixture of the good and the bad. It cannot do the good at all, only the bad. Sin has taken over so completely that the "I" is imprisoned.[37] Contrariwise, those who are in Christ "do not walk according to the flesh, but according to the Spirit" (8:4). The wording is exclusive.

Nevertheless, those who are in Christ need exhortations not to walk according to the flesh, but according to the Spirit. There is an ambiguity, then; but it is not so much an eschatological one as an ambiguity arising out of the possibility of false profession and the consequent possibility of apostasy. Ultimately, of course, the overlapping of the ages gives rise to these possibilities. But it is the ambiguity of profession vis-à-vis reality which provides the immediate reason for exhortations not to forfeit salvation by failing to live holily. These exhortations crop up throughout the NT (Matt. 5:19–20; 13:24–30, 36–43; 22:11–14; 25:1–13; John 15:1–6; Rom. 6:12–13; 13:14; 1 Cor. 9:27; 15:2; 2 Cor. 13:5; Gal. 5:16–6:10; Heb. 4:11–13; 6:1–12; 10:26–31; 2 Pet. 1:4–11; Revelation 2–3 are representative).

One of them merits special discussion because some have used it to argue for the Christian view of Rom. 7:14–25. It is Gal. 5:16–17, which, according to the argument, describes the same tension we find in Rom. 7:14–25 yet incontestably deals with Christian experience. But wide differences separate the two passages. The desire of the Spirit figures prominently in Gal. 5:16–17; but delight in God's law is related to the inner man or mind, not the Spirit, in Rom. 7:14–25.[38] In Gal. 5:16–17 the Spirit opposes the flesh; in Rom. 7:14–25 the mind, or inner man, opposes sin. In Gal. 5:16–17 the flesh is virtually equivalent to sin (cf. verses 19–21); in Rom. 7:14–25 flesh is equivalent to the members and the body, differs from sin as its dwelling place and means of action, and is sin's victim rather than the Spirit's opponent. The "I" suffers defeat in Rom. 7:14–25; the Spirit gives victory in Gal. 5:16, 22–24. Rom. 7:14–25 is a dismal description, Gal. 5:16–17 a confident exhortation. In Rom. 7:14–25 Paul speaks of actualities; in Gal. 5:16–17, about purposes—the desire of the flesh, the desire of the Spirit, ἵνα μή + the subjunctive.[39] When actualities finally come into view in Galatians 5, Paul makes clear that the person whose life is characterized by the deeds of the flesh is not regenerate: "Now the deeds of the flesh are evident . . . those who practise such things will not inherit the kingdom of God" (verses 19–21). Since "those who belong to Christ Jesus have crucified the flesh with its passions and desires" (Gal. 5:24), the power of sin in Rom. 7:14–25 makes Gal. 5:16–24 damaging rather than helpful to the case for regenerate experience in Rom. 7:14–25.

The power of sin leads to the outcry, "Wretched man that I am! Who will rescue me from the body of this death?" (verse 24). Some have seen a parallel with "the body is dead because of sin" in 8:10 and reasoned that since this statement, introduced with the clause "but if Christ is in you," has to do with Christians, "the body of this death" in 7:24 must also belong to a Christian. His cry for deliverance and the thanksgiving in verse 25a look forward, then, to translation and resurrection (cf. 8:23; 1 Cor. 15:50–58).

But in 8:10 the body is dead in the sense that it is mortal, under the sentence of death (see verse 11 and 6:12[40]). Physical death is in view. But "*this* death" in 7:24 looks back to a different kind of death, the one mentioned in verses 10, 11, and 13 (cf. 8:2): Paul's inability to carry out his designs when sin sprang to life. (The word-order in 7:24 and the antecedents in verses 10, 11, and 13 favor "the body of this death" over "this body of death.") Therefore the pre-Christian "I," shackled by a body that sin dominates, cries out for a deliverance that would consist in a body which, though mortal, is freed and filled by the Spirit, its members "instruments of righteousness to God" (see 6:12–23 for the best commentary; also 1 Cor. 6:19–20). Such a deliverance takes place at conversion, not at the last day. And it is God who effects that deliverance through Jesus Christ our Lord—therefore the thanksgiving in verse 25a (cf. the similar thanksgiving in 6:17, which unquestionably deals with conversion).

The thanksgiving in verse 25a follows naturally upon the outcry and question in verse 24. But the stepping back in verse 25b to summarize verses 7–23 or 14–23 has seemed so awkward that it has been considered a gloss.[41] No textual critical evidence supports the theory of a gloss, however; and if verse 25b were a gloss, some such evidence would probably bear witness to the pure text.[42] Furthermore, Dahl points out that verses 6b and 25b bracket verses 7–25a:

> Drawing the conclusion of the section, v. 25b corrects a possible misunderstanding of what was said in v. 6b. To be enslaved *palaiotēti grammatos* is not really to be subservient to the law of God, which is served by the *nous* only; in the sphere of the flesh (in which actions are done), "I serve the law of sin." A delayed conclusion, inserted after the beginning of a new trend of thought, would not be without analogy (cf. e.g. Rom 10:17).[43]

Therefore the argument that under the pre-Christian view verse 25b is anticlimactic proves weak. Those who put it forward fail to recognize that under *any* view, Paul steps back in verse 25b to draw a conclusion concerning verses 7–24 or 14–24. We would have to say so even though a Christian were speaking in ch. 7 as well as ch. 8. Either the backward step is radical from the chronological standpoint (a Christian "I" looks forward to his resurrection at the last day in verse 25a and reverts to his present struggle in verse 25b), or it is radical in the shifting role of the speaker (the "I" speaks as a victorious Christian in verse 25a but as a wretchedly defeated Christian or non-Christian in verse 25b). In fact, there is a backward step in 8:1, too—all the way back to justification—before Paul takes up sanctification again (cf. the parallel between "Therefore then" in 7:25b and "Now then" in 8:1). Since not even a Christian view of 7:14–25 can avoid the backward step in 8:1, little room is left for denying what is inherently likely, viz., that at an emotional pitch Paul felt his lament and question in verse 24 needed an immediate response before the drawing of a conclusion and the building of a counter theme.[44]

The outcome: Rom. 7:14–25 does not describe, let alone excuse, moral defeat as a necessary experience of true Christians. Rather, the whole of Rom. 7:7–25 leads up to the availability of moral victory in Rom. 8:1–17, a victory that is characteristic as well as possible. Hence, the extended suffering of moral defeat should cause either a questioning of Christian profession or a questioning of the petty standards by which Christians often evaluate their lives.

Notes

1. Kümmel, *Römer 7 und die Bekehrung des Paulus* (1929), reprinted in *Römer 7 und das Bild des Menschen im Neuen Testament* (TBü 53; Munich,

Kaiser, 1974). Typical of the announcements that Kümmel settled the matter are R. Schnackenburg's ("Römer 7 im Zusammenhang des Römerbriefes," *Jesus und Paulus*, Festschrift for W. G. Kümmel [2nd ed.; eds. E. E. Ellis and E. Grässer; Göttingen, Vandenhoeck & Ruprecht, 1978], 293) and G. Schunack's (*Das hermeneutische Problem des Todes* [Tübingen, Mohr, 1967], 108–109).

2. Especially noteworthy is the support given to one or both sides of the interpretation by A. Nygren, *Commentary on Romans* (Philadelphia, Muhlenberg, 1949), 277–303; K. Stalder, *Das Werk des Geistes in der Heiligung bei Paulus* (Zürich, EVZ-Verlag, 1962), 295–307; C. E. B. Cranfield, *A Critical and Exegetical Commentary on the Epistle to the Romans* (ICC; Edinburgh, T. & T. Clark, 1975), 1. 340–370; J. D. G. Dunn, "Rom. 7,14–25 in the Theology of Paul," *TZ* 5 (1975), 257–273; idem, *Jesus and the Spirit* (Philadelphia, Westminster, 1975), 313–316.

3. F. F. Bruce, "Paul and the Law of Moses," *BJRL* 57 (1974–75), 273, n. 1.

4. Cranfield, *Romans*, 1.344–345. Dunn's arguing that ᾔδειν in verse 7 probably implies an experience of lust that has continuēd into the present ("Rom. 7,14–25," 261) flounders in its failure to maintain the difference between verses 7–13 and 14–25 that would be indispensable to an argument from the present tense, and in its requiring the imperfect force of the pluperfect ᾔδειν to carry the action into the present.

5. N. A. Dahl, "The Pauline Letters: Proposal for a Study Project of an SBL Seminar on Paul" (unpublished paper), 17. Similar opinions may be found in C. L. Mitton, "Romans vii Reconsidered," *ExpT* 65 (1953–54), 78; M. Goguel, *The Birth of Christianity* (New York, Macmillan, 1954), 213–214; S. Sandmel, *The Genius of Paul* (New York, Farrar, Straus, and Cudahy, 1958), 28, 56; J. I. Packer, "The 'Wretched Man' in Romans 7," *SE* 2/1 (1964), 621–627; K. Kertelge, "Exegetische Überlegungen zum Verständnis der paulinischen Anthropologie nach Römer 7," *ZNW* 62 (1971), 106–107; J. Lambrecht, "Man Before and Without Christ: Rom 7 and Pauline Anthropology," *Louvain Studies* 5 (1974), 29, 31–32.

6. Cf. T. W. Manson, "Romans," *Peake's Commentary on the Bible*, eds. M. Black and H. H. Rowley (London, Nelson, 1962), 945.

7. αὐτὸς ἐγώ hardly means "I by myself" (i.e., without the help of the Holy Spirit), despite Mitton's lengthy attempt to establish that understanding ("Romans vii Reconsidered," 78–80, 99–103, 132–135). Under it, the preceding bulk of the passage would be unintelligible so far as this sense of "I" is concerned; and elsewhere in Paul the expression is simply intensive, not technical in the sense suggested (see U. Luz, *Das Geschichtsverständnis des Paulus* [BEvT 49; Munich, Kaiser, 1968], 160; R. Y.-K. Fung, "The Impotence of the Law: Toward a Fresh Understanding of Romans 7:14–25," *Scripture, Tradition, and Interpretation*, Essays Presented to E. F. Harrison, eds. W. W. Gasque and W. S. LaSor [Grand Rapids, Eerdmans, 1978], 39–40).

8. Dunn makes this point very well ("Rom. 7,14–25," 260–261; *Jesus and the Spirit*, 314).

9. S. Lyonnet, "Quaestiones ad Rom 7, 7–13," *VD* 40 (1962), 163–183; idem, "L'histoire du salut selon le chapitre vii de l'Epître aux Romains," *Bib* 43 (1962), 117–151; idem, "Tu ne convoiteras pas," *Neotestamentica et Patristica*, Festschrift for O. Cullmann (NovTSup 6; Leiden, Brill, 1962), 157–165; idem, "History of Salvation in Romans 7," *Theology Digest* 13 (1965), 35–38 (a summary of the article in *Biblica*); idem, *Les étapes de l'histoire du salut selon l'Epître aux Romains* (Bibliothèque oecuménique 8; Paris, Cerf, 1969), 113–137.

10. Gen. 3:6; cf. 1 John 2:15–17; *Tg. Neof.* Exod. 20:17 and Deut. 5:18[21]; *Apoc. Mos.* 19:3; Philo, *De decal.* 142, 150, 173; 4 Macc. 2:6, *b. Šabb.* 145b–146a

242 PAULINE STUDIES

11. See, e.g., P. von der Osten-Sacken, *Römer 8 als Beispiel paulinischer Soteriologie* (FRLANT 112; Göttingen, Vandenhoeck & Ruprecht, 1975), 198–199; G. Bornkamm, *Early Christian Experience* (New York, Harper & Row, 1969), 93–94.

12. E. Stauffer, among others, propounds this view ("ἐγώ," *TDNT* 2 [1964], 358).

13. "Sin is dead" does not mean "sin is not imputed" (Rom. 5:13). Here, sin's power is in view; in 5:13, sin's penalty.

14. F. Godet, *Commentary on the Epistle to the Romans* (1883; reprint, Grand Rapids, Zondervan, 1969), 280.

15. According to H. Schlier (*Der Römerbrief* [HTKNT; Freiburg, Herder, 1977], 224), "the commandment *came*" (Rom. 7:9b) makes sense only in terms of Genesis 1–3. But the argument requires a discrete period from Creation to the prohibiting of the tree of knowledge, *not* up to the Fall; for at the Fall the commandment could not have come in the sense of being given, but only in that of impinging on Adam's consciousness—yet the latter sense would agree with a Pauline autobiography. On the other hand, we have already noted the lack of evidence for a discrete period from Creation to the prohibiting of the tree of knowledge. At the opposite extreme, E. Brandenburger illegitimately modernizes Paul by making him dehistoricize Adam's Fall and treat it as typical of what happens to post-Mosaic man when the law comes (*Adam und Christus* [WMANT 7; Neukirchen, Neukirchener Verlag, 1962], 215–216).

16. Bornkamm says that Paul omits particular objects from the tenth commandment in order to leave room for "the possibility that 'desire' can express itself nomistically just as much as antinomistically, i.e. in the zeal for one's own righteousness (Rom. 10.3)" (*Early Christian Experience*, 90). This ties in with his adopting Bultmann's trans-subjective interpretation and the attempt to see the doctrine of justification at every possible turn in Paul. Whether or not Paul's theology centers on justification, he can talk about other topics; and here he is discussing sanctification. See R. Bultmann, *Theology of the New Testament* (New York, Scribner's 1951), 1.247–248; idem, *The Old and New Man in the Letters of Paul* (1932; reprinted, Richmond, John Knox, 1967), 16, 33ff.; and, for sufficient criticisms, H. Ridderbos, *Paul* (Grand Rapids, Eerdmans, 1975), 146; Kertelge, "Exegetische Überlegungen," 107; A. van Dülmen, *Die Theologie des Gesetzes bei Paulus* (Stuttgart, Katholisches Bibelwerk, 1968), 114, n. 134; O. Kuss, *Der Römerbrief* (Regensburg, Pustet, 1959), 2.469–470. Similarly, see Luz, *Geschichtsverständnis*, 162, against interpretation in terms of a person who is developing into a Christian, a Christian who has not yet received the Spirit, or a Christian who has fallen away or lapsed into dependence on the law.

17. Z. Kaplan, "Bar Mitzvah, Bat Mitzvah," *Enc Jud* 4.243–244.

18. W. D. Davies, *Paul and Rabbinic Judaism* (2nd ed.; London, SPCK, 1962), 24–26, 30–31.

19. G. W. Buchanan, *The Consequences of the Covenant* (NovTSup 20; Leiden, Brill, 1970), 182–184.

20. S. Lyonnet, "L'histoire du salut . . . ," 122, n. 2.

21. Concerning extra-biblical parallels, see Bruce, "Paul and the Law of Moses," 271. The objection that Paul does not elsewhere engage in introspection is ill-founded (see Rom. 9:1–3; 1 Cor. 4:4a; 2 Cor. 1:8–9, 12, 17; 4:16; 10:1; 12:1–10; Phil. 1:23–26; 3:7–14; 4:11–13; Col. 2:1; 1 Thess. 2:3–12; 3:1, 5; 2 Tim. 1:3).

22. On the physical connotations of these terms, see R. H. Gundry, *Sōma in Biblical Theology* (SNTSMS 29; Cambridge, Cambridge University Press, 1976), 137–140. Verse 25a shows that deliverance did not come till conversion.

23. Cf. E. P. Sanders, *Paul and Palestinian Judaism* (Philadelphia, Fortress, 1977), passim.

24. Cf. A. C. Purdy, "Paul the Apostle," *IDB*, 3.685.

25. Strangely, E. P. Sanders (*Paul and Palestinian Judaism*, 443, n. 4) overlooks Gal. 3:10 in appealing to Gal. 3:11–12 for the position that Paul repudiates the law on grounds of Christology and soteriology, but not on the ground of the unfulfillability of the law. Verse 10 affirms what Sanders denies and subverts his primary thesis that Paul did not start with man's need of salvation, but with God's deed of salvation. Do we need to put either one ahead of the other in Paul's thought?

26. For this reason, Paul can say on the one hand, "It is no longer I that do it [the bad]," and on the other hand, "What I hate [the bad], this I do." It is not regeneration that splits the "I" from its actions, as Nygren argues (*Romans*, 286), but a constitutional distinction true of all human beings—a distinction between physical and non-physical parts, so that the "I" may identify itself with the inner man, or mind, and distance itself from the flesh, members, or body, whose actions sin determines much to the distress of the inner man, or mind.

27. See a much fuller discussion in Gundry, *Sōma*, 135–140.

28. In favor of later Christian analysis, Luz argues that a *dead* "I" could have neither spoken of its death nor distinguished between life and death (*Geschichtsverständnis*, 162). The argument misconstrues "I died" (verse 10). Paul does not mean that he lost consciousness. He means he lost control. Later Christian analysis would allow a temporal meaning of "now" and "no longer" in verses 17 and 20; but since the logical meaning would remain possible, no point of argument arises.

29. With all due respect to Stalder (*Das Werk des Geistes*, 292–293), who denies that justification takes place once for all (but see Rom. 5:1, 9) and therefore assigns even Rom. 7:4–5 to present Christian experience.

30. Strictly speaking, the fleshly "I" in 7:14 is not a sinful "I," but an "I" whose physical weakness and needs make it easy prey for sin (see Gundry, *Sōma*, 137–138).

31. For example, C. E. B. Cranfield, "The Freedom of the Christian according to Romans 8.2," *New Testament Christianity for Africa and the World*, Essays in honour of Harry Sawyerr, eds. M. E. Glasswell and E. W. Fasholé-Luke (London, SPCK, 1974), 94–96. Cf. further minimization of the difference by saying that 7:7–25 shows the "tainting" with sin of even the Christian's best actions (Cranfield, *Romans*, 1.361; cf. Packer, "The 'Wretched Man' in Romans 7," 626; Stalder, *Das Werk des Geistes*, 293–294).

32. Dunn ("Rom. 7, 14–25," 261–262) thinks the battle with sin in 7:14–25 contrasts with a lack of resistance to sin in 7:7–13 and implies that the Spirit is joining battle in Paul with the flesh (cf. Gal. 5:16–17). But the admission that Paul "is still defeated" casts doubt on the Spirit's combat. And, as already noted, Paul joins rather than breaks apart 7:7–13 and 14–25; hence, his discussion simply progresses with the addition of a new element. The victory of sin (verses 14–25) does not disagree with the deceit of sin (verses 7–13). More than one battle has been won by deceit. Cranfield's attempt to read the Spirit between the lines of 7:14–25 is equally weak: he reasons that the qualification "in my flesh" (verse 18) implies that the Holy Spirit dwells elsewhere in the "I" (Cranfield, *Romans*, 1.360–361). But in this passage "flesh" parallels "members" and "body," and the Christian's "body is a temple of the Holy Spirit" (1 Cor. 6:19).

33. J. Murray (*The Epistle to the Romans* [NICNT; Grand Rapids, Eerdmans, 1959], 1.260–261) tries to make an argument for the Christian view

out of being sold under sin and captive to it: since in 1 Kgs. 21:20, 25; 2 Kgs. 17:17 the wicked are active agents in selling themselves to sin but in Rom. 7:14 the self is victimized, and because the "I" in 7:14–23 is captive to sin rather than wicked *per se*, its true character must be regenerate. One wonders what would happen to "redemption" under such reasoning.

34. C. Hodge tries to eliminate the contrast between chs. 7 and 8 by settling on the "no condemnation" of 8:1 (*Commentary on the Epistle to the Romans* [1886; reprint, Grand Rapids, Eerdmans, 1968], 244–245). But though 8:1 refers to justification (so that the referent of the inferential "then" becomes a question), 8:2ff. immediately returns to sanctification and sustains the contrasts already evident in a comparison of 6:1–7:6 and 7:7–25.

35. The wretchedness of a captive to the law of sin and of death differs from the sighing of Christians, liberated from that law but suffering with the rest of creation the pains of the old age while waiting for the new (contrast 7:23–24 with 8:18–25).

36. Dunn's discussion suffers at this point, however, because he confuses Christians' sharing in the death of Jesus through their persecutions and their suffering death as the lingering effect of their own and Adam's sin ("Rom. 7, 14–25," 269–271).

37. The contextual restriction to the particular commandment used by sin qualifies this inability; but those who appeal to eschatological tension usually cut 7:14–25 loose from 7:7–13, since 7:7–13 most naturally antedates conversion. The consequent generalizing of 7:14–25 exacerbates the problem of inability. Without the restriction, totally sinful conduct is required in 7:14–25 and sinless perfection in 8:1ff.; for Paul's language brooks no softening.

38. We have already seen that "mind" and "inner man" do not imply regeneration.

39. "In order that you may not do the things that you want" apparently means that the flesh aims to thwart the Spirit when you want to do good and that the Spirit aims to thwart the flesh when you want to do evil. Some interpret ἵνα μή as ecbatic here; but in the thirty-eight other places where Paul uses the construction, it is telic. The sole exception comes in 1 Cor. 1:10. There it is epexegetical, however, and does not make a real exception; for the epexegetical is a brand of the telic in that purpose is wrapped up in the content of what ἵνα μή introduces. In a few other Pauline passages the ecbatic meaning is possible, but the normal telic meaning more natural. Even Fung, who takes the ecbatic meaning and interprets Rom. 7:14–25 as the experience of a Christian who tries to keep God's law by his own efforts, admits that Gal. 5:16–17 envisions a different situation ("The Impotence of the Law," 36–37).

40. See also Gundry, *Sōma*, 37–47, though the interpretation of 7:24 needs modification by the following comments here.

41. See, e.g., R. Bultmann, *Exegetica* (Tübingen, Mohr, 1967), 278–279. His drawing a line between serving God's law with the mind (verse 25b) and agreeing with and delighting in God's law according to the inner man (verses 16, 22) is forced.

42. K. Aland, "Glosse, Interpolation, Redaktion und Komposition in der Sicht der neutestamentlichen Textkritik," *Apophoreta*, Festschrift for E. Haenchen (BZNW 30; Berlin, Töpelmann, 1964), 27–31.

43. Dahl, "The Pauline Letters," 25. Cf. also the doxology in 1:25b, after which Paul goes back to finish his former line of thought. Dahl's explanation is better than W. Keuk's attempt to make 7:25b a question beginning a new section

("Dienst des Geistes und des Fleisches. Zur Auslegungsgeschichte und Auslegung von Rm 7,25 b," *TQ* 141 [1961], 257–280).

44. Cranfield (*Romans*, 1. 345) thinks the emotional pitch "highly melodramatic" if a Christian "I" is not crying for deliverance from present distress. But is the cry any less melodramatic on the lips of a Christian "I" for whom deliverance from the power of sin is readily available and whose bodily resurrection is assured and believed in as a matter of creed? The further argument that if 7:14–25 were pre-Christian it would have appeared in Paul's discussion of humanity without Christ (1:18–3:20) deserves treatment only in a footnote. The argument either leaves 7:7–13 pre-Christian, and by doing so forfeits itself, or demands a Christian referent for 7:7–13, which goes against the wording of the passage. In 1:18–3:20 Paul shows the powerlessness of the law to justify, in 7:7–25 its powerlessness to sanctify: there is no duplication (Godet, *Romans*, 271). Chapter 7 helps ch. 6 draw out 5:20–21: ch. 6 seeks to counteract the domination of sin; ch. 7 describes the role of the law in that domination (Schnackenburg, "Römer 7," 297). And 7:5 sets the theme for 7:7–25; similarly, 7:6 sets the theme for 8:1ff. (Luz, *Geschichtsverständnis*, 161; idem, "Zum Aufbau von Röm. 1–8," *TZ* 25 [1969], 161–181).

Chapter 15

JUSTIFICATION BY FAITH IN 1 & 2 CORINTHIANS

RONALD Y.-K. FUNG

JUSTIFICATION BY FAITH HAS, TRADITIONALLY, been held to be the centre of Paul's theology. In modern times, however, the view has been gaining ground which regards this doctrine as being of merely subsidiary significance to Paul. The most notable exponents of this new appraisal of its status in the apostle's thought include Carl von Weizsäcker,[1] William Wrede,[2] Wilhelm Heitmüller[3] and Albert Schweitzer.[4] In their down-grading of the doctrine these scholars have been followed in more recent years by H. J. Schoeps[5] and, in the English-speaking world, by C. H. Buck, Jr.,[6] Krister Stendahl,[7] W. D. Davies[8] and E. P. Sanders.[9]

On the other side, the fundamental significance and centrality of justification by faith in Paul's thought has been maintained by scholars like J. Gresham Machen,[10] H. D. Wendland,[11] J. I. Packer,[12] Karl Kertelge,[13] Hans Conzelmann,[14] Günther Bornkamm,[15] Ernst Käsemann[16] and, last but not least, F. F. Bruce. Professor Bruce regards as properly given the emphasis which Bornkamm and Käsemann place on the centrality of Paul's doctrine of justification to his whole concept of the gospel, not only in polemical situations; against the view of Buck and Wrede, Bruce maintains that "the essence of justification by faith was probably implicit in the logic of his [i.e. Paul's] conversion."[17] At the same time, Professor Bruce holds that crucial as the doctrine of justification by faith is to Paul's understanding of the gospel, it does not exhaust that gospel:

> Paul sets his doctrine of justification, together with his other doctrines, in the context of the new creation that has come into being with Christ. That

246

the acquittal of the day of judgment is pronounced here and now on those who put their faith in Jesus is part and parcel of the truth that for them "the old order has gone, and a new order has already begun" (2 Cor. v. 17, NEB).[18]

This estimate of the status of justification in Paul is similar to the view of Herman N. Ridderbos, who, whilst affirming that the doctrine "unmistakably belongs to the very heart of Paul's preaching," judges that it nevertheless is but one aspect, although a very central aspect, of the great redemption accomplished by Christ, and that the perspective of *Heilsgeschichte* "alone can illuminate the many facets and interrelations of his preaching."[19]

With this all-too-brief introduction to the modern debate on the status of justification by faith in Paul's thought[20] as background, we offer in the following pages a study of the doctrine as it finds expression in 1 and 2 Corinthians. Since the fact that the doctrine is set forth in detail only in Galatians and Romans might seem to lend support to the claim that the doctrine is of merely polemical significance, it is important not to overlook Paul's teaching on the subject in his other epistles. Here we shall confine our attention to the other two *Hauptbriefe*, where four passages are to be considered.

I. 1 Corinthians 1:18-31

In dealing with the report received from Chloe's people that there were quarrels among the Corinthians, Paul exposes the root cause of the divisions as basically twofold: the Corinthian converts had a wrong conception both of wisdom (1:18-2:16) and of the Christian ministry (3:1-4:13). The passage before us sets forth the contrast between God's wisdom and the wisdom of the world, first in terms of the message of the cross (1:18-25) and then in terms of God's choice of the Corinthian community (1:26-31).

The word of the cross is described from two points of view: to those who are on the way to ruin, it is folly; but to those who are on the way to salvation, it is the power of God (verse 18, cf. NEB). By implication, it is also weakness to the former category of people and wisdom to the latter. This word of the cross, which proclaims Christ crucified, is a stumbling block (because it speaks of apparent weakness) to Jews in their demand for signs, and folly to Greeks in their quest for wisdom; but to those whom God has called, both Jew and Greek, Christ as proclaimed by the apostles is God's power and God's wisdom (verses 23-24). What the former category of people regard as "wisdom" is of no avail in the matter of salvation, as Scripture attests (verses 19-20a); for secular wisdom cannot attain to the knowledge of God, while salvation is attained through faith in the preached word, and it is exactly by thus accomplishing through the gospel what secular wisdom had been unable to accomplish that God has exposed the latter as folly (verses 20b–21). The ultimate explanation of all this paradox lies in the fact that the cross is God's act: what to human wisdom is unintelligible (τὸ μωρόν) and to human notions of power bespeaks weakness (τὸ ἀσθενές, cf. 2 Cor. 13:4) is wiser and stronger than men with all their wisdom and might (verse 25).

Clinching the argument of the preceding verses, and especially the comprehensive principle of verse 25, Paul now appeals to the Corinthians' own experience of God's call (verses 26–28). The threefold ἐξελέξατο ὁ θεός emphasizes that the community in its outwardly feeble condition has been the object of God's election, while the καταισχύνη–καταργήσῃ emphasis underlines the fact that God has set aside human wisdom, power and distinction as totally ineffective and inoperative as means of salvation. God's ultimate purpose in this mode of operation is that all flesh should be prevented from boasting before him (verse 29), and it is in accordance with this that the Corinthian Christians on their part (ὑμεῖς) have been chosen by God, from whom they have their being (i.e. as God's children) by virtue of their incorporation in Christ Jesus (verse 30, cf. RSV).

To believers, God has made Christ to be true wisdom which embraces three aspects: both δικαιοσύνη and ἁγιασμός, and also ἀπολύτρωσις. While the fact that ἡγιασμένοις in 1:2 refers not to the Corinthians' holiness in character or conduct but to their having been set apart to be God's holy people (cf. κλητοῖς ἁγίοις) might seem to create a presumption in favour of ἁγιασμός having in 1:30 a relational, not ethical, meaning, it has been observed that "the term ἁγιασμός is always distinguished from ἅγιος and ἁγιάζειν by the emphasis on the moral element,"[21] and there seems to be no compelling reason why we should deviate from this sense here. Perhaps we shall not go far astray if we take ἁγιασμός here to denote the process of sanctification, but with primary emphasis on its commencement. But ἁγιασμός would be repeating the same idea as δικαιοσύνη if the latter were understood in the sense of ethical righteousness; hence it is preferable to take δικαιοσύνη in the sense of forensic righteousness, i.e. the status of being in the right with God. As for ἀπολύτρωσις, which has been variously interpreted, it is probably best (in view of ἐγενήθη, which clearly points to the historic act of Christ, and of the fact that in Romans 3:24 believers are said to be justified διὰ τῆς ἀπολυτρώσεως which is in Christ Jesus) to understand the term here of the believers' deliverance through the death of Christ on the cross, which thus furnishes the ground both of justification and sanctification and sets the other terms "in the only context in which they can be rightly understood."[22] On this interpretation, we have in justification (an act) and sanctification (considered as the commencement of a process) not so much two successive stages of Christian experience as two coincident facets or aspects of the one act of redemption accomplished by Christ and, correspondingly, of the believer's one experience of incorporation in and union with Christ.

Finally, picking up the ὅπως of verse 29, Paul states that the divine purpose in Christ's becoming the believers' wisdom, righteousness, sanctification and redemption is the same as the ultimate goal of God's dealing as he does with the world and with the church, viz. the destruction of all καύχησις and his own glorification (verse 31).

Scholars have correctly observed that there is a parallel between Paul's polemic against secular wisdom in this passage and his polemic against justification by works elsewhere in his epistles: both secular wisdom and justification by works are characteristic of man in independence of God, and both have been done away in Christ.[23] It should be noted that Paul actually defines true wisdom *in terms of* justification as well as sanctification and redemption (verse 30). Since even in polemicizing against the Corinthians' false estimate of secular wisdom Paul thus uses the juridical category of justification to clarify his meaning, it is impossible to maintain that justification by faith is something merely occasional and secondary for Paul, something which he employs only when engaged in argument with Jewish legalists; certainly our passage tends rather to support the conclusion that "however much Paul's doctrine of the law is polemic in character, it... contains his central thoughts."[24]

To this we may add two other conclusions to be drawn from our study of the passage: (1) Righteousness (or justification) is attainable by faith: it is to those who believe (verse 21b), i.e. respond positively to the proclamation of Christ crucified (verse 23) in the word of the cross (verse 18), to those whom God has called and chosen (verses 26–28), that Christ became true wisdom which embraces justification, sanctification and redemption. And the twofold emphasis (a) on the exclusion of boasting on the basis of secular wisdom, power or distinction and (b) on the Lord as the sole ground of boasting implies that righteousness is by faith alone, apart from any merit on man's part. (2) Justification and sanctification (the latter viewed as the commencement of a process) appear to be alike based on redemption, and are closely connected as two coincident aspects of this redemption (verse 30b) and, correspondingly, of the believer's incorporation in Christ (verse 30a).

II. 1 Corinthians 6:11

One of the matters Paul had to deal with in 1 Corinthians was that some Christians were bringing their disputes before heathen judge

(6:1–11). Against such a practice of law-suits, one of the arguments Paul employs is that they should live as those who have been redeemed, with their past put behind them (verses 9–11). In the verse before us, Paul flatly declares that some among the Corinthian believers had been such as could never inherit the kingdom of God, but he immediately follows this with a triple ἀλλά, which sharply contrasts their present state and their seamy past.

In ἀπελούσασθε we probably have not the middle used for the passive so that the sense is "you were washed," but a genuine middle with some such sense as "you got (or allowed) yourselves (to be) washed." It suggests that baptism is in mind; but, as C. K. Barrett observes, the use of the non-technical word instead of the more technical ἐβαπτίσθητε shows that Paul attaches importance to the inward meaning rather than the outward circumstances of the rite.[25] The reference, it would seem, is to a spiritual cleansing from sin which is "sacramentally signified in baptism."[26] The two succeeding aorist verbs probably refer to the same event of baptism as is reflected in ἀπελούσασθε. Ἡγιάσθητε represents the Corinthians' sanctification as a definite act; in contrast to 1:30, here "sanctification is not moral action on the part of man, but a divinely effected state."[27] But if the word ἁγιάζειν itself does not here signify practical holiness on the part of the Corinthians, yet in view of the paraenetic nature of the context we may believe that Paul thinks at the same time of the ethical consequences which result from their state of being consecrated to God.[28] And since, in point of fact, being relationally consecrated to God means being separated to holiness of life, consecration (in the relational sense) may be regarded as but the commencement of sanctification (considered as a process of ethical transformation).

To the acts of cleansing and sanctification Paul adds ἐδικαιώθητε. It has been suggested that 1 Corinthians 6:11 is to be regarded as a statement of early Christian baptismal instruction, which understood justification, not yet in the Pauline sense of justification by faith, but as forgiveness of sins on the ground of Christ's atoning death.[29] But it is hard to think that Paul could speak of justification in a sense that is unrelated to its characteristic meaning. It has also been maintained, in view of the position of ἐδικαιώθητε (coming after the other two verbs), that it has a causative sense,[30] but this is not a necessary conclusion. We are probably not intended to take the three verbs in any chronological order at all (cf. the order in 1:30), since the aorists are best taken as denoting coincidental action; and the order of the verbs is perhaps best explained in terms of the apostle's sequence of thought, as O. Pfleiderer suggested: in contrast to the Corinthians' sinful past, the sanctifying effect of their conversion is described first in negative and then in positive terms (ἀπελούσασθε, ἡγιάσθητε), and ἐδικαιώθητε is added "because it was a necessary part of the full statement of the effects of God's favour."[31]

The two prepositional phrases which follow are naturally (especially in view of the threefold ἀλλά) to be taken as qualifying all three verbs, and are thus related to the baptismal event as a whole. If here Paul apparently presents the three coincident actions as occurring at baptism, this may be due to the fact that since "baptism is the visible sign of visible incorporation into the visible church"[32] it can be more effectively appealed to than faith as marking the believers' decisive break with the past. Hence, although formally Paul's statement is a reference to baptism, yet substantially it is really a description of what, in strict analysis, lies behind baptism, viz. the believers' (in this case, the Corinthians') conversion-experience.[33] On this showing, ἐν τῷ ὀνόματι κτλ. indicates the work of God in Jesus Christ which is the basis of the work of grace experienced by the Corinthian Christians, while ἐν τῷ πνεύματι κτλ. reflects the work of the Spirit who brings the believer into relation with Christ (cf. 1 Cor. 12:3, 13) and both separates him to God (cf. 2 Thess. 2:13) and leads him in the life of progressive sanctification (cf. 2 Cor. 3:18; Rom. 8:13–14; Gal. 5:17–18, 22–25). If this be the case, then we have in the three verbs of our text not three steps or stages of Christian experience, but different aspects of the Spirit's action or, to state it from the recipient's standpoint, of the believer's union with Christ.

Thus we find presented here in juxtaposition cleansing, sanctification and justification as different aspects of a single act of grace at the outset of the Christian life, as coincident facets of the believer's one experience of union with Christ. Since faith is implied both in ἀπελούσασθε and in the confession of the name of the Lord in baptism (cf. Rom. 10:10), it is implied that justification is by faith. The phrase ἐν τῷ ὀνόματι κτλ. also implies that justification is based on the work of Christ. On all these points, there is complete consistency between this passage and what we have found in 1:18–31.

III. 2 Corinthians 3:4–11

Following on the introduction (1:1–11) and an explanation of Paul's recent conduct towards the Corinthians (1:12–2:13), the third main section of 2 Corinthians is in large part a sustained exposition of the ministry as exercised by Paul and his colleagues (2:14–7:4). In the verses before us, Paul describes himself and his colleagues as ministers of the new covenant and begins to contrast the ministry of this new covenant with that of the old, the contrast being carried further and completed in the following verses (3:12-18), which stress the openness of the new ministry over against the veiledness of the old.

At the beginning of our passage, Paul explains that the confidence which he and his colleagues have before God (3:1-3) comes through the enabling of Christ (verse 4). This thought is expanded in both its negative and its positive aspect (verses 5-6): self-competence on the part of the workers is ruled out; their adequacy is from God—it is he who has made them adequate to be ministers of a new covenant. The reference is to Jeremiah's prophecy of a new covenant (Jer. 31:31-34) which is now fulfilled in Christ; that Paul here "but not in Romans refers to a *new* covenant is due to the fact that he is dealing with Judaizers."[34] Paul brings out the essential difference between the new covenant and the old by the phrase οὐ γράμματος ἀλλὰ πνεύματος, which contrasts not the letter of the law and the spirit of the law, but the law of God and the Spirit of God:[35] the law as γράμμα, i.e. a written code "carved in letters on stone" (verse 7a), only exacts obedience to its demands without imparting the power to fulfil them and pronounces the death-sentence on all transgressors (cf. Deut. 27:26; 30:17-18; Gal. 3:10; Rom. 7:5, 9-11); it is the Spirit—not the law (cf. Gal. 3:21)—who imparts life. The crucial difference that Paul brings out in verse 6, then, is this: under the old order of legal observance, an external code dispenses death; under the new order of divine grace, the Spirit gives life.

The contrast stated in the simple terms of verse 6 is expounded (verses 7-18) in a midrash on Exodus 34:29-35. In the first part of this Christian midrash (verses 7-11) Paul shows the superiority of the new ministry to the old by reference to its greater glory, and this for three reasons, the second of which is explanatory of the first. (a) If even the old ministry, which, based as it was on a covenant "engraved letter by letter upon stone" (NEB), is a ministry (or service) of death as dispensing death (τὸ γὰρ γράμμα ἀποκτείνει), had a glorious inauguration (ἐγενήθη ἐν δόξῃ), so much so that the Israelites could not gaze steadily on Moses' face because of its brightness, fading as this was (verse 7),[36] much more must the ministry that is marked by the Spirit be invested with glory (verse 8). (b) That the old ministry is a ministry of death is due to the fact that it is a ministry of condemnation—the law being both the criterion of judgment (cf. Rom. 2:12-13) and the instrument of condemnation (cf. Rom. 3:19-20); but if even the ministry of condemnation was glorious, much more will the ministry of δικαιοσύνη abound in glory (verse 9).

The Greek term here is most commonly understood to mean forensic righteousness, i.e. the righteous status conferred in justification; and the antithesis between δικαιοσύνη and κατάκρισις puts it beyond reasonable doubt that the former term at least includes the idea of justification. Two considerations, however, suggest that something more is here involved. First, the strict counterpart of κατάκρισις is not δικαιοσύνη but δικαίωσις, as in Romans 5:18; and while δικαιοσύνη certainly could mean the righteousness conferred in justification (cf. Gal. 2:21), yet the fact that Paul uses δικαιοσύνη instead of δικαίωσις when the latter would have been the obvious word to use to convey the idea of justification in opposition to condemnation, at least opens the possibility that he intends to convey more than the idea of justification here. Second, the "ministry of death" and the "ministry of the Spirit" in verses 7a and 8a become in verse 9 the "ministry of condemnation" and the "ministry of δικαιοσύνη" respectively. Since not only are the two statements parallel to each other but there is a logical connection between verses 7a and 9a (the "ministry of death" is lethal in its effect because it is a "ministry of condemnation"; condemnation leads to death), it is reasonable to assume that some logical connection similarly exists between verses 8 and 9b, i.e. between the "ministry of the Spirit" and the "ministry of δικαιοσύνη." Now if by analogy we may say that the new ministry is a ministry of δικαιοσύνη because it is a "ministry of the Spirit," then, since the Spirit is life-giving (ζωοποιεῖ, verse 6b), δικαιοσύνη will assume the meaning of righteousness of life. For these two reasons, we submit that δικαιοσύνη in verse 9 is to be understood as embracing both forensic and ethical righteousness: as antithetical to κατάκρισις it has the meaning of justification; at the same time, being logically connected with the Spirit it acquires the sense of righteousness of life, for the Spirit is not only the source of life (cf. Gal. 5:25a) but also the regulative principle of the believer's conduct (cf. Gal. 5:25b, 17–18, 22–23; Rom. 8:13–14) and the power by which the believer is enabled to fulfil the righteous requirement of the law (Rom. 8:4).

(c) A third reason for the greater splendour of the new ministry is its permanence, over against the transitoriness of the old (verses 10–11): the old ministry has, as it were, been paled into non-glory (καὶ ... οὐ δεδόξασται), as something which only once had glory (τὸ δεδοξασμένον), by the far superior glory of the new ministry. Now if that which was being done away (τὸ καταργούμενον)—viz. the entire order which had its basis in, and was characterized by, the law, and thus the old covenant and the old ministry together[37]—was accompanied by glory (διὰ δόξης), much more must the new order, the order which remains (τὸ μένον), continue in a state of glory (ἐν δόξῃ).

Without following Paul into the second half of his midrash (3:12–18), we may make two observations by way of conclusion. (1) If the old ministry is said to be a ministry of condemnation and death because it is based on a covenant epitomized by the law as a written code, the logical inference to be drawn is that there can be no justification on the basis of the law. In the words τὸ γὰρ γράμμα ἀποκτείνει (verse 6b) alone we have a clear and succinct statement of the impossibility of justification by works of the law. The very choice of γράμμα to refer to the law is well calculated to emphasize the negative value of the law. (2) The contrast between the old order and the new is the contrast between the old covenant and the new, which in turn means the contrast between the ministry of condemnation and death and the ministry of righteousness and the Spirit; in other words, if the old order is characterized by condemnation and death the new order is marked by righteousness and the life-giving Spirit. Whether δικαιοσύνη be taken to mean forensic righteousness alone or, as we suggest, both forensic and ethical righteousness, it is clear that the idea of justification occupies an essential place in Paul's understanding of the gospel. Even when due allowance has been made for the polemical orientation in what Paul says here, the very fact that he can characterize the entire gospel dispensation *as* a dispensation of righteousness must mean that justification, as an aspect of that righteousness, is of crucial importance to the gospel as Paul conceived it. If our interpretation of the term δικαιοσύνη here is correct, then we see that justification and sanctification are firmly linked together as the most essential blessings of the new order.

IV. 2 Corinthians 5:18-21

This paragraph (cf. NEB) is part of Paul's sustained exposition of the apostolic ministry (2:14-7:4). In its narrower context, it concludes a section (5:11-21) in which Paul enunciates the love of God as a motivating principle of all Christian conduct and therefore of apostolic service as well (verses 11-15), announces the new creation that has come in Christ (verses 16-17), and speaks of the ministry of reconciliation that has been committed to him and his colleagues (verses 18-21).

All that is involved in the new order (τὰ πάντα, verse 18)[38] is, like the original creation, God's handiwork. That a man can become a new creation in Christ is due to the fact that God has, on his own initiative, completed the work of reconciling men to himself through Christ. On the basis of this finished work God has also given to Paul and his colleagues (ἡμῖν), as recipients of the benefits of his reconciling work (ἡμᾶς), the ministry of reconciliation. In verses 19-21 Paul further explains what he has said in verse 18. The salient features may be noted as follows.

(1) In Christ God was engaged in reconciling (ἦν ... καταλλάσσων) the world to himself (verse 19a). Though Paul's primary concern is doubtless with the world of men (as the next phrase shows), God's work of reconciliation in Christ is represented as cosmic in its

effect (cf. Col. 1:20). Here "the very universality of the expression ... is consistent only with an objective reconciliation. ... it means that God is putting away His own condemnation and wrath."[39]

(2) God was reconciling a world to himself by not counting men's (αὐτῶν) trespasses against them. This already points to the thought of verse 21. What is suggested by Paul's words here is the idea of an objective general justification of mankind on the ground of Christ's atoning death.[40] From the juxtaposition of justification and reconciliation here (and again in verses 20–21) some have concluded that the two are one and the same thing.[41] Reconciliation is not, however, really described *as* justification; rather, justification is conceived of as providing the logical foundation for reconciliation. As Barrett explains, "since transgressions no longer counted against men (cf. Exod. xxix. 10) the way was open for reconciliation."[42]

(3) Since the "saving facts must be proclaimed in order that they may become saving reality for individuals,"[43] God also deposited in Paul and his colleagues (θέμενος ἐν ἡμῖν) the word or message of reconciliation (verse 19c), which is "not the conciliatory and reconciling word but the proclamation of the already accomplished reconciliation."[44] It follows (οὖν, verse 20a) from this divine commissioning that Paul and his colleagues are ambassadors ὑπὲρ Χριστοῦ—Christ's representatives acting in his place:[45] as they proclaim the message of reconciliation, God is in fact exhorting through them.[46] There is thus a complete unity of action and purpose between God and Christ (cf. verse 20b).

(4) The apostolic messenger's entreaty is an invitation to be reconciled to God (verse 20b), i.e. to accept the reconciliation which he offers, which is objectively complete but has to be appropriated by personal response to become subjectively true for the individual. This invitation to faith is not, however, the entire content of the message of reconciliation: the latter contains also a declaration of the ground on which the appeal can be made. That ground is supplied in (the asyndetic) verse 21. The main clause (verse 21a) states that God made Christ, who came to no personal, practical acquaintance with sin either inwardly in conscience (cf. 1 John 3:5) or outwardly in action (cf. 1 Pet. 2:22),[47] to be sin for our sake. Although a sacrificial allusion cannot be ruled out as impossible, ἁμαρτίαν ἐποίησεν probably means that God made Christ the object of his wrath and condemnation as he bore our sins and submitted to death;[48] this is the most natural interpretation, especially in view of the close similarity between the present verse and Galatians 3:13, where Christ is said to have redeemed us from the curse of the law by becoming a curse for us. God's intention in making Christ our sin-bearer—ὑπὲρ ἡμῶν probably includes both the idea of "for our sake" (RSV, NEB) and that of "on our behalf" (RV, NASB)[49]—is that we

might become the righteousness of God in Christ (verse 21b). It is by analogy with the preceding statement that God made Christ ἁμαρτίαν, and
for the sake of parallelism in construction, that believers are now said to
become δικαιοσύνη θεοῦ; "Paul has chosen this exceptional wording in
order to emphasize the 'sweet exchange' whereby sinners are given a
righteous status before God through the righteous one who absorbed
their sin (and its judgment) in himself."⁵⁰ The last phrase, ἐν αὐτῷ,
indicates that justification takes place in the sphere of Christ, i.e.
through identification with Christ in his death and resurrection.

    Thus we have in verse 21b a positive statement (of which verse 19b
is a negative counterpart and anticipation) of justification in Christ.⁵¹
Since (as noted earlier) verse 21 provides the ground for the appeal of
verse 20 to be reconciled to God, it is clear that Christ's death as sin-
bearer is the objective basis for reconciliation; but it is also the objective
basis for our justification (verse 21b). This raises again (cf. verse 19b) the
question of the exact relationship between justification and reconciliation implied here. Barrett seems to suggest that the two are synonymous: "Reconciliation," he writes, "if located within God's court and
expressed in forensic terms, becomes justification."⁵² The two are doubtless parallel to each other to the extent that both are based on Christ's
death, but they are not exactly identical in content: the conferment of a
righteous status on the believer and restoration to God's favour are as a
matter of fact indissolubly linked together but are nevertheless concep-
tually distinct. The logical relationship between the two has been correctly stated by Barrett himself when (in commenting on verse 19b) he
saw the not-counting of transgressions as opening the way for justification. Justification, in other words, is the logical basis for reconciliation.
Since justification takes place "in Christ," faith is implied as the means
of identification with him; it is also implied in the response to the call to
"be reconciled with God," which is an invitation to faith. When by faith
a man appropriates the reconciliation proffered in the word of reconciliation, he is at the same time justified. As F. Büchsel puts it, "The God
who reconciles us to Himself is always at the same time the God who
judges us. For this reason reconciliation *includes* justification both in
2 C. 5:21 . . . and in v. 19."⁵³

    Justification and reconciliation are thus inseparably linked together
as different but coincident aspects of faith in Christ, though logically
justification is the foundation for, and therefore prior to, reconciliation.
Since reconciliation is itself that which makes the "new creation" of
verse 17 possible, it follows that justification is the logical basis for the
new creation as well, and thus the ἐν αὐτῷ of verse 21b links up with the
ἐν Χριστῷ of verse 17a: by faith-union with Christ the believer is justified, he is reconciled to God, and he becomes a new creation. These do

not happen in successive stages, but as coincident aspects of the single experience of faith-union with Christ. Nevertheless, the logical relationships between them are such that justification appears to be the most fundamental aspect of this union.

We may sum up by saying that, according to this passage, (1) justification is by faith in Christ and on the basis of his death; (2) it is coincident with, but logically prior to, reconciliation; (3) it is the most fundamental aspect of the believer's union with Christ and appears to be Paul's first step in analyzing its meaning.

Summary and Conclusion

On the basis of the foregoing study of the four Corinthians passages (I) 1 Corinthians 1:18–31, (II) 1 Corinthians 6:11, (III) 2 Corinthians 3:4–11, (IV) 2 Corinthians 5:18–21, we offer the following observations by way of summary and conclusion:

(1) Justification can never be attained on the basis of the law (III).

(2) Justification is by faith in Christ alone and on the basis of his atoning death (I, II, IV). This is not expressly stated but clearly implied.

(3) Justification stands at the beginning of the Christian life coincidentally with sanctification (and cleansing) as an aspect of the believer's incorporation in Christ (I, II); it is also coincident with reconciliation, but logically precedes it as its basis, and thus appears to be the most fundamental aspect of union with Christ and Paul's first step in analyzing its meaning (IV).

(4) Justification and sanctification are conjoined as coincident aspects of redemption in Christ (I) and as the fundamental blessings of the new order (III). Justification is an essential aspect of that true wisdom which Christ has become for believers (I); it is also an essential aspect of that δικαιοσύνη which characterizes the entire new dispensation (III).

(5) The fact that Paul freely employs the concept of justification even in contexts where the legalistic point of view is not discussed at all (I, II, IV; the first passage is particularly important in this regard) strongly argues that it cannot fairly be regarded as a purely polemical doctrine born of, and intended for use in, debate with Jews and Jewish Christian legalists only. In the light of the previous two observations ([3], [4]), it is much rather to be considered as of central significance to Paul.

(6) Justification by faith does not exhaust the content of Paul's gospel: like reconciliation and sanctification, and coincident with these, justification is one aspect of redemption in Christ. At the same time, it is

not just one aspect like any other, but rather stands out as the most fundamental aspect of that redemption and of the believer's incorporation in Christ; it is the first step in Paul's analysis of the meaning of union with Christ, which in fact is the central motif and probably the best summarizing concept of Pauline soteriology.[54]

Notes

1. Weizsäcker, *The Apostolic Age of the Christian Church* (2 vols.; E. T., London, Williams & Norgate, 1894–95), 1.141, 165–166, 373–374.

2. Wrede, *Paul* (E.T., London, Philip Green, 1907), 123, 147, 177–178.

3. Heitmüller, *Luthers Stellung in der Religionsgeschichte des Christentums* (Marburg, N. G. Elwert, 1917), 19.

4. Schweitzer, *The Mysticism of Paul the Apostle* (E. T., 1931; reprinted, London, Adam & Charles Black, 1967), 220–226.

5. H. J. Schoeps, *Paul: The Theology of the Apostle in the Light of Jewish Religious History* (E.T., Philadelphia, Westminster, 1961), 123, 196, 206.

6. Charles Henry Buck, Jr., "The Date of Galatians," *JBL* 70 (1951), 113–122, esp. 121–122.

7. Stendahl, "The Apostle Paul and the Introspective Conscience of the West," *HTR* 56 (1963), 199–215, esp. 204 (= *Paul among Jews and Gentiles* [London, SCM, 1977], 78–96 [84]).

8. W. D. Davies, *Paul and Rabbinic Judaism* (2d ed.; London, SPCK, 1955), 221–223.

9. E. P. Sanders, *Paul and Palestinian Judaism* (London, SCM, 1977), 438–441, 490–495, 502–508 (cf. 452–463).

Particularly reminiscent in some ways of the theory of W. Wrede is the view of Georg Strecker as expressed in his recent essay, "Befreiung und Rechtfertigung: Zur Stellung der Rechtfertigungslehre in der Theologie des Paulus," in *Rechtfertigung. Festschrift für Ernst Käsemann zum 70. Geburtstag*, eds. Johannes Friedrich, Wolfgang Pöhlmann and Peter Stuhlmacher (Tübingen, J. C. B. Mohr [Paul Siebeck] and Göttingen, Vandenhoeck & Ruprecht, 1976), 479–508.

10. Machen, *The Origin of Paul's Religion* (London, Hodder & Stoughton, 1921), 278–279.

11. H. D. Wendland, *Die Mitte der paulinischen Botschaft* (Göttingen, Vandenhoeck & Ruprecht, 1935), esp. 6, 48.

12. J. I. Packer, *NBD* (1962), 684a–685a, s.v. "Justification."

13. Kertelge, *"Rechtfertigung" bei Paulus* (2d ed.; Münster, Aschendorff, 1971), 286, 295–304, 306.

14. Conzelmann, "Current Problems in Pauline Research," *Int* 22 (1968), 171–186, esp. 175–178, 186; idem, "Die Rechtfertigungslehre des Paulus. Theologie oder Anthropologie?" *EvT* 28 (1968), 389–404, esp. 394–397, 404.

15. Bornkamm, *Paul* (E.T., London, Hodder & Stoughton, 1971), 115–117, 152, 249.

16. Käsemann, *Perspectives on Paul* (E.T., London, SCM, 1971), 70 n. 27, 71–73, 76, 80, 164.

17. F. F. Bruce, "Galatian Problems. 4. The Date of the Epistle," *BJRL* 54 (1971–72), 250–267, esp. 261–264 (quotation from 262). See also his *The Epistle of Paul to the Romans* (TNTC; London, Tyndale, 1963), 35–37; and "Some Thoughts

on Paul and Paulinism," *Vox Evangelica* 7 (1971), 5–16, esp. 10. In John Reumann, "The Gospel of the Righteousness of God. Pauline Interpretation in Rom. 3:21–31," *Int* 20 (1966), 432–452, Bruce (*Romans*, 35–36) is erroneously cited (446 n. 45) as having stated that justification was merely a polemical doctrine deriving from disputes with the Judaizers.

18. Bruce, *Romans*, 40. Cf. idem, "The Epistles of Paul," in *PCB*, 927–939, esp. 934*a* (§810*c*).

19. See Ridderbos, *Paul and Jesus* (E.T., Philadelphia, Presbyterian & Reformed, 1958), 63–65; cf. idem, *Paul: An Outline of His Theology* (E.T., Grand Rapids, William B. Eerdmans, 1975), 161–162, 166–167, 173–174. See also Richard B. Gaffin, Jr., *Resurrection and Redemption* (Th.D. thesis, Westminster Theological Seminary, 1969; printed by Westminster Student Service, 1971), 143, cf. 1–15. On the subject of *Heilsgeschichte* in Paul, cf. F. F. Bruce, "Salvation History in the New Testament," in *Man and His Salvation. Studies in Memory of S. G. F. Brandon*, eds. E. J. Sharpe and J. R. Hinnells (Manchester, University Press, 1973), 75–90, esp. 82–85.

20. For a fuller account reference may perhaps be allowed to the author's unpublished Ph.D. thesis, "The Relationship between Righteousness and Faith in the Thought of Paul, as expressed in the Letters to the Galatians and the Romans" (2 vols.; Manchester University, 1975), 1.1–18, with corresponding notes in 2.1–6. Cf. idem, "The Status of Justification by Faith in Paul's Thought: A Brief Survey of a Modern Debate" (forthcoming).

21. O. Procksch, *TDNT* 1 (1964), 113, s.v. ἁγιασμός.

22. C. K. Barrett, *The First Epistle to the Corinthians* (HNTC; New York, Harper & Row, 1968), 61. Cf. P. Stuhlmacher, "Achtzehn Thesen zur paulinischen Kreuzestheologie," in *Rechtfertigung. Festschrift für Ernst Käsemann* (see n. 9 above), 509–523, esp. 512–513. For redemption as the basis of sanctification, cf. O. Procksch, *TDNT* 1 (1964), 113, s.v. ἁγιασμός. For ἀπολύτρωσις in the sense of initial redemption, cf. F. Büchsel, *TDNT* 4 (1967), 353, s.v. ἀπολύτρωσις.

One may note with F. Hahn, "Taufe und Rechtfertigung: Ein Beitrag zur paulinischen Theologie in ihrer Vor- und Nachgeschichte," in *Rechtfertigung. Festschrift für Ernst Käsemann*, 95–124, that the three concepts (δικαιοσύνη, ἁγιασμός, ἀπολύτρωσις) "in umgekehrter Reihenfolge so auffällig den Taufaussagen in 1Kor 6,11b entsprechen," without entirely subscribing to his conclusion that 1 Cor. 1:30b has "die Funktion einer christologischen Korrespondenzformel zu der Tauftradition, die in 1Kor 6,11 zitiert wird" (107, 108).

23. Cf. G. Bornkamm, *Early Christian Experience* (E.T., London, SCM, 1969), 29; A. Schlatter, *Der Glaube im Neuen Testament* (5th ed.; Stuttgart, Calwer, 1963), 388.

24. R. Bultmann, *Existence and Faith. Shorter Writings of Rudolf Bultmann* (E.T., London, Hodder & Stoughton, 1961), 137.

25. Barrett, *First Corinthians*, 141.

26. F. F. Bruce, *1 & 2 Corinthians* (NCB; London, Oliphants, 1971), 62.

27. O. Procksch, *TDNT* 1 (1964), 112, s.v. ἁγιάζω.

28. Cf. Kertelge, *Rechtfertigung*, 243–244.

29. So Kertelge, *Rechtfertigung*, 244; Rudolf Bultmann, *Theology of the New Testament* (2 vols.; E.T., London, SCM, 1971), 1.136; F. Hahn, "Taufe und Rechtfertigung," 105–107 with n. 47. Cf. also Sanders, *Paul and Palestinian Judaism*, 471–472, where the verb in 1 Corinthians 6:11 (as also in Romans 5:9 and 8:30) is considered as referring to "being cleansed of or forgiven for past transgressions" and thus being equivalent to "sanctified."

30. H. Braun, *Gerichtsgedanke und Rechtfertigungslehre bei Paulus* (Leipzig, J. C. Hinrichs, 1930), 83. Cf. BAG 197a, s.v. δικαιόω 3c.

31. O. Pfleiderer, *Paulinism* (2 vols.; E.T., London, Williams & Norgate, 1891), 1.180.

32. Hans Küng, *Justification* (E.T., London, Thomas Nelson & Sons, 1964), 245.

33. Cf. Barrett, *First Corinthians*, 142.

34. Barrett, *The Second Epistle to the Corinthians* (BNTC; London, Adam & Charles Black, 1973), 112. On this identification of Paul's opponents cf. ibid., 28–30; idem, "Cephas and Corinth," in *Abraham unser Vater. Festschrift für Otto Michel*, eds. Otto Betz, Martin Hengel and Peter Schmidt (Leiden, E. J. Brill, 1963), 1–12, esp. 11–12; idem, "Paul's Opponents in 2 Corinthians," *NTS* 17 (1970–71), 233–254. Cf. also F. F. Bruce, "Paul and Jerusalem," *Tyndale Bulletin* 19 (1968), 3–25, esp. 12–13; *1 & 2 Corinthians*, 174.

35. So, correctly, e.g. G. Schrenk, *TDNT* 1 (1964), 766–767, s.v. γράμμα. On πνεῦμα as a reference to the Holy Spirit, cf. Karl Prümm, "Röm 1–11 und 2 Kor 3," *Biblica* 31 (1950), 164–203, esp. 184.

36. In speaking of the δόξα of Moses' face Paul follows the Septuagint (Exod. 34:29–30), but the thought of the glory as fading from Moses' face seems to have been an inference from Exod. 34:33–34. Cf. F. F. Bruce, *1 & 2 Corinthians*, 191; Barrett, *Second Corinthians*, 114–116.

37. *Pace* C. E. B. Cranfield, "St. Paul and the Law," in *New Testament Issues*, ed. Richard Batey (London, SCM, 1970), 148–172, who refers τὸ καταρ-γούμενον exclusively "to the ministry of Moses at the giving of the law" (160). It is true that in verses 7–9 the explicit contrast is between the two ministries, but having spoken of "ministers of a new covenant" (verse 6), Paul immediately passes on to contrast the two ministries of the old and new covenants respectively; and the old ministry itself is said to be "carved in letters on stone" (verse 7a)—words more suitable as a description of the old covenant. Since ministry is based on covenant, the two stand or fall together. Cf. J. Behm, *TDNT* 2 (1964), 130, s.v. διαθήκη; G. Delling, *TDNT* 1 (1964), 454, s.v. καταργέω.

38. The existence of the new order is implied in verse 17, though its primary reference is to the individual man in Christ.

39. J. Denney, *The Second Epistle to the Corinthians* (London, Hodder & Stoughton, 1894), 215.

40. A. B. Bruce, *St. Paul's Conception of Christianity* (New York, Charles Scribner's Sons, 1894), 159.

41. Cf. e.g. Victor Paul Furnish, *Theology and Ethics in Paul* (Nashville, Abingdon, 1968), 149; Bultmann, *Theology*, 1.285–286.

42. Barrett, *Second Corinthians*, 177.

43. G. Friedrich, *TDNT* 3 (1965), 710, s.v. κηρύσσω.

44. Bultmann, *Theology*, 1.287.

45. Cf. G. Bornkamm, *TDNT* 6 (1968), 683, s.v. πρεσβεύω; H. Riesenfeld, *TDNT* 8 (1972), 513, s.v. ὑπέρ.

46. On the rendering "exhort" as preferable to "appeal" (RSV, NEB) and "entreat" (NASB), see O. Schmitz, *TDNT* 5 (1967), 795, s.v. παρακαλέω.

47. Cf. F. F. Bruce, *1 & 2 Corinthians*, 210–211.

48. So e.g. H. Braun, *TDNT* 6 (1968), 464, s.v. ποιέω; H. Riesenfeld, *TDNT* 8 (1972), 510, s.v. ὑπέρ; Bultmann, *Theology*, 1.277.

49. So, correctly, Otto Kuss, *Der Römerbrief* (2 vols.; Regensburg, Friedrich Pustet, 1963), 125. Cf. H. Riesenfeld, *TDNT* 8 (1972), 510, s.v. ὑπέρ.

50. F. F. Bruce, *1 & 2 Corinthians*, 211.

51. This is how most interpreters see it. For other interpretations, cf. e.g. (1) G. Schrenk, *TDNT* 2 (1964), 208–209, s.v. δικαιοσύνη; (2) Charles Archibald Anderson Scott, *Christianity According to St. Paul* (1927; reprinted, Cambridge, The University Press, 1966), 60 n. 1; Edgar Johnson Goodspeed, "Some Greek Notes," *JBL* 73 (1954), 84–92, esp. 88; (3) Ernst Käsemann, *New Testament Questions of Today* (E.T., London, SCM, 1969), 169; (4) Karl Kertelge, *Rechtfertigung*, 104–106; (5) J. A. Ziesler, *The Meaning of Righteousness in Paul* (Cambridge, The University Press, 1972), 159–161. A criticism which applies to each of these views, all of which agree in giving δικαιοσύνη a sense other than that of forensic righteousness, is that they take insufficient account of the fact that the language of verse 21b is largely conditioned by that of the preceding clause: since Christ's being made sin cannot be understood except in a forensic sense, our becoming God's righteousness in him is (in view of the parallel structure) most reasonably interpreted in a forensic sense, or in terms of a relationship.

52. Barrett, *Second Corinthians*, 176.

53. F. Büchsel, *TDNT* 1 (1964), 257, s.v. καταλλάσσω (italics supplied).

54. The teaching of justification by faith as expressed in the Corinthian letters will be found to be endorsed and more fully and systematically developed in Galatians and (especially) Romans.

Chapter 16

TITUS 2:13
AND THE DEITY OF CHRIST

MURRAY J. HARRIS

ON MANY OCCASIONS THE BIBLICAL SCHOLAR IS CALLED on to express an opinion, whether orally or in print, on a disputed point of Biblical interpretation. Usually the time or space available in such circumstances permits only the statement of a conclusion, not the detailed exposition of all the reasons supporting that conclusion. Professor Bruce's students or readers, however, have always had confidence that behind the simple statement of his opinion lay not only a great weight of scholarship but also highly trained literary acumen. The interpretation of Titus 2:13 affords an interesting case in point. As far as I am aware, nowhere in print has the Professor had the opportunity of justifying in exegetical detail his view, expressed briefly in several places,[1] that the phrase "great God and Saviour" refers to Jesus Christ. That this understanding of the passage is well founded may perhaps be shown by what follows.

Titus 2:11–14 reads thus:

11 Ἐπεφάνη γὰρ ἡ χάρις τοῦ θεοῦ σωτήριος πᾶσιν
ἀνθρώποις, 12 παιδεύουσα ἡμᾶς ἵνα ἀρνησάμενοι τὴν
ἀσέβειαν καὶ τὰς κοσμικὰς ἐπιθυμίας σωφρόνως καὶ
δικαίως καὶ εὐσεβῶς ζήσωμεν ἐν τῷ νῦν αἰῶνι, 13 προσδε-
χόμενοι τὴν μακαρίαν ἐλπίδα καὶ ἐπιφάνειαν τῆς δόξης
τοῦ μεγάλου θεοῦ καὶ σωτῆρος ἡμῶν Ἰησοῦ Χριστοῦ,
14 ὃς ἔδωκεν ἑαυτὸν ὑπὲρ ἡμῶν ἵνα λυτρώσηται ἡμᾶς
ἀπὸ πάσης ἀνομίας καὶ καθαρίσῃ ἑαυτῷ λαὸν περιούσιον,
ζηλωτὴν καλῶν ἔργων.

In this sentence Paul[2] specifies the ground (γάρ, verse 11) for his injunctions to holy living that Titus was to communicate to the older men and women, the younger men and the slaves in the churches of Crete (verses 1–10). God's grace has appeared with a view to achieving the salvation of all men (verse 11), viz. their ransom from moral evil and purification as the new People of God (verse 14a), their repudiation of irreligion and worldly passions (verse 12), and their devotion to the doing of good (verse 14b). M. Dibelius-H. Conzelmann[3] give this section the appropriate heading "Conduct based on the history of salvation".

From an analysis of the syntax of the crucial phrase . . . ἐπιφάνειαν τῆς δόξης τοῦ μεγάλου θεοῦ καὶ σωτῆρος ἡμῶν 'Ιησοῦ Χριστοῦ several different translations may be proposed that will be assessed in turn.

I

Construing δόξης and σωτῆρος as dependent on ἐπιφάνειαν (with θεοῦ dependent on δόξης):

"... the appearing of the glory of the great God (=the Father) and (the appearing) of our Saviour, Jesus Christ"

While there are NT parallels for the idea of a future ἐπιφάνεια of Christ (2 Thess. 2:8; 1 Tim. 6:14; 2 Tim. 4:1, 8) and a concomitant display of the Father's glory (Matt. 16:27; Mark 8:38; Luke 9:26), it would be strange for any NT writer to conjoin an impersonal or quasi-personal subject (δόξα) and a distinctly personal subject (σωτήρ) in a double epiphany. The only exit from this dilemma is to take ἡ δόξα τοῦ μεγάλου θεοῦ as a christological title and treat καί as epexegetic ("the appearing of the Glory of the great God, namely [or, which Glory is] our Saviour, Jesus Christ),[4] or, with J. N. D. Kelly,[5] to regard "the glory of the great God" as a description of "the divine radiance with which Christ is invested at his coming". Two distinct manifestations are therefore not contemplated.

Another difficulty with this view is the anarthrous state of σωτῆρος, which tends to associate this noun closely with either δόξης or θεοῦ.[6] One might have expected, *ex hypothesi*, that καὶ τοῦ σωτῆρος ἡμῶν 'Ιησοῦ Χριστοῦ would balance τῆς δόξης τοῦ μεγάλου θεοῦ as a second subject, especially since the phrase σωτὴρ ἡμῶν is articular in the NT unless it follows an anarthrous θεός,[7] a point which also counts against the first proposed "exit".[8] Moreover, given the widespread use of the phrase θεὸς καὶ σωτήρ in first-century cultic terminology[9]—"no living person could escape contact with some *theos soter*"[10]—it seems unnatural to separate σωτῆρος from θεοῦ. And Kelly's proposal would better accord with some such expression as . . . ἐπιφάνειαν τοῦ σωτῆρος ἡμῶν 'Ιησοῦ Χριστοῦ ἐν τῇ δόξῃ τοῦ μεγάλου θεοῦ.

II

Construing θεοῦ and σωτῆρος as dependent on ἐπιφάνειαν (with τῆς δόξης as a "Hebrew" genitive[11]) and as referring to either *one* or *two* persons:

"... the glorious appearing of our great God and Saviour, Jesus Christ" (NIV; similarly Goodspeed, Berkeley)
"... the glorious appearing of the great God and [of] our Saviour Jesus Christ" (KJV; similarly Phillips)

Within the thirteen letters of the Pauline corpus the genitive form δόξης occurs twenty times as *nomen rectum*. In seven of these cases (excluding the present verse), the genitive is possibly or probably "Hebrew" or adjectival ("glorious," "resplendent").[12] But although it is grammatically admissible to understand τῆς δόξης in this sense,[13] there remain two objections to this rendering.

First, the verbal parallelism between verses 11 and 13 is compromised. As things stand, (ἡ) ἐπιφάνεια τῆς δόξης τοῦ μεγάλου θεοῦ (verse 13) clearly corresponds to ἐπεφάνη ... ἡ χάρις τοῦ θεοῦ (verse 11). The first advent of Christ was an appearance of God's grace; the second advent of Christ will be an appearance of God's glory. Secondly, to render τῆς δόξης by the adjective "glorious" not only obscures the relation between verses 11 and 13 but also weakens the import of the term δόξα. Embedded in the church's tradition regarding the parousia of Christ was the belief that it would involve an open display of his Father's δόξα (Matt. 16:27; Mark 8:38; Luke 9:26). It is one thing to say that a person's appearance will be "resplendent" or "attended by glory". It is another thing to assert that his *own* "glory" will be revealed. A further problem with the KJV rendering is that nowhere in the NT is ἐπιφάνεια used of the Father (but five times of Christ) or are two persons said to appear at the Last Day.[14]

The question of whether θεὸς καὶ σωτήρ refers to one or to two persons will be discussed below (under III.A and III.C.2).

III

A. Construing θεοῦ and σωτῆρος as dependent on δόξης and as referring to *two persons*:

"... the appearing of the glory of the great God and [the glory of] our Saviour Jesus Christ" (RSV mg; similarly RV mg, ASV, Moffatt, Knox, Phillips, NEB mg, NAB)

There are two principal arguments generally cited in support of this translation.

1. "In *no single* passage is θεός connected directly with Ἰησοῦς

Χριστός as an attribute" (J. E. Huther[15]).

Now it is true that no NT writer refers to Jesus Christ as Ἰησοῦς Χριστὸς ὁ θεὸς ἡμῶν, not to speak of the undefined ὁ θεὸς ἡμῶν. But it must be allowed that the first step towards the bold christological expressions of Ignatius would be the use of θεός in a titular sense in reference to Christ, particularly if the term θεός were incorporated within a traditional formula. In the phrase ὁ θεὸς ἡμῶν καὶ σωτὴρ Ἰησοῦς Χριστός in 2 Peter 1:1 and ὁ μέγας θεὸς καὶ σωτὴρ ἡμῶν Ἰησοῦς Χριστός in Titus 2:13 we may have just such an intermediate step. Here θεός is a descriptive title, not a proper name; it is part of the stereotyped formula θεὸς καὶ σωτήρ; it is not used absolutely but is followed by an identification of the person so titled. No one will doubt that if these two verses afford instances of a christological use of θεός, such usage is exceptional in the NT. But there is an ever-present danger in literary research of making a writer's "habitual usage" so normative that he is disallowed the privilege of creating the exception that proves the rule. Every NT author must be permitted the luxury of some stylistic, verbal, or theological *hapax* (or *dis* or *tris*) *legomena*. In the case of Paul in Titus 2:13, we have a comparable (probable) application of the title θεός to Jesus in Romans 9:5,[16] although the point is vigorously debated.[17]

2. "Is it probable that within one (Greek) sentence the same word once denotes the Father (verse 11) and once the Son (verse 13)?" (a summary of E. Abbot's point[18]).

Abbot reinforces his argument by pointing to the parallelism between verses 11 and 13, which, it is implied, would be destroyed if θεός referred to two persons: Christ's first advent was a visible manifestation of God the Father's grace; his second advent would be an appearing of God the Father's (and his own) glory. There are, however, several elements in the parallelism besides the reference to θεός, viz. the χάρις– δόξα antithesis, the ἐπεφάνη–ἐπιφάνεια and σωτήριος–σωτήρ correspondences. It is no more necessary to make the θεός of verse 13 refer to the Father on the basis of the undoubted reference to him in the θεός of verse 11 than it is to argue from the identification of the σωτήρ as Jesus Christ in verse 13 to the equation of ἡ χάρις τοῦ θεοῦ σωτηρίος with the salvific grace of Christ (= τοῦ θεοῦ) in verse 11.

Any NT use of θεός as a christological title will produce certain linguistic anomalies and ambiguities, for in all strands of the NT θεός generally signifies the Father. Short of coining a new theological term to denote deity, writers who believed in the divinity of Jesus were forced to employ current terminology and run the risk of being branded ditheistic.[19] One reason for the relative infrequency of the NT use of θεός in reference to Jesus may in fact have been the danger recognized by the early church that if θεός were applied to Jesus as regularly as to the Father, Jews would have tended to regard Christianity as incurably deuterotheological, and Gentiles would probably have viewed it as polytheistic. Also significant is the fact that in those cases in which it is certain (John 1:1; 20:28), highly probable (Heb. 1:8; 2 Pet. 1:1), or probable (John 1:18; Rom. 9:5; Titus 2:13) that (ὁ) θεός refers to Jesus, the usage is usually accompanied by a statement in the immediate context that makes an explicit personal distinction between the Son and God the Father.[20] Thus, for example, we find ὁ λόγος ἦν πρὸς τὸν θεόν immediately before θεὸς ἦν ὁ λόγος (John 1:1), while the verse that follows 2 Pet. 1:1 where Ἰησοῦς Χριστός is called ὁ θεὸς ἡμῶν καὶ σωτήρ distinguishes ὁ θεός from Ἰησοῦς ὁ κύριος ἡμῶν (2 Pet. 1:2).

B. Construing θεοῦ and σωτῆρος as dependent on δόξης and as referring to *one person* (with Ἰησοῦ Χριστοῦ in apposition to τῆς δόξης):

" . . . the appearing of [him who is] the Glory of our great God and Saviour [= the Father], [which Glory is/that is] Jesus Christ" (F. J. A. Hort).[21]

This novel interpretation has a *prima facie* attractiveness, since (1) it preserves intact the θεὸς καὶ σωτήρ formula; (2) in identifying "our great God and Saviour" as the Father, it reflects the usage of the Pastorals (1 Tim. 1:1; 2:3; Titus 1:3; 2:10; 3:4) where the phrases ὁ σωτὴρ ἡμῶν θεός and θεὸς σωτὴρ ἡμῶν denote the Father; and (3) δόξα θεοῦ may have been a primitive christological title.[22]

Although this view is attractive, it is not without difficulties. (1) While nouns in epexegetic apposition need not be juxtaposed,[23] ἥτις ἐστιν might have removed the ambiguity that arises, *ex hypothesi*, from the genitives that occur between δόξης and Ἰησοῦ Χριστοῦ. (2) Since the relative clause following Ἰησοῦ Χριστοῦ (viz. "who gave himself for us . . .") defines the work of Jesus Christ as Saviour, it is unnatural to dissociate σωτῆρος from Ἰησοῦ Χριστοῦ. (3) The title σωτήρ is elsewhere applied to Jesus in the Pastorals (2 Tim. 1:10; Titus 1:4; 3:6), but nowhere in the NT is the title δόξα θεοῦ explicitly used of Jesus.

C. Construing θεοῦ and σωτῆρος as dependent on δόξης and as referring to *one person* (with Ἰησοῦ Χριστοῦ in apposition to θεοῦ καὶ σωτῆρος):

" . . . the appearing of the glory of our great God and Saviour Jesus Christ" (RSV; similarly RV, ASV mg, NASB, TCNT, Weymouth, NEB, JB, TEV)

Several considerations support this rendering.

1. The expression θεὸς καὶ σωτήρ was a stereotyped formula common in first-century religious terminology,[24] was (apparently) used by both Diaspora and Palestinian Jews in reference to Yahweh,[25] and invariably denoted one deity, not two.[26] If no Ἰησοῦς Χριστός followed the expression, undoubtedly it would be taken to refer to one person; yet Ἰησοῦς Χριστός is simply added in epexegesis.

That Paul is here borrowing and applying to Christ a formula derived from the current terminology of pagan apotheosis cannot of course be finally demonstrated but seems probable for two reasons. (a) In the immediate context Paul uses several semi-technical terms associated with the royal epiphany, viz. ἐπιφαίνομαι ("appear", verse 11), ἐπιφάνεια ("appearance", verse 13), χάρις ("favour", verse 11), σωτήριος ("bringing aid", verse 11), ἐλπίς ("high expectation", verse 13).[27] (b) Some seven or eight years earlier, Paul had been personally confronted with the Demetrius riot at Ephesus when the people had chanted their credo, Μεγάλη ἡ Ἄρτεμις Ἐφεσίων (Acts 19:28, 34). Provoked by this pagan profession of faith which may have awakened memories of the cult of Artemis in Tarsus,[28] Paul had wished to mingle with the crowd, gain a hearing (Acts 19:30), and, one may suggest, speak of ὁ μέγας θεὸς καὶ σωτὴρ ἡμῶν, Ἰησοῦς Χριστός. Even if, as B. S. Easton suggests, verse 13 is a citation of a Christian liturgical formula or credal hymn,[29] it is difficult to avoid the conclusion that, whatever the date of Titus, one impulse behind this particular verse was the desire to combat the extravagant titular endowment that had been accorded to human rulers such as Antiochus Epiphanes (θεὸς ἐπιφανής), Ptolemy I (σωτὴρ καὶ θεός), or Julius Caesar (θεὸς καὶ σωτήρ), or to claim exclusively for the Christians' Lord the divine honours freely granted to goddesses such as Aphrodite and Artemis or to gods such as Asclepius and Zeus.[30]

Consequently, if one reason for the use of the phrase θεὸς καὶ σωτήρ was polemical, it is unlikely that the two elements in the phrase should be divorced, with θεός denoting God the Father and σωτήρ Jesus Christ.

2. The most satisfactory explanation of the anarthrous σωτῆρος is that two co-ordinate nouns referring to the same person are customarily linked by a single article.

When two (or more) nouns in the same case are linked by καί, the repetition of the article with the second noun shows unambiguously that the nouns are separate items, while its non-repetition indicates that the nouns are being considered corporately, not separately, or that they have a single referent.[31] For example, the repeated article in the phrase οἱ ἀπόστολοι καὶ οἱ πρεσβύτεροι (Acts 15:4, 6, 22) shows that the apostles of the Jerusalem church were a group distinct from the elders. On the other hand the single article in the expression οἱ ἀπόστολοι καὶ πρεσβύτεροι (Acts 15:2; 16:4) indicates that the Jerusalem apostles and elders could also be regarded (by the Antiochian church?) as a single administrative unit, not as two distinct groups. But in the case of the combination ὁ θεὸς καὶ πατὴρ (τοῦ κυρίου ἡμῶν Ἰησοῦ Χριστοῦ) (2 Cor. 1:3) it is clearly a matter of personal identity—God is the Father, as the preceding phrase ἀπὸ θεοῦ πατρὸς ἡμῶν (2 Cor. 1:2) shows—not simply a matter of conceptual unity. In Titus 2:13 the difficulty lies in deciding whether the non-repetition of the article before σωτῆρος points to a conceptual association of two separate items, or to their actual equation, with the second element affording an additional description of the first. That is, are θεός and σωτήρ here distinct entities being conceived of unitarily as joint possessors of δόξα, or is σωτήρ a further description of one and the same θεός? The reason for preferring the second of these alternatives is that in contemporary usage the θεὸς καὶ σωτήρ formula never referred to two persons or deities.

Alternative ways of accounting for the anarthrous σωτῆρος are not lacking but they fail to carry comparable conviction.

(a) Σωτήρ was already a semi-technical term[32] or "a quasi proper name",[33] and as such tended to be anarthrous. The absence of the article is therefore insignificant.

But, to judge from the NT use of σωτήρ, evidence is wanting that in the first century σωτήρ was a proper name as well as a title of Jesus. Apart from Titus 2:13, the word is used only fifteen times in reference to Jesus.[34] In nine of these cases it is a title accompanying proper names (such as Ἰησοῦς Χριστός);[35] in the remaining six cases it is used simply as a descriptive title.[36] Nor is there proof that as a quasi-technical word σωτήρ "speedily became anarthrous".[37] In fact, in the Pastorals σωτήρ is articular seven times[38] but anarthrous only twice (excluding Titus 2:13).[39] Only if it could be established that σωτὴρ (ἡμῶν) Ἰησοῦς Χριστός was an early credal formula comparable to κύριος Ἰησοῦς Χριστός could one argue that σωτήρ was anarthrous in Titus 2:13 because of its widespread technical use.[40]

(b) Σωτήρ is anarthrous because there was no need to distinguish different subjects, the writer assuming a distinction between ὁ μέγας θεός and σωτὴρ ἡμῶν Ἰησοῦς Χριστός.[41]

No one will deny that the repetition of the article is not essential to ensure that two items be considered separately,[42] but it is difficult to prove what an author was or was not assuming. What is indisputable is that the combination σωτὴρ ἡμῶν is generally articular in the Pastorals (seven examples), being anarthrous only in 1 Timothy 1:1 (where there is no possibility that two persons are referred to) and in Titus 2:13. Consequently the exceptional nature of the usage in this verse calls for a positive explanation. But the affirmation that the article is absent because it was not needed does not account for this departure from the idiom of the Pastorals which suggests that the article would normally be found with σωτὴρ ἡμῶν.[43]

(c) A single article is found with θεός and σωτήρ because Father and Son are regarded as equal sharers in or joint possessors of the divine glory to be manifested at Christ's parousia.[44]

Luke 9:26 shows this to be a permissible view, although it fails to take sufficiently seriously the *ex hypothesi* ambiguity of diction that arises from the non-use of the second article. The inference that a first-century reader or hearer would first draw from the phrase ἡ δόξα τοῦ μεγάλου θεοῦ καὶ σωτῆρος ἡμῶν would probably not be that two divine figures jointly possessed δόξα but that the θεός who was also their σωτήρ possessed δόξα.

(d) By using the anarthrous σωτήρ the writer is stressing the saviourhood of Jesus Christ, his distinctive character as σωτήρ.[45] This explanation would be more convincing if θεοῦ also were anarthrous: ... ἐπιφάνειαν δόξης μεγάλου θεοῦ καὶ σωτῆρος ἡμῶν Ἰησοῦ Χριστοῦ.

(e) The prefixing of the appositional substantive σωτῆρος to the proper name Ἰησοῦ Χριστοῦ has led to the anarthrous state of σωτῆρος.[46] It is not clear, however, that an appositional noun that precedes a proper name is necessarily anarthrous. In 2 Timothy 1:10 we have διὰ τῆς ἐπιφανείας τοῦ σωτῆρος ἡμῶν Ἰησοῦ Χριστοῦ,[47] while in four other passages in the Pastorals σωτὴρ ἡμῶν is articular preceding the anarthrous quasi-proper name θεός.[48]

Two observations may fitly conclude this discussion of a complex grammatical point. First, if Paul had wished to speak unambiguously of two persons, he could have written either τοῦ μεγάλου θεοῦ καὶ Ἰησοῦ Χριστοῦ τοῦ σωτῆρος ἡμῶν, or τοῦ μεγάλου θεοῦ ἡμῶν καὶ τοῦ σωτῆρος Ἰησοῦ Χριστοῦ.[49] Secondly, it must remain improbable that Paul would have acquiesced in a form of words that would naturally be construed as depicting Jesus as ὁ μέγας θεὸς καὶ σωτὴρ ἡμῶν if in fact he believed that Jesus was in no sense θεός.

3. The exceptional use of μέγας with θεός may be more easily explained if θεός refers to Christ than if it signifies the Father.[50]

As a description of the Father, μέγας is not elsewhere used in the NT,[51] although it occurs relatively often in the LXX (especially in the Psalms) as a divine epithet.[52] Given the widespread use by Jews of this epithet in reference to Yahweh, one cannot say that μέγας would be redundant if applied to the Father, especially since it aptly summarizes the description of God given in 1 Timothy 6:15–16 in connection with the ἐπιφάνεια of Jesus Christ.[53] Yet against this must be set two points.

(a) If there is a use of the θεὸς καὶ σωτήρ formula and therefore exclusive reference to Christ,[54] it would occasion no surprise if μέγας (and ἡμῶν) were added in opposition to the pagan applications of the formula: "*our great* God and Saviour, Jesus Christ."[55]

(b) In describing the atoning work of Christ, verse 14 explicates that in which the greatness of Jesus Christ as "our God and Saviour" is displayed. Not only will Jesus Christ as Saviour fulfil Christians' "hope of glory" (cf. Rom. 5:2) at his appearance (verse 13) by transforming their lowly bodies into glorious bodies like his own body (Phil. 3:20–21). He has already proved himself a μέγας σωτήρ, a unique bearer of God's saving grace (verse 11), by his sacrificial self-surrender to achieve their redemption and sanctification (verse 14).

4. There is a significant parallelism between the two parts of the verse, viz. τὴν... δόξης and τοῦ... ἡμῶν. In each case we have: article–adjective–noun–καί–anarthrous noun–genitive. Whether τὴν... ἐλπίδα καὶ ἐπιφάνειαν is a hendiadys[56] or καί is epexegetic,[57] the sense of verse 13a seems to be: "we await the hope[58] that brings and will bring blessing[59]—the appearing of the glory...". If the parallelism is intentional, ὁ μέγας θεός is the σωτήρ, just as ἡ μακαρία ἐλτίς is the ἐπιφάνεια.

Sometimes adduced in favour of understanding θεός of Jesus Christ in this verse are four further arguments, each of which is of dubious validity.

5. W. Lock alleges that the relative clause ὃς ἔδωκεν κτλ. (verse 14) implies a single referent, θεὸς καὶ σωτήρ, for a second article would seem to be required before σωτῆρος if θεός designated the Father but σωτὴρ ἡμῶν... ὃς ἔδωκεν denoted Jesus.[60]

However, a similar conjunction of two persons (this time under the bond of a single preposition, not a single article) followed by a predicate referring to only one of the two is found in Galatians 1:3–4: χάρις ὑμῖν καὶ εἰρήνη ἀπὸ θεοῦ πατρὸς ἡμῶν καὶ κυρίου Ἰησοῦ Χριστοῦ, τοῦ δόντος ἑαυτὸν κτλ.

6. In the NT the word ἐπιφάνεια is never applied to the Father, but on several occasions to the Son, in reference to his first advent[61] or his second advent.[62]

What this argument overlooks is that it is not the Father himself who will be visibly manifested but the *glory* that belongs to the great God. It is unlikely that τῆς δόξης is a "Hebrew" genitive ("the glorious appearing of the great God")[63] or that "the appearance of the glory of the great God" is simply a circumlocution for "the great God will appear".[64] In any case, nowhere does a NT writer speak of a dual epiphany of Father and Son. And in Jewish apocalyptic, where appearances of Yahweh and of the Messiah are mentioned, never are both said to appear together.[65]

7. In the OT the work of redemption and purification is attributed to Yahweh (e.g., Exod. 19:5; Deut. 7:6; 14:2), but in Titus 2:14 Christ is said to have redeemed and purified his People: Christ and his Church replace Yahweh and Israel. Consequently it would be natural for Paul to

apply to Jesus two of the OT appellations of Yahweh, viz. θεός and σωτήρ.[66]

In reply, we may observe that what is "natural" for a writer to say is not always what he does say. Moreover, similarity of function does not prove interchangeability of titles any more than identity of person.

8. The majority of post-Nicene writers support the identification of ὁ μέγας θεὸς καὶ σωτὴρ ἡμῶν as Christ.[67]

Against this, however, must be set the fact that the principal ancient versions (except the Ethiopic) distinguish θεός from σωτήρ, as do Justin Martyr[68] and Ambrosiaster. If anything, the testimony of the versions is more important than that of the Fathers on this point, given the widespread use of θεός as an appellation of Christ in the fourth century and the post-Nicene concern for the scriptural buttressing of orthodox teaching on the deity of Christ.

IV. Concluding Remarks

In the light of the foregoing evidence, it seems probable that in Titus 2:13 Jesus Christ is called "our great God and Saviour", a verdict shared, with varying degrees of assurance, by almost all grammarians[69] and lexicographers,[70] many commentators,[71] and most writers on NT christology,[72] although there are some dissenting voices.[73] Certainly the NT doctrine of the deity of Christ does not stand or fall depending on the number of times Jesus is called θεός or ὁ θεός. In the present passage, for example, even if ὁ μέγας θεός denotes the Father, not Jesus, the verse still contains evidence of the deity of Christ, for the personal equality of the Son and the Father is implied by: (a) the single article which (on that view) links θεός and σωτὴρ ἡμῶν Ἰησοῦς Χριστός in a conceptual unit (and only two divine persons could be so conjoined); (b) the idea of the manifestation of jointly shared glory; and (c) the sixfold repetition of the phrase ὁ σωτὴρ ἡμῶν in Titus, applied first to the Father (Titus 1:3; 2:10; 3:4), then to the Son (Titus 1:4; 2:13; 3:6).[74]

Even if the early church had never applied the title θεός to Jesus, his deity would still be apparent in his being the object of human and angelic worship[75] and of saving faith;[76] the exerciser of exclusively divine functions such as creatorial agency,[77] the forgiveness of sins,[78] and the final judgment;[79] the addressee in petitionary prayer;[80] the possessor of all divine attributes;[81] the bearer of numerous titles used of Yahweh in the OT;[82] and the co-author of divine blessing.[83] Faith in the deity of Jesus does not rest on the existence or validity of a series of "proof-texts" in which Jesus may receive the title θεός but on the general testimony of the NT corroborated at the bar of personal experience.[84]

With this said, the significance of θεός as a christological appellation must not be minimized. The use of θεός in reference to Jesus confirms what may be established on other grounds and makes explicit what is implied in other christological titles such as κύριος and υἱὸς θεοῦ, viz. the deity of Jesus Christ.

Notes

1. *An Expanded Paraphrase of the Epistles of Paul* (Exeter, Paternoster, 1965), 293; "'Our God and Saviour': A Recurring Biblical Pattern" in *The Saviour God*, ed. S. G. F. Brandon (Manchester, Manchester University, 1963), 51; *Answers to Questions* (Exeter, Paternoster, 1972), 173.

2. The Pauline authorship of the Pastoral epistles is here assumed. See the detailed defence of this position by C. Spicq, *Les Épîtres Pastorales* (Paris, Gabalda, 1969⁴), I. 157–214, and the article by B. M. Metzger, "A Reconsideration of Certain Arguments against the Pauline Authorship of the Pastoral Epistles", *ExpT* 70 (1958–1959), 91–94.

3. *The Pastoral Epistles* (E.T., Philadelphia, Fortress, 1972), 142.

4. This is a variation of the view associated with the name of F. J. A. Hort, on which see III.B.

5. *The Pastoral Epistles* (BNTC, London, 1963), 246–47.

6. On the reasons for the anarthrous σωτῆρος, see III.C.2.

7. Viz. 1 Tim. 2:3; 2 Tim. 1:10; Titus 1:3, 4; 2:10; 3:4, 6. In each case where σωτὴρ ἡμῶν is anarthrous (viz. 1 Tim. 1:1; Jude 25), it follows an anarthrous θεός.

8. That is, one might have expected ἐπιφάνειαν τῆς δόξης τοῦ μεγάλου θεοῦ, τοῦ σωτῆρος ἡμῶν Ἰησοῦ Χριστοῦ.

9. See below, nn. 24, 25.

10. C. H. Moehlmann, *The Combination* THEOS SOTER *as Explanation of the Primitive Christian Use of* SOTER *as Title and Name of Jesus* (Rochester, N.Y., Du Bois, 1920), 32.

11. On this "Hebrew" genitive (also called "adjectival," "qualitative," or "attributive"), see M. Zerwick, *Biblical Greek* (E.T., Rome, Pontifical Biblical Institute, 1963), 14–15, paras. 40–41.

12. Rom. 8:21 (RSV); 2 Cor. 4:4 (KJV, Knox); Eph. 1:17 (TCNT); 3:16 (Phillips); Phil. 3:21 (KJV, RSV, NEB); Col. 1:11 (KJV, RSV, Weymouth, Moffatt); 1 Tim. 1:11 (KJV, TCNT, RSV, Goodspeed).

13. Since ἐλπίδα and ἐπιφάνειαν are joined by a single article, it would be possible to argue that τῆς δόξης is parallel to μακαρίαν and therefore adjectival in sense.

14. These two points are further developed (III.C.6).

15. *Critical and Exegetical Handbook to the Epistles of St. Paul to Timothy and Titus* (E.T., Edinburgh, T. & T. Clark, 1881), 360. A similar but less precise statement of this argument is found in E. Abbot, "On the Construction of Titus II. 13" in his book *The Authorship of the Fourth Gospel and other Critical Essays* (Boston, Ellis, 1888): "While the word θεός occurs more than five hundred times in the Epistles of Paul . . . , there is not a single instance in which it is *clearly* applied to Christ" (447); "The habitual, and I believe *uniform*, usage of Paul corresponds with his language [in] 1 Cor. viii.6" (447 n.). Note also G. B. Winer's candid comment (*A Grammar of the Idiom of the New Testament* [E.T., Andover, Draper, 1872], 130 n. 2): "Doctrinal conviction, deduced from Paul's teaching, that this

apostle could not have called Christ *the great God*, induced me to show that there is . . . no grammatical obstacle to taking καὶ σωτ. . . . Χριστοῦ by itself as a second subject."

16. If θεοῦ be read in Acts 20:28 (which is part of Luke's account of Paul's speech to the Ephesian elders), it is possible that the referent is Jesus, but it seems more likely that God the Father is referred to and that either Ἰησοῦς Χριστός is the unexpressed subject of περιεποιήσατο, or ὁ ἴδιος is a christological title.

17. All the issues raised in this paragraph are discussed in the author's forthcoming monograph *Jesus as 'God' in the New Testament: A Study of the Use of* THEOS *as a Christological Title.*

18. *Critical Essays*, 448.

19. It is just possible that in the unique affixing of the adjective μέγας to θεός we have Paul's (unconscious?) acknowledgment that he was indulging in an exceptional use of θεός.

20. The one exception is Rom. 9:5. But even though this verse lacks any explicit distinction between Son and Father, ὁ Χριστός is qualified by τὸ κατὰ σάρκα, a phrase that could not be predicated of the Father.

21. *The Epistle of St. James* (London, Macmillan, 1909), 47, 103f; followed by R. St John Parry, *The Pastoral Epistles* (Cambridge, C.U.P., 1920), 81, and (apparently) A. E. J. Rawlinson, *The NT Doctrine of the Church* (London, Longmans, 1929), 172 n. 3. Hort adduces Titus 2:13 in support of his interpretation of τῆς δόξης in Jas. 2:1 in a titular sense (". . . who is the Glory").

22. See John 1:14; 12:41; Acts 7:55; 2 Cor. 4:6; Eph. 1:3 compared with Eph. 1:17; Heb. 1:3.

23. In Col. 2:2, for instance, τοῦ θεοῦ intervenes between τοῦ μυστηρίου and Χριστοῦ, yet the sense is "God's mystery, which is Christ."

24. P. Wendland, 'Σωτήρ: Eine religionsgeschichtliche Untersuchung", ZNW 5 (1904), 335–53.

25. Dibelius-Conzelmann, *Pastoral Epistles*, 100–102 (in an excursus on "Saviour" in the Pastoral epistles).

26. Θεός and σωτήρ are two separate titles of one and the same deity. This is why the καί in the formula is not epexegetic (which would produce the sense: ". . . the appearing of the glory of the great God, our Saviour Jesus Christ").

27. Cf. Spicq, *Épîtres Pastorales*, 2.251–52, 640.

28. See references in Spicq, *Épîtres Pastorales*, 2.251 n. 2.

29. *The Pastoral Epistles* (New York, Scribner's, 1947), 94. Cf. the observation of Spicq (*Épîtres Pastorales*, 2.245) that the christology of the Pastorals is expressed in traditional terminology.

30. On this theme, see L. Cerfaux and J. Tondriau, *Le culte des souverains dans la civilisation gréco-romaine* (Paris, Desclée, 1957).

31. For a discussion of these issues, see Zerwick, *Biblical Greek*, 59–60, paras. 183–85, and especially A. T. Robertson, *A Grammar of the Greek NT* (Nashville, Broadman, 1934[4]), 785–88.

32. So J. H. Bernard, *The Pastoral Epistles* (CGT; Cambridge, C.U.P., 1899), 172.

33. H. Alford, *Greek Testament* (1856; reprinted, Grand Rapids, Guardian, 1976), 3.420.

34. V. Taylor (*The Names of Jesus* [London, Macmillan, 1954], 109) explains the sparing use of σωτήρ as a title of Jesus for more than half a century by suggesting that the use of the name in Greek religion and especially in the

emperor cult "restricted and delayed its currency in the primitive tradition". But Moehlmann (Theos Soter, 40–41) rejects such an explanation, proposing rather that not until Jesus had been called θεός (subsequent to the death of Paul, according to Moehlmann) did the early church give him the title σωτήρ (42–65; cf. the similar sentiment expressed earlier by W. Bousset, *Kyrios Christos* [E.T., Nashville, Abingdon, 1970], 317): "During the first decades of its life, Christianity promulgated a soterless soteriology" (2). The association of the terms θεός and σωτήρ in the θεὸς σωτήρ formula of Graeco-Roman civilization forms the key for Moehlmann's hypothesis (see esp. 25–39). But in substantiating his thesis, Moehlmann rejects the apostolic authorship of Titus and 2 Peter. Perhaps the relevant data are better accommodated by saying that Christ was given σωτήρ as a *proper name* and as a *frequent* appellation only when he was regularly called θεός, i.e. not until the second century.

35. Phil. 3:20; 2 Tim. 1:10; Titus 1:4; 3:6; 2 Pet. 1:1, 11; 2:20; 3:2, 18. Moehlmann, however, believes (Theos Soter, 20) that in 2 Pet. 3:2 σωτήρ is a proper name but that even there it occurs with another title (κύριος). From the data of the Pastoral Epistles and 2 Peter, Moehlmann traces the evolution of the early Christian use of σωτήρ: God our *soter*; Jesus Christ our *soter*; our Lord and *soter*, Jesus Christ; our God and *soter*, Jesus Christ (17). Significantly, in each case σωτήρ is found with a proper name.

36. Luke 2:11; John 4:42; Acts 5:31; 13:23; Eph. 5:23; 1 John 4:14.

37. As Bernard (*Pastoral Epistles*, 172) claims.

38. Ὁ σωτὴρ ἡμῶν occurs in 1 Tim. 2:3; 2 Tim. 1:10; Titus 1:3, 4; 2:10; 3:4, 6 (the fact that ἡμῶν is generally attached to an articular noun does not diminish the force of this statistic).

39. 1 Tim. 1:1, where σωτήρ is anarthrous as being in apposition to θεός which lacks the article in accordance with the canon of Apollonius; 1 Tim. 4:10, where σωτήρ is anarthrous because it is predicative and adjectival.

40. Similarly A. W. Wainwright, *The Trinity in the New Testament* (London, SPCK, 1962), 64.

41. Abbot (*Critical Essays*, 451) formulates the general principle thus: "The definite article is inserted before the second attributive when it is *felt to be needed to distinguish different subjects;* but when the two terms connected by a copulative are *shown by any circumstance* to denote distinct subjects, then the article may be omitted, for the excellent reason that it is not needed."

42. N. Turner, *A Grammar of New Testament Greek, III. Syntax* (Edinburgh, T. & T. Clark, 1963), 181. H. Cremer (*Biblico-Theological Lexicon of New Testament Greek* [E.T., Edinburgh, T. & T. Clark, 1895⁴], 280) cites (among other passages) Matt. 16:21; 20:18; 27:3; Acts 15:22 in support of this principle.

43. The same objection may be levelled against G. B. Winer's proposal (*Grammar*, 130) that since ἡμῶν makes σωτῆρος definite, the article is superfluous with σωτῆρος.

44. Abbot, *Critical Essays*, 452.

45. Abbot, *Critical Essays*, 441, 452–53.

46. An argument of Winer (*Grammar*, 130) that is followed by Alford (*Greek Testament*, 3.420). An anarthrous σωτήρ precedes Ἰησοῦς Χριστός or Χριστὸς Ἰησοῦς in 2 Pet. 1:1, 11; 3:18 (as in Titus 2:13), while in Titus 1:4; 3:6 this name precedes the articular ὁ σωτὴρ ἡμῶν.

47. Here the presence of the article with σωτῆρος illustrates the canon of Apollonius that nouns in *regimen* generally either both have the article or both lack it.

48. Viz. 1 Tim. 2:3; Titus 1:3; 2:10; 3:4 (each rendered in the RSV by "God our Saviour", which construes τοῦ σωτῆρος as an appositional substantive).

49. In the latter case, the article inserted before σωτῆρος, in addition to the altered position of ἡμῶν, would indicate two distinct subjects.

50. Cf. C. J. Ellicott, The Pastoral Epistles of St Paul (London, Longmans, 1883⁵), 207.

51. The substantival form μεγαλειότης is used of Christ in 2 Pet. 1:16, of God in Luke 9:43, and μεγαλωσύνη of God in Heb. 1:3; 8:1; Jude 25.

52. E.g., Deut. 10:17; Neh. 4:14; 8:6; 9:32; Ps. 47:1; 76:13; 85:10; Isa. 26:4; Jer. 39:19; Dan. 2:45; 9:4; Mal. 1:14.

53. Cf. Abbot, Critical Essays, 443–44.

54. Only on Hort's view (discussed above, III.B) could θεοῦ and σωτῆρος both refer to the Father.

55. E. F. Scott (The Pastoral Epistles [MNTC, London, Hodder, 1936], 170) maintains that the idea of "greatness" really belongs to δόξα but has been transferred to θεός from whom the δόξα emanates.

56. According to C. J. Ellicott (Pastoral Epistles, 207), Theodoret construed the whole phrase as a hendiadys: "the hope of his glorious coming".

57. This understanding of the verse is reflected in several translations: TCNT, RSV, NAB, Moffatt, Goodspeed, Weymouth, Berkeley.

58. Ἐλπίς here is no subjective sentiment but the objective fulfilment of divine promise, res sperata not spes (cf. Col. 1:5). Goodspeed has the rendering "the fulfilment of our blessed hope"; and the NEB, "the happy fulfilment of our hopes".

59. The present expectation of realized hope brings blessing, as does the actual future realization of hope.

60. A Critical and Exegetical Commentary on the Pastoral Epistles (ICC, Edinburgh, T. & T. Clark, 1924), 145; similarly Spicq, Épîtres Pastorales, 2.640. But Parry (Pastoral Epistles, 81) refers ὃς ἔδωκεν to Ἰησοῦς Χριστός alone, because he finds in verse 14 an indication of the sense in which Christ is the glory of God, viz. in his manifestation of the grace of God.

61. 2 Tim. 1:10.

62. 2 Thess. 2:8; 1 Tim. 6:14; 2 Tim. 4:1, 8.

63. For the reasons why it is improbable that τῆς δόξης is a "Hebrew" or attributive genitive ("glorious"), see above, II.

64. Pace Easton (Pastoral Epistles, 94) who compares Acts 7:55; 2 Pet. 1:17.

65. Spicq, Épîtres Pastorales, 2.640.

66. This argument is adduced by Cremer (Lexicon, 281), Lock (Pastoral Epistles, 145) and G. Kittel, "δόξα", TDNT 2 (1964), 248.

67. Ellicott (Pastoral Epistles, 207) who also cites Clement of Alexandria and Hippolytus as supporting this identification, but Abbot (Critical Essays, 444) has shown their testimony to be suspect.

68. Apol. 1.61.

69. T. F. Middleton, The Doctrine of the Greek Article (London, Rivington, 1841²), 307–09; J. H. Moulton, A Grammar of NT Greek, Vol. I. Prolegomena (Edinburgh, T. & T. Clark, 1908³), 84; A. T. Robertson, Grammar, 786; "The Greek Article and the Deity of Christ", Expositor, 8th series, 21 (1921), 186–87; BDF, 145 para. 276 (3); M. Zerwick, Biblical Greek, 60, para. 185 (the single article "seem(s) to suggest the divinity of Christ"; cf. his Analysis Philologica Novi Testamenti Graeci [Rome, Pontifical Biblical Institute, 1966³], 488 ad loc.); C. F. D. Moule, An Idiom Book of NT Greek (Cambridge, Cambridge University, 1960²), 109–10; N. Turner,

Grammatical Insights into the NT (Edinburgh, T. & T. Clark, 1965), 15–16; cf. his *Syntax*, 181; B. Weiss, "Der Gebrauch des Artikels bei den Gottesnamen", *StKr* 84 (1911), 365.

70. Cremer, *Lexicon*, 279–81; BAG, 357, s.v. θεός 2; 555, s.v. ὁ II.10.b; E. Stauffer, "θεός," *TDNT* 3 (1965), 106 (see also his *NT Theology* [E.T., New York, Macmillan, 1955], 324 n. 803); W. Grundmann, "μέγας", *TDNT* 4 (1967), 538–40; idem, "χρίω", *TDNT* 9 (1974), 565 n. 464.

71. Ellicott, *Pastoral Epistles*, 207–08 ("a direct, definite, and even *studied* declaration of the divinity of the Eternal Son"); A. Wiesinger, *Biblical Commentary on St Paul's Epistles* (Edinburgh, T. & T. Clark, 1851), 307–10; Bernard, *Pastoral Epistles*, 171–73 ("with great hesitation"); M. Dibelius, *Die Pastoralbriefe* (HNT, Tübingen, Mohr, 1931²), 90, 92; Easton, *Pastoral Epistles*, 94–95; Lock, *Pastoral Epistles*, 144–46; Spicq, *Épîtres Pastorales*, 2.249, 251, 254, 640–41; W. Hendriksen, *Commentary on I & II Timothy and Titus* (London, Banner of Truth, 1959), 373–75; E. K. Simpson, *The Pastoral Epistles* (Grand Rapids, Eerdmans, 1954), 108f. ("a studied assertion"); F. D. Gealy, "Titus," *The Interpreter's Bible*, ed. G. A. Buttrick, *et al.* (New York, Abingdon, 1955), 11.539–40; D. Guthrie, *The Pastoral Epistles* (TNTC; Grand Rapids, Eerdmans, 1957), 200 (a slight preference); A. R. C. Leaney, *The Epistles to Timothy, Titus and Philemon* (London, SCM, 1960), 123; C. K. Barrett, *The Pastoral Epistles* (Oxford, Clarendon, 1963), 138; A. T. Hanson, *The Pastoral Letters* (CBC; Cambridge, Cambridge University, 1966), 116; J. L. Houlden, *The Pastoral Epistles* (PNTC; London, Penguin, 1976), 150–51.

72. Bousset, *Kyrios*, 314, 316; B. B. Warfield, *The Lord of Glory* (London, Hodder & Stoughton, 1907), 245, 254–55; E. Meyer, *Ursprung und Anfänge des Christentums* (Stuttgart, J. G. Cotta'sche, 1921–3), 3.396; J. Lebreton, *History of the Dogma of the Trinity, I. The Origins* (E.T., London, Burns, Oates & Washbourne, 1939), 371; Moehlmann, THEOS SOTER 17, 39, 57; F. Prat, *The Theology of Saint Paul* (E.T., London, Burns, Oates & Washbourne, 1945), 2.127–28; J. Bonsirven, *Théologie du Nouveau Testament* (Paris, Aubier, 1951), 251 and n. 10; R. Bultmann, *Theology of the New Testament* (E.T., London, SCM, 1952), 1.129; K. Rahner, *Theological Investigations* (London, Darton, Longman & Todd, 1961), 1.135, 136, n. 2; O. Cullmann, *The Christology of the New Testament* (E.T., London, SCM, 1959), 313–14; Wainwright, *Trinity*, 63–65; W. Barclay, *Jesus As They Saw Him* (London, SCM, 1962), 31–33; R. E. Brown, "Does the NT call Jesus God?" *TS* 26 (1965), 556–57, 561; F. F. Bruce, in *The Saviour God*, 51; L. Sabourin, *The Names and Titles of Jesus* (E.T., New York, Macmillan, 1967), 302; R. N. Longenecker, *The Christology of Early Jewish Christianity* (SBT 2/17; London, SCM, 1970), 138–39; K. Romaniuk, *L'Amour du Père et du Fils dans la Sotériologie de Saint Paul* (AB 15A; Rome, Pontifical Biblical Institute, 1974²), 66–67.

73. The only grammarian seems to be Winer, *Grammar*, 130. Among the commentators we find Alford, *Greek Testament*, 3.419–21; Huther, *Timothy and Titus*, 359–62; E. Abbot, *Critical Essays*, 439–57; Hort, *James*, 47, 103–04; N. J. D. White, "The Epistle to Titus" in *EGT* 4 (1910; reprinted, Grand Rapids, Eerdmans, 1970), 195–96; Parry, *Pastoral Epistles*, 81; Scott, *Pastoral Epistles*, 169–70; Kelly, *Pastoral Epistles*, 246–47; H. Conzelmann in Dibelius-Conzelmann, *Pastoral Epistles*, 143. So also V. Taylor, *The Person of Christ in NT Teaching* (London, Macmillan, 1959), 131–33; cf. his *NT Essays* (Grand Rapids, Eerdmans, 1972), 86; and Rawlinson, *Christ*, 172 n. 3 (apparently).

74. Attention is drawn to this latter fact by Simpson, *Pastoral Epistles*, 109, and Romaniuk, *L'Amour*, 67.

75. E.g., John 5:23; 20:28; Phil. 2:9–11.

76. E.g., John 14:1; Acts 10:43; 16:31; Rom. 10:8–13.

77. E.g., John 1:3; Col. 1:16; Heb. 1:2–3.

78. E.g., Mark 2:5, 10; Col. 3:13.

79. E.g., John 5:22; Acts 10:42; 17:31; 1 Cor. 4:4–5; 2 Cor. 5:10; 2 Thess. 1:7–9.

80. E.g., Acts 1:24; 7:59; 22:19; 1 Cor. 1:2; 16:22; 2 Cor. 12:8.

81. E.g., John 1:4; 10:30; Eph. 4:10; Col. 1:19; 2:9; Heb. 13:8.

82. See V. Taylor, *The Names of Jesus* (London, Macmillan, 1953).

83. E.g., in the customary Pauline salutation "Grace to you and peace from God the Father and our Lord Jesus Christ" (Gal. 1:3), or in the remarkable "*enallage* of number" in 1 Thess. 3:11–12; 2 Thess. 2:16–17.

84. Cf. W. Temple, *Christus Veritas* (London, Macmillan, 1924), 112, 113 and n. 2.

INDEX OF REFERENCES

A. THE OLD TESTAMENT

279

B. OT APOCRYPHA AND PSEUDEPIGRAPHA

C. THE NEW TESTAMENT

D. DEAD SEA SCROLLS AND RELATED TEXTS

E. RABBINICAL SOURCES

F. OTHER ANCIENT AUTHORS AND WRITINGS

INDEX OF MODERN AUTHORS

290